D1538218

IMMIGRATION AND ILLEGAL ALIENS

BURDEN OR BLESSING?

ISSN 1536-5263

IMMIGRATION AND ILLEGAL ALIENS

BURDEN OR BLESSING?

Cynthia S. Becker

INFORMATION PLUS® REFERENCE SERIES
Formerly Published by Information Plus, Wylie, Texas

THOMSON

GALE

Detroit • New York • San Francisco • New Haven, Conn. • Waterville, Maine • London

Immigration and Illegal Aliens: Burden or Blessing?
Cynthia S. Becker
Paula Kepos, Series Editor

Project Editors
Kathleen J. Edgar, John McCoy

Permissions
Tracie Richardson, Jhanay Williams

Composition and Electronic Prepress
Evi Seoud

Manufacturing
Cynde Bishop

© 2008 The Gale Group.

Thomson and Star logos are trademarks and Gale is a registered trademark used herein under license.

For more information, contact
The Gale Group
27500 Drake Rd.
Farmington Hills, MI 48331-3535
Or you can visit our Internet site at http://www.gale.com

ALL RIGHTS RESERVED
No part of this work covered by the copyright hereon may be reproduced or used in any form or by any means–graphic, electronic, or mechanical, including photocopying, recording, taping, Web distribution, or information storage retrieval systems–without the written permission of the publisher.

For permission to use material from this product, submit your request via Web at http://www.gale-edit.com/permissions, or you may download our Permissions request form and submit your request by fax or mail to:

Permissions Department
The Gale Group
27500 Drake Rd.
Farmington Hills, MI 48331-3535
Permissions Hotline: 248-699-8006 or 800-877-4253, ext. 8006
Fax: 248-699-8074 or 800-762-4058

Cover photo reproduced by permission of Digital Stock.

While every effort has been made to ensure the reliability of the information presented in this publication, the Gale Group does not guarantee the accuracy of the data contained herein. The Gale Group accepts no payment for listing; and inclusion in the publication of any organization, agency, institution, publication, service, or individual does not imply endorsement of the editors or publisher. Errors brought to the attention of the publisher and verified to the satisfaction of the publisher will be corrected in future editions.

ISBN-13: 978-0-7876-5103-9 (set)
ISBN-10: 0-7876-5103-6 (set)
ISBN-13: 978-1-4144-0764-7
ISBN-10: 1-4144-0764-5
ISSN 1536-5263

This title is also available as an e-book.
ISBN-13: 978-1-4144-2948-9 (set), ISBN-10: 1-4144-2948-7 (set)
Contact your Gale Group sales representative for ordering information.

Printed in the United States of America
10 9 8 7 6 5 4 3 2 1

TABLE OF CONTENTS

PREFACE vii

CHAPTER 1

Immigration—Almost Four Hundred Years of U.S.
History 1

The history of the United States has been shaped by immigrants. Immigration policy, however, has varied from the unrestricted flow of colonial times to exclusions and restrictive quota systems, to preference systems, and to post–September 11 security consciousness. This chapter outlines the history of immigration in the United States, discussing attitudes toward immigration and the varying demographic characteristics of immigrants up to 1980.

CHAPTER 2

Immigration Laws and Policies since the 1980s 15

Current immigration issues have resulted in new immigration legislation. This chapter details recent federal and state laws pertaining to legal and illegal immigration, marriage fraud, the preference system, welfare reform, terrorism, and identity documents, explaining and investigating the impact of each.

CHAPTER 3

Current Immigration Statistics 31

This chapter describes immigration quantitatively, providing data on the rate of immigration, the place of origin of immigrants, the categories under which these immigrants are admitted, and other topics of interest. The naturalization process, nonimmigrants, and aliens denied entry to the United States are also discussed.

CHAPTER 4

The Refugee Influx. 53

Immigration policy has allowed for the admission of refugees since the end of World War II. This chapter explains the legislation under which they are admitted, details how many there are and from where they come, and evaluates their adjustment to the United States. The process of asylum-seeking and several legal challenges are outlined.

CHAPTER 5

Illegal Aliens. 65

Illegal aliens reside in the United States in violation of immigration law. Tracking where they are is a challenge, and their numbers are uncertain. This chapter considers barriers to legal immigration, issues in the southwestern border counties, and the flow of emigrants from Mexico. The chapter compares the plight of and the impact of illegal workers in New Orleans after Hurricane Katrina and in Georgia, a new migrant destination.

CHAPTER 6

The Cost of Immigration. 85

This chapter explores the benefits of immigrant labor and taxes compared with the federal and state costs of public assistance, education of immigrant children, and detention of illegal aliens. It also explores immigrant impact on native wages and the flow of U.S. dollars sent to families in immigrants' home countries.

CHAPTER 7

The Impact of Immigration on the United States in the
Twenty-first Century 101

Immigration has changed the United States in many ways. The influence of Latin American immigrants and the Spanish language is described in this chapter, along with the importance of immigrant entrepreneurs and foreign students. The chapter includes public opinion about immigration, the debate over amnesty and guest worker programs, and solutions to the illegal immigration problem.

CHAPTER 8

More Liberal Policies Will Solve the Problem of Illegal
Immigration 115

This chapter reprints various statements and testimonies that are in favor of immigration. Presented by select government officials, academics, specialists in the field, and other individuals before such bodies as Congress and the U.S. House Subcommittee on Immigration and Claims, these statements detail why it is important for the United States to keep its doors open to immigrants.

CHAPTER 9

Stricter Policies Will Solve the Problem of Illegal
Immigration 125

This chapter reprints various statements and testimonies that are opposed to immigration. Presented by select government officials, academics, specialists in the field, and other individuals before such bodies as Congress and the U.S. House Subcommittee on Immigration and Claims, these statements detail why the United States should make it more difficult for people to immigrate to the United States and why the country should rethink its immigration policy.

APPENDIX I. U.S. DEPARTMENT OF JUSTICE BROCHURE: FEDERAL PROTECTIONS AGAINST NATIONAL ORIGIN DISCRIMINATION 135

APPENDIX II. MAPS OF THE WORLD 139

IMPORTANT NAMES AND ADDRESSES 147

RESOURCES 149

INDEX 151

PREFACE

Immigration and Illegal Aliens: Burden or Blessing? is part of the *Information Plus Reference Series*. The purpose of each volume of the series is to present the latest facts on a topic of pressing concern in modern American life. These topics include today's most controversial and most studied social issues: abortion, capital punishment, care of senior citizens, crime, the environment, health care, immigration, minorities, national security, social welfare, women, youth, and many more. Although written especially for the high school and undergraduate student, this series is an excellent resource for anyone in need of factual information on current affairs.

By presenting the facts, it is the Gale Group's intention to provide its readers with everything they need to reach an informed opinion on current issues. To that end, there is a particular emphasis in this series on the presentation of scientific studies, surveys, and statistics. These data are generally presented in the form of tables, charts, and other graphics placed within the text of each book. Every graphic is directly referred to and carefully explained in the text. The source of each graphic is presented within the graphic itself. The data used in these graphics are drawn from the most reputable and reliable sources, in particular from the various branches of the U.S. government and from major independent polling organizations. Every effort has been made to secure the most recent information available. The reader should bear in mind that many major studies take years to conduct and that additional years often pass before the data from these studies are made available to the public. Therefore, in many cases the most recent information available in 2007 dated from 2004 or 2005. Older statistics are sometimes presented as well, if they are of particular interest and no more-recent information exists.

Although statistics are a major focus of the *Information Plus Reference Series*, they are by no means its only content. Each book also presents the widely held positions and important ideas that shape how the book's subject is discussed in the United States. These positions are explained in detail and, where possible, in the words of their proponents. Some of the other material to be found in these books includes: historical background; descriptions of major events related to the subject; relevant laws and court cases; and examples of how these issues play out in American life. Some books also feature primary documents or have pro and con debate sections giving the words and opinions of prominent Americans on both sides of a controversial topic. All material is presented in an even-handed and unbiased manner; the reader will never be encouraged to accept one view of an issue over another.

HOW TO USE THIS BOOK

America is known as a melting pot, a place where people of different nationalities, cultures, ethnicities, and races have come together to form one nation. This process has been shaped by the influx of both legal immigrants and illegal aliens, and American attitudes toward both groups have varied over time. Legal immigrants have faced discrimination based on prevailing social and political trends; illegal aliens have been seen by some as undesirable, particularly after it became apparent that some or all of the terrorists behind the September 11, 2001, attacks had entered the United States legally but had overstayed their allotted time. This book discusses these and other legal, social, and political aspects of immigration and illegal aliens.

Immigration and Illegal Aliens: Burden or Blessing? consists of nine chapters and five appendixes. Each of the chapters is devoted to a particular aspect of immigration in the United States. For a summary of the information covered in each chapter, please see the synopses provided in the Table of Contents at the front of the book. Chapters generally begin with an overview of the basic facts and background information on the chapter's topic, then proceed to examine subtopics of particular interest. For example, Chapter 5, Illegal Aliens, begins with a discussion of the barriers to legal immigration then explains what an illegal alien is and how many are in the United States. It then presents information on monitoring who comes and goes, how the country's borders are protected, and the impact of illegal immigration along the southwestern border of the United States. This is followed by an overview of how disasters present special challenges to illegal immigrants. The chapter concludes with sections on illegal aliens and crime and whether undocumented workers take jobs away from low-skilled U.S. workers. Throughout the chapter, changes to immigration law and enforcement systems since September 11, 2001, are highlighted. Readers can find their way through a chapter by looking for the section and subsection headings, which are clearly set off from the text. Or, they can also refer to the book's extensive Index, if they already know what they are looking for.

Statistical Information

The tables and figures featured throughout *Immigration and Illegal Aliens: Burden or Blessing?* will be of particular use to the reader in learning about this topic. These tables and figures represent an extensive collection of the most recent and valuable statistics on immigration and illegal aliens and related issues—for example, graphics in the book cover the number of immigrant orphans adopted by U.S. citizens, the percentage of native-born and foreign-born workers employed in various industries, the living arrangements of native- and foreign-born children, and use of welfare programs for native and immigrant households. The Gale Group believes that making this information available to the reader is the most important way in which we fulfill the goal of this book: to help readers understand the issues and controversies surrounding immigration and illegal aliens in the United States and to reach their own conclusions.

Each table or figure has a unique identifier appearing above it for ease of identification and reference. Titles for the tables and figures explain their purpose. At the end of each table or figure, the original source of the data is provided.

In order to help readers understand these often complicated statistics, all tables and figures are explained in the text. References in the text direct the reader to the relevant statistics. Furthermore, the contents of all tables and figures are fully indexed. Please see the opening section of the Index at the back of this volume for a description of how to find tables and figures within it.

Appendixes

In addition to the main body text and images, *Immigration and Illegal Aliens: Burden or Blessing?* has five appendixes. The first is a reproduction of a pamphlet published by the U.S. Department of Justice titled *Federal Protections against National Origin Discrimination*. The second appendix features maps of the world to assist the reader in pinpointing the places of birth of America's immigrant population. The third is the Important Names and Addresses directory. Here the reader will find contact information for a number of government and private organizations that can provide further information on aspects of immigration and illegal aliens. The fourth appendix is the Resources section, which can also assist the reader in conducting his or her own research. In this section the author and editors of *Immigration and Illegal Aliens: Burden or Blessing?* describe some of the sources that were most useful during the compilation of this book. The final appendix is the Index.

ADVISORY BOARD CONTRIBUTIONS

The staff of Information Plus would like to extend its heartfelt appreciation to the Information Plus Advisory Board. This dedicated group of media professionals provides feedback on the series on an ongoing basis. Their comments allow the editorial staff who work on the project to make the series better and more user-friendly. Our top priorities are to produce the highest-quality and most useful books possible, and the Advisory Board's contributions to this process are invaluable.

The members of the Information Plus Advisory Board are:

- Kathleen R. Bonn, Librarian, Newbury Park High School, Newbury Park, California

- Madelyn Garner, Librarian, San Jacinto College— North Campus, Houston, Texas

- Anne Oxenrider, Media Specialist, Dundee High School, Dundee, Michigan

- Charles R. Rodgers, Director of Libraries, Pasco-Hernando Community College, Dade City, Florida

- James N. Zitzelsberger, Library Media Department Chairman, Oshkosh West High School, Oshkosh, Wisconsin

COMMENTS AND SUGGESTIONS

The editors of the *Information Plus Reference Series* welcome your feedback on *Immigration and Illegal Aliens: Burden or Blessing?* Please direct all correspondence to:

Editors
Information Plus Reference Series
27500 Drake Rd.
Farmington Hills, MI 48331-3535

CHAPTER 1

IMMIGRATION—ALMOST FOUR HUNDRED YEARS OF U.S. HISTORY

From its beginning the United States has been a land of immigrants. People have come from all nations seeking free choice of worship, escape from cruel governments, and relief from war, famine, or poverty. All came with dreams of a better life for themselves and their families. The United States has accommodated these people of diverse backgrounds, customs, and beliefs, although not without considerable friction along the way.

On the eastern shore of the peninsula that is now Florida, Spanish conquistadors established a settlement in 1565. The city of St. Augustine survived to become the oldest continuously occupied settlement of European origin in North America. However, the series of northern colonies gained far more attention in history. In *Immigration: From the Founding of Virginia to the Closing of Ellis Island* (2002), Dennis Wepman chronicles the immigrants who built the United States. Not long after English settlers established the first permanent colony on the James River in 1607, the French developed a settlement on the St. Lawrence River in what is now Canada. Dutch explorers soon built a fur trading post along the Hudson River. Swedes settled on the Delaware River. German Quakers and Mennonites joined William Penn's experimental Pennsylvania colony. Jews from Brazil, Protestant Huguenots from France, and Puritans and Catholics from England all came to escape persecution of their religious beliefs and practices.

During the colonial period many immigrants came as indentured servants—meaning that they were required to work for four to seven years to earn back the cost of their passage. To the great aggravation of the colonists, some were convicts who accepted being shipped across the ocean as an alternative to imprisonment or death. Wepman estimates that as many as fifty thousand British felons were sent to the colonies. The first Africans arrived at Jamestown in 1619 as indentured servants, but other Africans were soon brought in chains to be slaves.

A continual flow of immigrants provided settlers to develop communities along the Atlantic coast, pioneers to push the United States westward, builders for the Erie Canal and the transcontinental railways, pickers for cotton in the South and vegetables in the Southwest, laborers for U.S. industrialization, and intellectuals in all fields. Together, these immigrants have built, in the opinion of many people, the most diverse nation in the world.

The 1790 census in the United States showed a population of 3.2 million white people and 757,000 slaves, according to Campbell Gibson and Kay Jung, in *Historical Census Statistics on Population Totals by Race, 1790 to 1990, and by Hispanic Origin, 1790 to 1990, for the United States, Regions, Division, and States* (September 2002, http://www.census.gov/population/www/documentation/twps0056.html). All were immigrants or descendants of earlier seventeenth- and eighteenth-century arrivals. The population was predominantly English but also included people of German, Irish, Scottish, Dutch, French, and Spanish descent. Native Americans were not counted.

ATTITUDES TOWARD IMMIGRANTS

Even though immigration was the way of life in the country's first century, negative attitudes began to appear among the already settled English population. Officially, however, with the major exception of the Alien and Sedition Acts of 1798, the United States encouraged immigration. The Articles of Confederation (drafted in 1777) made citizens of each state citizens of every other state. The U.S. Constitution (written in 1787) made only one direct reference to immigration. Article I, Section 9, Clause I provided that the "Migration or Importation of such Persons as any of the States now existing shall think proper to admit, shall not be prohibited by the Congress prior to the Year one thousand eight hundred and eight, but a Tax or duty may be imposed on such Importation, not exceeding ten dollars for each Person." Article I also gave Congress power to establish "a uniform rule of naturalization" to grant U.S. citizenship.

Alien and Sedition Acts of 1798

Early federal legislation established basic criteria for naturalization: five years' residence in the United States, good moral character, and loyalty to the U.S. Constitution. These requirements were based on state naturalization laws. In 1798 the Federalist-controlled Congress proposed four laws, collectively called the Alien and Sedition Acts:

- The Naturalization Act lengthened the residence requirement for naturalization from five to fourteen years.

- The Alien Act authorized the president to arrest and/or expel allegedly dangerous aliens.

- The Alien Enemies Act allowed the imprisonment or deportation of aliens who were subjects of an enemy nation during wartime.

- The Sedition Act authorized fines and imprisonment for acts of treason including "any false, scandalous and malicious writing."

The Sedition Act was used by the Federalist administration to arrest and silence a number of newspaper editors who publicly opposed the new laws. The strong public outcry against the Alien and Sedition Acts was partly responsible for the election of Thomas Jefferson, the Democratic-Republican presidential candidate, in the election of 1800. Jefferson pardoned the individuals convicted under the Sedition Act. The Naturalization Act was repealed by Congress, and the other three laws were allowed to lapse.

FIRST CENTURY OF IMMIGRATION

In the early 1800s U.S. territory more than doubled in size with the addition of 828,000 square miles of land, which came to be known as the Louisiana Purchase. Reports of rich farmland and virgin forests provided by explorers such as Meriwether Lewis and William Clark drew struggling farmers and skilled craftsmen, merchants and miners, laborers, and wealthy investors to leave Europe for the land of opportunity. The Office of Immigration Statistics reports in *2005 Yearbook of Immigration Statistics* (November 2006, http://www.dhs.gov/xlibrary/assets/statistics/yearbook/2005/OIS_2005_Yearbook.pdf) that in 1820, the year when immigration records were first kept, only 8,385 immigrants entered the United States. During the 1820s the number began to rise slowly, an increase that generally continued for more than a century, until the Great Depression in 1929.

Wave of Irish and German Immigration

Europe suffered from a population explosion in the 1800s. As land in Europe became more and more scarce, tenant farmers were pushed off their farms into poverty.

Some immigrated to the United States to start a new life. This situation was made worse in Ireland, when a fungus that caused potato crops to rot struck in 1845. Many of the Irish were poor farmers who depended on potatoes for food. They suffered greatly from famine when their crops rotted, and epidemics of cholera and typhoid spread from village to village. The Irish Potato Famine forced people to choose between starving to death and leaving their country. In the ten-year period between 1830 and 1839, 170,672 Irish people arrived in the United States. (See Table 1.1.) Driven by the potato famine, between 1840 and 1849 the number of Irish immigrants rose more than 284% to 656,145. The flow of emigrants from Ireland peaked at more than 1,029,486 in the 1850s.

Also affected by a potato famine and failed political revolutions, increasing numbers of German immigrants paralleled that of the Irish. Between 1850 and 1859 the number of German immigrants (976,072) was not far behind the Irish (1,029,486). (See Table 1.1.) The influx of Germans continued to rise to a peak of more than 1.4 million immigrants between 1880 and 1889.

Immigration, Politics, and the Civil War

This new wave of immigration led to intense anti-Irish, anti-German, and anti-Catholic sentiments among Americans, many of whom had been in the United States for only a few generations. It also triggered the creation of secret nativist societies (groups professing to protect the interests of the native-born against immigrants). Out of these groups grew a new political party, the Know Nothing movement (later known as the American Party), which claimed to support the rights of Protestant, American-born voters (and by implication, men, as women were not allowed to vote in federal elections until ratification of the Nineteenth Amendment in 1920). The American Party managed to win seventy-five seats in Congress and six governorships in 1855 before the party dissolved.

Felix S. Cohen explains in *Immigration and National Welfare* (1940) that in contrast to the nativists, the 1864 Republican Party platform, written in part by Abraham Lincoln, stated, "Resolved, That foreign immigration, which in the past has added so much to the wealth, development of resources, and increase of power to the nation, the asylum of the oppressed of all nations, shall be fostered and encouraged by a liberal and just policy."

In 1862 Lincoln had signed the Homestead Law, which offered 160 acres of free land to any adult citizen or prospective citizen who agreed to occupy and improve the land for five years. Wepman notes that between 1862 and 1904 more than 147 million acres of western land were claimed by adventurous citizens and eager new immigrants. In addition, efforts to complete a transcontinental railroad during the 1860s provided work for predominantly Irish and Chinese laborers.

TABLE 1.1

Immigration by region and selected country of last residence, 1820–2005

Region and country of last residence[a]	1820 to 1829	1830 to 1839	1840 to 1849	1850 to 1859	1860 to 1869	1870 to 1879	1880 to 1889	1890 to 1899	1900 to 1909
Total	128,502	538,381	1,427,337	2,814,554	2,081,261	2,742,137	5,248,568	3,694,294	8,202,388
Europe	99,272	422,771	1,369,259	2,619,680	1,877,726	2,251,878	4,638,677	3,576,411	7,572,569
Austria-Hungary[b, c, d]	—	—	—	—	3,375	60,127	314,787	534,059	2,001,376
Austria[b, d]	—	—	—	—	2,700	54,529	204,805	268,218	532,416
Hungary[b]	—	—	—	—	483	5,598	109,982	203,350	685,567
Belgium	28	20	3,996	5,765	5,785	6,991	18,738	19,642	37,429
Bulgaria[e]	—	—	—	—	—	—	—	52	34,651
Czechoslovakia[f]	—	—	—	—	—	—	—	—	—
Denmark	173	927	671	3,227	13,553	29,278	85,342	56,671	61,227
Finland	—	—	—	—	—	—	—	—	—
France[g]	7,694	39,330	75,300	81,778	35,938	71,901	48,193	35,616	67,735
Germany[c, d]	5,753	124,726	385,434	976,072	723,734	751,769	1,445,181	579,072	328,722
Greece	17	49	17	32	51	209	1,807	12,732	145,402
Ireland[h]	51,617	170,672	656,145	1,029,486	427,419	422,264	674,061	405,710	344,940
Italy	430	2,225	1,476	8,643	9,853	46,296	267,660	603,761	1,930,475
Netherlands	1,105	1,377	7,624	11,122	8,387	14,267	52,715	29,349	42,463
Norway-Sweden[i]	91	1,149	12,389	22,202	82,937	178,823	586,441	334,058	426,981
Norway[i]	—	—	—	—	16,068	88,644	185,111	96,810	182,542
Sweden[i]	—	—	—	—	24,224	90,179	401,330	237,248	244,439
Poland[c]	19	366	105	1,087	1,886	11,016	42,910	107,793	—
Portugal[j]	177	820	196	1,299	2,083	13,971	15,186	25,874	65,154
Romania	—	—	—	—	—	—	5,842	6,808	57,322
Russia[c, k]	86	280	520	423	1,670	35,177	182,698	450,101	1,501,301
Spain[l]	2,595	2,010	1,916	8,795	6,966	5,540	3,995	9,189	24,818
Switzerland	3,148	4,430	4,819	24,423	21,124	25,212	81,151	37,020	32,541
United Kingdom[h, m]	26,336	74,350	218,572	445,322	532,956	578,447	810,900	328,759	469,518
Yugoslavia[n]	—	—	—	—	—	—	—	—	—
Other Europe	3	40	79	4	9	590	1,070	145	514
Asia	34	55	121	36,080	54,408	134,128	71,151	61,285	299,836
China	3	8	32	35,933	54,028	133,139	65,797	15,268	19,884
Hong Kong	—	—	—	—	—	—	—	—	—
India	9	38	33	42	50	166	247	102	3,026
Iran	—	—	—	—	—	—	—	—	—
Israel	—	—	—	—	—	—	—	—	—
Japan	—	—	—	—	138	193	1,583	13,998	139,712
Jordan	—	—	—	—	—	—	—	—	—
Korea	—	—	—	—	—	—	—	—	—
Philippines	—	—	—	—	—	—	—	—	—
Syria	—	—	—	—	—	—	—	—	—
Taiwan	—	—	—	—	—	—	—	—	—
Turkey	19	8	45	94	129	382	2,478	27,510	127,999
Vietnam	—	—	—	—	—	—	—	—	—
Other Asia	3	1	11	11	63	248	1,046	4,407	9,215
America	9,655	31,905	50,516	84,145	130,292	345,010	524,826	37,350	277,809
Canada and Newfoundland[o, p]	2,297	11,875	34,285	64,171	117,978	324,310	492,865	3,098	123,067
Mexico[p, q]	3,835	7,187	3,069	3,446	1,957	5,133	2,405	734	31,188
Caribbean	3,061	11,792	11,803	12,447	8,751	14,285	27,323	31,480	100,960
Cuba	—	—	—	—	—	—	—	—	—
Dominican Republic	—	—	—	—	—	—	—	—	—
Haiti	—	—	—	—	—	—	—	—	—
Jamaica[r]	—	—	—	—	—	—	—	—	—
Other Caribbean[r]	3,061	11,792	11,803	12,447	8,751	14,285	27,323	31,480	100,960
Central America	57	94	297	512	70	173	279	649	7,341
Belize	—	—	—	—	—	—	—	—	77
Costa Rica	—	—	—	—	—	—	—	—	—
El Salvador	—	—	—	—	—	—	—	—	—
Guatemala	—	—	—	—	—	—	—	—	—
Honduras	—	—	—	—	—	—	—	—	—
Nicaragua	—	—	—	—	—	—	—	—	—
Panama[s]	—	—	—	—	—	—	—	—	—
Other Central America	57	94	297	512	70	173	279	649	7,264

The Civil War (1861–65) seemed to have little impact on immigration. The U.S. Department of Homeland Security, in *2005 Yearbook of Immigration Statistics* (2006, http://www.dhs.gov/xlibrary/assets/statistics/yearbook/2005/OIS_2005_Yearbook.pdf), notes that even though the number of immigrants dropped from 153,640 in 1860 to just under 92,000 in both 1861 and 1862, there were 176,282 new arrivals in 1863, and the numbers continued to grow.

TABLE 1.1

Immigration by region and selected country of last residence, 1820–2005 [CONTINUED]

Region and country of last residence[a]	1820 to 1829	1830 to 1839	1840 to 1849	1850 to 1859	1860 to 1869	1870 to 1879	1880 to 1889	1890 to 1899	1900 to 1909
South America	405	957	1,062	3,569	1,536	1,109	1,954	1,389	15,253
Argentina	—	—	—	—	—	—	—	—	—
Bolivia	—	—	—	—	—	—	—	—	—
Brazil	—	—	—	—	—	—	—	—	—
Chile	—	—	—	—	—	—	—	—	—
Colombia	—	—	—	—	—	—	—	—	—
Ecuador	—	—	—	—	—	—	—	—	—
Guyana	—	—	—	—	—	—	—	—	—
Paraguay	—	—	—	—	—	—	—	—	—
Peru	—	—	—	—	—	—	—	—	—
Suriname	—	—	—	—	—	—	—	—	—
Uruguay	—	—	—	—	—	—	—	—	—
Venezuela	—	—	—	—	—	—	—	—	—
Other South America	405	957	1,062	3,569	1,536	1,109	1,954	1,389	15,253
Other America[t]	—	—	—	—	—	—	—	—	—
Africa	15	50	61	84	407	371	763	432	6,326
Egypt	—	—	—	—	4	29	145	51	—
Ethiopia	—	—	—	—	—	—	—	—	—
Liberia	1	8	5	7	43	52	21	9	—
Morocco	—	—	—	—	—	—	—	—	—
South Africa	—	—	—	—	35	48	23	9	—
Other Africa	14	42	56	77	325	242	574	363	6,326
Oceania	3	7	14	166	187	9,996	12,361	4,704	12,355
Australia	2	1	2	15	—	8,930	7,250	3,098	11,191
New Zealand	—	—	—	—	—	39	21	12	—
Other Oceania	1	6	12	151	187	1,027	5,090	1,594	1,164
Not specified[t, u]	19,523	83,593	7,366	74,399	18,241	754	790	14,112	33,493

Region and country of last residence[a]	1910 to 1919	1920 to 1929	1930 to 1939	1940 to 1949	1950 to 1959	1960 to 1969	1970 to 1979	1980 to 1989	1890 to 1999
Total	6,347,380	4,295,510	699,375	856,608	2,499,268	3,213,749	4,248,203	6,244,379	9,775,398
Europe	4,985,411	2,560,340	444,399	472,524	1,404,973	1,133,443	825,590	668,866	1,348,612
Austria-Hungary[b, c, d]	1,154,727	60,891	12,531	13,574	113,015	27,590	20,387	20,437	27,529
Austria[b, d]	589,174	31,392	5,307	8,393	81,354	17,571	14,239	15,374	18,234
Hungary[b]	565,553	29,499	7,224	5,181	31,661	10,019	6,148	5,063	9,295
Belgium	32,574	21,511	4,013	12,473	18,885	9,647	5,413	7,028	7,077
Bulgaria[e]	27,180	2,824	1,062	449	97	598	1,011	1,124	16,948
Czechoslovakia[f]	—	101,182	17,757	8,475	1,624	2,758	5,654	5,678	8,970
Denmark	45,830	34,406	3,470	4,549	10,918	9,797	4,405	4,847	6,189
Finland	—	16,922	2,438	2,230	4,923	4,310	2,829	2,569	3,970
France[g]	60,335	54,842	13,761	36,954	50,113	46,975	26,281	32,066	35,945
Germany[c, d]	174,227	386,634	119,107	119,506	576,905	209,616	77,142	85,752	92,207
Greece	198,108	60,774	10,599	8,605	45,153	74,173	102,370	37,729	25,403
Ireland[h]	166,445	202,854	28,195	15,701	47,189	37,788	11,461	22,210	65,384
Italy	1,229,916	528,133	85,053	50,509	184,576	200,111	150,031	55,562	75,992
Netherlands	46,065	29,397	7,791	13,877	46,703	37,918	10,373	11,234	13,345
Norway-Sweden[i]	192,445	170,329	13,452	17,326	44,224	36,150	10,298	13,941	17,825
Norway[i]	79,488	70,327	6,901	8,326	22,806	17,371	3,927	3,835	5,211
Sweden[i]	112,957	100,002	6,551	9,000	21,418	18,779	6,371	10,106	12,614
Poland[c]	—	223,316	25,555	7,577	6,465	55,742	33,696	63,483	172,249
Portugal[j]	82,489	44,829	3,518	6,765	13,928	70,568	104,754	42,685	25,497
Romania	13,566	67,810	5,264	1,254	914	2,339	10,774	24,753	48,136
Russia[c, k]	1,106,998	61,604	2,463	605	453	2,329	28,132	33,311	433,427
Spain[l]	53,262	47,109	3,669	2,774	6,880	40,793	41,718	22,783	18,443
Switzerland	22,839	31,772	5,990	9,904	17,577	19,193	8,536	8,316	11,768
United Kingdom[h, m]	371,878	341,552	61,813	131,794	195,709	220,213	133,218	153,644	156,182
Yugoslavia[n]	—	49,215	6,920	2,039	6,966	17,990	31,862	16,267	57,039
Other Europe	6,527	22,434	9,978	5,584	11,756	6,845	5,245	3,447	29,087
Asia	269,736	126,740	19,231	34,532	135,844	358,605	1,406,544	2,391,356	2,859,899
China	20,916	30,648	5,874	16,072	8,836	14,060	17,627	170,897	342,058
Hong Kong	—	—	—	—	13,781	67,047	117,350	112,132	116,894

Post–Civil War Growth in Immigration

Post–Civil War America was characterized by the rapid growth of the Industrial Revolution, which fueled the need for workers in the nation's flourishing factories. The number of arriving immigrants continued to grow in the 1870s, dominated by people from Germany, the United

Region and country of last residence[a]	1910 to 1919	1920 to 1929	1930 to 1939	1940 to 1949	1950 to 1959	1960 to 1969	1970 to 1979	1980 to 1989	1990 to 1999
India	3,478	2,076	554	1,692	1,850	18,638	147,997	231,649	352,528
Iran	—	208	198	1,144	3,195	9,059	33,763	98,141	76,899
Israel	—	—	—	98	21,376	30,911	36,306	43,669	41,340
Japan	77,125	42,057	2,683	1,557	40,651	40,956	49,392	44,150	66,582
Jordan	—	—	—	—	4,899	9,230	25,541	28,928	42,755
Korea	—	—	—	83	4,845	27,048	241,192	322,708	179,770
Philippines	—	—	391	4,099	17,245	70,660	337,726	502,056	534,338
Syria	—	5,307	2,188	1,179	1,091	2,432	8,086	14,534	22,906
Taiwan	—	—	—	—	721	15,657	83,155	119,051	132,647
Turkey	160,717	40,450	1,327	754	2,980	9,464	12,209	19,208	38,687
Vietnam	—	—	—	—	290	2,949	121,716	200,632	275,379
Other Asia	7,500	5,994	6,016	7,854	14,084	40,494	174,484	483,601	637,116
America	1,070,539	1,591,278	230,319	328,435	921,610	1,674,172	1,904,355	2,695,329	5,137,743
Canada and Newfoundland[o, p]	708,715	949,286	162,703	160,911	353,169	433,128	179,267	156,313	194,788
Mexico[p, q]	185,334	498,945	32,709	56,158	273,847	441,824	621,218	1,009,586	2,757,418
Caribbean	120,860	83,482	18,052	46,194	115,661	427,235	708,850	790,109	1,004,687
Cuba	—	12,769	10,641	25,976	73,221	202,030	256,497	132,552	159,037
Dominican Republic	—	—	1,026	4,802	10,219	83,552	139,249	221,552	359,818
Haiti	—	—	156	823	3,787	28,992	55,166	121,406	177,446
Jamaica[r]	—	—	—	—	7,397	62,218	130,226	193,874	177,143
Other Caribbean[r]	120,860	70,713	6,229	14,593	21,037	50,443	127,712	120,725	131,243
Central America	15,692	16,511	6,840	20,135	40,201	98,560	120,374	339,376	610,189
Belize	40	285	193	433	1,133	4,185	6,747	14,964	12,600
Costa Rica	—	—	431	1,965	4,044	17,975	12,405	25,017	17,054
El Salvador	—	—	597	4,885	5,094	14,405	29,428	137,418	273,017
Guatemala	—	—	423	1,303	4,197	14,357	23,837	58,847	126,043
Honduras	—	—	679	1,874	5,320	15,078	15,651	39,071	72,880
Nicaragua	—	—	405	4,393	7,812	10,383	10,911	31,102	80,446
Panama[s]	—	—	1,452	5,282	12,601	22,177	21,395	32,957	28,149
Other Central America	15,652	16,226	2,660	—	—	—	—	—	—
South America	39,938	43,025	9,990	19,662	78,418	250,754	273,608	399,862	570,624
Argentina	—	—	1,067	3,108	16,346	49,384	30,303	23,442	30,065
Bolivia	—	—	50	893	2,759	6,205	5,635	9,798	18,111
Brazil	—	4,627	1,468	3,653	11,547	29,238	18,600	22,944	50,744
Chile	—	—	347	1,320	4,669	12,384	15,032	19,749	18,200
Colombia	—	—	1,027	3,454	15,567	68,371	71,265	105,494	137,985
Ecuador	—	—	244	2,207	8,574	34,107	47,464	48,015	81,358
Guyana	—	—	131	596	1,131	4,546	38,278	85,886	74,407
Paraguay	—	—	33	85	576	1,249	1,486	3,518	6,082
Peru	—	—	321	1,273	5,980	19,783	25,311	49,958	110,117
Suriname	—	—	25	130	299	612	714	1,357	2,285
Uruguay	—	—	112	754	1,026	4,089	8,416	7,235	6,062
Venezuela	—	—	1,155	2,182	9,927	20,758	11,007	22,405	35,180
Other South America	39,938	38,398	4,010	7	17	28	97	61	28
Other America[t]	—	29	25	25,375	60,314	22,671	1,038	83	37
Africa	8,867	6,362	2,120	6,720	13,016	23,780	71,408	141,990	346,416
Egypt	—	1,063	781	1,613	1,996	5,581	23,543	26,744	44,604
Ethiopia	—	—	10	28	302	804	2,588	12,927	40,097
Liberia	—	—	35	37	289	841	2,391	6,420	13,587
Morocco	—	—	73	879	2,703	2,880	1,967	3,471	15,768
South Africa	—	—	312	1,022	2,278	4,360	10,002	15,505	21,964
Other Africa	8,867	5,299	909	3,141	5,448	9,314	30,917	76,923	210,396
Oceania	12,339	9,860	3,306	14,262	11,353	23,630	39,980	41,432	56,800
Australia	11,280	8,404	2,260	11,201	8,275	14,986	18,708	16,901	24,288
New Zealand	—	935	790	2,351	1,799	3,775	5,018	6,129	8,600
Other Oceania	1,059	521	256	710	1,279	4,869	16,254	18,402	23,912
Not specified[t, u]	488	930	—	135	12,472	119	326	305,406	25,928

Kingdom, Ireland, Sweden, and Norway. (See Table 1.1.) Opposition to immigration continued among some factions of established citizens. Secret societies of white supremacists, such as the Ku Klux Klan, formed throughout the South to oppose not only African-American suffrage but also the influence of the Roman Catholic Church and rapid naturalization of foreign immigrants.

Eastern European Influx during the 1880s

The decade from 1880 to 1889 marked a new era in immigration to the United States. The volume of immigrants nearly doubled from 2,742,137 in the 1870s to 5,248,568 in the 1880s. (See Table 1.1.) German arrivals peaked at over 1.4 million, and emigration from Norway, Sweden, and the United Kingdom also reached their

TABLE 1.1

Immigration by region and selected country of last residence, 1820–2005 [CONTINUED]

Region and country of last residence[a]	2000	2001	2002	2003	2004	2005
Total	**841,002**	**1,058,902**	**1,059,356**	**703,542**	**957,883**	**1,122,373**
Europe	131,920	176,892	177,059	102,546	135,663	180,449
Austria-Hungary[b, c, d]	2,009	2,303	4,004	2,176	3,689	4,569
Austria[b, d]	986	996	2,650	1,160	2,442	3,002
Hungary[b]	1,023	1,307	1,354	1,016	1,247	1,567
Belgium	817	997	834	515	746	1,031
Bulgaria[e]	4,779	4,273	3,476	3,706	4,042	5,451
Czechoslovakia[f]	1,407	1,911	1,854	1,472	1,871	2,182
Denmark	549	732	651	435	568	714
Finland	377	497	365	230	346	549
France[g]	4,063	5,379	4,567	2,926	4,209	5,035
Germany[c, d]	12,230	21,992	20,977	8,061	10,270	12,864
Greece	5,113	1,941	1,486	900	1,213	1,473
Ireland[h]	1,264	1,531	1,400	1,002	1,518	2,083
Italy	2,652	3,332	2,812	1,890	2,495	3,179
Netherlands	1,455	1,888	2,296	1,321	1,713	2,150
Norway-Sweden[i]	1,967	2,544	2,082	1,516	2,011	2,264
Norway[i]	508	582	460	385	457	472
Sweden[i]	1,459	1,962	1,622	1,131	1,554	1,792
Poland[c]	9,750	12,308	13,274	11,004	14,048	14,837
Portugal[j]	1,373	1,611	1,301	808	1,062	1,084
Romania	6,506	6,206	4,515	3,305	4,078	6,431
Russia[c, k]	43,156	54,838	55,370	33,513	41,959	60,395
Spain[l]	1,390	1,875	1,588	1,102	1,453	2,002
Switzerland	1,339	1,786	1,493	862	1,193	1,465
United Kingdom[h, m]	14,427	20,118	17,940	11,155	16,680	21,956
Yugoslavia[n]	11,960	21,854	28,051	8,270	13,213	19,249
Other Europe	3,337	6,976	6,723	6,377	7,286	9,486
Asia	254,932	336,112	325,749	235,339	319,025	382,744
China	41,804	50,677	55,901	37,342	50,280	64,921
Hong Kong	7,181	10,282	7,938	5,015	5,421	5,004
India	38,938	65,673	66,644	47,032	65,507	79,140
Iran	6,481	8,003	7,684	4,696	5,898	7,306
Israel	3,871	4,892	4,907	3,686	5,206	6,963
Japan	7,688	10,424	9,106	6,702	8,655	9,929
Jordan	4,476	5,106	4,774	4,008	5,186	5,430
Korea	15,107	19,728	19,917	12,076	19,441	26,002
Philippines	40,465	50,644	48,493	43,133	54,651	57,656
Syria	2,255	3,542	3,350	2,046	2,549	3,350
Taiwan	9,457	12,457	9,932	7,168	9,314	9,389
Turkey	2,702	3,463	3,914	3,318	4,491	6,449
Vietnam	25,159	34,537	32,372	21,227	30,074	30,832
Other Asia	49,348	56,684	50,817	37,890	52,352	70,373
America	392,461	470,794	477,363	305,936	408,972	432,748
Canada and Newfoundland[o, p]	21,289	29,991	27,142	16,447	22,439	29,930
Mexico[p, q]	171,445	204,032	216,924	114,758	173,711	157,992
Caribbean	84,250	96,384	93,914	67,498	82,116	91,378
Cuba	17,897	25,832	27,435	8,685	15,385	20,651
Dominican Republic	17,373	21,139	22,386	26,112	30,063	27,366
Haiti	21,977	22,470	19,151	11,924	13,695	13,496
Jamaica[r]	15,603	15,031	14,507	13,045	13,581	17,775
Other Caribbean[r]	11,400	11,912	10,435	7,732	9,392	12,090
Central America	60,331	72,504	66,298	53,283	61,253	52,636
Belize	774	982	983	616	888	901
Costa Rica	1,390	1,863	1,686	1,322	1,811	2,479
El Salvador	22,301	30,876	30,472	27,854	29,297	20,891
Guatemala	9,861	13,399	15,870	14,195	18,655	16,475
Honduras	5,851	6,546	6,355	4,582	5,339	6,825
Nicaragua	18,258	16,908	9,171	3,503	3,842	3,196
Panama[s]	1,896	1,930	1,761	1,211	1,421	1,869
Other Central America	—	—	—	—	—	—
South America	55,143	67,880	73,082	53,946	69,452	100,811
Argentina	2,472	3,426	3,791	3,193	4,672	6,945
Bolivia	1,744	1,804	1,660	1,365	1,719	2,164
Brazil	6,767	9,391	9,034	6,108	10,247	16,331
Chile	1,660	1,881	1,766	1,255	1,719	2,354
Colombia	14,125	16,234	18,409	14,400	18,055	24,710

TABLE 1.1

Immigration by region and selected country of last residence, 1820–2005 [CONTINUED]

Region and country of last residence[a]	2000	2001	2002	2003	2004	2005
Ecuador	7,624	9,654	10,524	7,022	8,366	11,528
Guyana	5,255	7,835	9,492	6,373	5,721	8,772
Paraguay	394	464	413	222	324	523
Peru	9,361	10,838	11,737	9,169	11,369	15,205
Suriname	281	254	223	175	170	287
Uruguay	396	516	499	470	750	1,110
Venezuela	5,052	5,576	5,529	4,190	6,335	10,870
Other South America	12	7	5	4	5	12
Other America[t]	3	3	3	4	1	1
Africa	40,790	50,009	56,002	45,559	62,623	79,701
Egypt	4,323	5,333	6,215	3,928	6,590	10,296
Ethiopia	3,645	4,620	6,308	5,969	7,180	8,380
Liberia	1,225	1,477	1,467	1,081	1,540	1,846
Morocco	3,423	4,752	3,188	2,969	3,910	4,165
South Africa	2,814	4,046	3,685	2,088	3,035	4,425
Other Africa	25,360	29,781	35,139	29,524	40,068	50,589
Oceania	5,928	7,201	6,495	5,076	6,954	7,432
Australia	2,694	3,714	3,420	2,488	3,397	4,090
New Zealand	1,080	1,347	1,364	1,030	1,420	1,457
Other Oceania	2,154	2,140	1,711	1,558	2,137	1,885
Not specified[t, u]	14,971	17,894	16,688	9,086	24,646	39,299

— Represents zero or not available.

[a]Data for years prior to 1906 refer to country of origin; data from 1906 to 2005 refer to country of last residence.
[b]Data for Austria and Hungary not reported separately for all years during 1860 to 1869, 1890 to 1899, 1900 to 1909.
[c]From 1899 to 1919, data for Poland included in Austria-Hungary, Germany, and the Soviet Union.
[d]From 1938 to 1945, data for Austria included in Germany.
[e]From 1899 to 1910, included Serbia and Montenegro.
[f]Currently includes the Czech Republic and Slovak Republic.
[g]From 1820 to 1910, included Corsica.
[h]Prior to 1926, data for Northern Ireland included in Ireland.
[i]Data for Norway and Sweden not reported separately until 1869.
[j]From 1820 to 1910, included Cape Verde and Azores Islands.
[k]From 1820 to 1920, data refer to the Russian Empire. Between 1920 and 1990 data refer to the Soviet Union. From 1991 to present, the data refer to the Russian Federation, Armenia, Azerbaijan, Belarus, Georgia, Kazakhstan, Kyrgyzstan, Moldova, Russia, Tajikistan, Ukraine, and Uzbekistan.
[l]From 1820 to 1910, included the Canary Islands and Balearic Islands.
[m]Since 1925, data for United Kingdom refer to England, Scotland, Wales and Northern Ireland.
[n]Currently includes Bosnia-Herzegovina, Croatia, Macedonia, Slovenia, Serbia, and Montenegro.
[o]Prior to 1911, data refer to British North America. From 1911, data includes Newfoundland.
[p]Land arrivals not completely enumerated until 1908.
[q]No data available for Mexico from 1886 to 1893.
[r]Data for Jamaica not reported separately until 1953. Prior to 1953, Jamaica was included in British West Indies.
[s]From 1932 to 1972, data for the Panama Canal zone included in Panama.
[t]Included in 'Not specified' until 1925.
[u]Includes 32,897 persons returning in 1906 to their homes in the United States.
Note: From 1820 to 1867, figures represent alien passenger arrivals at sea ports; from 1868 to 1891 and 1895 to 1897, immigrant alien arrivals; from 1892 to 1894 and 1898 to 2005, immigrant aliens admitted for permanent residence; from 1892 to 1903, aliens entering by cabin class were not counted as immigrants. Land arrivals were not completely enumerated until 1908. For this table, fiscal year 1843 covers 9 months ending September, 1843; fiscal years 1832 and 1850 cover 15 months ending December 31 of the respective years; and fiscal year 1868 covers 6 months ending June 30, 1868.

SOURCE: "Table 2. Persons Obtaining Legal Permanent Resident Status by Region and Selected Country of Last Residence: Fiscal Years 1820 to 2005," in *2005 Yearbook of Immigration Statistics*, U.S. Department of Homeland Security, Office of Immigration Statistics, November 2006, http://www.dhs.gov/xlibrary/assets/statistics/yearbook/2005/OIS_2005_Yearbook.pdf (accessed December 7, 2006)

highest levels. A new wave of emigrants began to arrive from Russia (including a significant number of Jews fleeing massacres called pogroms), Poland, Austria-Hungary, and Italy. The mass exodus from eastern Europe foretold events that would result in World War I (1914–18). These newcomers were different: they came from countries with limited public education and no sense of social equality; they were often unskilled and illiterate; and they tended to form tight ethnic communities within the large cities, where they clung to their own language and customs, which further limited their ability to assimilate into U.S. culture.

A Developing Federal Role in Immigration

The increasing numbers of immigrants prompted a belief that there should be some type of administrative order to the ever-growing influx. In 1864 Congress created the Commission of Immigration under the U.S. Department of State. A one-person office was set up in New York City to oversee immigration.

The 1870s witnessed a national debate over the importation of contract labor and limiting immigration for such purposes. In 1875, after considerable debate, Congress passed the Page Law. This first major piece of restrictive immigration legislation prohibited alien convicts and prostitutes from entering the country.

With the creation of the Commission of Immigration, the federal government began to play a central role in immigration, which had previously been handled by the individual states. Court decisions beginning in 1849 strengthened the federal government's role and limited the states' role in regulating immigration. In 1875 the U.S. Supreme Court ultimately ruled in *Henderson v. Mayor of the City of New York* (92 U.S. 259) that the immigration laws of New York, California, and Louisiana were unconstitutional. This ended the states' right to regulate immigration and exclude undesirable aliens. From then on Congress and the federal government had complete responsibility for immigration.

In 1882 Congress passed the first general immigration law. The Immigration Act of 1882 established a centralized immigration administration under the secretary of the treasury. The law also allowed the exclusion of "undesirables," such as paupers, criminals, and the insane. A head tax was added at $0.50 per arriving immigrant to defray the expenses of immigration regulation and caring for the immigrants after their arrival in the United States.

Influx of Emigrants from Asia

Before the discovery of gold in California in 1848, few Asians (only 121 between 1840 and 1849) came to the United States. (See Table 1.1.) Between 1849 and 1852 large numbers of Asian immigrants began arriving in the United States. These early arrivals came mostly from southern China, spurred on by economic depression, famine, war, and flooding. Thousands of Chinese immigrants were recruited to build railroads and work in mines, construction, or manufacturing. Many became domestic servants. Former mining camp cooks who had saved some of their income opened restaurants. Others invested small amounts in equipment to operate laundries, performing a service few other people wanted to tackle. Between 1850 and 1879 about a quarter of a million emigrants arrived from China, whereas only a few thousand arrived from other Asian countries.

Some people became alarmed by this increase in Chinese immigration. Their fears were fueled by a combination of racism and concerns among American-born workers that employers were bringing over foreign workers to replace them and keep unskilled wages low. The public began to call for restrictions on Chinese immigration.

Chinese Exclusion Act

In 1882 Congress passed the Chinese Exclusion Act, which prohibited further immigration of Chinese laborers to the United States for ten years. Exceptions included teachers, diplomats, students, merchants, and tourists.

The Chinese Exclusion Act marked the first time the United States barred immigration of a national group. The law also prohibited Chinese immigrants in the United States from becoming naturalized U.S. citizens. Fewer than sixteen thousand Chinese arrived during the last decade of the nineteenth century. (See Table 1.1.)

Four other laws that prohibited the immigration of Chinese laborers followed the Chinese Exclusion Act. The Geary Act of 1892 extended the Chinese Exclusion Act for ten more years. In cases brought before the Supreme Court, the Court upheld the constitutionality of these two laws. The Immigration Act of 1904 made the Chinese exclusion laws permanent. Under the Immigration Act of 1917 the United States suspended the immigration of laborers from almost all Asian countries.

During World War II (1939–45) the United States and China became allies against the Japanese in Asia. As a gesture of goodwill, on December 17, 1943, President Franklin D. Roosevelt signed the Act to Repeal the Chinese Exclusion Acts, to Establish Quotas, and for Other Purposes. The new law lifted the ban on naturalization of Chinese nationals but established a quota or limit of 105 Chinese immigrants to be admitted per year.

Beginning of Japanese Immigration

Until the passage of the Chinese Exclusion Act, Japanese immigration was hardly noticeable, with the total flow at 331 between 1860 and 1879. (See Table 1.1.) Because Japanese immigrants were not covered by the Chinese Exclusion Act, Japanese laborers were brought in to replace Chinese workers. Consequently, Japanese immigration increased from 1,583 in the 1880s to over 139,000 during the first decade of the twentieth century. According to Marianne K. G. Tanabe, in *Health and Health Care of Japanese-American Elders* (2001, http://www.stanford.edu/group/ethnoger/japanese.html), the booming Hawaiian sugar industry offered so many jobs that by 1910 Hawaii had four times as many Japanese as the U.S. mainland.

The same anti-Asian attitudes that had led to the Chinese Exclusion Act culminated in President Theodore Roosevelt's Gentleman's Agreement of 1907, an informal arrangement between the United States and Japan that cut the flow of Japanese immigration to a trickle. This anti-Asian attitude resurfaced a generation later in the National Origins Act of 1924. The immigration quota for any nationality group had been based on the number of people of that nationality that were residents in the United States during the 1910 census. The new law reduced quotas from 3% to 2% and shifted the base for quota calculations from 1910 back to 1890. Because few Asians lived in the United States in 1890, the 1924 reduction in Asian immigration was particularly dramatic. Asian immigration was not permitted to increase until after World War II.

Greater Government Control

In "Overview of INS History" (January 20, 2006, http://149.101.23.2/graphics/aboutus/history/articles/oview.htm), Marion L. Smith describes the development of the federal role in control of immigration. Except for Asian immigration, the federal government had done little to restrict immigration. In 1891 the federal government assumed total control over immigration issues. The Immigration Act of 1891 authorized the establishment of the U.S. Office of Immigration under the U.S. Department of the Treasury. This first comprehensive immigration law added to the list of inadmissible people those suffering from certain contagious diseases, polygamists (married people who had more than one spouse at the same time), and aliens convicted of minor crimes. The law also prohibited using advertisements to encourage immigration.

On January 1, 1892, a new federal immigration station began operating on Ellis Island in New York. During its years of operation (1892–1954) over twelve million immigrants were processed through Ellis Island. That figure represents about half of the more than twenty-three million total immigrants tallied by Table 1.1 during that period.

In 1895 the Office of Immigration became the Bureau of Immigration under the commissioner-general of immigration. In 1903 the Bureau of Immigration was transferred to the U.S. Department of Commerce and Labor. The Basic Naturalization Act of 1906 consolidated the immigration and naturalization functions of the federal government under the Bureau of Immigration and Naturalization. When the Department of Commerce and Labor was separated into two cabinet departments in 1913, two bureaus were formed: the Bureau of Immigration and the Bureau of Naturalization. In 1933 the two bureaus were reunited as the U.S. Immigration and Naturalization Service (INS).

Emigrants from Eastern Europe Continued to Come

By the 1890s the origins of those arriving in the United States had changed. Fewer emigrants came from northern Europe, whereas emigrants from southern, central, and eastern European countries grew in numbers every year. Of the 7.5 million European immigrants who arrived between 1900 and 1909, 5.4 million (72%) came from Italy, Russia, and Austria-Hungary. (See Table 1.1.) The 1923 report *The Immigration Problem in the United States* (http://pds.harvard.edu:8080/pdx/servlet/pds?id=2581652) prepared by the National Industrial Conference Board (NICB) noted that immigration from northern and western Europe was referred to as "old" immigration, whereas immigration from southern and eastern European countries was commonly called "new" immigration. The same report noted racial problems between "old" and "new" immigrants; the term *race* generally included nationalities or ethnic groups. The NICB report displayed graphs of emigrant groups by race, including Hebrew, German, English, Irish, Scotch, Scandinavian, Slovak, and Armenian.

The exodus of Jews (called Hebrews in the NICB report) from eastern Europe was particularly significant. The NICB stated that an average of greater than fifty-seven thousand Hebrews per year arrived between 1908 and 1922. This was double the average arrivals of any other group. The American Immigration Law Foundation notes that many of these Jewish immigrants were merchants, shopkeepers, craftsmen, and professionals, contrary to the stereotype of poor, uneducated immigrants coming out of eastern Europe.

IMMIGRATION AT THE TURN OF THE TWENTIETH CENTURY

A Million Immigrants a Year

The DHS, in *2005 Yearbook of Immigration Statistics*, reports that the nation's already high immigration rate at the turn of the twentieth century nearly doubled between 1902 and 1907. Immigration reached a million per year in 1905, 1906, 1907, 1910, 1913, and 1914, but declined to less than 325,000 per year from 1915 through 1919 because of World War I. Many Americans worried about the growing influx of immigrants, whose customs were unfamiliar to most of the native population. Anti-Catholic, anti–political radicalism (usually expressed as antisocialism), and racist movements became more prevalent along with a resurgence of nativism.

The Immigration Act of 1907 barred the immigration of "feeble-minded" people, those with physical or mental defects that might prevent them from earning a living, and people with tuberculosis. Increasing the head tax on each arriving immigrant to $5, the 1907 law also officially classified the arriving aliens as immigrants (people planning to take up residence in the United States) and nonimmigrants (people visiting for a short period to attend school, conduct business, or travel as tourists). All arrivals were required to declare their intentions for permanent or temporary stays in the United States. The law further authorized the president to refuse admission to people he considered harmful to the labor conditions in the nation.

Reflecting national concerns about conflicts between old and new immigrant groups, Bureau of Immigration annual reports proposed that the immigrants should be more widely dispersed throughout the rest of the country, instead of being concentrated mostly in the northeastern urban areas. Not only would such a distribution of aliens help relieve the nation's urban problems but also the bureau thought it might promote greater racial and cultural assimilation.

TABLE 1.2

Aliens excluded, by administrative reason for exclusion, 1892–1990

Year	Total	Subversive or anarchist	Criminal or narcotics violations	Immoral	Mental or physical defect	Likely to become public charge	Stowaway	Attemped entry without inspection or without proper documents	Contract laborer	Unable to read (over 16 years of age)	Other
1892–1990	650,252	1,369	17,465	8,209	82,590	219,399	16,240	204,943	41,941	13,679	44,417
1892–1900	22,515	—	65	89	1,309	15,070	—	—	5,792	—	190
1901–10	108,211	10	1,681	1,277	24,425	63,311	—	—	12,991	—	4,516
1911–20	178,109	27	4,353	4,824	42,129	90,045	1,904	—	15,417	5,083	14,327
1921–30	189,307	9	2,082	1,281	11,044	37,175	8,447	94,084	6,274	8,202	20,709
1931–40	68,217	5	1,261	253	1,530	12,519	2,126	47,858	1,235	258	1,172
1941–50	30,263	60	1,134	80	1,021	1,072	3,182	22,441	219	108	946
1951–60	20,585	1,098	2,017	361	956	149	376	14,657	13	26	932
1961–70	4,831	128	383	24	145	27	175	3,706	—	2	241
1971–80	8,455	32	814	20	31	31	30	7,237	—	—	260
1981–90	19,759	NA	3,675	NA	NA	NA	NA	14,960	—	—	1,124

Note: From 1941–53, statistics represent all exclusions at sea and air ports and exclusions of aliens seeking entry for 30 days or longer at land ports. After 1953, includes aliens excluded after formal hearings.
— Represents zero.
NA Not available.

SOURCE: Adapted from "Table 44. Aliens Excluded by Administrative Reason for Exclusion: Fiscal Years 1892–1990," in *Enforcement Supplemental Tables for 2003 Yearbook of Immigration Statistics*, U.S. Department of Homeland Security, Office of Immigration Statistics, September 2004, http://www.dhs.gov/xlibrary/assets/statistics/yearbook/2003/2003ENF.pdf (accessed February 8, 2007)

Immigration Act of 1917

The mounting negative feelings toward immigrants resulted in the Immigration Act of 1917, which was passed despite President Woodrow Wilson's veto. Besides codifying previous immigration legislation, the 1917 act required that immigrants be able to read and write in their native language and pass a literacy test, which proved to be a controversial clause. The new act also added the following groups to the inadmissible classes of immigrants: "illiterates, persons of constitutional psychopathic inferiority, men and women entering for immoral reasons, chronic alcoholics, stowaways, vagrants, persons who had suffered a previous attack of insanity," and those coming from the designated Asiatic "barred zone," comprising mostly Asia and the Pacific Islands. This provision was a continuation of the Chinese Exclusion Act and the Gentleman's Agreement of 1907, in which the Japanese government had agreed to stop the flow of workers to the United States. In 1918 passports were required by presidential proclamation for all entries into the United States.

Denied Entry

Despite the restrictive immigration legislation, only a small percentage of those attempting to immigrate to the United States were turned away. Between 1892 and 1990, 650,252 people were denied entry for a variety of reasons. (See Table 1.2.) Aside from those attempting to enter without proper papers, the largest group excluded was 219,399 people considered "likely to become public charges." The thirty-year period from 1901 to 1930 was the peak era for exclusion of immigrants deemed likely to become public charges, mentally or physically defective, or immoral. The 1917 ban on illiterate immigrants excluded 13,679 aliens over the next fifty years.

RESTRICTIONS ON IMMIGRATION TIGHTEN

World War I temporarily stopped the influx of immigrants. In *2005 Yearbook of Immigration Statistics*, the DHS reports that in 1914, 1.2 million immigrants arrived; a year later the number dropped to 326,700. By 1918, the final year of the war, just over 110,000 immigrants ventured to the United States. However, the heavy flow of immigration started again after the war as people fled the war-ravaged European continent. Over 805,000 immigrants arrived in 1921.

The new wave of immigrants flocked to major cities where they hoped to find relatives or other emigrants from their native country as well as jobs. According to the Census Bureau's *Census Monograph I, 1922–1931* (2007, http://www2.census.gov/prod2/decennial/documents/00476515n1ch1.pdf), the 1920 census reported that for the first time in U.S. history the population living in cities exceeded that living in rural areas.

First Quota Law

Concern over whether the United States could continue to absorb such huge numbers of immigrants led Congress to introduce a major change in U.S. immigration policy. Other factors influencing Congress included racial fears about the new immigrants and apprehension over many of the immigrants' politically radical ideas.

The Quota Law of 1921 was the first quantitative immigration law. Congress limited the number of aliens of any nationality who could enter the United States to 3% of the number of foreign-born people of that nationality who lived in the United States in 1910 (based on the U.S. census). By 1910, however, many southern and eastern Europeans had already entered the country, a fact many legislators had overlooked. Consequently, to restructure the makeup of the immigrant population, Congress approved the National Origins Act of 1924. This act set the first permanent limitation on immigration, called the national origins quota system. The law immediately limited the number of people of each nationality to 2% of the population of that nationality who lived in the United States in 1890.

The 1924 law provided that after July 1, 1927, an overall cap would allow a total of 150,000 immigrants per year. Quotas for each national origin group were to be developed based on the 1920 census. Exempted from the quota limitation were spouses or dependents of U.S. citizens, returning alien residents, or natives of Western Hemisphere countries not subject to quotas (natives of Mexico, Canada, or other independent countries of Central or South America). The 1924 law further required that all arriving nonimmigrants present visas (government authorizations permitting entry into a country) obtained from a U.S. consulate abroad. U.S. immigration law consisted of the 1917 and 1924 acts until 1952.

Impact of Quotas

The new laws also barred all Asian immigration, which soon led to a shortage of farm and sugar plantation workers. Filipinos filled the gap; because the Philippines was a U.S. territory, it did not come under the immigration quota laws. In addition, large numbers of emigrants arrived from the Caribbean, peaking during the 1910 to 1919 period, when nearly 121,000 Caribbean immigrants entered the United States. (See Table 1.1.)

Before World War I Caribbean workers had moved among the islands and to parts of South and Central America. Following the war many went north in search of work. Similarly, after World War II, when agricultural changes in the Caribbean forced many people off the farms and into the cities, many traveled on to the United States or the United Kingdom in search of jobs.

With the new quota laws the problem of illegal aliens arose for the first time. Previously, only a few of the small number of immigrants who had failed the immigration standards tried to sneak in, usually across the U.S.-Mexican border. With the new laws, the number of illegal aliens began to increase. Subsequently, Congress created the Border Patrol in 1924 (under the Labor Appropriation Act) to oversee the nation's borders and prevent illegal

aliens from coming into the United States. This in turn resulted in a system of appeals and deportation actions.

DEPRESSION AND WAR
Changes at the INS

Immigration dropped well below one hundred thousand arrivals per year during the Great Depression (1929–41), because the United States offered no escape from the unemployment that was rampant throughout most of the world. However, in the latter half of the 1930s Nazi persecution caused a new round of emigrants to flee Europe. In 1940 the INS was transferred from the U.S. Department of Labor to the U.S. Department of Justice. This move reflected the growing fear of war, making surveillance of aliens a question of national security rather than of how many to admit. The job of the INS shifted from the exclusion of aliens to combating alien criminal and subversive elements. This required closer cooperation with the U.S. attorney general's office and the Federal Bureau of Investigation.

Alien Registration

World War II began with the German invasion of Poland in September 1939. Growing concern about an increase in refugees that might result from the war in Europe led Congress to pass the Alien Registration Act of 1940 (also known as the Smith Act). Among other provisions, this act required all aliens to register and those over fourteen years old to be fingerprinted. All registration and fingerprinting took place at local post offices between August 27 and December 26, 1940. In "This Month in Immigration History: June 1940" (January 20, 2006, http://149.101.23.2/graphics/aboutus/history/6june40.htm), the U.S. Citizenship and Immigration Service (USCIS) notes that during this four-month period, five million aliens registered, nearly 4% of the total U.S. population of 132 million people. Each alien was identified by an alien registration number, known as an A-number. For the first time the government had a means of identifying an individual immigrant. (The A-number system is still in use today.) Following registration each alien received by mail an Alien Registration Receipt Card, which he or she was required to keep to prove registration. Each alien was required to report any change of address within five days. Managing such a vast number of registrants and documents in a short time created a monumental challenge for the federal government. The ranks of employees in the Alien Registration Division of the INS swelled from 55 in August 1940 to a peak of 985 in July 1941.

The United States officially entered World War II on December 8, 1941, the day after the Japanese attack on Pearl Harbor. President Roosevelt immediately proclaimed all "nationals and subjects" of nations with which the country was at war to be enemy aliens. The INS states that on January 14, 1942, the president issued a proclamation requiring further registration of aliens from enemy nations (primarily Germany, Italy, and Japan). All such aliens aged fourteen and over were directed to apply for a Certificate of Identification during the month of February 1942.

Alien registrations were used by a variety of government agencies and private industry to locate possible enemy subversives, such as aliens working for defense contractors, aliens with radio operator licenses, and aliens trained to pilot aircraft. According to the INS, one out of every twenty-three workers in U.S. industry at that time was a noncitizen.

Japanese Internment

Following the recommendation of military advisers the president issued Executive Order 9066 on February 19, 1942, which authorized the forcible internment of people of Japanese ancestry. Lieutenant General John L. DeWitt was placed in charge of removal of the Japanese to internment camps, located in remote areas in western states, including Arizona, California, Colorado, Idaho, Wyoming, and Utah. Two camps were established in Arkansas. In the *Final Report: Japanese Evacuation from the West Coast 1942* (1943), DeWitt revealed that during a period of less than ninety days, 110,442 people of Japanese ancestry were evacuated from the West Coast. More than two-thirds were U.S. citizens. Relocation began in April 1942 and the last camp was vacated in March 1946.

Executive Order 9066 was never formally terminated after the war ended. Over the years many Japanese-Americans expressed concern that it could be implemented again. On February 19, 1976, President Gerald Ford issued a proclamation officially terminating the provisions of Executive Order 9066 retroactive to December 31, 1946. In 1988 President Ronald Reagan signed a bill into law providing restitution ($20,000) to each of the surviving internees.

POSTWAR IMMIGRATION LAW

A growing fear of communist infiltration arose during the post–World War II period. One result was the passage of the Internal Security Act of 1950, which made membership in communist or totalitarian organizations cause for exclusion (denial of an alien's entry into the United States), deportation, or denial of naturalization. The law also required resident aliens to report their addresses annually and made reading, writing, and speaking English prerequisites for naturalization.

The Immigration and Nationality Act of 1952 added preferences for relatives and skilled aliens, gave immigrants and aliens certain legal protections, made all races eligible for immigration and naturalization, and absorbed most of the Internal Security Act of 1950. The act changed the national origin quotas to only one-sixth of 1% of the number of people in the United States in 1920

whose ancestry or national origin was attributable to a specific area of the world. It also excluded aliens on ideological grounds, homosexuality, health restrictions, criminal records, narcotics addiction, and involvement in terrorism.

Once again, countries within the Western Hemisphere were not included in the quota system. President Harry Truman vetoed the legislation, but Congress overrode his veto. Although there were major amendments, the Immigration and Nationality Act remained the basic statute governing who could gain entry into the United States until the passage of new laws following the September 11, 2001, terrorist attacks.

During the 1950s a half dozen special laws allowed the entrance of additional refugees. Many of the laws resulted from World War II, but some stemmed from new developments. An example was the law affecting refugees fleeing the failed 1956 Hungarian revolution.

A TWO-HEMISPHERE SYSTEM

In 1963 President John F. Kennedy submitted a plan to change the quota system. Two years later Congress passed the Immigration and Nationality Act Amendments of 1965. Since 1924 sources of emigration had changed. In the 1950s emigration from Asia to the United States nearly quadrupled from 34,532 (between 1940 and 1949) to 135,844 (between 1950 and 1959). (See Table 1.1.) In the same period emigration from North, Central, and South America increased dramatically.

The 1965 legislation canceled the national origins quota system and made visas available on a first-come, first-served basis. A seven-category preference system was implemented for families of U.S. citizens and permanent resident aliens for the purpose of family reunification. In addition, the law set visa allocations for people with special occupational skills, abilities, or training needed in the United States. It also established an annual ceiling of 170,000 Eastern Hemisphere emigrants with a 20,000 per-country limit, and an annual limit of 120,000 for the Western Hemisphere without a per-country limit or preference system.

The Immigration and Nationality Act Amendments of 1976 extended the twenty thousand per-country limit to Western Hemisphere countries. Some legislators were concerned that the twenty-thousand-person limit for Mexico was inadequate, but their objections were overruled. The Immigration and Nationality Act Amendments of 1978 combined the separate ceilings for the Eastern and Western Hemispheres into a single worldwide ceiling of 290,000.

WAR CREATED REFUGEES

Official U.S. refugee programs began in response to the devastation of World War II, which created millions of refugees and displaced persons (DPs). (A displaced person was a person living in a foreign country as a result of having been driven from his or her home country because of war or political unrest.) This was the first time the United States formulated policy to admit people fleeing persecution. The Presidential Directive of December 22, 1945, gave priority in issuing visas to about forty thousand DPs. The directive was followed by the Displaced Persons Act of 1948, which authorized admission of 202,000 people from Eastern Europe, and the Refugee Relief Act of 1953, which approved entry of another 209,000 defectors from communist countries over a three-year period. The Displaced Persons Act counted the refugees in the existing immigration quotas, whereas the Refugee Relief Act admitted them outside the quota system.

Parole Authority—A Temporary Admission Policy

In 1956 the U.S. attorney general used the parole authority (temporary admission) under section 212(d) (15) of the Immigration and Nationality Act of 1952 for the first time on a large scale. This section authorized the attorney general to temporarily admit any alien to the United States. Even though parole was not admission for permanent residence, it could lead to permanent resident or immigrant status. Aliens already in the United States on a temporary basis could apply for asylum (to stay in the United States) on the grounds they were likely to suffer persecution if returned to their native lands. The attorney general was authorized to withhold deportation on the same grounds.

According to the INS, in *An Immigrant Nation: United States Regulation of Immigration, 1798–1991* (1991), this parole authority was used to admit approximately thirty-two thousand of the thirty-eight thousand Hungarians who fled the failed Hungarian revolution in 1956. The other six thousand entered under the Refugee Relief Act of 1953 and were automatically admitted as permanent residents. This parole provision was also used in 1962 to admit fifteen thousand refugees from Hong Kong to the United States.

Refugees as Conditional Entrants

In 1965, under the Immigration and Nationality Act Amendments, Congress added section 203(a) (7) to the Immigration and Nationality Act of 1952, creating a group of conditional entrant refugees from communist or Middle Eastern countries, with status similar to the refugee parolees. Sections 203(a) (7) and 212(d) (15) were used to admit thousands of refugees, including Czechoslovakians escaping their failed revolution in 1968, Ugandans fleeing their dictatorship in the 1970s, and Lebanese avoiding the civil war in their country in the 1980s.

Not until the Refugee Act of 1980 did the United States have a general policy governing the admission of refugees. The Refugee Act of 1980 eliminated refugees as a category in the preference system and set a worldwide ceiling on immigration of 270,000, not counting refugees. It also removed the requirement that refugees had to originate from a communist or Middle Eastern nation.

IMMIGRATION INTENSIFIES AS A POLITICAL ISSUE

In "This Month in Immigration History: May 1987" (January 20, 2006, http://149.101.23.2/graphics/aboutus/history/may1987.htm), the USCIS highlights issues of the 1960s and 1970s that elevated immigration's position on the political agenda into the twenty-first century. In 1964 the United States ended the twenty-two-year-old Bracero Program, an agreement with Mexico that allowed migrant workers to enter the United States to supply seasonal agricultural labor. However, ending the program did not stop migrants from crossing the border for work they had come to rely on. Those who could get visas often overstayed their time limits. Others simply crossed the border illegally and found jobs. A population of illegal immigrants began to develop.

During the 1970s the Vietnam War (1954–75) divided the nation, oil prices skyrocketed, and gasoline shortages caused long waiting lines at the pumps. Price controls were implemented and removed to control rampant inflation. In this period of political, social, and economic uncertainty many people saw immigrants as straining the already limited welfare and educational systems. States with growing immigrant populations, such as California, Florida, Illinois, New York, and Texas, pushed Congress for immigration reform.

A surge of refugees from Vietnam and Cambodia as well as Cubans escaping the Castro regime in the mid-1970s added to Americans' concerns. The major source of emigrants had changed from Europe to Latin America and Asia. Many people were uncomfortable with the faces and cultures of these new arrivals.

President Ford established a cabinet-level Domestic Council Committee on Illegal Aliens. Its December 1976 report recommended sanctions against employers who knowingly hired undocumented workers, increased border enforcement, and called for legalization for certain illegal aliens who arrived in the United States before July 1, 1968. In 1979 Congress established the Select Commission on Immigration and Refugee Policy (SCIRP). The commission spent the next two years evaluating the problem. The 1981 SCIRP Final Report fostered ideas that would become part of major new immigration reform legislation in 1986. Over twenty-five years later, however, Congress and the nation would still be debating issues of employers hiring undocumented workers, border enforcement, and legalization of long-term illegals.

CHAPTER 2
IMMIGRATION LAWS AND POLICIES
SINCE THE 1980s

In "Immigration: Shaping and Reshaping America" (*Population Bulletin*, June 2003), Philip Martin and Elizabeth Midgley point out that before the 1980s U.S. immigration laws might have changed once in a generation, but the quickening pace of global change since 1980 brought major new immigration legislation in 1986, 1990, and 1996. The September 11, 2001 (9/11), terrorist attacks led to antiterrorism laws that had considerable impact on immigration policies and procedures and that effected changes to immigration legislation. This chapter covers the most significant immigration laws from the 1980s through 2006.

IMMIGRATION REFORM AND CONTROL ACT OF 1986

On November 6, 1986, after thirty-four years with no new major immigration legislation and a six-year effort to send an acceptable bill through both houses of Congress, the Immigration Reform and Control Act of 1986 (IRCA) was signed into law by President Ronald Reagan.

To control illegal immigration, the IRCA adopted three major strategies:

- Legalization of a portion of the undocumented population (aliens in the country without legal papers), thereby reducing the number of aliens illegally resident in the United States

- Sanctions against employers who knowingly hired illegal aliens

- Additional border enforcement to impede further unlawful entries

Arrivals before 1982

Two groups of immigrants became eligible to apply for legalization under the IRCA. The largest group consisted of those who could prove they had continuously resided in the United States without authorization since January 1, 1982. This large group of aliens had entered the United States in one of two ways: they arrived as illegal aliens before January 1, 1982, or they arrived on temporary visas (government authorizations permitting entry into a country) that expired before January 1, 1982.

To adjust to the legal status of permanent resident, aliens were required to prove eligibility for admission as immigrants and have at least a minimal understanding and knowledge of the English language and U.S. history and government. They could apply for citizenship five years from the date permanent resident status was granted.

Special Agricultural Workers

The second group of immigrants to become eligible to apply for legalization under the IRCA were referred to as special agricultural workers (SAWs). This category was created because numerous fruit and vegetable farmers feared they would lose their workers, many of whom were illegal aliens, if the IRCA provisions regarding length of continuous residence were applied to seasonal laborers. Most of these workers were migrants who returned home to live in Mexico when there was no work available in the fields. The SAW program permitted aliens who had performed labor in perishable agricultural commodities for a minimum of ninety days between May 1985 and May 1986 to apply for legalization.

HOW MANY WERE LEGALIZED? Nancy Rytina estimates in *IRCA Legalization Effects: Lawful Permanent Residence and Naturalization through 2001* (October 25, 2002, http://www.dhs.gov/xlibrary/assets/statistics/publications/irca0114int.pdf) that three to five million illegal aliens were living in the United States in 1986. Over three million aliens applied for temporary residence status under the IRCA. Nearly 2.7 million (88%) of these applicants were eventually approved for permanent residence. By 2001 one-third (889,033) of these residents had become naturalized citizens. Rytina notes that a majority (75%) of applicants under the IRCA provisions were born in Mexico.

The IRCA barred newly legalized aliens from receiving most federally funded public assistance for five years. Exceptions included access to Medicaid for children, pregnant women, the elderly, the handicapped, and for emergency care. The State Legalization Impact Assistance Grant program reimbursed state and local governments the costs for providing public assistance, education, and public health services to the legalized aliens. David Simcox reports in *Measuring the Fallout: The Cost of IRCA Amnesty after 10 Years* (May 1997, http://www.cis.org/articles/1997/back197.htm) that the program reimbursed states $3.5 billion, averaging $1,167 per eligible legalized alien, during its seven years of operation.

Employer Sanctions

The employer sanctions provision of the IRCA was intended to correct a double standard that prohibited unauthorized aliens from working in the United States but permitted employers to hire them. The IRCA prohibited employers from hiring, recruiting, or referring for a fee aliens known to be unauthorized to work in the United States. Employers who violated the law were subject to a series of civil fines or criminal penalties when a pattern or practice of violations was found.

The burden of proof was on employers to demonstrate that their employees had valid proof of identity and were authorized to work. The IRCA required employers to complete the Employment Eligibility Verification form, known as Form I-9, for each employee hired. (See Figure 2.1.) In completing the form the employer certified that the employee had presented valid proof of identity and eligibility for employment and that these documents appeared genuine. The IRCA also required employers to retain the completed I-9 forms and produce them in response to an official government request.

Challenges of Verifying Employee Eligibility for Work

Because employers had to verify employee eligibility for work, some ineligible workers illegally assumed the identities of individuals whose status could be documented. The Federal Trade Commission reports that in 2005 there were 255,565 nationwide complaints of identity theft, a 19% increase over the 215,177 complaints in 2003 (*Identity Theft Victim Complaint Data: Figures and Trends, January 1–December 31, 2005*, January 25, 2006, http://www.consumer.gov/idtheft/pdf/clearinghouse_2005.pdf). Of the complaints registered in 2005, 12% included use of a stolen identity for employment-related fraud.

Identity theft gained national attention as victims reported their struggles to resolve credit card charges for purchases they did not make and negative entries on credit reports for debts they did not incur. Some citizens were questioned by the Internal Revenue Service about failure to report income related to taxes deposited to their Social Security accounts. Many responded that they had never worked for the companies that made the tax deposits. Demands for government action to stop identity theft increased.

Some complaints by citizens who had received Social Security tax contributions from companies that weren't their employers were traced to Swift &Company®, a beef and pork processor headquartered in Colorado. According to U.S. Immigration and Customs Enforcement (ICE; December 13, 2006, http://www.ice.gov/pi/news/newsreleases/articles/061213dc.htm), armed ICE agents surrounded Swift meat processing plants in six states in December 2006. The agents arrested 1,282 illegal aliens in the Swift raids, and 65 people were arrested on criminal charges that included identity theft. According to ICE, the raids culminated a ten-month investigation of identity theft complaints filed with the Federal Trade Commission.

To assist employers in complying with the Illegal Immigration Reform and Immigrant Responsibility Act and the IRCA, the Social Security Administration in 1966 began the Basic Pilot Program, a computerized system that allowed employers to check the validity of Social Security numbers (SSNs) presented by new hires. It was tested with employers in California, Florida, Illinois, and Texas before being expanded on December 1, 2004, to voluntary employers in all states. The program returned a "tentative nonconfirmation" if the name, date of birth, or gender of the new hire did not match Social Security records; if the SSN had never been issued; or if records indicated the person issued that SSN was deceased. The new hire had a set time limit for resolving the problem with the Social Security Administration before the employer could terminate the individual.

Bruce Finley and Tom McGhee report in "Raids at Swift Plants Target Identity Theft" (*Denver Post*, December 13, 2006) that Swift had participated in the Basic Pilot Program for nearly a decade but the raids showed that the system did not recognize identity theft. Basic Pilot confirmed the validity of the SSN but did not check to see how many times and in what locations the number had been used for employment. Thus, several people could be using the same number on fraudulent identification (IDs). Even though the Swift raids left employers feeling threatened, they were assured that by using the tools provided by the government, they would be hiring legally eligible workers.

IMMIGRATION MARRIAGE FRAUD AMENDMENTS OF 1986

Before 1986 the U.S. Immigration and Naturalization Service (INS) granted permanent residence fairly quickly to the foreign spouses of U.S. citizens or lawful permanent residents (LPRs). However, a number of marriages between Americans and foreigners occurred purely to

FIGURE 2.1

Department of Homeland Security U.S. Citizenship and Immigration Services	Form I-9

OMB No. 1615-0047; Expires 03/31/07

Employment Eligibility Verification

INSTRUCTIONS

PLEASE READ ALL INSTRUCTIONS CAREFULLY BEFORE COMPLETING THIS FORM.

Anti-Discrimination Notice. It is illegal to discriminate against any individual (other than an alien not authorized to work in the U.S.) in hiring, discharging, or recruiting or referring for a fee because of that individual's national origin or citizenship status. It is illegal to discriminate against work eligible individuals. Employers **CANNOT** specify which document(s) they will accept from an employee. The refusal to hire an individual because of a future expiration date may also constitute illegal discrimination.

Section 1- Employee. All employees, citizens and noncitizens, hired after November 6, 1986, must complete Section 1 of this form at the time of hire, which is the actual beginning of employment. **The employer is responsible for ensuring that Section 1 is timely and properly completed.**

Preparer/Translator Certification. The Preparer/Translator Certification must be completed if Section 1 is prepared by a person other than the employee. A preparer/translator may be used only when the employee is unable to complete Section 1 on his/her own. However, the employee must still sign Section 1 personally.

Section 2 - Employer. For the purpose of completing this form, the term "employer" includes those recruiters and referrers for a fee who are agricultural associations, agricultural employers or farm labor contractors.

Employers must complete Section 2 by examining evidence of identity and employment eligibility within three (3) business days of the date employment begins. If employees are authorized to work, but are unable to present the required document(s) within three business days, they must present a receipt for the application of the document(s) within three business days and the actual document(s) within ninety (90) days. However, if employers hire individuals for a duration of less than three business days, Section 2 must be completed at the time employment begins. **Employers must record: 1)** document title; **2)** issuing authority; **3)** document number, **4)** expiration date, if any; and **5)** the date employment begins. Employers must sign and date the certification. Employees must present original documents. Employers may, but are not required to, photocopy the document(s) presented. These photocopies may only be used for the verification process and must be retained with the I-9. **However, employers are still responsible for completing the I-9.**

Section 3 - Updating and Reverification. Employers must complete Section 3 when updating and/or reverifying the I-9. Employers must reverify employment eligibility of their employees on or before the expiration date recorded in Section 1. Employers **CANNOT** specify which document(s) they will accept from an employee.

- If an employee's name has changed at the time this form is being updated/reverified, complete Block A.

- If an employee is rehired within three (3) years of the date this form was originally completed and the employee is still eligible to be employed on the same basis as previously indicated on this form (updating), complete Block B and the signature block.

- If an employee is rehired within three (3) years of the date this form was originally completed and the employee's work authorization has expired **or** if a current employee's work authorization is about to expire (reverification), complete Block B and:

- examine any document that reflects that the employee is authorized to work in the U.S. (see List A **or** C),

- record the document title, document number and expiration date (if any) in Block C, and

- complete the signature block.

Photocopying and Retaining Form I-9. A blank I-9 may be reproduced, provided both sides are copied. The Instructions must be available to all employees completing this form. Employers must retain completed I-9s for three (3) years after the date of hire or one (1) year after the date employment ends, whichever is later.

For more detailed information, you may refer to the Department of Homeland Security (DHS) Handbook for Employers, (Form M-274). You may obtain the handbook at your local U.S. Citizenship and Immigration Services (USCIS) office.

Privacy Act Notice. The authority for collecting this information is the Immigration Reform and Control Act of 1986, Pub. L. 99-603 (8 USC 1324a).

This information is for employers to verify the eligibility of individuals for employment to preclude the unlawful hiring, or recruiting or referring for a fee, of aliens who are not authorized to work in the United States.

This information will be used by employers as a record of their basis for determining eligibility of an employee to work in the United States. The form will be kept by the employer and made available for inspection by officials of the U.S. Immigration and Customs Enforcement, Department of Labor and Office of Special Counsel for Immigration Related Unfair Employment Practices.

Submission of the information required in this form is voluntary. However, an individual may not begin employment unless this form is completed, since employers are subject to civil or criminal penalties if they do not comply with the Immigration Reform and Control Act of 1986.

Reporting Burden. We try to create forms and instructions that are accurate, can be easily understood and which impose the least possible burden on you to provide us with information. Often this is difficult because some immigration laws are very complex. Accordingly, the reporting burden for this collection of information is computed as follows: **1)** learning about this form, 5 minutes; **2)** completing the form, 5 minutes; and **3)** assembling and filing (recordkeeping) the form, 5 minutes, for an average of 15 minutes per response. If you have comments regarding the accuracy of this burden estimate, or suggestions for making this form simpler, you can write to U.S. Citizenship and Immigration Services, Regulatory Management Division, 111 Massachusetts Avenue, N.W., Washington, DC 20529. OMB No. 1615-0047.

NOTE: This is the 1991 edition of the Form I-9 that has been rebranded with a current printing date to reflect the recent transition from the INS to DHS and its components.

EMPLOYERS MUST RETAIN COMPLETED FORM I-9
PLEASE DO NOT MAIL COMPLETED FORM I-9 TO ICE OR USCIS

Form I-9 (Rev. 05/31/05)Y

FIGURE 2.1

Form I-9

OMB No. 1615-0047; Expires 03/31/07

Employment Eligibility Verification

Please read instructions carefully before completing this form. The instructions must be available during completion of this form. ANTI-DISCRIMINATION NOTICE: It is illegal to discriminate against work eligible individuals. Employers CANNOT specify which document(s) they will accept from an employee. The refusal to hire an individual because of a future expiration date may also constitute illegal discrimination.

Section 1. Employee Information and Verification. To be completed and signed by employee at the time employment begins.

Print Name: Last	First	Middle Initial	Maiden Name

Address (Street Name and Number)	Apt. #	Date of Birth (month/day/year)

City	State	Zip Code	Social Security #

I am aware that federal law provides for imprisonment and/or fines for false statements or use of false documents in connection with the completion of this form.

I attest, under penalty of perjury, that I am (check one of the following):

☐ A citizen or national of the United States
☐ A Lawful Permanent Resident (Alien #) A _____
☐ An alien authorized to work until _____

(Alien # or Admission #) _____

Employee's Signature	Date (month/day/year)

Preparer and/or Translator Certification. *(To be completed and signed if Section 1 is prepared by a person other than the employee.) I attest, under penalty of perjury, that I have assisted in the completion of this form and that to the best of my knowledge the information is true and correct.*

Preparer's/Translator's Signature	Print Name

Address (Street Name and Number, City, State, Zip Code)	Date (month/day/year)

Section 2. Employer Review and Verification. To be completed and signed by employer. Examine one document from List A OR examine one document from List B and one from List C, as listed on the reverse of this form, and record the title, number and expiration date, if any, of the document(s).

	List A	OR	List B	AND	List C
Document title:					
Issuing authority:					
Document #:					
Expiration Date (if any):					
Document #:					
Expiration Date (if any):					

CERTIFICATION - I attest, under penalty of perjury, that I have examined the document(s) presented by the above-named employee, that the above-listed document(s) appear to be genuine and to relate to the employee named, that the employee began employment on *(month/day/year)* _____ **and that to the best of my knowledge the employee is eligible to work in the United States. (State employment agencies may omit the date the employee began employment.)**

Signature of Employer or Authorized Representative	Print Name	Title

Business or Organization Name	Address (Street Name and Number, City, State, Zip Code)	Date (month/day/year)

Section 3. Updating and Reverification. To be completed and signed by employer.

A. New Name (if applicable)	B. Date of Rehire (month/day/year) (if applicable)

C. If employee's previous grant of work authorization has expired, provide the information below for the document that establishes current employment eligibility.

Document Title:	Document #:	Expiration Date (if any):

I attest, under penalty of perjury, that to the best of my knowledge, this employee is eligible to work in the United States, and if the employee presented document(s), the document(s) I have examined appear to be genuine and to relate to the individual.

Signature of Employer or Authorized Representative	Date (month/day/year)

NOTE: This is the 1991 edition of the Form I-9 that has been rebranded with a current printing date to reflect the recent transition from the INS to DHS and its components.

Form I-9 (Rev. 05/31/05)Y Page 2

FIGURE 2.1

Form I-9

LISTS OF ACCEPTABLE DOCUMENTS

LIST A		LIST B		LIST C
Documents that Establish Both Identity and Employment Eligibility	**OR**	**Documents that Establish Identity**	**AND**	**Documents that Establish Employment Eligibility**

LIST A — Documents that Establish Both Identity and Employment Eligibility

1. U.S. Passport (unexpired or expired)

2. Certificate of U.S. Citizenship (Form N-560 or N-561)

3. Certificate of Naturalization (Form N-550 or N-570)

4. Unexpired foreign passport, with I-551 stamp or attached Form I-94 indicating unexpired employment authorization

5. Permanent Resident Card or Alien Registration Receipt Card with photograph (Form I-151 or I-551)

6. Unexpired Temporary Resident Card (Form I-688)

7. Unexpired Employment Authorization Card (Form I-688A)

8. Unexpired Reentry Permit (Form I-327)

9. Unexpired Refugee Travel Document (Form 1-571)

10. Unexpired Employment Authorization Document issued by DHS that contains a photograph (Form I-688B)

OR

LIST B — Documents that Establish Identity

1. Driver's license or ID card issued by a state or outlying possession of the United States provided it contains a photograph or information such as name, date of birth, gender, height, eye color and address

2. ID card issued by federal, state or local government agencies or entities, provided it contains a photograph or information such as name, date of birth, gender, height, eye color and address

3. School ID card with a photograph

4. Voter's registration card

5. U.S. Military card or draft record

6. Military dependent's ID card

7. U.S. Coast Guard Merchant Mariner Card

8. Native American tribal document

9. Driver's license issued by a Canadian government authority

For persons under age 18 who are unable to present a document listed above:

10. School record or report card

11. Clinic, doctor or hospital record

12. Day-care or nursery school record

AND

LIST C — Documents that Establish Employment Eligibility

1. U.S. social security card issued by the Social Security Administration (other than a card stating it is not valid for employment)

2. Certification of Birth Abroad issued by the Department of State (Form FS-545 or Form DS-1350)

3. Original or certified copy of a birth certificate issued by a state, county, municipal authority or outlying possession of the United States bearing an official seal

4. Native American tribal document

5. U.S. Citizen ID Card (Form I-197)

6. ID Card for use of Resident Citizen in the United States (Form I-179)

7. Unexpired employment authorization document issued by DHS (other than those listed under List A)

Illustrations of many of these documents appear in Part 8 of the Handbook for Employers (M-274)

Form I-9 (Rev. 05/31/05)Y Page 3

SOURCE: "Form I-9," U.S. Department of Homeland Security, U.S. Citizenship and Immigration Services, http://www.uscis.gov/files/form/i-9.pdf (accessed January 29, 2007)

attain U.S. permanent residence status for the foreigner. Some U.S. citizens or LPRs agreed to marry aliens for money. After the alien gained permanent residence, the marriage was dissolved. Other cases involved aliens entering into marriages by deceiving U.S. citizens or LPRs with declarations of love, only to seek divorce after gaining permanent residence.

The Immigration Marriage Fraud Amendments of 1986 specified that aliens basing their immigrant status on a marriage of less than two years were considered conditional immigrants. To remove the conditional immigrant status, the alien had to apply for permanent residence within ninety days after the second-year anniversary of receiving conditional status. The alien and his or her spouse were required to show that the marriage was and continued to be a valid one; otherwise, conditional immigrant status was terminated and the alien could be deported.

Wendy Koch notes in "Va. Case Highlights Fraudulent Marriages" (*USA Today*, November 8, 2006, http://www.usatoday.com/news/nation/2006-11-08-greencard_x.htm) that during fiscal year (FY) 2004 through FY2006 ICE investigated seven hundred cases of marriage fraud. ICE found that marriage fraud organizations typically charged $2,500 to $6,000 to arrange a marriage for immigration purposes. Marriage fraud took on more serious implications after 9/11. Koch reports that according to the Center for Immigration Studies, half of the thirty-six suspected 9/11 terrorists gained legal status by marrying Americans, ten through sham marriages.

Battered Brides

Spousal abuse sometimes results from the two-year conditional immigrant status. Particularly in cases of mail-order brides and brides from countries where women have few, if any, rights, some husbands take advantage of the power they have as the wife's sponsor. The new wives are dependent on their husbands to obtain permanent U.S. residence. The U.S. Department of Justice finds cases of alien wives who are virtual prisoners, afraid they will be deported if they defy their husbands or report abuse. In addition, some of the women come from cultures in which divorced women are outcasts with no place in society.

The Violence against Women Act of 1994—which is part of the Violent Crime Control and Law Enforcement Act of 1994—and the Victims of Trafficking and Violence Prevention Act of 2000 were enacted to address the plight of such abused women and their children. The 1994 law allows the women and/or children to self-petition for immigrant status without the abuser's participation or consent. Abused males can also file a self-petition under this law. The 2000 law created a new nonimmigrant U-visa for victims of serious crimes. Recipients of the U-visa, including victims of crimes against women, can adjust to lawful

permanent resident status based on humanitarian grounds as determined by the U.S. attorney general.

IMMIGRATION ACT OF 1990

Shortly afte the IRCA was passed, Senators Edward Kennedy (D-Massachusetts) and Alan Simpson (R-Wyoming) began work to change the Immigration and Nationality Act Amendments of 1965, which determined legal immigration into the United States. The senators asserted that the family-oriented system allowed one legal immigrant to bring too many relatives into the country. They proposed to cut the number of dependents admitted and replace them with individuals who had the skills or money to immediately benefit the U.S. economy. The result of their efforts was the Immigration Act of 1990 (IMMACT).

Enacted on November 29, 1990, IMMACT represented a major overhaul of immigration law. The focus of the new law was to raise the annual number of immigrants allowed and give greater priority to employment-based immigration. A diversity program encouraged applications for emigration from countries with low immigration history.

Michael J. Greenwood and Fred A. Ziel, in *The Impact of the Immigration Act of 1990 on U.S. Immigration* (January 2, 1998, http://migration.ucdavis.edu/mn/cir/Greenwood/combined.htm), indicate that the total number of immigrants was set at 700,000 annually from FY1992 through FY1994 with an annual level of 675,000 beginning in FY1995. At the 675,000 level, the annual immigrant pool was roughly 70% family sponsored immigrants (480,000), 20% employment-based immigrants (140,000), and 10% diversity immigrants (55,000).

Employment-Based Immigration

IMMACT nearly tripled the allowed level of employment-based immigration—from 54,000 to 140,000. The goal was to attract professional people with skills that would promote U.S. economic development rather than the unskilled workers who were legalized through the IRCA. However, the allotment of 140,000 included both workers and their families, so the actual number of workers was considerably lower.

Diversity Visa Program

IMMACT made new provisions for the admission of immigrants from countries with low rates of immigration to the United States. The program was introduced as a transitional measure from 1992 to 1994. Ruth Ellen Wasem and Karma Ester report in "Immigration: Diversity Visa Lottery" (April 22, 2004, http://www.ilw.com/immigdaily/news/2005,0809-crs.pdf) that under the permanent program, which began in 1995, no country was permitted more than 7% (3,850) of the total 55,000 visas, and Northern Ireland was treated as a separate state. To be eligible, aliens were required to have at least a high school education or equivalent, or at least two years of work experience in an occupation that required a minimum of two years' training or two years' experience within the past five years. An alien selected under the lottery program could apply for permanent residence and, if granted, was authorized to work in the United States. The alien's spouse and unmarried children under age twenty-one were also allowed to enter the United States.

Beginning with FY1999, five thousand visas were reserved for participants in the 1997 Nicaraguan Adjustment and Central American Relief Act. This law provided various immigration benefits and relief from deportation to certain Nicaraguans, Cubans, Salvadorans, Guatemalans, nationals of former Soviet-bloc countries, and their dependents.

RESULTS OF THE 2007 DIVERSITY LOTTERY. According to the U.S. Department of State in "Diversity Visa Lottery 2007 (DV-2007) Results" (2007, http://travel.state .gov/visa/immigrants/types/types_1317.html), over 5.5 million qualified entries for DV-2007 were received during the sixty-day application period (October 5, 2005, to December 4, 2005). Natives of Canada, China (mainland born, excluding Hong Kong and Taiwan), Colombia, the Dominican Republic, El Salvador, Haiti, India, Jamaica, Mexico, Pakistan, the Philippines, Poland, Russia, South Korea, the United Kingdom (except Northern Ireland) and its dependent territories, and Vietnam were not eligible. Eighty-two thousand of the 5.5 million people who entered DV-2007 were notified that they may apply for an immigrant visa; even though only 50,000 visas are available through the lottery, the Department of State contacts a larger number of applicants to ensure that none of the 50,000 visas go unused. The countries with the highest representation among the 82,000 potential immigrants in DV-2007 included Nigeria (9,849), Egypt (7,229), Ukraine (7,205), Ethiopia (6,871), and Bangladesh (5,901).

Efforts to End the Diversity Visa Program

In 2004 the House Judiciary Committee issued *House Report 108-747—Security and Fairness Enhancement for America Act of 2003* (October 6, 2004, http://thomas.loc .gov/cgi-bin/cpquery/R?cp108:FLD010:@1(hr747)), which supported a bill to end the Diversity Lottery Program. The report noted many aliens filed multiple applications using a variety of aliases, and fraudulent documents were common in many countries because of poor control of vital records and identity documents. The report also said the Diversity Visa Program posed a threat to national security. According to the report, among the 2004 applicants selected were 1,183 Sudanese, 1,431 Iranians, 674 Cubans, 64 Syrians, 24 Libyans, and 4 North Koreans—all from countries that the United States considered state sponsors of terrorism. However, no legislation to end the program was enacted by the close of the 2006 legislative session.

Changing Grounds for Entry

IMMACT changed the political and ideological grounds for exclusion and deportation. The law repealed the ban against the admission of communists and representatives of other totalitarian regimes that had been in place since 1950. In addition, immigration applicants who had been excluded previously because of associations with communism were provided exceptions if the applicants had been involuntary members of the communist party, had terminated membership, or merely had close family relationships with people affiliated with communism.

Temporary Protected Status

IMMACT authorized the U.S. attorney general to grant temporary protected status (TPS) to undocumented aliens present in the United States when a natural disaster, ongoing armed conflict, or other extraordinary occurrence in their countries posed a danger to their personal safety.

TPS lasts for six to eighteen months unless conditions in the alien national's country warrants an extension of stay. TPS does not lead to permanent resident status, although such aliens can obtain work authorization. Once the TPS designation ends, the foreign nationals resume the same immigrant status they had before TPS (unless that status has expired) or any new status obtained while in TPS. According to the U.S. Citizenship and Immigration Services (USCIS), as of April 2007 applicants from seven nations—Burundi, El Salvador, Honduras, Liberia, Nicaragua, Somalia, and Sudan—were eligible for temporary protected status (http://www.uscis.gov).

WELFARE REFORM LAW OF 1996

Under Title IV of the Personal Responsibility and Work Opportunity Reconciliation Act of 1996 federal welfare benefits for legal immigrants were cut substantially and the responsibility for public assistance was shifted from the federal government to the states. (Illegal immigrants were already ineligible for most major welfare programs.) The law was designed to ensure that available welfare benefits did not serve as an incentive for immigration and that immigrants admitted to the United States would be self-reliant.

In the past legal immigrants had generally been eligible for the same welfare benefits as citizens. Under the new rules immigrants who had become naturalized citizens remained eligible for federal benefits, but most noncitizens were barred from participating in federal programs such as Temporary Assistance for Needy Families (TANF), food stamps, Supplemental Security Income (SSI), and Medicaid. (TANF is a federal block grant program for needy families with dependent children that replaced the Aid to Families with Dependent Children, Emergency Assistance, and Job Opportunities and Basic Skills programs, whereas Medicaid is a joint federal-state health insurance program for certain

TABLE 2.1

State-funded food programs for legal immigrants, April–June 2006

[Programs states have initiated to provide food assistance to legal immigrants who are ineligible for federal food stamp benefits as a result of welfare reform]

States	Starting date	Targeted population	Persons served (monthly estimate)*	Issuance (monthly estimate)*
California	9-1-97	Legal immigrants otherwise eligible.	27,947	$1,978,927
Nebraska	8-1-97	Legal immigrants otherwise eligible.	168	$17,297
New York	9-1-97	Immigrants legally residing in the U.S. on 8/22/96 who are victims of domestic violence or 60 years of age or older and born after 8/22/31.	0	$0
Wisconsin	8-1-98	Legal immigrants otherwise eligible.	503	$33,626
Total			**28,618**	**$2,029,850**

* Estimates are based on information reported by states to the United States Department of Agriculture (USDA) and are an average of the prior 3 months.

SOURCE: "State-Funded Food Programs for Legal Immigrants, April through June 2006," *Food Stamp Program*, U.S. Department of Agriculture, Food & Nutrition Service, http://www.fns.usda.gov/FSP/rules/Memo/PRWORA/StatePrograms.htm (accessed January 29, 2007)

low-income and needy people; SSI is a federal income supplement program funded by general tax revenues—not Social Security taxes—that assists aged, blind, and disabled people who have little or no income.) States were given the option of using federal funds for TANF and Medicaid for immigrants who arrived before the act took effect. Immigrants who arrived legally after the law took effect were ineligible for any federal funds for five years; states then had the option of granting their applications for TANF and/or Medicaid.

Restoration of Government Benefits

On August 15, 1997, the Balanced Budget Act restored SSI and Medicaid benefits to legal immigrants who had been receiving these benefits when the welfare reform law was passed. The Noncitizen Benefit Clarification and Other Technical Amendments Act of 1998 amended the welfare reform law, requiring that nonqualified aliens who were receiving SSI and Medicaid benefits on August 22, 1996, could retain these benefits.

EMERGENCY CARE FOR UNAUTHORIZED IMMIGRANTS. In May 2005 the Centers for Medicare and Medicaid Services (CMS) issued final guidance on Section 1011 of the Medicare Prescription Drug, Improvement, and Modernization Act of 2003. This section provides $250 million annually for FY2005 to FY2008 to reimburse eligible hospitals, physicians, and ambulance services for costs incurred from treating unauthorized immigrants. According to the CMS, in "Emergency Health Services for Undocumented Aliens" (May 9, 2005, http://www. cms.hhs.gov/apps/media/press/release.asp?Counter=1452), states that received the highest allocations in FY2005 included California ($70.8 million), Texas ($46 million), Arizona ($45 million), New York ($12.2 million), Illinois ($10.3 million), and Florida ($8.7 million).

FOOD STAMPS. In 1997, when the food stamp restrictions went into effect, an estimated 940,000 of the 1.4 million legal immigrants receiving food stamps lost their eligibility, as reported in *Welfare Reform: Many States Continue Some Federal or State Benefits for Immigrants* (U.S. General Accounting Office, July 1998, http://www.gao.gov/archive/1998/he98132.pdf). Nearly one-fifth were immigrant children. During 1997 and 1998 fourteen states created food stamp programs that served about one-quarter of this immigrant group nationwide. Most recipients were children, the elderly, and the disabled. Some states continued to provide food assistance to ineligible legal immigrants.

The Agricultural Research, Extension, and Education Reform Act of 1998 and the Farm Security and Rural Investment Act of 2002 restored access to food stamps to many legal immigrants. As of June 2006 four states—California, Nebraska, New York, and Wisconsin—provided food assistance to certain immigrants who were ineligible for federal food stamp benefits as a result of welfare reform. (See Table 2.1.) From April through June 2006 California assisted 27,947 people, whereas Nebraska aided 168. New York had a program in place but reported no assistance used.

ILLEGAL IMMIGRATION REFORM AND IMMIGRANT RESPONSIBILITY ACT OF 1996

On September 30, 1996, the Illegal Immigration Reform and Immigrant Responsibility Act (IIRIRA) became law. In an effort to reduce illegal immigration, the IIRIRA included the following among its many provisions:

• Required doubling the number of U.S. Border Patrol agents to five thousand by 2001 and increasing equipment and technology at air and land ports of entry

• Authorized improvements of southwest border barriers

• Toughened penalties for immigrant smuggling (up to ten years in prison, fifteen years for third and subsequent offenses) and document fraud (up to fifteen years in prison)

- Increased the number of INS investigators for work site enforcement, tracking aliens who overstayed visas, and investigating alien smuggling

- Instituted a new "expedited removal" proceeding (denial of an alien's entry into the United States without a hearing) to speed deportation of aliens with no documents or with fraudulent documents

- Authorized three voluntary pilot programs to enable employers to verify the immigrant status of job applicants and to reduce the number and types of documents needed for identification and employment eligibility

- Instituted a bar on admissibility for aliens seeking to reenter the United States after having been unlawfully present in the country—a bar of three years for aliens unlawfully present from six months to a year and a bar of ten years for those unlawfully present for more than a year

Tuition Rules Limit Undocumented Students

The IIRIRA restricted states' residency requirements and in-state tuition benefits for undocumented students unless the same benefit was available to any U.S. citizen or national. This potentially forced unauthorized students to pay out-of-state tuition in the states where they resided. These students had received free primary and secondary education regardless of immigration status based on the 1982 Supreme Court decision in *Plyler v. Doe* (457 U.S. 202). However, after graduation from high school they were barred from receiving federal financial aid and were required to pay nonresident tuition at schools in the state where they lived.

According to the University of Houston Law Center (2006, http://www.law.uh.edu/ihelg/state.html), in 2001 Texas became the first state to pass legislation granting resident tuition to any student who had been a Texas resident for a minimum of two years and graduated from a Texas high school. By 2006 ten states had passed similar legislation. Other states legislated against tuition benefits for undocumented students. Virginia allowed in-state tuition only for students holding legal immigration visas or classified as political refugees. Georgia prohibited in-state tuition for any student who was not a citizen or legal permanent resident.

GREEN CARD

According to the USCIS (2007, http://www.uscis.gov/), "a 'green card' gives you official immigration status (Lawful Permanent Residency [LPR]) in the United States." An LPR carries this document as proof of legal status in the country. Yet, the card is not green. What is known as a "green card" came in a variety of different colors at differ-

ent times in history. The card, formally known as the Alien Registration Receipt Card, Form I-151 or I-551, entitles an alien to certain benefits, and those benefits originated at a time when the card was actually green. The USCIS provides a history of this important document in "Q: Green Card Not Green?" (2007, http://www. uscis.gov).

The first receipt card, Form AR-3, resulted from the Alien Registration Act of 1940, a World War II–era national defense measure. The act required all non-U.S. citizens (legal or illegal) to register at post offices. From there the registration forms were forwarded to the INS. The receipt card was mailed to each alien as proof of his or her compliance with the law. These receipts were printed on white paper.

When the war ended, alien registration became part of the regular immigration procedure. Aliens registered at ports of entry and the INS issued different types of Alien Registration Receipt Cards based on each alien's admission status. Temporary foreign laborers, for example, received an I-100a card and visitors received an I-94c. Permanent residents received the I-151. Cards were different colors to make it easy to identify the immigration status of each alien. The permanent resident card was green and was necessary to get a job.

The Internal Security Act of 1950 made the I-151 even more valuable. Effective April 17, 1951, any alien holding an AR-3 card (the type issued to all aliens during the war) had to apply to have it replaced with the green I-151 card. Anyone who could not prove his or her legal admission to the United States did not qualify for a green card and could be subject to prosecution for violation of immigration laws.

By 1951 the green card represented security for an alien. It indicated the right to permanently live and work in the United States and instantly communicated that right to law enforcement officials. The Alien Registration Receipt Card, Form I-151, became commonly known to aliens, immigration attorneys, enforcement officers, and employers by its color. The term *green card* designated not only the document but also the official status so desired by many legal nonimmigrants (students, tourists, and temporary workers) and by illegal aliens.

The green card was so desirable that counterfeiting became a problem. To combat this fraud the INS issued nineteen different designs of the card between 1940 and 1977. The 1964 version was pale blue and in 1965 the card became dark blue. In January 1977 the INS introduced the new style, machine-readable Alien Registration Receipt Card, Form I-551, which has since been issued in a variety of colors, including pink and a pink and blue combination. Form I-151 and its successor, Form I-551, have such vital meaning to immigrants that despite changes in form number, design, and color it will probably always be known as a green card.

USA PATRIOT ACT OF 2001

Following 9/11 it became apparent that some, if not all, of the perpetrators had entered the United States legally and many had overstayed their visas with no notice taken by the INS or any other enforcement agency. As a result, several laws were enacted to address immigration concerns related to terrorism. The first such law was the Uniting and Strengthening America by Providing Appropriate Tools Required to Intercept and Obstruct Terrorism, more commonly known as the USA PATRIOT Act, which was signed into law in October 2001. With reference to immigration, the act:

- Mandated that the number of personnel at the northern border be tripled, appropriated funds for technology improvements, and gave the INS access to the Federal Bureau of Investigation's (FBI) criminal databases. The INS was to begin the task of locating hundreds of thousands of foreigners who had been ordered deported and entering their names into the FBI database.

- Amended the Immigration and Nationality Act to clarify that an alien who solicited funds or membership or provided material support to a certified terrorist organization could be detained or removed from the country.

- Directed the U.S. attorney general to implement an entry-exit system, with particular focus on biometric information gathered during the visa application process, and develop tamper-resistant documents. The new system would require certain nonimmigrants to register with the INS and submit fingerprints and photographs on arrival in the United States; report to the INS in person within thirty days of arrival and annually thereafter; and notify an INS agent of their departure. Those who failed to comply could face criminal prosecution.

- Appropriated $36.8 million to implement a foreign-student monitoring system with mandatory participation by all institutions of higher education that enrolled foreign students or exchange visitors. The act expanded the list of participating institutions to include air flight schools, language training schools, and vocational schools.

- Established provisions to ensure that the immigration status of 9/11 victims and their families was not adversely affected as a result of the attacks. The family members of some victims were facing deportation.

HOMELAND SECURITY ACT OF 2002

On November 25, 2002, President Bush signed into law the Homeland Security Act of 2002, which implemented the largest restructuring of the government in several decades. The Homeland Security Act created the cabinet-level U.S. Department of Homeland Security (DHS) and consolidated the functions of more than twenty federal agencies into one department employing over 170,000 people. One of the affected agencies was the INS.

INS Reorganization

Title IV, Section 402 of the Homeland Security Act transferred the responsibilities of the INS from the Justice Department to the DHS. With the goal of separating immigration services from immigration law enforcement, on March 1, 2003, the INS became the USCIS, responsible for processing visas and petitions for naturalization, asylum, and refugee status. Immigration enforcement became the responsibility of ICE (called the Bureau of Border Security in the act).

Border Security

Section 402 of the Homeland Security Act outlined the responsibilities of the Under Secretary for Border and Transportation Security. These included:

- Preventing the entry of terrorists and the instruments of terrorism into the United States

- Securing the borders, territorial waters, ports, terminals, waterways, and air, land, and sea transportation systems of the United States

- Administering the immigration and naturalization laws of the United States, including the establishment of rules governing the granting of visas and other forms of permission to enter the United States to individuals who are not citizens or lawful permanent residents

- Administering the customs laws of the United States

- Ensuring the speedy, orderly, and efficient flow of lawful traffic and commerce in carrying out these responsibilities

OTHER POST-9/11 CHANGES

Since 9/11 hundreds of policy changes have been inaugurated by the Justice Department, the DHS, and the INS/USCIS.

In November 2001 the State Department mandated background checks on all male visa applicants between the ages of sixteen and forty-five from twenty-six mostly Muslim countries. The Enhanced Border Security and Visa Entry Reform Act of 2002 prohibited issuing nonimmigrant visas to nationals of seven countries (Cuba, Iran, Iraq, Libya, North Korea, Sudan, and Syria) unless it was determined after a thorough background check that the individuals were not security threats. The list of prohibited countries could change as directed by the attorney general.

Foreign Students Face Increased Visa Restrictions

The IIRIRA had mandated the creation of a database that stored information about international students, but the system had not yet been launched when 9/11 occurred. In May 2002 the INS launched the Student and Exchange Visitor Information System to track foreigners who enter the country on student visas. New rules required that foreign students present a confirmation of acceptance from an American school before a visa would be issued and colleges were required to report enrollment information and dates of students' arrivals or failure to arrive.

Reporting Change of Address

The INS took steps to enforce the long-standing but essentially ignored requirement that all noncitizens in the country for more than thirty days must report any change of address within ten days of moving. Failure to report could be grounds for fines, penalties, or deportation.

Police Enforcement of Immigration Laws

The Justice Department ruled that effective August 2002 local police could detain individuals for immigration violations, a right formerly reserved for federal agents. The measure was part of the IIRIRA but had not previously been finalized. Florida became the test state, initiating a Memorandum of Understanding with the Justice Department, which authorized specially trained local police officers to assist federal agents in locating and detaining wanted aliens.

INTELLIGENCE REFORM AND TERRORISM PREVENTION ACT OF 2004

On December 17, 2004, President Bush signed the Intelligence Reform and Terrorism Prevention Act of 2004. This act set national standards for driver's licenses, Social Security cards, and birth certificates.

The law required the secretary of transportation to issue within eighteen months regulations governing any driver's license or identification cards to be accepted for any official purpose by a federal agency. The documents were required to include full legal name, date of birth, gender, license or ID card number, digital photograph, address, and signature of the individual; contain physical security features designed to prevent tampering, counterfeiting, or duplicating for fraudulent purposes; and conform to specified requirements for a common machine-readable technology. States would be required to confiscate a driver's license or ID card if any of the security features were compromised. The regulations would include standards for documentation required by the applicant for a license or ID card and procedures for verifying the documents. States retained the right to determine what categories of individuals (e.g., legal or illegal immigrants) were eligible for a license.

The law required that within one year the commissioner of social security would restrict issuance of replacement Social Security cards for any individual to three in one year or ten in a lifetime; create minimum standards for verification of documents to be submitted to obtain initial or replacement Social Security cards; and add death and fraud indicators to verification systems used by employers, state agencies, and other entities. The commissioner was also required to improve controls for issuing SSNs to newborns to prevent multiple numbers being issued to one child and to avoid fraud. The law also created an interagency task force to develop methods to prevent counterfeiting, tampering, theft, and alteration of Social Security cards. Finally, it amended the Social Security Act to prevent states from displaying SSNs on driver's licenses, motor vehicle registrations, or any other document issued to an individual for identification.

The law charged the secretary of health and human services with establishing minimum standards for birth certificates for use by federal agencies for any official purpose. This included requiring state or local issuing officials to certify the birth certificate. States would be required to use safety paper or other methods to prevent tampering, counterfeiting, or other birth certificate fraud. Also, procedures would be established for verifying proof of identity in issuing birth certificates, with additional security measures for issuing a birth certificate to someone other than the applicant (parents, adoptive parents, and so on).

REAL ID ACT OF 2005

The National Commission on Terrorist Attacks upon the United States (also known as the 9/11 Commission), an independent, bipartisan group, was created in late 2002 by Congress and the president to prepare a complete account of the circumstances surrounding the September 11, 2001, terrorist attacks and the nation's response. The Commission was also mandated to provide recommendations designed to guard against future attacks. One recommendation of the 9/11 Commission was improved: secure identification for all Americans. The Intelligence Reform and Terrorism Prevention Act of 2004 established a committee of federal and state officials to set new security and verification standards for driver's licenses. In 2005 a bill called the Real ID Act passed through Congress attached to an emergency appropriations bill for defense spending, tsunami relief, and terror prevention. On May 11, 2005, President Bush signed the REAL ID Act of 2005, which dismantled many of the provisions of the Intelligence Reform and Terrorism Prevention Act of 2004 and mandated federal standards for state-issued driver's licenses. The new act transferred responsibility for driver's license security from the U.S. Department of Transportation to the DHS.

The new law also required states to: develop security upgrades and security clearances for Department of Motor Vehicles (DMV) personnel; verify all documents with the original issuing agency and verify U.S. citizenship or lawful immigration status before issuing a driver's license or non-driver's identification card; and establish new data management, storage, and sharing protocols. States were prohibited from accepting any foreign documents other than an official passport for identity purposes. States are required to be certified by May 11, 2008, in compliance with the DHS and the Transportation Department. After this date, licenses and ID cards issued by noncertified states will not be accepted for federal purposes, including boarding an airplane, receiving federal benefits such as Social Security, or filing an employment eligibility verification form (the I-9).

Cost Projections for the REAL ID Act

The Congressional Budget Office estimates in "Cost Estimate H.R. 418" (February 9, 2005, http://www.cbo .gov/showdoc.cfm?index=6072) the cost of the REAL ID Act at $100 million over an implementation period from 2005 to 2010. This cost includes $80 million to reimburse states for the expense of establishing and maintaining the Driver License Agreement, an interstate database to share driver information, and $20 million in additional grants to states to cover other costs of compliance.

The REAL ID Act: National Impact Analysis (September 2006, http://www.nga.org/Files/pdf/0609REALID.pdf), the result of a survey jointly sponsored by the National Governors Association, the National Conference of State Legislatures, and the National Association of Motor Vehicle Administrators, projects that implementation of the act will cost more than $11 billion over five years. Besides new applicants, all 245 million current holders of state driver's licenses or ID cards will be required to make a personal visit to a DMV office to present original documents verifying identity and be reenrolled in the state's computer system. The cost of additional staff and work hours necessary to reenroll that number of people within the five-year deadline was projected at $8.5 billion. Upgrading state and national systems to facilitate verification of each document presented by a driver's license applicant or reenrollee was estimated to cost $1.4 billion. The price tag for license redesign to comply with required security features was projected at $1.1 billion. Other items, such as security clearances and fraudulent document training for employees processing license applications, added an additional $40 million.

SUSPICIONS OF GOVERNMENT INVASION OF PRIVACY. Following on the heels of the Patriot Act, civil libertarians viewed the REAL ID Act as one more example of the erosion of privacy rights allowed by Congress under the guise of fighting terrorism. According to Angela French of Citizens Against Government Waste in *REAL ID: Big*

Brother Could Cost Big Money (October 17, 2005, http:// www.cagw.org/site/DocServer/Real_ID_FINAL_with_cover .pdf?docID=1281:

> Some view the implementation of the REAL ID Act as a chance to convince the government that the best way to secure licenses is to embed them with a tiny little chip, creating a "smartcard," which has the potential to track every movement and decision made by the card-holder. ... The Orwellian plot seems far-fetched, but the government already made the mistake of mandating that U.S. passports will be updated using this technology. ... If the government opts to use these brittle chips, ... U.S. drivers will be forced to carry a license that has the memory to store every detail about the person, including health records, family history, bank and credit card transactions, as well as a wealth of other information.

REBELLION IN THE STATES. Reports on the impact of the REAL ID Act generated a stir in state legislatures. Shaun Waterman notes in "Analysis: Maine Says 'No' to REAL ID Act" (United Press International, January 26, 2007) that the Maine legislature passed a resolution in 2006 rejecting proposed federal standards for driver's licenses and calling on Congress to repeal the REAL ID Act. According to Waterman, the American Civil Liberties Union (ACLU) reported that similar initiatives were under way in eleven other states: Georgia, Hawaii, Massachusetts, Missouri, Montana, New Hampshire, New Mexico, Oklahoma, Vermont, Washington, and Wyoming.

SECURE FENCE ACT OF 2006

The U.S. Customs and Border Patrol (CBP) reports that during the 2006 fiscal year 12,300 agents guarded the U.S. borders ("On a Typical Day ... ," 2006, http:// www.cbp.gov/linkhandler/cgov/newsroom/fact_sheets/ typical_day.ctt/typical_day.pdf). On May 15, 2006, President Bush supplemented this staffing by calling up six thousand National Guard troops to support the Border Patrol in an all-out effort to stop the flow of illegal immigrants across the U.S.-Mexican border.

In a further effort to close the porous southwestern border, President Bush signed the Secure Fence Act of 2006, which authorized construction of hundreds of miles of additional fencing along the U.S.-Mexican border and more vehicle barriers, checkpoints, and lighting to help prevent people from entering the country illegally. The act also authorized the Department of Homeland Security to increase use of advanced technology such as cameras, satellites, and unmanned aerial vehicles to reinforce infrastructure at the border. The DHS secretary was directed to conduct a study on construction of a state-of-the-art barrier system along the northern international land and maritime border.

The border fence legislation met with controversy. As noted by Jamie Reno in *Newsweek* (October 12, 2006,

http://www.msnbc.msn.com/id/15240665/site/newsweek/):
"Pro-immigration border activists are calling the measure
an outrage, a political stunt, a gimmick that has everything to do with the congressional elections drawing
near, while anti-immigration groups counter that the
fence is a positive first step to securing the porous southern border. Environmentalists decry the potential hazards
of the fence, while Mexico's outgoing President Vicente
Fox condemns it as 'shameful.'"

LEGISLATION IN THE STATES
California's Efforts to Legislate against Illegal Aliens

In November 1994 increasing concern about the
effects of a large population of illegal aliens culminated
in California voters approving Proposition 187. The ballot initiative prohibited illegal aliens and their children
from receiving any welfare services, education, or emergency health care. It further required local law enforcement authorities, educators, medical professionals, and
social service workers to report suspected illegal aliens
to state and federal authorities. It also considered the
manufacture, distribution, and sale of fraudulent documents to be a state felony punishable by up to five years
in prison.

The day after California voters approved Proposition
187, civil rights groups filed suit in federal district court
to block implementation of the ballot initiative. One
week later a temporary restraining order was issued.

In November 1995 U.S. district judge Mariana R.
Pfaelzer ruled unconstitutional Proposition 187's provision denying elementary and secondary education for
undocumented children. Pfaelzer cited the Supreme
Court decision in *Plyler v. Doe*, which held that the equal
protection clause of the Fourteenth Amendment prohibited states from denying education to illegal immigrants.
Civil rights and education groups had argued that states
had no legal rights to regulate immigration, which was a
federal responsibility.

In March 1998 Pfaelzer permanently barred Proposition 187's restrictions on benefits for aliens and declared
much of the legislation unconstitutional. Pfaelzer did allow,
however, the criminal provision to consider as a felony the
manufacture, distribution, and use of false documents.

Arizona Succeeds Where California Failed

In November 2004 Arizona voters approved Proposition 200, which required proof of citizenship when
registering to vote and applying for public benefits. It
also required state, county, and municipal employees to
report suspected undocumented immigrants to immigration authorities. The Mexican American Legal Defense
and Educational Fund filed suit to block implementation
of Proposition 200. In December 2004 the U.S. district
judge David Bury lifted a temporary order barring imple-

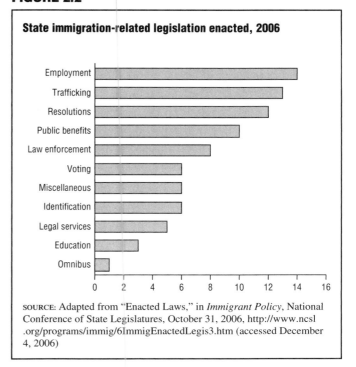

FIGURE 2.2

State immigration-related legislation enacted, 2006

SOURCE: Adapted from "Enacted Laws," in *Immigrant Policy*, National
Conference of State Legislatures, October 31, 2006, http://www.ncsl
.org/programs/immig/6ImmigEnactedLegis3.htm (accessed December
4, 2006)

mentation of Proposition 200, which allowed it to become
law in Arizona.

The apparent success of Arizona's Proposition 200
sparked interest in similar laws in other states. Tyche Hendricks notes, for example, in "Issue of Illegals Roiling
Arizona: New Law Denies Public Services to Such Immigrants" (*San Francisco Chronicle*, February 28, 2005) that
similar initiatives were being developed in Colorado, Georgia, Louisiana, Mississippi, Oregon, and Washington.

Flurry of New Immigration Legislation in 2006

In "Immigrant Policy" (October 31, 2006, http://www
.ncsl.org/programs/immig/6ImmigEnactedLegis3.htm), the
National Conference of State Legislatures reports that
570 pieces of legislation concerning immigrants were
introduced in state legislatures during 2006. Particular
subjects included education, employment, identification
and driver's licenses, law enforcement, legal services,
public benefits, trafficking, and voting procedures as
related to immigrants. Only a handful of these bills were
vetoed, whereas eighty-four bills were enacted by thirty-
two states in 2006. Colorado enacted seventeen new bills,
or 20% of all new immigration bills, enacted by the
states.

Employment (17%) and trafficking (15%) issues
accounted for one-third of new immigration-related state
legislation. (See Figure 2.2.) Employment laws were
adopted by nine states. Colorado led the way with five
new employment laws and five prohibiting trafficking.
Employment legislation required employers to verify

legal work status of new hires, prohibited hiring illegal immigrants, added penalties for hiring illegal immigrants, or restricted unemployment and worker compensation benefits to people lawfully present. Washington State enacted one of the few pro-immigrant pieces of employment legislation. Noting significant inequities suffered by people of color (generally anyone who does not have light skin or appear Caucasian) in almost all aspects of daily life, the new law mandated multicultural education for health care professionals to increase understanding of the relationship between culture and health. Trafficking legislation set penalties for human smuggling and forced employment and established task forces to investigate ways to deter trafficking.

Twelve resolutions passed by state legislatures generally affirmed support of specific legislation to be considered by Congress. Unique among these was Georgia's SR 1426, which recognized "the great value of continued immigration into Georgia."

REPERCUSSIONS OF POST-9/11 POLICIES

The U.S. government was aggressive in its pursuit of terrorism suspects. Allison Parker and Jamie Fellner of Human Rights Watch note in "Above the Law: Executive Power after September 11 in the United States" (January 2004, http://hrw.org/wr2k4/8.htm) that in the year following 9/11 the Justice Department apprehended approximately twelve hundred aliens. More than seven hundred individuals were confined on immigration-related charges. On April 17, 2003, the U.S. attorney general John Ashcroft issued a decision that illegal aliens could be detained indefinitely, whether they were known to have ties to terrorist groups or not (http://www.usdoj.gov/eoir/efoia/bia/Decisions/Revdec/pdfDEC/3488.pdf). The attorney general ordered officials to keep the names of detainees secret. In certain cases the detainees' mail and communications with their attorneys were monitored.

Interested parties charged that the government's policies were unconstitutional or in violation of civil liberties or laws regarding public disclosure. Many lawsuits were filed seeking information about the 9/11 detainees and protesting secret deportation hearings.

Secret Deportation Hearings

In September 2001 Chief Immigration Judge Michael Creppy issued an order stating that typically open deportation hearings should be closed in any case deemed of "special interest" in the investigation of the 9/11 attacks. The ACLU filed suit on behalf of Representative John Conyers (D-Michigan) and Michigan newspapers challenging Judge Creppy's order after the public and press were denied access to the deportation hearing of a Muslim fundraiser who had overstayed a tourist visa.

In August 2002 the U.S. Court of Appeals for the Sixth Circuit ruled in *Detroit News, Inc., et al., v. Ashcroft, et al.* (2002 FED App. 0291P [6th Cir.] No. 02-1437) that the Bush administration acted unlawfully in holding hundreds of deportation hearings in secret on the sole grounds that those involved were terrorism suspects. This ruling characterized the 9/11 attacks as "egregious, deplorable, and despicable" events that led to vigorous prosecution of immigration laws and described governmental secrecy as "profoundly undemocratic."

In a separate suit the ACLU represented the media seeking information on special interest detainees taken into custody in New Jersey. A lower court judge in Newark ordered the government to open all such hearings to the public unless it could offer case-by-case proof of the need for secrecy. In *North Jersey Media Group, Inc.; New Jersey Law Journal v. John Ashcroft, Attorney General of the United States; Michael Creppy, Hon.* (2002 No. 02-2524), the Third U.S. Circuit Court of Appeals reversed the lower court ruling. The case was appealed to the U.S. Supreme Court, which declined to review it.

The decisions of the courts in these two cases restricted the government's power to hold secret hearings in the four states belonging to the Sixth Circuit (Tennessee, Michigan, Ohio, and Kentucky) but not in the remaining forty-six states.

Voluntary Interviews?

According to *Homeland Security: Justice Department's Project to Interview Aliens after September 11, 2001* (April 2003, http://www.gao.gov/new.items/d03459.pdf), the General Accounting Office (now the Government Accountability Office) reports that between September 11 and November 9, 2001, the INS compiled a list of 7,602 names of aliens in the United States with characteristics similar to those of the 9/11 hijackers and requested that the individuals on the list make themselves available for voluntary interviews. Even though many individuals expressed understanding regarding the need for such interviews, others were apprehensive. The GAO notes that "attorneys for interviewees and immigration advocates ... expressed the view that interviewed aliens did not perceive the interviews to be truly voluntary. ... They worried about repercussions, such as future INS denials for visa extensions or permanent residence, if they refused to be interviewed."

Civil Rights Violations

After 9/11 Americans began to take greater notice of foreign-born residents. People who appeared to be from the Middle East were suddenly suspect. Those who appeared different in dress or behavior became the subject of particular attention, suspicion, and sometimes even violence. Communities, and particularly law enforcement agencies, across the nation were faced with

TABLE 2.2

Fact sheet regarding post-9/11 backlash discrimination

OSC	EEOC
Office of Special Counsel for Immigration Related Unfair Employment Practices, Civil Rights Division, U.S. Dept. of Justice	Equal Employment Opportunity Commission

OSC

Jurisdiction:

Prohibited conduct: Citizenship/immigration status and national origin discrimination with respect to hiring, firing, and recruitment or referral for a fee; unfair documentary practices during the employment eligibility verification (Form I-9) process; and retaliation.

Employers covered: Employers with four or more employees are covered by the prohibition against citizenship/immigration status discrimination and unfair documentary practices. Employers with four to fourteen employees are covered by the prohibition against national origin discrimination.

Covered persons: U.S. citizens and work authorized aliens are protected from national origin discrimination and document abuse. U.S. citizens, many lawful permanent residents, asylees and refugees are protected from citizenship/immigration status discrimination.

EEOC

Jurisdiction:

Prohibited conduct: Religious, national origin, and race discrimination with respect to any aspect of employment, including the terms and conditions of employment.

Employers covered: Employers with fifteen or more employees.

Covered persons: All individuals, regardless of immigration status.

Examples of employment discrimination

OSC

Citizenship/immigration status discrimination:

Anwar, an asylee from Egypt, applies for a position with a financial services company. He is refused hire because he is not a U.S. citizen and does not have a green card. What should Anwar do?

Anwar can file a charge with OSC alleging citizenship/immigration status discrimination. Employers may not deny hire to asylees or refugees because they are not U.S. citizens or lawful permanent residents, or because they do not possess a green card.

Employers should verify the employment eligibility of all new hires, whether or not U.S. citizens, by completing the Form I-9. Employers may not require green cards from non-citizens for this purpose. Individuals may choose from lists of acceptable documents, including an unrestricted Social Security card and driver's license.

Citizenship/immigration status discrimination:

- An employer posts a sign that states, "We hire Americans only."
- An employer refuses to hire a job applicant because he or she does not look like an "American citizen."
- An employer fires employees who are not U.S. citizens or who appear "foreign."

National origin discrimination:

- An employer refuses to hire applicants because they are, or appear to be, of Arab or South Asian descent.
- An employer fires an employee who wears a head scarf, veil or turban
- An employer refuses to hire anyone with a foreign accent.
- An employer continuously uses ethnic slurs when referring to an employee who was born in Pakistan, resulting in the forced resignation of the employee.

Unfair documentary practices:

- An employer scrutinizes and rejects the documents presented by Arab Americans to establish employment eligibility in the United States (Form I-9) to a far greater extent than those of other new hires.
- An employer requires all South Asians to complete a new Form I-9, while not requiring other employees to do so.
- An employer requires applicants or new employees who appear "Muslim" to provide documents establishing U.S. citizenship, while allowing other job applicants to present any combination of legally acceptable documents (such as a Social Security card and driver's license) to complete the Form I-9.
- An employer requires non-citizens to provide a document issued by the INS or DHS to complete the Form I-9, rather than allowing such individuals the opportunity to present any combination of acceptable documentation (including an unrestricted Social Security card and a driver's license).

EEOC

Religious discrimination:

Narinder, a South Asian man who wears a Sikh turban, applies for a position as a cashier at XYZ. He is denied hire because XYZ fears Narinder's religious attire will make customers uncomfortable. What should XYZ do?

XYZ may not deny Narinder the job due to customer preferences about religious attire. That would be unlawful. It would be the same as refusing to hire Narinder because he is a Sikh. It is unlawful to treat individuals differently in the workplace based upon perceptions about their religion, race or national origin.

Religious discrimination:

Like employees of other religions, Muslim employees may need accommodations such as time off for religious holidays or exceptions to dress and grooming codes.

Muslim employees in XYZ corporation approach their supervisor and ask that they be allowed to use a conference room in an adjacent building for prayer. Until making the request, those employees prayed at their work stations. What should XYZ do?

When the room is needed for business purposes, XYZ can deny its use for personal religious purposes. However, allowing the employees to use the conference room for prayers likely would not impose an undue hardship on XYZ in many other circumstances. Similarly, prayer often can be performed during breaks, so that providing sufficient time during work hours for prayer would not result in an undue hardship. If going to another building for prayer takes longer than the allotted break periods, the employees still can be accommodated if the nature of work makes flexible scheduling feasible. XYZ can require employees to make up any work time missed for religious observance.

Examples of workplace harassment:

Muhammad works for XYZ. Muhammad meets with his manager and complains that one of his coworkers, Bill, regularly calls him names like "camel jockey," "the local terrorist," and "the ayatollah," and has intentionally embarrassed him in front of customers by claiming that he is incompetent. How should the supervisor respond?

Managers and supervisors who learn about objectionable workplace conduct based on religion or national origin are responsible for taking steps to correct the conduct by anyone under their control. Muhammad's manager should relay Muhammad's complaint to the appropriate manager if he does not supervise Bill. If XYZ determines that harassment occurred, it should take disciplinary action against Bill that is significant enough to ensure that the harassment does not continue.

SOURCE: "Fact Sheet Regarding Post–9/11 Backlash Discrimination," U.S. Equal Employment Opportunity Commission and Department of Justice, June 2002, http://www.usdoj.gov/crt/osc/pdf/publications/ee_post911_english.pdf (accessed December 14, 2006)

the challenges of fair treatment and protection of foreign-born residents.

Even the Justice Department, the enforcement agency for such civil rights violations, was not immune to complaints. Philip Shenon notes in "Report on U.S. Antiterrorism Law Alleges Violations of Civil Rights" (*New York Times*, July 20, 2003) that the Justice Department's inspector general reported to Congress in July 2003 that in the six-month period that ended on June 15, 2003, the inspector general's office had received thirty-four credible complaints of violations of the civil rights and liberties of individuals held in connection with terrorism investigations. According to Shenon, Muslim and Arab immigrants held in detention had allegedly been beaten; the accused perpetrators were Justice Department employees. As a result, the Justice Department developed the "Fact Sheet Regarding Post-9/11 Backlash Discrimination" (June 2002, http://www.usdoj.gov/crt/osc/pdf/publications/ee_post911_english.pdf) to help employers understand such discrimination and how to avoid it. (See Table 2.2.)

CULTURAL AND RELIGIOUS AWARENESS FOR LAW ENFORCEMENT. The Chicago Police Department, recognizing the need to understand and more effectively communicate with the diverse ethnic and religious groups that populate the city, developed a program to increase officers' ability to do so. In "Chicago Police Videos Offer Insights into Various Faiths" (*New York Times*, January 23, 2005), Stephen Kinzer reports that the department produced a series of short videos about religious groups with a significant presence in Chicago—Sikhs, Muslims, Jews, Buddhists, and Hindus. Many members of these faiths appeared to be from the Middle East and/or wore particular clothing that made them look "different." The videos provided a look into homes and houses of worship and interviews with religious and community leaders. A police narrator gave tips on things to do or to avoid when interacting with people of each faith. The intent was to help police officers respect people's cultural heritage while protecting the community and the city.

Viewing the tapes was required training for all Chicago police officers and had a noticeable effect. Kinzer reports that one Sikh leader said the training helped the police understand that the display of swords in homes and as part of men's clothing was a religious tradition rather than intended for criminal activity. A leader of Chicago's Islamic community said the training "changed our community's relationship with the police ... people are beginning to see the Chicago Police Department as an ally rather than an opposing force."

The Chicago videos became a two-DVD training program (2007, http://www.pluralism.org/research/profiles/display.php?profile=74371) on both religions and cultures for use by other law enforcement organizations across the nation. For information on national origin discrimination, see appendix I.

CHAPTER 3
CURRENT IMMIGRATION STATISTICS

To understand the scope of the immigration issue in the United States, it is important to know the number of immigrants in the country, where they came from, why they came, and why some did not get to stay. Because immigrant statistics have been the basis for legislation and project funding, information about immigrants' ages, skills, ability to work, and location of settlement in the United States is collected in a variety of forms. The U.S. Bureau of the Census uses statistical methods to estimate the nation's population size based on the most recent census counts and also estimates the foreign-born population.

In October 2006 the Census Bureau announced that the population of the United States had reached a new milestone: 300 million people ("Nation's Population to Reach 300 Million on Oct. 17," October 12, 2006, http://www.census.gov/Press-Release/www/releases/archives/population/007616.html). The Census Bureau based the nation's headcount on statistical averages it had developed, including one birth every seven seconds, one death every thirteen seconds, and one new immigrant arriving in the country every thirty-one seconds.

When the U.S. population reached 100 million in 1915, immigrants comprised 15% of the total ("Special Edition: 300 Million," August 9, 2006, http://www.census.gov/Press-Release/www/2006/cb06ffse-06.pdf). The U.S. population reached 200 million in 1967; at that time only 5% were foreign born, and the greatest share of immigrants had come from Italy. As of 2006 the Census Bureau estimated the foreign-born population at 31.2 million, with the largest share having been born in Mexico. The foreign-born population is projected to rise from 10.8% of the total U.S. population in 2006 to 13.3% in 2050, and then drop to 10.9% by 2100. The immigrant population is projected to top fifty million by 2050. (See Table 3.1.)

WHO IS AN IMMIGRANT?

U.S. immigration law defines an immigrant as a person legally admitted for permanent residence in the United States. Some arrive in the country with immigrant visas (government authorizations permitting entry into a country) issued abroad by U.S. Department of State consular offices. Others who already reside in the United States become immigrants when they adjust their status from temporary to permanent residence. These include individuals who enter the country as foreign students, temporary workers, refugees and asylees (those seeking asylum), and illegal immigrants.

FOREIGN-BORN POPULATION
Region of Birth

In *A Statistical Portrait of the Foreign-Born Population at Mid-Decade* (October 2006, http://pewhispanic.org/files/other/foreignborn/Table-2.pdf), the Pew Hispanic Center estimates that more than one-third (38%) of the U.S. foreign-born population in 2005 came from Central American countries, including Mexico, which represented the largest single source of immigrants. (See Figure 3.1.) Asia was the birthplace of 23% of foreign-born people living in the United States. These numbers reflect a major shift in immigration patterns during the twentieth century. Between 1900 and 1909 the vast majority (93%) of immigrants came from Europe. (See Table 1.1 in Chapter 1.) The 38,529 immigrants who arrived between 1900 and 1909 from Central America and Mexico represented only 0.5% of the 8.2 million immigrants who arrived in the United States during that time.

Where the Foreign-Born Population Chooses to Live

Table 3.2 offers greater detail from the Pew Hispanic Center study about the birthplaces of the foreign-born population and where they lived in 2005. States are listed

TABLE 3.1

Population projections for native and foreign-born, selected years 2006–2100

[Numbers in thousands]

	July 1, 2006	July 1, 2025	July 1, 2050	July 1, 2075	July 1, 2100
Total					
Population	290,152	337,814	403,686	480,504	570,954
Percent of total	100.0	100.0	100.0	100.0	100.0
Native population	258,917	296,999	349,890	420,957	508,694
Percent of total	89.2	87.9	86.7	87.6	89.1
Foreign-born population	31,235	40,814	53,796	59,546	62,259
Percent of total	10.8	12.1	13.3	12.4	10.9

SOURCE: Adapted from "Projections of the Resident Population by Race, Hispanic Origin, and Nativity: Middle Series, 1999–2100 (NP-T5-C; NP-T5-F; NP-T5-G; NP-T5-H)," U.S. Census Bureau, http://www.census.gov/population/www/projections/natsum-T5.html (accessed February 8, 2007)

FIGURE 3.1

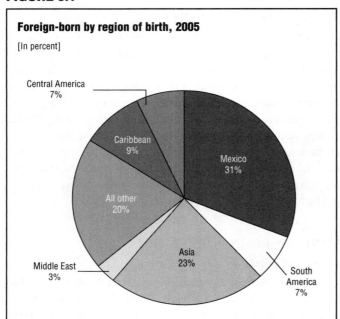

Foreign-born by region of birth, 2005

[In percent]

Central America 7%
Caribbean 9%
Mexico 31%
All other 20%
Asia 23%
Middle East 3%
South America 7%

Note: Middle East includes Afghanistan, Cyprus, Iran, Iraq, Israel, Jordan, Kuwait, Lebanon, Saudi Arabia, Syria, Turkey, Yemen, Algeria, Egypt, Libya, Morocco, and Sudan.

SOURCE: Adapted from "Table 2. Foreign Born by Region of Birth: 2000 and 2005," in *A Statistical Portrait of the Foreign-Born Population at Mid-Decade*, Pew Hispanic Center, October 2006, http://pewhispanic .org/files/other/foreignborn/complete.pdf (accessed December 12, 2006). © 2006 Pew Hispanic Center, a Pew Research Center project, www .pewhispanic.org.

in rank order by the size of their foreign-born populations. California was home to 9.6 million immigrants, including the largest populations from Mexico (4.3 million) and Asia (2.9 million). Florida, with the fourth largest total foreign-born population, had the largest population born in Caribbean countries (1.2 million). The greatest concentrations of people born in South America lived in New York and Florida. Table 3.3 shows that between 2000 and 2005 Georgia and Arizona experienced increases in their foreign-born population of

38.1% and 30.5%, respectively. The number of foreign-born in California increased as well, but at a much slower rate (9.5%).

Families

The Pew Hispanic Center reports that foreign-born residents are more likely than natives to be married and less likely to be divorced. (See Table 3.4.) In 2005, 61.8% of foreign-born residents were married, compared with 51.9% of natives. Just 6.7% of the foreign born were divorced, compared with 10.8% of natives (this data refers to current marital status and does not record previous divorces). The lowest share of foreign-born divorced residents were from Mexico (4.4%) and Asia (4.8%).

Foreign-born families tended to be larger than native families in 2005, according to the Pew Hispanic Center in *A Statistical Portrait of the Foreign-Born Population at Mid-Decade*. Just 11.4% of native families had five or more people, compared with 24.2% of foreign-born families. (See Table 3.5.) The greatest share of foreign-born families with five or more members were from Mexico (37.8%) and Central America (27.4%). Foreign-born women were more likely to have given birth within the past year. Of foreign-born women in 2005, 9.1% had given birth during the past year, compared with 6.6% of native women. (See Table 3.6.) Mexican women accounted for 43.1% of all births to foreign-born women.

The Pew study found little difference among native and foreign-born people regarding the share of children living in 2005 with at least one parent (89% and 85%, respectively). (See Table 3.7.) However, 6.5% of native children lived with a grandparent, compared with 3% of foreign-born children. A significant difference between the two groups was that 11.9% of foreign-born children lived with someone other than a parent or grandparent, compared with just 4.5% of native children. Foreign-born children most frequently living with someone other than a parent or grandparent in 2005 were from Central America (16.8%) and Mexico (16.3%).

TABLE 3.2

Foreign-born by state and region of birth, 2005

[2005 household population]

	Total population		Region of birth						
	Native born	Foreign born	Mexico	South and East Asia	Caribbean	Central America	South America	Middle East	All other
California	25,692,798	9,647,768	4,260,240	2,874,108	68,520	788,140	220,321	366,436	1,070,003
New York	14,716,444	3,962,767	194,504	842,885	967,645	238,709	564,539	146,347	1,008,138
Texas	18,700,012	3,550,140	2,264,889	522,694	50,674	273,167	93,480	57,785	287,451
Florida	14,143,512	3,220,141	284,155	246,013	1,246,311	299,009	546,459	61,394	536,800
Illinois	10,738,316	1,703,548	708,126	369,617	28,741	42,147	54,084	52,630	448,203
New Jersey	6,869,031	1,655,837	90,588	448,343	250,699	107,439	273,800	68,121	416,847
Massachusetts	5,293,890	907,054	14,667	210,187	134,745	57,619	129,733	32,907	327,196
Arizona	4,951,910	854,356	582,692	83,240	10,334	22,549	14,613	13,730	127,198
Georgia	8,019,942	791,706	271,357	174,393	52,532	54,749	59,106	15,735	163,834
Washington	5,400,551	757,235	194,098	268,343	6,849	14,231	11,704	15,926	246,084
Virginia	6,599,005	721,843	54,819	254,380	20,672	107,411	70,827	52,387	161,347
Maryland	4,808,463	644,978	33,862	184,119	49,573	99,967	57,963	29,166	190,328
Pennsylvania	11,326,966	621,896	45,877	212,433	45,480	20,676	37,547	26,959	232,924
Michigan	9,249,820	607,657	81,402	174,960	10,212	10,802	13,247	85,616	231,418
North Carolina	7,838,442	559,343	226,090	95,258	19,403	58,037	23,280	17,468	119,807
Colorado	4,080,259	460,380	241,700	74,995	2,666	18,848	11,290	11,357	99,524
Connecticut	2,951,931	413,837	17,727	76,706	56,813	23,661	66,725	11,322	160,883
Nevada	1,965,460	410,557	198,296	91,714	10,445	27,822	11,914	7,750	62,616
Ohio	10,754,496	391,554	39,802	119,725	12,621	6,806	14,137	26,448	172,015
Oregon	3,216,600	344,322	146,600	87,361	2,997	10,578	8,250	9,755	78,781
Minnesota	4,641,179	327,973	62,274	120,216	1,951	14,319	16,489	9,508	103,216
Indiana	5,843,819	237,393	94,065	51,858	4,336	9,211	6,869	7,579	63,475
Wisconsin	5,177,908	223,832	75,735	69,559	4,667	4,078	8,517	4,117	57,159
Hawaii	1,038,552	219,976	7,300	177,969	742	1,704	2,956	545	28,760
Tennessee	5,598,624	217,735	62,390	50,845	8,489	19,237	8,213	15,859	52,702
Missouri	5,430,426	202,177	41,706	59,838	7,612	8,927	5,576	9,650	68,868
Utah	2,259,877	192,272	81,982	30,208	334	13,172	22,649	3,380	40,547
South Carolina	3,954,211	173,180	58,018	31,379	5,837	13,642	9,607	6,911	47,786
New Mexico	1,721,769	165,020	117,880	16,341	2,089	4,430	3,280	2,086	18,914
Oklahoma	3,276,122	153,852	76,084	36,061	2,378	7,382	7,698	4,626	19,623
Kansas	2,524,029	145,670	67,499	37,681	868	5,752	3,514	4,500	25,856
Rhode Island	905,097	128,187	4,955	16,463	20,487	18,890	13,510	2,248	51,634
Louisiana	4,263,846	123,335	12,912	44,176	6,442	25,229	5,268	4,823	24,485
Alabama	4,328,559	119,516	35,677	29,230	4,713	10,904	5,063	2,959	30,970
Arkansas	2,589,778	104,887	50,170	17,040	872	15,631	3,882	2,688	14,604
Kentucky	3,963,854	101,781	24,645	27,522	4,623	3,730	1,585	4,439	35,237
Iowa	2,749,890	98,376	28,620	28,598	418	8,527	1,535	2,681	27,997
Nebraska	1,612,103	94,240	39,398	20,120	468	9,013	1,491	5,836	17,914
Idaho	1,324,177	84,473	53,159	6,436	168	2,571	2,162	2,285	17,692
New Hampshire	1,196,511	75,386	528	19,496	4,599	3,273	4,256	2,925	40,309
District of Columbia	442,831	65,741	3,429	10,289	7,840	15,308	6,121	1,655	21,099
Delaware	765,296	60,302	15,199	13,142	5,006	3,720	3,493	1,084	18,658
Mississippi	2,784,158	46,230	14,191	13,418	3,178	3,899	2,463	964	8,117
Maine	1,244,157	38,317	304	5,985	1,161	784	3,483	1,220	25,380
Alaska	622,684	35,318	2,063	15,880	2,082	1,247	1,049	306	12,691
West Virginia	1,760,398	21,419	1,851	6,774	970	261	387	2,237	8,939
Vermont	589,051	20,806	0	5,174	233	157	340	807	14,095
Montana	877,116	20,251	1,278	3,663	0	0	1,314	410	13,586
South Dakota	735,766	19,386	2,581	3,321	0	950	134	2,260	10,140
North Dakota	606,564	14,499	935	3,969	154	949	355	672	7,465
Wyoming	483,016	11,154	5,532	1,040	143	62	0	277	4,100
Total	**252,629,216**	**35,769,603**	**10,993,851**	**8,385,165**	**3,150,792**	**2,509,326**	**2,436,278**	**1,220,776**	**7,073,415**

Note: Middle East includes Afghanistan, Cyprus, Iran, Iraq, Israel, Jordan, Kuwait, Lebanon, Saudi Arabia, Syria, Turkey, Yemen, Algeria, Egypt, Libya, Morocco, and Sudan.

SOURCE: "Table 9. Foreign Born by State and Region of Birth: 2005," in *A Statistical Portrait of the Foreign-Born Population at Mid-Decade*, Pew Hispanic Center, October 2006, http://pewhispanic.org/files/other/foreignborn/complete.pdf (accessed December 12, 2006). © 2006 Pew Hispanic Center, a Pew Research Center project, www.pewhispanic.org.

Employment

Native and foreign-born residents find work in varied occupations, according to the Pew report. Educational levels and English-language skills are likely factors in some of the occupational differences. The greatest percentage of native workers in 2005 were found in office and administrative support (15.4%), sales (12.1%), and management (8.9%) occupations. (See Table 3.8.) A larger share of people from the Middle East (11.4%) held management positions than native born (8.9%) and people from Asia (8.3%). Foreign-born workers were found in greatest numbers in production (10.5%), office and

TABLE 3.3

Top ten states by percentage growth of foreign-born population, 2000 and 2005

	2005	2000	Change 2000–2005	Percent change 2000–2005
California	9,647,768	8,809,641	838,127	9.5
New York	3,962,767	3,819,028	143,739	3.8
Texas	3,550,140	2,878,503	671,637	23.3
Florida	3,220,141	2,634,349	585,792	22.2
Illinois	1,703,548	1,518,500	185,048	12.2
New Jersey	1,655,837	1,459,007	196,830	13.5
Massachusetts	907,054	752,899	154,155	20.5
Arizona	854,356	654,746	199,610	30.5
Georgia	791,706	573,161	218,545	38.1
Washington	757,235	608,622	148,613	24.4

SOURCE: Adapted from "Table 11. Change in Foreign-Born Population by State: 2000 and 2005," in *A Statistical Portrait of the Foreign-Born Population at Mid-Decade*, Pew Hispanic Center, October 2006, http://pewhispanic.org/files/other/foreignborn/complete.pdf (accessed December 12, 2006). © 2006 Pew Hispanic Center, a Pew Research Center project, www.pewhispanic.org.

TABLE 3.5

Family size for native and foreign-born residents by region of birth, 2005

	Two person families	Three to four person families	Five or more person families
Percent distribution			
Total native born	47.7	40.9	11.4
Total foreign born	28.9	47.0	24.2
Mexico	16.9	45.3	37.8
South and East Asia	28.3	52.6	19.0
Caribbean	34.0	47.6	18.4
Central America	23.9	48.7	27.4
South America	31.8	50.1	18.0
Middle East	30.9	46.9	22.2
All other	47.1	40.7	12.2

SOURCE: Adapted from "Table 17. Family Size by Region of Birth: 2005," in *A Statistical Portrait of the Foreign-Born Population at Mid-Decade*, Pew Hispanic Center, October 2006, http://pewhispanic.org/files/other/foreignborn/complete.pdf (accessed December 12, 2006). © 2006 Pew Hispanic Center, a Pew Research Center project, www.pewhispanic.org.

TABLE 3.4

Marital status of native and foreign-born by region of birth, 2005

	Now married	Widowed	Divorced	Separated	Never married
Percent distribution					
Total native born	51.9	6.2	10.8	2.1	29.0
Total foreign born	61.8	4.8	6.7	3.2	23.5
Mexico	61.7	2.8	4.4	4.0	27.1
South and East Asia	68.9	4.6	4.8	1.4	20.3
Caribbean	51.2	6.0	11.8	6.0	25.0
Central America	51.5	2.7	6.7	5.2	33.9
South America	57.5	3.5	9.6	4.2	25.1
Middle East	67.8	4.9	6.8	1.6	18.9
All other	62.5	8.8	9.0	2.0	17.7

SOURCE: Adapted from "Table 12. Marital Status by Region of Birth: 2005," in *A Statistical Portrait of the Foreign-Born Population at Mid-Decade*, Pew Hispanic Center, October 2006, http://pewhispanic.org/files/other/foreignborn/complete.pdf (accessed December 12, 2006). © 2006 Pew Hispanic Center, a Pew Research Center project, www.pewhispanic.org.

administrative support (9.7%), and construction trades (9.4%). In 2005 the education, health, and human services industry attracted the largest share of people from the Caribbean (25.5%), other countries (22.2%), South and East Asia (20.9%), the Middle East (20.1%), and South America (16.8%). (See Table 3.9.) The largest share of people from Mexico (19.1%) and Central America (16.3%) worked in construction.

HOUSEHOLD INCOME. The Pew Hispanic Center notes that the median 2005 income for native households was $46,000, compared with $42,000 for all foreign-born households. Median income was highest for Asian households ($59,000) and Middle Eastern households ($49,000).

Mexican households had the lowest median income at $32,000. Household incomes varied by the number of people in the household with jobs and whether jobs were full time, part time, or seasonal. Table 3.10 offers more comparative detail about household incomes. Native households were evenly distributed across the scale with about 20% in each earning category. Among Middle Eastern households the largest income groups were at the bottom and top ends of the scale (21% with incomes less than $18,999 and 27.2% with incomes greater than $89,600). The share of Asian households grew progressively larger at each income quartile, ending with 30.4% in the top income quartile.

In *A Statistical Portrait of the Foreign-Born Population at Mid-Decade* the Pew Hispanic Center reports that the 2005 poverty rate for natives was 12.8%, compared with 17.1% for foreign-born residents. (See Table 3.11.) The lowest poverty rate (11.6%) was found among people from "all other" countries. Among the population aged sixty-five and over, 23.4% of Caribbean-born people and 22.6% of Mexican-born lived in poverty.

Age

Figure 3.2 illustrates age differences between the foreign-born and native populations in 2005. Most foreign born were in the prime working ages—midtwenties to midforties—represented by the great bulge in the middle of the stacked bar graphs. By contrast the graph for the native population is heavy with children at the bottom and narrows with increasing age, except for a slight bulge of baby boomers in the forty to fifty-five age range. Past age sixty-five the two graphs appear similar. The Census Bureau, whose data was the basis for these graphs, notes that the small proportion of foreign-born children can be

TABLE 3.6

Fertility in past year for native and foreign-born women, 2005

[By maternal birth region]

	Women with a birth	Percent of women with a birth	Share of foreign-born women with a birth
Mexico	372,378	11.5	43.1
South and East Asia	184,534	7.9	21.4
Caribbean	59,781	7.8	6.9
Central America	66,210	8.9	7.7
South America	50,443	7.3	5.8
Middle East	25,597	9.3	3.0
All other	104,125	6.9	12.1
Total foreign-born	**863,068**	**9.1**	
Total native-born	**3,359,012**	**6.6**	

Note: Middle East includes Afghanistan, Cyprus, Iran, Iraq, Israel, Jordan, Kuwait, Lebanon, Saudi Arabia, Syria, Turkey, Yemen, Algeria, Egypt, Libya, Morocco, and Sudan.

SOURCE: "Table 13. Fertility in the Past Year by Region of Birth: 2005," in *A Statistical Portrait of the Foreign-Born Population at Mid-Decade*, Pew Hispanic Center, October 2006, http://pewhispanic.org/files/other/foreignborn/complete.pdf (accessed December 12, 2006). © 2006 Pew Hispanic Center, a Pew Research Center project, www.pewhispanic.org.

TABLE 3.7

Living arrangements of native and foreign-born children by region of birth, 2005

	Parent householder	Grandparent householder	Other
Percent distribution			
Total native born	**89.0**	**6.5**	**4.5**
Total foreign born	**85.0**	**3.0**	**11.9**
Mexico	81.0	2.7	16.3
South and East Asia	88.3	3.5	8.1
Caribbean	78.2	8.1	13.7
Central America	79.5	3.7	16.8
South America	86.5	3.6	9.9
Middle East	93.0	0.9	6.1
All other	91.9	1.4	6.7

SOURCE: Adapted from "Table 18. Living Arrangements of Children by Region of Birth: 2005," in *A Statistical Portrait of the Foreign-Born Population at Mid-Decade*, Pew Hispanic Center, October 2006, http://pewhispanic.org/files/other/foreignborn/complete.pdf (accessed December 12, 2006). © 2006 Pew Hispanic Center, a Pew Research Center project, www.pewhispanic.org.

explained by the fact that most young children of immigrant parents are born in the United States and are counted as natives.

COUNTING IMMIGRANTS

There are various ways to qualify for immigration to the United States, but the U.S. Citizenship and Immigration Services (USCIS) generally classifies admissions into four major groups:

- Family-sponsored preference
- Employment-based preference
- Diversity Program
- Other—including Amerasians (typically children of Asian mothers and U.S. military or civilian personnel), parolees, refugees and asylees, individuals whose order for removal was canceled, and other legal provisions

With the passage of the Immigration Act of 1990 (IMMACT), the number of immigrants was limited to a total of 675,000 per year. However, the annual limit is flexible; it can exceed 675,000 if the maximum number of visas are not issued in the preceding year. For example, Table 3.12 reports the total immigrants from 2000 to 2005; in 2001, 2002, and 2005 the number of immigrants admitted exceeded one million. How did this happen?

The USCIS reports that some major categories of immigrants are exempt from the annual limits. These include:

- Immediate relatives of U.S. citizens
- Refugee and asylee adjustments
- Certain parolees from Indochina and the former Soviet Union
- Certain special agricultural workers
- Canceled removals
- Aliens who applied for adjustment of status after having unlawfully resided in the United States since January 1, 1982

In 2002 the number of immediate relatives admitted hit a high of 483,676. (See Table 3.12.) In 2002 and 2005 the number of refugees admitted exceeded 100,000, compared with a low of 34,362 in 2003. The 30,286 asylees admitted in 2005 was nearly triple the number admitted in this category in any of the previous five years.

New Arrivals

The United States offers two general methods for foreign-born people to attain immigrant status. In the first method aliens living abroad can apply for an immigrant visa and then become legal residents when approved for admission at a U.S. port of entry. In 2005, 384,071 such people entered the United States; identified in statistics as "new arrivals," they accounted for 34% of all immigrants admitted in 2005. (See Table 3.12.)

Adjustment of Status

The second method of gaining immigrant status is by "adjustment of status." This procedure allows certain aliens already in the United States to apply for immigrant status, including certain undocumented residents, temporary workers, foreign students, and refugees. The 738,302 individuals who had their status

TABLE 3.8

Occupation for native and foreign-born by region of birth, 2005

Percent distribution

Occupation group	Total		Region of birth						
	Native born	Foreign born	Mexico	South and East Asia	Caribbean	Central America	South America	Middle East	All other
Management	8.9	6.3	2.6	8.3	5.7	3.3	6.4	11.4	10.6
Business operations	1.9	1.2	0.4	1.7	1.1	0.7	1.2	1.9	1.9
Financial	2.2	1.9	0.3	3.8	2.0	0.7	2.0	2.3	2.5
Computer and mathematics	1.9	3.0	0.2	8.0	1.1	0.5	1.7	3.4	3.6
Architecture and engineering	1.7	2.0	0.4	4.2	1.2	0.5	1.4	4.3	2.9
Life, physical, and social sciences	0.8	1.1	0.1	2.3	0.4	0.2	0.9	1.6	1.7
Community and social services	1.6	0.9	0.3	0.9	1.4	0.8	1.1	1.2	1.4
Legal	1.1	0.4	0.1	0.5	0.5	0.2	0.5	0.6	0.8
Education, training, and library	6.0	3.6	1.3	4.7	3.5	1.8	4.1	7.2	6.0
Arts, design, entertainment, sports, and media	2.0	1.5	0.6	1.8	1.3	0.8	2.1	2.0	2.9
Healthcare practitioners and technical	4.5	4.1	0.6	8.0	5.2	1.3	3.0	6.5	5.8
Healthcare support	2.2	2.3	1.0	2.1	7.0	2.0	2.2	1.0	3.0
Protective services	2.3	0.9	0.4	0.7	2.3	0.9	0.9	0.9	1.3
Food preparation and serving	5.3	7.3	10.5	6.4	4.9	8.2	7.2	4.5	4.3
Building and grounds cleaning and maintenance	3.4	8.0	12.8	2.4	8.0	15.4	9.8	1.7	4.2
Personal care and services	3.3	3.9	2.5	4.7	5.3	4.0	4.6	3.5	4.0
Sales	12.1	9.3	5.8	11.5	9.9	6.9	10.6	19.7	11.0
Office and administrative support	15.4	9.7	6.1	11.3	12.9	9.0	12.6	9.6	11.5
Farming, fishing, and forestry	0.6	2.0	5.7	0.2	0.2	1.3	0.3	0.0	0.2
Construction trades	5.6	9.4	18.5	1.4	5.7	15.6	9.2	2.5	5.1
Extraction workers	0.1	0.0	0.1	0.0	0.0	0.0	0.0	0.0	0.0
Installation, maintenance, and repair workers	3.5	2.8	3.4	1.9	3.6	3.5	2.7	2.1	2.6
Production	6.4	10.5	15.5	9.0	7.2	12.1	8.1	5.4	6.6
Transportation and material moving	6.2	6.7	9.5	3.2	8.1	9.0	6.3	5.6	5.0
Military	0.3	0.1	0.0	0.1	0.1	0.2	0.1	0.1	0.1
Unemployed	0.7	1.0	1.1	0.8	1.4	1.1	1.0	0.9	0.7
Total	**100.0**	**100.0**	**100.0**	**100.0**	**100.0**	**100.0**	**100.0**	**100.0**	**100.0**

Note: Middle East includes Afghanistan, Cyprus, Iran, Iraq, Israel, Jordan, Kuwait, Lebanon, Saudi Arabia, Syria, Turkey, Yemen, Algeria, Egypt, Libya, Morocco, and Sudan.

SOURCE: Adapted from "Table 22. Occupation by Region of Birth: 2005," in *A Statistical Portrait of the Foreign-Born Population at Mid-Decade*, Pew Hispanic Center, October 2006, http://pewhispanic.org/files/other/foreignborn/complete.pdf (accessed December 12, 2006). © 2006 Pew Hispanic Center, a Pew Research Center project, www.pewhispanic.org.

adjusted in 2005 accounted for about two-thirds (66%) of all immigrants admitted. (See Table 3.12.)

There was a noticeable dip in the number of adjustments in status in 2003. (See Table 3.12.) The sudden decrease resulted from the Legal Immigration Family Equity (LIFE) Act of 2002, which resolved three class action lawsuits. Eligible people had one year (until June 4, 2003) to apply for this particular adjustment of status. Key to eligibility was proof that by October 1, 2000, the applicant had filed a written claim for class membership in one of three lawsuits commonly referred to as CSS, LULAC, and Zambrano. Applicants also had to prove they entered the United States before January 1, 1982, resided in continuous unlawful status through May 4, 1988, and were continuously physically present in the United States from November 6, 1986, through May 4, 1988. Eligible applicants, and certain spouses and children, were protected from removal or deportation while their adjustment applications were pending. Also, they could be eligible for employment authorization while waiting.

LIFE Act applications were submitted by the tens of thousands. In the *2003 Yearbook of Immigration Statistics* (September 2004), the Office of Immigration Statistics notes a backlog of 1.2 million adjustment-of-status cases pending decisions at the end of fiscal year (FY) 2003. The volume of applications clogged the system, resulting in fewer approved adjustments in 2003.

New Arrivals by Adoption

Included in the category of immediate relatives are orphans adopted by U.S. citizens. In October 2000 Congress passed the Child Citizenship Act of 2000, granting automatic U.S. citizenship to foreign-born biological and adopted children of U.S. citizens.

In FY2005 the number of foreign adopted children who were admitted to the United States totaled 22,710. As shown in Table 3.13, girls outnumbered boys 2 to 1 (14,982 to 7,728). The vast majority of foreign adopted children were four years of age or younger. According to the Office of Immigration Statistics, in *2005 Yearbook of*

TABLE 3.9

Industry of employment for native and foreign-born by region of birth, 2005

Percent distribution

Industry	Total — Percent of native born	Total — Percent of foreign born	Mexico	South and East Asia	Caribbean	Central America	South America	Middle East	All other
Agriculture, forestry, fishing and hunting	1.3	2.2	6.0	0.4	0.3	1.5	0.3	0.1	0.6
Mining	0.4	0.2	0.3	0.1	0.0	0.1	0.2	0.1	0.2
Utilities	0.8	0.3	0.2	0.4	0.3	0.2	0.3	0.3	0.4
Construction	7.0	10.2	19.1	2.0	6.5	16.3	10.0	4.1	6.4
Nondurable goods manufacturing	4.3	6.1	8.9	5.0	4.0	7.2	4.8	3.4	4.4
Durable goods	7.0	8.0	8.4	10.5	4.2	6.4	5.5	6.0	7.9
Wholesale trade	3.3	3.7	4.4	3.5	3.2	3.9	3.7	3.6	2.9
Retail trade	12.4	9.9	7.5	11.3	10.5	9.0	10.5	19.4	10.4
Transportation and warehousing	4.1	3.9	2.5	3.6	6.8	4.2	4.7	5.1	4.3
Information and communications	2.5	1.8	0.8	2.6	1.9	1.3	2.1	2.0	2.6
Finance, insurance, real estate, and rental and leasing	7.0	5.6	2.3	7.2	7.8	4.1	7.1	7.2	7.7
Professional, scientific, management, administrative, and waste management services	9.5	10.9	9.8	11.7	9.2	11.2	11.0	10.0	12.3
Educational, health and social services	20.8	16.3	7.2	20.9	25.5	11.6	16.8	20.1	22.2
Arts, entertainment, recreation, accommodations, and food services	8.9	11.5	14.4	11.0	9.2	11.8	11.3	9.4	8.8
Other services (except public administration)	4.6	6.3	6.1	6.1	5.9	8.7	8.7	5.5	5.3
Public administration	5.0	2.0	0.9	2.8	3.1	1.2	1.9	2.5	2.7
Active duty military	0.5	0.2	0.1	0.3	0.2	0.2	0.2	0.1	0.2
Unemployed, no work experience in past five years	0.7	1.0	1.1	0.8	1.4	1.1	1.0	0.9	0.7
Total	**100.0**	**100.0**	**100.0**	**100.0**	**100.0**	**100.0**	**100.0**	**100.0**	**100.0**

Note: Middle East includes Afghanistan, Cyprus, Iran, Iraq, Israel, Jordan, Kuwait, Lebanon, Saudi Arabia, Syria, Turkey, Yemen, Algeria, Egypt, Libya, Morocco, and Sudan.

SOURCE: Adapted from "Table 23. Industry by Region of Birth: 2005," in *A Statistical Portrait of the Foreign-Born Population at Mid-Decade*, Pew Hispanic Center, October 2006, http://pewhispanic.org/files/other/foreignborn/complete.pdf (accessed December 12, 2006). © 2006 Pew Hispanic Center, a Pew Research Center project, www.pewhispanic.org.

TABLE 3.10

Household income for native and foreign-born by region of birth, 2005

	1st quintile ($0–$18,999)	2nd quintile ($19,000–$35,999)	3rd quintile ($36,000–$56,499)	4th quintile ($56,500–$89,599)	5th quintile ($89,600+)	Total
Percent distribution						
Total native born	19.6	19.9	20.0	20.3	20.2	100.0
Total foreign born	21.1	22.3	20.0	18.0	18.6	100.0
Mexico	24.7	30.7	23.0	14.8	6.9	100.0
South and East Asia	16.5	14.7	17.3	21.1	30.4	100.0
Caribbean	26.7	22.6	19.5	17.2	14.0	100.0
Central America	20.1	27.8	23.6	18.0	10.5	100.0
South America	16.9	22.5	22.7	20.3	17.6	100.0
Middle East	21.0	16.9	17.5	17.4	27.2	100.0
All other	20.5	18.7	17.9	18.7	24.3	100.0

Note: Middle East includes Afghanistan, Cyprus, Iran, Iraq, Israel, Jordan, Kuwait, Lebanon, Saudi Arabia, Syria, Turkey, Yemen, Algeria, Egypt, Libya, Morocco, and Sudan. Quintiles are based upon 2005 total household income distribution. Figures based on reported incomes, not adjusted incomes.

SOURCE: "Table 28. Household Income Distribution by Region of Birth: 2005," in *A Statistical Portrait of the Foreign-Born Population at Mid-Decade*, Pew Hispanic Center, October 2006, http://pewhispanic.org/files/other/foreignborn/complete.pdf (accessed December 12, 2006). © 2006 Pew Hispanic Center, a Pew Research Center project, www.pewhispanic.org.

TABLE 3.11

Persons living in poverty for native and foreign-born by age and region of birth, 2005

	Poverty rate (%)			
	Under 18 years	18 to 64 years	65 and over	Total
Total native born	18.2	11.2	9.1	12.8
Total foreign born	29.3	15.9	16.2	17.1
Mexico	42.3	23.6	22.6	25.5
South and East Asia	16.8	11.2	15.0	12.0
Caribbean	28.8	15.5	23.4	17.6
Central America	25.8	16.3	16.6	17.0
South America	17.6	10.7	17.6	11.9
Middle East	33.2	15.4	16.6	17.0
All other	21.5	10.2	12.3	11.6

Note: Middle East includes Afghanistan, Cyprus, Iran, Iraq, Israel, Jordan, Kuwait, Lebanon, Saudi Arabia, Syria, Turkey, Yemen, Algeria, Egypt, Libya, Morocco, and Sudan.

SOURCE: "Table 30. Poverty by Age and Region of Birth: 2005," in *A Statistical Portrait of the Foreign-Born Population at Mid-Decade*, Pew Hispanic Center, October 2006, http://pewhispanic.org/files/other/foreignborn/complete.pdf (accessed December 12, 2006). © 2006 Pew Hispanic Center, a Pew Research Center project, www.pewhispanic.org.

Immigration Statistics (November 2006, http://www.dhs.gov/xlibrary/assets/statistics/yearbook/2005/OIS_2005_Yearbook.pdf), of the 3,537 children aged five years and over, more than one-third (38%) came from Russia, the second leading source country for children adopted by American families. Figure 3.3 shows the leading countries of origin for orphans adopted by U.S. citizens during FY2005. Nearly half of all foreign adopted children (10,558) came from Asia. The People's Republic of China was the largest single source with 7,939 children adopted, or 35% of the total for all ages. Ninety-five percent of adopted Chinese children were females, primarily under the age of four years. Holt International Children's Services, a nonprofit adoption service, notes in "FAQs about the China Adoption Process: How Do Children Come into Care?" (2006, http://www.holtintl.org/china/chinafaq.shtml) that nearly all children available for adoption from China were abandoned, usually left in public places with no identifying information.

In "China: Population May Peak under 'One-Child' Policy" (Radio Free Europe/Radio Liberty, January 6, 2005), Daisy Sindelar explains China's efforts at population control. Fear of widespread famine if the population continued to grow at the 1950s birth rate of six children

FIGURE 3.2

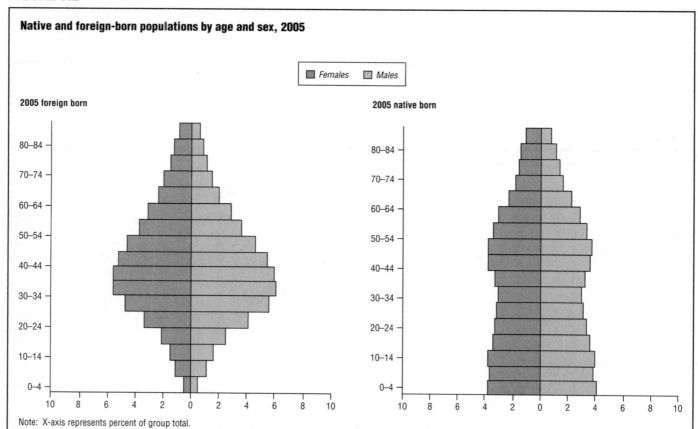

Native and foreign-born populations by age and sex, 2005

Note: X-axis represents percent of group total.

SOURCE: "Table 6a. Population Pyramids by Nativity Groups: 2005," in *A Statistical Portrait of the Foreign-Born Population at Mid-Decade*, Pew Hispanic Center, October 2006, http://pewhispanic.org/files/other/foreignborn/complete.pdf (accessed December 12, 2006). © 2006 Pew Hispanic Center, a Pew Research Center project, www.pewhispanic.org.

TABLE 3.12

Immigrants admitted by class of admission, fiscal years 2000–05

Class of admission	2000	2001	2002	2003	2004	2005
Total	841,002	1,058,902	1,059,356	703,542	957,883	1,122,373
New arrivals	407,279	410,816	384,289	358,333	373,962	384,071
Adjustments	433,723	648,086	675,067	345,209	583,921	738,302
Family-sponsored preferences	235,092	231,699	186,880	158,796	214,355	212,970
Unmarried sons/daughters of U.S. citizens and their children	27,635	27,003	23,517	21,471	26,380	24,729
Spouses, unmarried sons/daughters of alien residents and their children	124,540	112,015	84,785	53,195	93,609	100,139
Married sons/daughters of U.S. citizens[a]	22,804	24,830	21,041	27,287	28,695	22,953
Brothers or sisters of U.S. citizens[a]	60,113	67,851	57,537	56,843	65,671	65,149
Employment-based preferences	106,642	178,702	173,814	81,727	155,330	246,878
Priority workers[a]	27,566	41,672	34,168	14,453	31,291	64,731
Professionals with advanced degrees or aliens of exceptional ability[a]	20,255	42,550	44,316	15,406	32,534	42,597
Skilled workers, professionals, unskilled workers[a]	49,589	85,847	88,002	46,415	85,969	129,070
Special immigrants[a]	9,014	8,442	7,186	5,389	5,407	10,134
Employment creation (investors)[a]	218	191	142	64	129	346
Immediate relatives of U.S. citizens	346,350	439,972	483,676	331,286	417,815	436,231
Spouses	196,405	268,294	293,219	183,796	252,193	259,144
Children[b]	82,638	91,275	96,941	77,948	88,088	94,974
Parents	67,307	80,403	93,516	69,542	77,534	82,113
Refugees	56,091	96,870	115,601	34,362	61,013	112,676
Asylees	6,837	11,111	10,197	10,402	10,21 7	30,286
Diversity[c]	50,920	41,989	42,820	46,335	50,084	46,234
Cancellation of removal	12,154	22,188	23,642	28,990	32,702	20,785
Parolees	3,162	5,349	6,018	4,196	7,121	7,715
Nicaraguan Adjustment and Central American Relief Act (NACARA)	20,364	18,663	9,307	2,498	2,292	1,155
Haitian Refugee Immigration Fairness Act (HRIFA)	435	10,064	5,345	1,406	2,451	2,820
Other	2,955	2,295	2,056	3,544	4,503	4,623

[a]Includes spouses and children.
[b]Includes orphans.
[c]Includes categories of immigrants admitted under three laws intended to diversify immigration: P.L. 99-603, P.L. 100-658, and P.L. 101-649.

SOURCE: "Table 6. Immigrants Admitted by Class of Admission: 2000 to 2005," in *Statistical Abstract of the United States: 2007*, U.S. Census Bureau, http://www.census.gov/prod/2006pubs/07statab/pop.pdf (accessed December 21, 2006)

TABLE 3.13

Immigrant orphans adopted by U.S. citizens, by gender, age, and region of birth, fiscal year 2005

		Gender		Age			
	Total	Male	Female	Under 1 year	1 to 4 years	5 years and over	Unknown
Region							
Total	22,710	7,728	14,982	9,059	10,113	3,537	1
Africa	812	367	445	196	253	362	1
Asia	10,558	1,805	8,753	4,416	5,639	503	—
Europe	6,591	3,276	3,315	1,293	3,257	2,041	—
North America	4,261	2,052	2,209	2,999	846	416	—
Oceania	22	9	13	7	D	D	—
South America	453	211	242	141	107	205	—
Unknown	13	8	5	7	D	D	—

— Represents zero.
D Data withheld to limit disclosure.

SOURCE: Adapted from "Table 12. Immigrant Orphans Adopted by U.S. Citizens by Gender, Age, and Region and Country of Birth: Fiscal Year 2005," in *2005 Yearbook of Immigration Statistics*, U.S. Department of Homeland Security, Office of Immigration Statistics, November 2006, http://www.dhs.gov/xlibrary/assets/statistics/yearbook/2005/OIS_2005_Yearbook.pdf (accessed December 7, 2006)

FIGURE 3.3

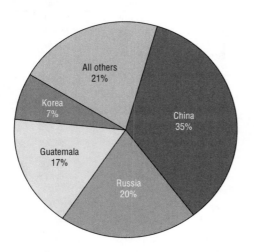

Top countries supplying orphans adopted by U.S. citizens, fiscal year 2005

All others 21%

Korea 7%

Guatemala 17%

China 35%

Russia 20%

SOURCE: Adapted from "Table 12. Immigrant Orphans Adopted by U.S. Citizens by Gender, Age, and Region and Country of Birth: Fiscal Year 2005," in *2005 Yearbook of Immigration Statistics*, U.S. Department of Homeland Security, Office of Immigration Statistics, November 2006, http://www.dhs.gov/xlibrary/assets/statistics/yearbook/2005/OIS_2005 _Yearbook.pdf (accessed December 7, 2006)

per woman drove the Chinese government to implement a policy of one child per family in 1979. Even though some rural families were allowed a second child if the first was a girl, in most areas enforcement was strict. Punishment for exceeding the limit included forced abortions, beating of men whose wives gave birth to too many children, and sometimes jail terms or sterilization. The restrictions brought the fertility rate down to 1.8 by 2005 but not without negative side effects. The strong cultural preference for a son resulted in the abortion of female fetuses and the killing or abandonment of infant girls.

In December 2006 Chinese officials began briefing foreign adoption agencies about new rules for adopting Chinese orphans to be implemented by May 2007. In "China Tightens Adoption Rules for Foreigners" (*New York Times*, December 20, 2006), Pam Belluck and Jim Yardley report that these changes are intended to provide the greatest chances that adopted children will be raised by healthy, economically stable parents. The new rules bar adoption by people who are single, obese, older than fifty, or have criminal records. Couples applying to adopt Chinese orphans have to be married at least two years and have no more than two divorces between them. If either is divorced, the required years currently married increases to five. Health requirements include freedom from the acquired immunodeficiency syndrome (AIDS), cancer, and certain mental health conditions. New financial minimums include a net worth of at least $80,000

and household income equivalent to at least $10,000 per person, including the prospective adoptive child. Belluck and Yardley note that other countries, such as Guatemala and Vietnam, have even stricter foreign adoption rules.

Despite adoption fees of about $15,000, China has long been a top source of orphan adoptions. According to Belluck and Yardley, Americans have adopted some fifty-five thousand Chinese children since 1991. In FY2006 the State Department granted 6,493 visas to Chinese orphans.

Employment-Based Admissions

In the decade before 1991 employment-based admissions accounted for a small percentage of total immigration. One of the major goals of IMMACT was to increase the number of highly skilled workers entering the United States. In 2005, 246,877 individuals (22% of all admissions for the fiscal year) entered the United States under employment-based preferences, according to the Office of Immigration Statistics. (See Table 3.14.) However, spouses and children continued to claim a significant portion of this class of admission.

Thirty-eight percent (94,910) of 2005 employment-based admissions were identified as having "no occupation/not working outside the home"; most were homemakers and students or children. (See Table 3.14.) The remaining 151,967 employment-based admissions who were actually seeking jobs represented just 13% of total immigrants admitted for the fiscal year. The majority (84,753 or 56%) of the actual job seekers in this category were prepared by training and experience to fill management, professional, and related occupations.

NATURALIZATION—BECOMING A CITIZEN

Naturalization refers to the conferring of U.S. citizenship on a person after birth. A naturalization court grants citizenship if the naturalization occurs within the United States, whereas a representative of the USCIS confers naturalization if it is performed outside the United States. Beginning in 1992 IMMACT also permitted people to naturalize through administrative hearings with the U.S. Immigration and Naturalization Service (now the USCIS). When individuals become U.S. citizens, they pledge allegiance to the United States and renounce allegiance to their former country of nationality.

General Requirements

To naturalize, most immigrants must meet certain general requirements. They must be at least eighteen years old, have been legally admitted to the United States for permanent residence, and have lived in the country continuously for at least five years. They must also be able to speak, read, and write English; know how the U.S.

TABLE 3.14

Persons obtaining legal permanent resident status by broad class of admission and occupation, fiscal year 2005

Characteristic	Total	Family-sponsored preferences	Employment-based preferences	Immediate relatives of U.S. citizens	Diversity	Refugees and asylees	Other
Occupation							
Total	1,122,373	212,970	246,877	436,231	46,234	142,962	37,099
Management, professional, and related occupations	134,861	11,084	84,753	24,750	9,844	3,742	688
Service occupations	49,589	10,945	9,338	14,521	4,164	9,029	1,592
Sales and office occupations	34,923	9,467	3,978	13,006	2,715	5,158	599
Farming, fishing, and forestry occupations	12,362	6,009	596	4,993	278	242	244
Construction, extraction, maintenance and repair occupations	10,472	1,108	2,869	3,417	258	2,182	638
Production, transportation, and material moving occupations	51,040	15,658	4,379	16,008	1,800	10,582	2,613
Military	206	48	21	101	13	14	9
No occupation/not working outside home	514,340	120,513	94,910	219,738	18,434	54,202	6,543
Homemakers	139,788	28,707	31,232	72,037	1,705	5,150	957
Students or children	292,227	81,109	57,604	91,252	15,012	42,653	4,597
Retirees	8,829	418	118	6,381	54	1,783	75
Unemployed	73,496	10,279	5,956	50,068	1,663	4,616	914
Unknown	314,580	38,138	46,033	139,697	8,728	57,811	24,173

SOURCE: Adapted from "Table 9. Persons Obtaining Legal Permanent Resident Status by Broad Class of Admission and Selected Demographic Characteristics: Fiscal Year 2005," in *2005 Yearbook of Immigration Statistics*, U.S. Department of Homeland Security, Office of Immigration Statistics, November 2006, http://www.dhs.gov/xlibrary/assets/statistics/yearbook/2005/OIS_2005_Yearbook.pdf (accessed December 7, 2006)

government works; have a basic knowledge of U.S. history; and be of good moral character.

Special Provisions

A small share of people are naturalized under special provisions of the naturalization laws that exempt them from one or more of the general requirements. Spouses of U.S. citizens can become naturalized in three years instead of the normal five. Children who immigrated with their parents generally receive their U.S. citizenship through the naturalization of their parents. Aliens with lawful permanent resident status who served honorably in the U.S. military are also entitled to certain exemptions from the naturalization requirements.

Expedited Naturalization of Active-Duty Military

In testimony before the Senate Committee on Armed Services, the USCIS director Emilio T. Gonzalez estimated that more than 45,000 noncitizen, immigrant personnel were on active or reserve duty in the U.S. armed forces during 2006 (July 10, 2006, http://www.uscis.gov/files/testimony/mil_natz_060710.pdf). In 2002 President George W. Bush issued an executive order that provided "expedited naturalization" of noncitizen men and women serving on active-duty status since September 11, 2001 (9/11). Gonzalez stated that under the new guidelines, USCIS had "naturalized more than 26,000 service men and women since September 11, 2001 in the U.S. and overseas."

Naturalization Rates

The longer immigrants live in the United States, the more likely they are to become naturalized citizens. Luke J. Larsen reports in *The Foreign-Born Population in the United States: 2003* (August 2004, http://www.census.gov/prod/2004pubs/p20-551.pdf) that 81% of those who entered the United States before 1970 were naturalized, compared with 15% of those who arrived in 1990 or later.

National Origins of Naturalized Citizens

For much of the twentieth century quotas established by immigration legislation favored people from Europe, resulting in higher numbers of naturalizations among immigrants from European countries. Once the quotas ended with the Immigration and Nationality Act Amendments in 1965, the regional origin of people immigrating and naturalizing shifted to Asian countries. The rapid growth of the Asian share of naturalizations from 12.9% in the 1961–70 decade to 48.8% in the 1981–90 decade is illustrated in Figure 3.4. Legal immigrants to the United States from North American countries, primarily Canada and Mexico, began to increase in the mid-1980s, resulting in North American immigrants accounting for 40% of naturalizations in the 1991–2000 decade. From 2001 through 2005 Asian immigrants claimed the greatest share (41%) of naturalizations, whereas naturalization of immigrants from North America declined to 30%. (See Figure 3.5.) According to the *2005 Yearbook of Immigration Statistics*, the top

FIGURE 3.4

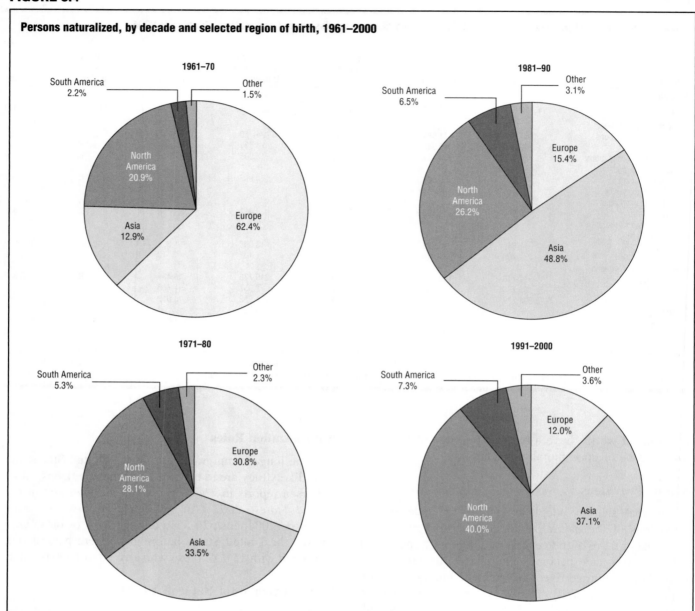

Persons naturalized, by decade and selected region of birth, 1961–2000

SOURCE: "Chart M. Persons Naturalized by Decade and Selected Region of Birth: Fiscal Years 1961–2000," in *2000 Statistical Yearbook of the Immigration and Naturalization Service*, U.S. Department of Justice, Immigration and Naturalization Service, September 2002, http://www.dhs.gov/xlibrary/assets/statistics/yearbook/2000/Yearbook2000.pdf (accessed February 8, 2007)

countries of origin for people becoming naturalized U.S. citizens in 2005 were Mexico (77,089), the Philippines (36,673), India (35,962), Vietnam (32,926), and China (31,708).

Trends in Naturalization

Michael E. Fix, Jeffrey S. Passel, and Kenneth Sucher of the Urban Institute identify three areas of concern about future candidates for naturalization: limited English skills, little formal education, and low incomes (*Trends in Naturalization*, August 2003, http://www.urban.org/UploadedPDF/310847_trends_in_naturalization.pdf). They find

that 52% of naturalized citizens who had arrived recently (that is, had lived in the United States less than fourteen years) had limited English proficiency. Even greater English-language limitations were noted among the legal immigrant population eligible to naturalize, that is, those aged eighteen and older who had had resided in the United States at least five years or who had lived in the United States for three years and were married to a U.S. citizen. Among those eligible to naturalize, six out of ten (3.5 million adults) had limited English proficiency. For those who would soon be eligible for citizenship (defined as legal permanent residents who had not lived

FIGURE 3.5

Persons naturalized by selected region of birth, 2001–05

Europe 16%
Other 6%
South America 7%
North America 30%
Asia 41%

SOURCE: Adapted from "Table 21. Persons Naturalized by Region and Country of Birth: Fiscal Years 1996 to 2005," in *2005 Yearbook of Immigration Statistics*, U.S. Department of Homeland Security, Office of Immigration Statistics, November 2006, http://www.dhs.gov/xlibrary/assets/statistics/yearbook/2005/OIS_2005_Yearbook.pdf (accessed December 7, 2006)

FIGURE 3.6

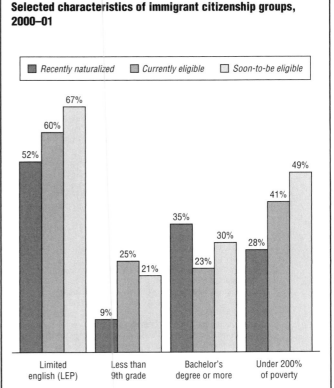

Selected characteristics of immigrant citizenship groups, 2000–01

■ Recently naturalized   ■ Currently eligible   □ Soon-to-be eligible

Limited english (LEP): 52%, 60%, 67%
Less than 9th grade: 9%, 25%, 21%
Bachelor's degree or more: 35%, 23%, 30%
Under 200% of poverty: 28%, 41%, 49%

SOURCE: Michael Fix, Jeffrey S. Passel, and Kenneth Sucher, "Figure 4. Selected Characteristics of Immigrant Citizenship Groups: 2000–2001," in *Trends in Naturalization*, Brief No. 3, Immigrant Families and Workers: Facts and Perspectives, Immigration Studies Program, The Urban Institute, September 2003, http://urban.org/UploadedPDF/310847_trends_in_naturalization.pdf (accessed February 3, 2006)

in the United States long enough to qualify for citizenship), 67% (1.5 million adults) had limited English. Fix, Passel, and Sucher suggest that publicly supported English classes and civics courses might be needed to help this population achieve the language skills and knowledge of U.S. history and government required for citizenship.

In education Fix, Passel, and Sucher describe two significant clusters of immigrants: those with less than a high school education and those with college degrees. Compared with 9% of the recently naturalized with less than a ninth-grade education, 25% of current and 21% of soon-to-be eligible candidates for naturalization had less than a ninth-grade education. (See Figure 3.6.) This suggests that literacy is a significant issue, besides English-language skills, in preparing this group of immigrants to qualify for future citizenship. Fix, Passel, and Sucher also find that, even though 35% of the recently naturalized had bachelor's degrees or higher, just 23% of currently eligible and 30% of the soon-to-be eligible held such degrees.

In addition, Fix, Passel, and Sucher indicate that a far greater share of the future naturalization candidates had incomes under 200% of the poverty level. They note that the combination of limited English skills, low level of education, and low income present greater barriers to naturalization among the pool of future candidates for naturalization.

NONIMMIGRANTS

Tourists, Business People, Foreign Government Officials, and Foreign Students

Table 3.15 lists nonimmigrant visa classifications and numbers of nonimmigrant visas issued by the State Department for FY2001 to FY2005. The impact of increased security following 9/11 can be seen in the almost 24% drop from 7.6 million total visas issued in 2001 to a total of 5.8 million in 2002. Totals continued to drop to a low of 4.9 million in 2003. By the end of 2005 nonimmigrant visas still had not regained the 2002 level.

Half (50.3%) of all nonimmigrant visas issued in 2005 went to 2.7 million visitors who came to the United States for business combined with pleasure (B1/B2 visas). (See Table 3.15.) Another 1.7% of visas were issued to 94,222 officials of foreign governments, their families, and employees (A1, A2, and A3 visas). Students and their family members totaled 255,951 in 2005, or 4.7% of all visas issued.

There are no restrictions on the number of nonimmigrants allowed to enter the United States. In fact, the United States, like most other countries, encourages tourism and

TABLE 3.15

Nonimmigrant visas issues by classification, fiscal years 2001–05

Visa symbol/class		2001	2002	2003	2004	2005
A1	Ambassador, public minister, career diplomat, consul, and immediate family	9,662	10,452	9,152	9,562	9,944
A2	Other foreign government official or employee, and immediate family	66,398	71,728	73,092	81,536	83,051
A3	Attendant, servant, or personal employee of A1 and A2, and immediate family	2,228	1,971	1,259	1,258	1,227
B1	Temporary visitor for business	84,201	75,642	60,892	53,245	52,649
B1/B2	Temporary visitor for business and pleasure	3,527,118	2,528,103	2,207,303	2,340,795	2,709,468
B1/B2/BCC	Combination B1/B2 and border crossing card	1,990,402	1,399,819	836,407	740,616	732,566
B2	Temporary visitor for pleasure	381,431	255,487	271,358	279,106	245,816
C1	Person in transit	27,231	24,207	34,664	81,292	65,272
C1/D	Combination transit/crew member (indiv. iss.)	167,435	175,446	210,648	228,778	229,115
C2	Person in transit to United Nations headquarters	24	8	15	21	44
C3	Foreign government official, immediate family, attendant, servant, or personal employee in transit	5,697	6,024	6,160	7,963	10,537
D	Crew member (sea or air) (individual issuance)	21,615	13,671	16,125	16,896	19,988
DCREW	Crewlist visas	8,480	8,399	4,631	1,055	0
E1	Treaty trader, spouse and children	9,309	7,811	7,590	8,608	8,867
E2	Treaty investor, spouse and children	27,577	25,633	24,506	28,213	28,290
E3	Australian specialty occupation professional	0	0	0	0	4
E3D	Spouse or child of Australian specialty occupation professional	0	0	0	0	3
E3R	Returning Australian specialty occupation professional	0	0	0	0	0
F1	Student (academic or language training program)	293,357	234,322	215,695	218,898	237,890
F2	Spouse or child of student	26,160	22,212	19,885	18,893	18,061
F3	Border commuter academic or language student	0	0	0	16	42
G1	Principal resident represenive of recognized foreign member government to international organization, staff, and immediate family	5,274	4,905	4,555	5,018	4,995
G2	Other representative of recognized foreign member government to international organization, and immediate family	8,825	9,144	7,194	10,899	13,703
G3	Representative of nonrecognized or nonmember foreign government to international organization, and immediate family	134	99	146	266	309
G4	International organization officer or employee, and immediate family	16,999	17,374	18,091	20,017	20,930
G5	Attendant, servant, or personal employee of G1 through G4, and immediate family	1,645	1,482	1,117	945	998
H1A	Temporary worker performing services as a registered nurse	0	0	0	0	0
H1B	Temporary worker of distinguished merit and ability performing services other than as a registered nurse	161,643	118,352	107,196	138,965	124,100
H1B1	Free Trade Agreement professional	0	0	0	72	274
H1C	Shortage area nurse	34	212	191	110	63
H2A	Temporary worker performing agricultural services	31,523	31,538	29,882	31,774	31,892
H2B	Temporary worker performing other services	58,215	62,591	78,955	76,169	87,492
H2R	Returning H2B worker	0	0	0	0	1,643
H3	Trainee	1,613	1,387	1,417	1,410	1,763
H4	Spouse or child of H1A/B/B1/C, H2A/B/R, or H3	95,967	79,725	69,289	83,128	70,266
I	Representative of foreign information media, spouse and children	13,799	18,187	12,329	16,390	16,975
J1	Exchange visitor	261,769	253,841	253,866	254,504	275,161
J2	Spouse or child of exchange visitor	38,189	32,539	29,796	27,875	28,661
K1	Fiance(e) of U.S. citizen	24,973	28,338	25,304	29,658	33,910
K2	Child of K1	3,735	4,298	3,752	4,694	5,308
K3	Certain spouse of U.S. citizen	3	5,078	12,403	13,623	11,312
K4	Child of K3	1	1,294	3,174	3,827	3,438
L1	Intracompany transferee (executive, managerial, and specialized personnel continuing employment with international firm or corporation)	59,384	57,721	57,245	62,700	65,458
L2	Spouse or child of intracompany transferee	61,154	54,903	53,571	59,164	57,523
M1	Vocational and other nonacademic student	5,373	4,116	4,157	4,817	5,822
M2	Spouse or child of vocational student	285	161	144	95	153
M3	Border commuter vocational or nonacademic student	0	0	0	0	0
N8	Parent of SK3 special immigrant	8	8	11	8	10
N9	Child of N8 or of SK1, SK2 or SK4 special immigrant	6	4	7	3	4

tries to attract as many visitors as possible. Even though it is easy to get in, strict rules do apply to the conditions of the visit. For example, students can stay only long enough to complete their studies, and business people can stay only six months (although a six-month extension is available). Most nonimmigrants are not allowed to hold jobs while in

TABLE 3.15

Nonimmigrant visas issues by classification, fiscal years 2001–05 [CONTINUED]

Visa symbol/class		2001	2002	2003	2004	2005
NATO1	Principal permanent representative of member state to NATO* (including any of its subsidiary bodies) resident in the U.S., and resident members of official staff; principal NATO officers; and immediate family	4	24	16	12	28
NATO2	Other representatives of member states to NATO (including any of its subsidiary bodies), and immediate family; dependents of member of a force entering in accordance with provisions of NATO agreements; members of such force if issued visas	4,282	5,195	5,364	6,234	5,893
NATO3	Official clerical staff accompanying a representative of member state to NATO, and immediate family	0	0	2	4	1
NATO4	Officials of NATO (other than those classifiable as NATO1), and immediate family	95	89	133	255	353
NATO5	Experts, other than NATO4 officials, employed in missions on behalf of NATO, and their dependents	121	179	91	49	69
NATO6	Members of a civilian component accompanying a force entering in accordance with the provisions of NATO agreements, and their dependents	220	192	93	168	201
NATO7	Attendant, servant, or personal employee of NATO1 through NATO6, and immediate family	1	8	3	1	5
O1	Person with extraordinary ability in the sciences, art, education, business, or athletics	6,666	6,026	6,126	6,437	6,712
O2	Person accompanying and assisting in the artistic or athletic performance by O1	1,918	1,972	2,472	2,611	3,387
O3	Spouse or child of O1 or O2	2,287	1,760	1,552	1,679	1,861
P1	Internationally recognized athlete or member of an internationally recognized entertainment group	24,378	24,287	25,643	22,269	23,907
P2	Artist or entertainer in a reciprocal exchange program	125	119	93	211	125
P3	Artist or entertainer in a culturally unique program	8,495	8,131	7,727	8,689	9,611
P4	Spouse or child of P1, P2, or P3	1,020	938	895	871	1,022
Q1	Participant in an international cultural exchange program	1,432	1,469	1,579	1,570	1,972
Q2	Irish peace process trainee	186	329	389	11	6
Q3	Spouse or child of Q2	0	1	2	0	0
R1	Person in a religious occupation	8,503	8,646	8,636	8,806	8,538
R2	Spouse or child of R1	3,009	3,175	3,162	2,976	3,267
S5	Informant processing critical reliable information concerning criminal organization or enterprise	0	0	0	0	0
S6	Informant processing critical reliable information concerning terrorist organization, enterprise, or operation	0	0	0	0	0
S7	Spouse, married or unmarried son or daughter, or parent of S5 or S6	0	0	0	0	0
T1	Victim of a severe form of trafficking in persons	0	0	0	0	0
T2	Spouse of T1	0	0	20	74	35
T3	Child of T1	0	0	38	145	65
T4	Parent of T1	0	0	0	0	7
T5	Unmarried sibling under 18 years of age on date T1 applied	0	0	0	0	5
TD	Spouse or child of TN	1,041	856	796	1,268	1,941
TN	NAFTA professional	787	699	423	908	1,902
U1	Victim of criminal activity	0	0	0	0	0
U2	Spouse of U1	0	0	0	0	0
U3	Child of U1	0	0	0	0	0
U4	Parent of U1	0	0	0	0	0
V1	Certain spouse of legal permanent resident	9,127	18,020	13,983	6,896	911
V2	Certain child of legal permanent resident	14,805	19,523	12,918	7,217	951
V3	Child of V1 or V2	1,400	19,567	16,302	6,856	1,165
Other nonimmigrant classes						
BCC	Border crossing card	0	0	0	0	0
Grand total		**7,588,778**	**5,769,437**	**4,881,632**	**5,049,099**	**5,388,937**

*North Atlantic Treaty Organisation.

SOURCE: "Table XVI(B). Nonimmigrant Visas Issued by Classification (Including Crewlist Visas and Border Crossing Cards) Fiscal Years 2001–2005," in *Report of the VISA Office 2005*, U.S. Department of State, Bureau of Consular Affairs, 2005 Preliminary Data, http://travel.state.gov/pdf/FY05tableXVIb.pdf (accessed December 24, 2006)

the United States, although exceptions are made for students and the families of diplomats. An undetermined number of visitors, amounting to many tens of thousands, overstay their nonimmigrant visas and continue to live in the United States illegally.

Temporary Foreign Workers

A temporary worker is an alien coming to the United States to work for a limited period. The major nonimmigrant visa category for legal temporary workers is the H visa, which includes the H2/H2A, H1B/H1B1, and H1C visas.

H2/H2A PROGRAM. The H2 Temporary Agricultural Worker Program, authorized by the Immigration and Nationality Act of 1952, was a flexible response to seasonal agricultural labor demands. Since 1964 it has been the only legal temporary foreign agricultural worker program in the United States. In 1986 the H2 program was amended to specify categories of workers. H2A temporary workers perform agricultural services, H2B workers perform other services, and H2R workers are former H2B workers authorized to return. The H2 temporary program is based on employer needs and has no set numerical limit on the number of workers allowed per year.

Under the H2A program employers who anticipate a shortage of domestic workers file an application with the U.S. Department of Labor stating that there are not enough workers able, willing, qualified, and available. Employers must certify that the employment of aliens will not adversely affect the wages and working conditions of similarly employed U.S. workers. The employer must also certify that the jobs are not vacant because of a labor dispute. The employer pays a fee of $100, plus $10 for each job opportunity certified, up to a maximum fee of $1,000 for each certification granted.

Hiring foreign workers under the H2A program places a number of requirements on the employer, including advertising for and hiring qualified domestic workers, providing workers compensation insurance or equivalent insurance for all workers, and following specific pay and recordkeeping procedures. In some situations the employer may be required to pay for transportation and provide housing and meals for workers.

The employer is required to pay all workers the higher of (1) the Adverse Effect Wage Rate (AEWR) determined by the Labor Department for each state, (2) the applicable prevailing wage for the state, or (3) the statutory minimum wage. The federal minimum wage in 2006 was $5.15 per hour, an amount set by law in 1997. Table 3.16 lists the 2006 AEWR for all states. State hourly AEWRs ranged from a low of $7.58 in Arkansas, Louisiana, and Mississippi to $9.49 in Iowa and Missouri. Hawaii was highest at $9.99.

The Labor Department (November 8, 2006, http://www.foreignlaborcert.doleta.gov/h-2a_region2006.cfm) reports that in FY2006, 6,550 employers were certified under the H2A program to hire up to 64,146 foreign workers. A total of 59,112 workers gained visas for these jobs. Ten states employed 56% of H2A farm workers and one state, North Carolina, claimed 12% (7,803) of all H2A workers in 2006. (See Table 3.17.)

H1B PROGRAM. The H1 program allows employers to temporarily employ foreign workers on a nonimmigrant basis in a specialty occupation or as a model of distinguished merit and ability. A specialty occupation requires

TABLE 3.16

Adverse effect wage rates, 2006

State	2006	State	2006
Alabama	$8.37	Nebraska	9.23
Arizona	8.00	Nevada	8.37
Arkansas	7.58	New Hampshire	9.16
California	9.00	New Jersey	8.95
Colorado	8.37	New Mexico	8.00
Connecticut	9.16	New York	9.16
Delaware	8.95	North Carolina	8.51
Florida	8.56	North Dakota	9.23
Georgia	8.37	Ohio	9.21
Hawaii	9.99	Oklahoma	8.32
Idaho	8.47	Oregon	9.01
Illinois	9.21	Pennsylvania	8.95
Indiana	9.21	Rhode Island	9.16
Iowa	9.49	South Carolina	8.37
Kansas	9.23	South Dakota	9.23
Kentucky	8.24	Tennessee	8.24
Louisiana	7.58	Texas	8.32
Maine	9.16	Utah	8.37
Maryland	8.95	Vermont	9.16
Massachusetts	9.16	Virginia	8.51
Michigan	9.43	Washington	9.01
Minnesota	9.43	West Virginia	8.24
Mississippi	7.58	Wisconsin	9.43
Missouri	9.49	Wyoming	8.47
Montana	8.47		

SOURCE: "Adverse Effect Wage Rates—Year 2005," U.S. Department of Labor, March 16, 2006, http://www.foreignlaborcert.doleta.gov/adverse.cfm (accessed December 15, 2006)

TABLE 3.17

Top ten states by number of H-2A workers, fiscal year 2006

Top ten H-2A employer states	Number of H-2A workers
North Carolina	7,803
Georgia	5,320
Virginia	4,084
Louisiana	3,948
Kentucky	3,483
Arkansas	2,535
California	2,292
Florida	1,880
Tennessee	1,879
Total	**33,224**

SOURCE: Adapted from "H-2A Regional Summary, Fiscal Year 2006 Annual," U.S. Department of Labor, Employment & Training Administration, http://www.foreignlaborcert.doleta.gov/h-2a_region2006.cfm (accessed December 26, 2006)

the theoretical and practical application of a body of specialized knowledge and a bachelor's degree or the equivalent in the specific specialty (e.g., sciences, medicine and health care, education, biotechnology, business specialties, and so on). No visas were issued between 2001 and 2005 under the H1A program for temporary nurses. In 2000 the last such temporary nurses (a total of two) were issued visas. H1B visas are issued to professionals other than nurses. Effective January 1, 2004, the

H1B1 program became available, allowing employers to request specialty foreign workers from Chile and Singapore—called Free Trade Agreement Professionals. There were 72 H1B1 visas issued in 2004 and 274 in 2005. (See Table 3.15.)

A foreign worker can be in H1B status for a maximum continuous period of six years. After the H1B expires, the worker has to remain outside the United States for one year before another H1B petition can be approved. Certain foreign workers with labor certification applications or immigrant visa petitions in process for extended periods may stay in H1B status beyond the normal six-year limitation, in one-year increments. Extensions and renewals are allowed under the H1B program; however, adjustment of status to another nonimmigrant category or to legal permanent residency is not permitted.

The Immigration Act of 1990 set the ceiling on H1B admissions for initial employment at sixty-five thousand beginning in FY1992, but demand for H1B workers grew. The American Competitiveness and Workforce Improvement Act of 1998 temporarily raised the maximum number of petitions for initial H1B employment to 115,000 for FY1999 and FY2000.

The American Competitiveness in the Twenty-first Century Act of 2000 increased the H1B annual limit for initial employment to 195,000 for FY2001, FY2002, and FY2003. The cap reverted back to sixty-five thousand for FY2004. When the H1B1 visa was introduced in 2004, the 6,800 allowable H1B1 visas were deducted from the total H1B program. This left 58,200 H1B visas available per year. On October 1, 2004, the first day of FY2005, the USCIS announced that it had already received enough H1B petitions to meet the annual cap for FY2005. The H1B Visa Reform Act of 2004 made an additional twenty thousand visas for individuals with a master's degree or a more advanced degree from U.S. graduate institutions.

Figure 3.7 shows major source countries for H1B workers in 2005. Of the total 124,100 H1B workers admitted in FY2005 (see Table 3.15), the vast majority (66%) came from Asia. Europe was a distant second source for 20% of H1B workers.

MEETING LONG-TERM NEEDS FOR SCIENTISTS AND ENGINEERS WITH H1B VISAS. According to Stuart Anderson and Michaela Platzer in a survey commissioned by the National Venture Capital Association, foreign-born scientists and engineers play a key role in the U.S. economy (*American Made: The Impact of Immigrant Entrepreneurs and Professionals on U.S. Competitiveness*, November 15, 2006, http://www.nvca.org/pdf/American Made_study.pdf). Anderson and Platzer contacted 342 privately held venture-backed businesses. Sixty-five percent of respondents used H1B visas for specialty staffing. Nearly all reported that restrictive U.S. immigration laws

FIGURE 3.7

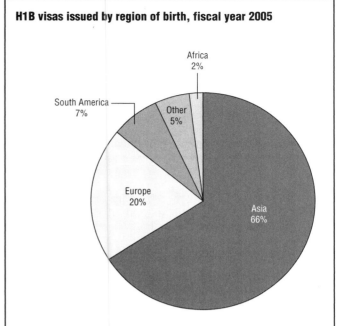

H1B visas issued by region of birth, fiscal year 2005

SOURCE: Adapted from "Table XVII. Nonimmigrant Visas Issued by Classification and Nationality (Including Border Crossing Cards) Fiscal Year 2005," in *Report of the VISA Office 2005*, U.S. Department of State, Bureau of Consular Affairs, 2005 Preliminary Data, http://travel.state.gov/pdf/FY05tableXVII.pdf (accessed December 24, 2006)

for skilled professionals harmed U.S. competitiveness. Forty percent said the lack of enough H1B visas to fill their staffing needs had negatively affected their ability to compete globally. One-third of responders said the lack of enough H1B visas had influenced their decision to staff facilities abroad or to outsource functions to other countries.

In discussing concerns about the future availability of scientists and engineers, Anderson and Platzer note that the number of first-time enrollments of international graduate students in science and engineering programs at U.S. universities declined 20% from 34,179 in 2001 to 27,486 in 2004. However, Table 3.18 shows that the number of doctorates awarded to noncitizens increased 25% in the same period. International students received 11,516 (or 41%) of U.S. science and engineering doctorates in 2005.

H1C PROGRAM ASSISTED HOSPITALS. The Nursing Relief for Disadvantaged Areas Act of 1999 allowed qualifying hospitals to employ foreign registered nurses for up to three years under H1C visas. Only five hundred H1C visas could be issued each year during the four-year period of the H1C program (2000–04). The sponsoring employer paid a filing fee of $250 for each application filed with the Labor Department. H1C nurses were admitted for a period of three years and the law did not provide for an extension of that time frame. The H1C program

TABLE 3.18

Doctorates in science and engineering awarded by U.S. universities to citizens and noncitizens, 2001–05

Characteristic of recipient	2001	2002	2003	2004	2005	% change 2001–05	% change 2004–05
All doctorates	25,496	24,582	25,274	26,272	27,974	9.7	6.5
U.S. citizen	15,049	14,341	14,635	14,741	14,912	−0.9	1.2
Non-U.S. citizen	9,213	8,861	9,480	10,154	11,516	25.0	13.4

SOURCE: Adapted from Susan T. Hill, "Table 1. S&E Doctorate Awards, by Selected Characteristics of Doctorate Recipients, 2001–05," in *InfoBrief: S&E Doctorates Hit All-Time High in 2005*, National Science Foundation, Directorate of Social, Behavioral, and Economic Sciences, NSF 07-301, November 2006, http://www.nsf.gov/statistics/infbrief/nsf07301/nsf07301.pdf (accessed December 8, 2006).

ended June 15, 2005, with a total of 610 visas issued since June 2001.

VISAS AND BASEBALL

"Americans have benefited from our nation's openness toward skilled immigrant baseball players, just as the country has gained from the entry of other skilled foreign-born professionals." This was the conclusion by Stuart Anderson and L. Brian Andrew of the National Foundation for American Policy in *Coming to America: Immigrants, Baseball, and the Contributions of Foreign-Born Players to America's Pastime* (October 2006, http://www.nfap.net/researchactivities/studies/BaseballComing 1006.pdf). Major league rosters offer a fixed number of jobs—750 (30 teams with a maximum 25 players on the active rosters)—unlike fluctuating jobs in other industries. According to Anderson and Andrew, "Even though only a fixed number of jobs exist on active major league rosters ... one never hears complaints about 'immigrants taking away jobs' from Americans in the major leagues."

Anderson and Andrew further note that increased competition from foreign-born players has not lowered salaries for native ballplayers. Even though the proportion of foreign-born players more than doubled from 1990 to 2006, major league salaries more than quadrupled. (See Figure 3.8.) Anderson and Andrew credit improved quality of play—contributed to by foreign-born players—for the increase in major league ballpark attendance from 54.8 million in 1990 to 74.9 million in 2005.

Number of Foreign-Born Players

As of August 2006, 175 (23%) of the 750 players on active major league team rosters were born outside the United States. This was an all-time high level of foreign-born players. Anderson and Andrew note that they use the term *foreign born* instead of *immigrants* because many players hold P1 temporary visas and have not yet received green cards.

Before 1960 foreign-born players comprised less than 5% of major league rosters. (See Figure 3.9.) Restrictive

FIGURE 3.8

Foreign-born players and baseball salaries, selected years 1980–2006

[Salaries in nominal dollars]

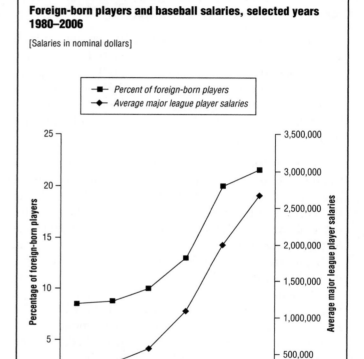

SOURCE: Stuart Anderson and L. Brian Andrew, "Foreign-Born Players and Rising Major League Salaries 1980–2006," in *Coming to America: Immigrants, Baseball and the Contributions of Foreign-Born Players to America's Pastime*, National Foundation for American Policy, October 2006, http://www.nfap.com/researchactivities/studies/BaseballComing 1006.pdf (accessed December 27, 2006). Data from National Foundation for American Policy; Baseball Oracle; Associated Press and Baseball Archive.

immigration laws passed in the 1920s, the Great Depression, and tighter State Department visa restrictions in the 1930s limited the entry of foreign-born players.

Until 1947 only light-skinned foreign-born players were accepted in the major leagues. Most Cuban players

FIGURE 3.9

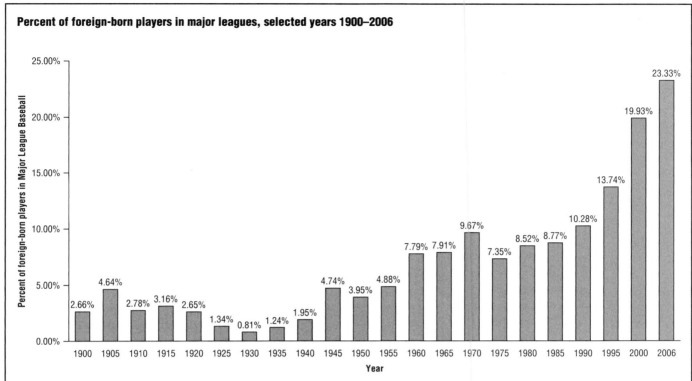

Percent of foreign-born players in major leagues, selected years 1900–2006

SOURCE: Stuart Anderson and L. Brian Andrew, "Percent of Foreign-Born Players in Major Leagues 1900–2006," in *Coming to America: Immigrants, Baseball and the Contributions of Foreign-Born Players to America's Pastime*, National Foundation for American Policy, October 2006, http://www.nfap .com/researchactivities/studies/BaseballComing1006.pdf (accessed December 27, 2006). Data from National Foundation for American Policy; Baseball Oracle; MLB.

joined Negro League teams. Then Jackie Robinson broke baseball's color barrier, and opportunities for other players of color expanded. In 2006, however, Cuban-born players represented only 2% of major leaguers. (See Figure 3.10.) The Dominican Republic was the greatest source of U.S. baseball talent, representing 46% of foreign-born major league players.

Success of Foreign-Born Players

Anderson and Andrew indicate that 31% of players selected for the 2006 All-Star Game were foreign born. In 2006 foreign-born players claimed seven of the top nine batting averages in the American League. Six foreign-born major league players have been elected to the National Baseball Hall of Fame.

The Major League Players Association complains that the limited availability of H2B temporary visas hampers the recruiting of foreign-born players. Most players are first hired in the minor leagues on H2B temporary visas, which can be extended for up to three years. If players move up to the major leagues, they can apply for P1 visas (internationally recognized athlete or member of an internationally recognized entertainment group), which are good for five years with extensions up to ten years. Part of the P1 application process requires the USCIS to consult any participating labor union to see if there are objec-

tions. The players' union assumes that anyone who receives an offer of a major league contract meets the P1 visa application criteria. Players who get to the major leagues and qualify for P1 visas can then apply for an employment-based permanent residency, usually under the category of "extraordinary ability."

ALIENS TURNED AWAY FROM THE UNITED STATES

State Department officials in foreign countries screen applicants and deny visas on a variety of bases. For example, in *Report of the Visa Office, 2005* (March 5, 2007, http:// travel.state.gov/visa/frvi/statistics/statistics_2787.html), the State Department reports that in 2005, 3,626 applicants for immigrant visas and 6,885 applicants for nonimmigrant visas were denied for misrepresentation of facts in their applications. Applicants were given the opportunity to correct any errors. Just 12% (1,307 of a total 10,511 applicants) were able to "overcome ineligibility" and obtain a visa.

U.S. Customs and Border Protection inspectors determine the admissibility of aliens who arrive at any of the approximately three hundred U.S. ports of entry. Aliens who arrive without required documents, present improper or fraudulent documents, or who are on criminal wanted lists are deemed inadmissible. New rules that became

FIGURE 3.10

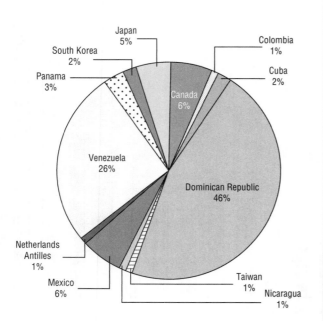

Source countries for major league foreign-born players, 2006

SOURCE: Stuart Anderson and L. Brian Andrew, "Source Countries for Major League Foreign-Born Players—2006," in *Coming to America: Immigrants, Baseball and the Contributions of Foreign-Born Players to America's Pastime*, National Foundation for American Policy, October 2006, http://www.nfap.com/researchactivities/studies/BaseballComing 1006.pdf (accessed December 27, 2006). Data from National Foundation for American Policy; Major League Baseball.

effective in 1997 under the Illegal Immigration Reform and Immigrant Responsibility Act (IIRIRA) provide two options to the inadmissible alien: voluntary departure or removal proceedings. The *2005 Yearbook of Immigration*

Statistics reports that over 965,000 inadmissible aliens chose voluntary departure in FY2005 (82% of the total 1.2 million inadmissible aliens). More than 208,000 remaining aliens were deported under removal proceedings.

Removal Proceedings

Most removal proceedings involve a hearing before an immigration judge, which could result in removal or adjustment to a legal status, such as granting asylum. Removal proceedings can also involve fines or imprisonment. The IIRIRA empowered immigration officers to order an alien removed without a hearing or review through a process called expedited removal. This process applies to cases in which the officers determine that the alien is inadmissible because the alien engaged in fraud or misrepresentation or lacked proper documents. In 2005, 208,521 aliens were removed by formal proceedings; nearly one-fifth (40,018) were removed for criminal violations. (See Table 3.19.) Nine countries accounted for 92.5% of all formal removals. (See Table 3.20.) With 144,840 aliens removed, Mexico alone accounted for the majority (69.5%) of the 208,521 alien removals in 2005.

Aliens with Communicable Diseases

Aliens with "communicable diseases of public health significance" are not permitted to enter the United States. In 1990 the U.S. Department of Health and Human Services, as part of the Immigration Act of 1990, declared that tuberculosis (TB) and AIDS were a public health threat. In 1993 Congress added the human immunodeficiency virus (the virus that causes AIDS) to the list of grounds for exclusion (denial of an alien's entry into the United States).

TABLE 3.19

Aliens formally removed by administrative reason for removal, fiscal years 1996–2005

Administrative reason for removal	1996	1997	1998	1999	2000	2001	2002	2003	2004	2005
Total	69,680	114,432	173,283	181,194	186,391	178,207	150,788	189,856	204,290	208,521
Attempted entry without proper documents or through fraud or misrepresentation	15,412	35,738	79,328	91,891	89,935	76,292	41,392	52,728	50,727	75,532
Criminal violations	27,655	34,113	35,984	42,028	41,155	40,196	37,816	40,356	42,835	40,018
Failed to maintain status	708	1,031	996	811	748	729	1,257	1,334	1,125	1,042
Previously removed, ineligible for reentry	2,006	3,340	7,201	9,483	11,906	10,827	13,239	18,595	21,504	18,203
Present without authorization	23,522	39,297	48,531	35,089	40,501	48,150	55,733	75,329	86,313	72,229
Public charge	10	372	578	1,261	1,461	1,296	560	676	857	824
National security and related grounds	36	30	15	10	13	12	11	15	12	10
Smuggling or aiding illegal entry	275	385	498	409	494	511	582	624	729	540
Other	42	116	149	202	173	188	175	193	182	120
Unknown	14	10	3	10	5	6	23	6	6	3

Note: Data for 1999 to 2005 reported as of January 2006. The administrative reason for formal removal is the legal basis for removal. Some aliens who are criminals may be removed under a different administrative reason (or charge) for the convenience of the government.

SOURCE: "Table 40. Aliens Formally Removed by Administrative Reason for Removal: Fiscal Years 1996–2005," in *2005 Yearbook of Immigration Statistics*, Office of Immigration Statistics, U.S. Department of Homeland Security, November 2006, http://www.dhs.gov/xlibrary/assets/statistics/yearbook/2005/ OIS_2005_Yearbook.pdf (accessed December 7, 2006)

TABLE 3.20

Aliens formally removed, by nationality, fiscal year 2005

Country	Number removed	Percent of total
Total all removals	208,521	
Total removals Central and South America	192,971	
Mexico	144,840	69.5%
Honduras	14,556	7.0%
Guatemala	12,529	6.0%
El Salvador	7,235	3.5%
Brazil	5,938	2.8%
Dominican Republic	2,929	1.4%
Colombia	1,879	0.9%
Jamaica	1,777	0.9%
Ecuador	1,288	0.6%

SOURCE: Adapted from "Table 41. Aliens Formally Removed by Criminal Status and Region and Country of Nationality: Fiscal Years 1998–2005," in *2005 Yearbook of Immigration Statistics*, U.S. Department of Homeland Security, Office of Immigration Statistics, November 2006, http://www.dhs.gov/xlibrary/assets/statistics/yearbook/2005/OIS_2005_Yearbook.pdf (accessed December 7, 2006)

FIGURE 3.11

Tuberculosis cases in U.S. by origin of birth, selected years 1993–2005

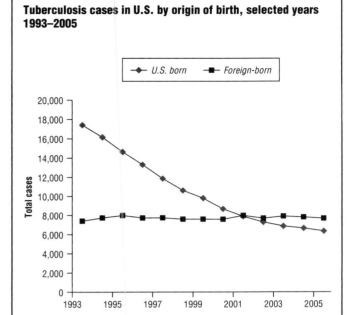

SOURCE: Adapted from "Table 5. Tuberculosis Cases, Percentages, and Case Rates per 100,000 Population by Origin of Birth: United States, 1993–2005," in *Reported Tuberculosis in the United States: 2005*, U.S. Department of Health and Human Services, Centers for Disease Control and Prevention, September 2006, http://www.cdc.gov/nchstp/tb/surv/surv2005/PDF/TBSurvFULLReport.pdf (accessed December 21, 2006)

The Centers for Disease Control and Prevention (CDC; December 12, 2005, http://www.cdc.gov/ncidod/dq/diseases.htm) lists the following as "Communicable Diseases of Public Health Significance": TB, HIV infection, gonorrhea, syphilis, chancroid (a sexually transmitted bacterial infection), granuloma inguinale (a sexually transmitted bacterial disease), lymphogranuloma venereum (a sexually transmitted infection involving the lymph glands in the genital area), and Hansen's disease (leprosy). A communicable disease of public health concern is not a legal ground for deportation of immigrants already in the country, and illegal aliens bypass any screening or treatment for communicable diseases.

TUBERCULOSIS. The CDC monitors TB cases in the United States. In *Reported Tuberculosis in the United States, 2005* (September 2006, http://www.cdc.gov/nchstp/tb/surv/surv2005/PDF/TBSurvFULLReport.pdf), the CDC states that the 14,097 cases of TB reported in 2005 represent a 47% decrease from the 26,673 cases reported in 1992. However, the number of TB cases in foreign-born people remains relatively constant. (See Figure 3.11.) With the continuing decline of TB cases among the native-born population, the foreign born represent an increasing percentage of all TB cases. In 1993 foreign-born people accounted for 29% of all TB cases; in 2005 they accounted for 55% of all TB cases.

The CDC indicates that in 2005 twenty states reported increases in TB cases. Four significant destination states for foreign-born people—California, New York, Texas, and Florida—tallied 48% of all TB cases in 2005. In twenty-two states foreign-born residents accounted for more than 50% of all TB cases, and in six states (California, Hawaii, Massachusetts, Minnesota, New Hampshire, and Utah) they accounted for more than 70%. The top five countries of

origin for foreign-born people with TB are Mexico, the Philippines, Vietnam, India, and China. The CDC notes that "fluxes in immigration patterns are leading to changes in the distribution of TB cases by global region of origin." From 1993 through 2005 the proportion of TB cases among people from Southeast Asia nearly doubled (from 6% in 1993 to 11% in 2005) and cases among people from Africa more than tripled (from 2% in 1993 to 7% in 2005).

Of further concern to the CDC are cases of TB that prove resistant to standard drugs used to treat the disease. As drug-resistant cases among natives dropped sharply, by 1995 cases of drug-resistant TB in foreign-born people became an increasingly greater share of total cases. (See Figure 3.12.) The drug-resistant strains of TB required more patients to be placed on an initial treatment regimen of three or more drugs.

To address the high rate of TB cases among the foreign born, the CDC is collaborating with other national and international public health organizations to:

1. Improve overseas screening of immigrants and refugees

2. Strengthen the internal system for alerting local health departments of the arrival of immigrants or refugees with suspected TB

FIGURE 3.12

Drug-resistant tuberculosis cases in U.S. by origin of birth, selected years 1993–2005

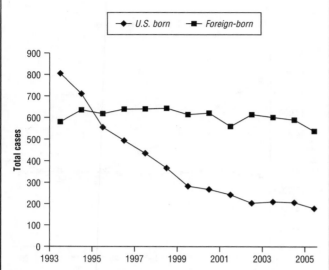

Note: Cases reported had no previous history of tuberculosis and demonstrated resistance to Isoniazid.

SOURCE: Adapted from "Table 10. Tuberculosis Cases and Percentages, by Resistance to INH or Multidrug Resistance in Persons with No Previous History of TB, by Origin of Birth: United States, 1993–2005," in *Reported Tuberculosis in the United States: 2005*, U.S. Department of Health and Human Services, Centers for Disease Control and Prevention, September 2006, http://www.cdc.gov/nchstp/tb/surv/surv2005/PDF/TBSurvFULLReport.pdf (accessed December 21, 2006)

3. Improve coordination of TB control activities between the United States and Mexico to ensure completion of treatment among TB patients who cross the border

4. Test recent arrivals from high-incidence countries for latent TB infection and treat them

5. Survey foreign-born TB patients in the United States to identify opportunities to improve prevention and control

CHAPTER 4

THE REFUGEE INFLUX

Library
Academy of the Holy Cross
4920 Strathmore Avenue
Kensington, MD 20895

In the October 2006 issue of *Refugees*, the magazine of the Office of the United Nations High Commissioner for Refugees (UNHCR), Rupert Colville reflects on the fiftieth anniversary of the Hungarian revolution—"the first major refugee relief operation of its kind" since the UNHCR was established by the UN General Assembly on December 14, 1950 (http://www.unhcr.org/publ/PUBL/4523caa32.pdf). The UNHCR grew out of the post–World War II efforts to deal with some forty million people displaced by the war.

On October 23, 1956, Hungarian citizens overthrew their communist government. Twelve days later the Soviet army crushed the revolution. Thousands of people were killed, arrested, or simply disappeared. Frightened Hungarians poured across the border into Austria. Within just nine weeks 200,000 Hungarians became refugees. The UNHCR and the French Red Cross took action to house refugees in Austria using camps with barracks recently vacated by post–World War II peacekeeping forces. The UNHCR set to work resettling the refugees. By the end of 1959, 180,000 refugees had been resettled in 37 countries. The UNHCR reported that the United States accepted the largest share (40,650 or 22%) of the refugees.

WHO IS A REFUGEE?

Every year millions of people around the world are displaced by war, famine, civil unrest, and political turmoil. Others are forced to flee their country to escape the risk of death and torture at the hands of persecutors on account of race, religion, nationality, membership in a particular social group, or political opinion.

The United States works with other governmental, international, and private organizations to provide food, health care, and shelter to millions of refugees throughout the world. Resettlement in another country, including the United States, is considered for refugees in urgent need of protection, refugees for whom other long-term solutions are not feasible, and refugees able to join close family members. The United States gives priority to the safe, voluntary return of refugees to their homelands. This policy, recognized in the Refugee Act of 1980, is also the preference of the UNHCR. If repatriation is not feasible, refugees can be resettled in countries within their geographic region or in more distant countries, such as the United States.

The UNHCR reports in *Measuring Protection by Numbers, 2005* (November 2006, http://www.unhcr.org/publ/PUBL/4579701b2.pdf) that in 2005 forty-six thousand refugees were referred to twenty-five countries for resettlement. The United States continued to take the lead in receiving refugees referred by the UNHCR, by accepting 23,289 cases in 2005. This was a significant decrease from the 28,253 refugees referred by the UNHCR in 2004 but still more than four times the number received by any other country. In 2005 Thailand replaced Kenya as the number-one source country from which refugees were resettled. The UNHCR notes that refugees from African countries comprised 51% of the worldwide total number of resettled refugees in 2005.

Legally Admitting Refugees

Before World War II the U.S. government had no arrangements for admitting people seeking refuge. The only way oppressed people were able to enter the United States was through regular immigration procedures.

After World War II refugees were admitted through special legislation passed by Congress. The Displaced Persons Act of 1948, which admitted 400,000 Eastern Europeans displaced by the war, was the first U.S. refugee legislation. The Immigration and Nationality Act of 1952 did not specifically mention refugees, but it did allow the U.S. attorney general parole authority (temporary admission) for oppressed people, such as Hungarians after their unsuccessful uprising in 1956. Other legislation—the Refugee Relief Act of 1953, the Fair Share Refugee Act of 1960, and the Indochinese Refugee Act of 1977—responded to particular world events and admitted specific groups.

Refugees were legally recognized for the first time in the Immigration and Nationality Act Amendments of 1965 with a preference category reserved for refugees from the Middle East or from countries ruled by a communist government.

Refugee Act of 1980

The Refugee Act of 1980 established a geographically and politically neutral adjudication standard for refugee status. The act redefined the term *refugee* as:

> (A) any person who is outside any country of such person's nationality or, in the case of a person having no nationality, is outside any country in which such person last habitually resided, and who is unable or unwilling to return to, and is unable or unwilling to avail himself or herself of the protection of, that country because of persecution or a well-founded fear of persecution on account of race, religion, nationality, membership in a particular social group, or political opinion, or (B) in such circumstances as the President after appropriate consultation ... may specify any person who is within the country of such person's nationality or, in the case of a person having no nationality, within the country in which such person is habitually residing, and who is persecuted or who has a well-founded fear of persecution on account of race, religion, nationality, membership in a particular social group, or political opinion.

The Refugee Act of 1980 required the president, at the beginning of each fiscal year, to determine the number of refugees to be admitted without consideration of any overall immigrant quota. The 1980 law also regulated U.S. asylum policy.

REFUGEES AND ASYLEES. The Refugee Act of 1980 made a distinction between refugees and asylees. A refugee is someone who applies for protection while outside the United States; an asylee is someone who is already in the United States when he or she applies for protection.

Lautenberg Amendment

Normal procedures required refugees to establish a well-founded fear of persecution on a case-by-case basis. A provision of the Foreign Operations, Export Financing, and Related Programs Appropriations Act of 1990, called the Lautenberg Amendment, addressed persecution based on group identity. Applicants are only required to prove that they are members of a protected category (or group) with a credible, but not necessarily individual, fear of persecution. According to the U.S. Department of State in "Refugee Admissions Program for Europe and Central Asia" (May 9, 2006, http://www.state.gov/g/prm/rls/fs/

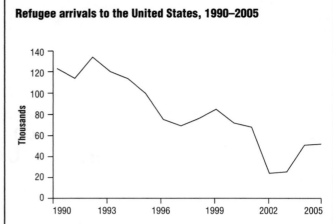

FIGURE 4.1

Refugee arrivals to the United States, 1990–2005

SOURCE: Kelly Jefferys, "Figure 1. Refugee Arrivals to the United States: 1990 to 2005," in *Annual Flow Report: Refugees and Asylees, 2005*, U.S. Department of Homeland Security, Office of Immigration Statistics, May 2006, http://www.dhs.gov/xlibrary/assets/statistics/publications/Refugee_Asylee_5.pdf (accessed January 3, 2007)

2006/66015.htm), since 1989 the United States has processed nearly 430,000 refugees under the Lautenberg Amendment, which applies to individuals within specified categories and who have qualifying relatives in the United States. In fiscal year (FY) 2005 most of the 11,316 refugees from Europe, Central Asia, and the Baltics who entered the United States came under the Lautenberg Amendment.

HOW MANY ARE ADMITTED?

The United States has resettled refugees for more than fifty years. Figure 4.1 shows recent trends in refugee arrivals from 1990 through 2005. The range is wide from a peak of roughly 135,000 refugee arrivals in 1992 to a low of about 25,000 in 2002.

Annual Refugee Admissions Limits

Before the start of a new fiscal year (October 1), the president sends to Congress a *Proposed Refugees Admissions* report, which sets limits on the maximum number of refugees to be admitted in the coming fiscal year. Table 4.1 compares actual refugee arrivals in FY2005, the approved number (ceiling) of refugees allowed for FY2006, projected 2006 arrivals, and the proposed FY2007 ceiling. Refugee numbers are established by geographic regions. The total refugee ceiling for 2005 (not shown in the chart) was 50,000. Actual arrivals exceeded the ceiling by 3,813 refugees. This was accomplished by applying the U.S. attorney general's parole authority.

By contrast, 2006 is an example of a year in which arrivals did not meet the ceiling. Because the president's request was prepared before the 2006 fiscal year ended, Table 4.1 estimates 41,500 arrivals in FY2006. The State

TABLE 4.1

Refugees admitted fiscal years (FY) 2005–06; proposed admissions for FY 2007, by region

Region	FY 2005 actual arrivals	FY 2006 ceiling	FY 2006 projected arrivals	Proposed FY 2007 ceiling
Africa	20,749	20,000	17,200	22,000
East Asia	12,071	15,000	5,800	11,000
Europe and Central Asia	11,316	15,000	11,500	6,500
Latin America/Caribbean	6,700	5,000	3,000	5,000
Near East/South Asia	2,977	5,000	4,000	5,500
Regional subtotal	53,813	60,000	41,500	50,000
Unallocated reserve		10,000		20,000
Total	**53,813**	**70,000**	**41,500**	**70,000**

SOURCE: "Table I. Refugee Admissions in FY2005 and FY2006, Proposed Refugee Admissions by Region for FY 2007," in *Proposed Refugees Admissions for Fiscal Year 2007: Report to Congress*, U.S. Department of State, U.S. Department of Homeland Security, U.S. Department of Health and Human Services, http://www.state.gov/documents/organization/74762.pdf (accessed December 30, 2006)

Department's *FY2006 Performance and Accountability Report* (November 2006, http://www.state.gov/s/d/rm/rls/perfrpt/2006/html/76611.htm) provides the final count of 41,277 refugees resettled in FY2006—69% of the 60,000 allowable refugee admissions by region. The State Department notes the reasons for the low number of 2006 admissions were "(1) delays due to material support issues; and (2) funding levels sufficient for only 54,000 refugees."

"Material support issues" refers to provisions of the 2001 USA PATRIOT Act and the 2005 REAL ID Act that prohibit granting entrance to the United States to anyone who has given money or other support to terrorists or terrorist organizations. In the *Material Support Backgrounder* (October 31, 2005, http://www.rcusa.org/finmatsupback10-31-05w.pdf), the Refugee Council USA argues that people who had been "coerced under extreme duress to make payments to armed groups on the State Department's list of foreign terrorist organizations" are being denied admission to the United States as refugees. The Refugee Council cites as an example Colombian refugees who gave money to the United Self-Defense Forces of Colombia, the Revolutionary Armed Forces of Colombia, or the National Liberation Army. Payments to these groups were made under threat of torture or death to self or a loved one. Making such payments became a necessity of survival for many Colombians. The Refugee Council contends that such nonvoluntary material support should not deny these refugees admission to the United States.

In the *Proposed Refugees Admissions*, the president specifies that certain otherwise qualified people may be considered refugees of special humanitarian concern to the United States, although they are still within their countries of nationality. In FY2007 (2006, http://www.state.gov/documents/organization/74762.pdf) the president recommended continuing such in-country processing for specified groups in Cuba, Vietnam, and the countries of the former Soviet Union.

The "unallocated reserve" in the *Proposed Refugees Admissions* is to be used at the discretion of the secretary of state (with notice to the congressional Judiciary Committee), where additional refugee needs arise.

Table 4.2 profiles FY2005 refugee admissions by median age and gender for the top twenty countries of origin. The youngest refugee population came from Burundi, with a median age of 18.4. Cuban refugees had the highest median age of 33. Even though most refugee groups hovered near a fifty-fifty mix of males and females, 75.7% of refugees from Eritrea were male. Most likely these men were escaping being forced into the military or rebel militias.

The largest share of refugee admissions between FY2003 through FY2005 were dependent children—a range from 44.8% in 2003 to 48.6% in 2004. In FY2005 dependent children accounted for 46.5% of the total 53,813 refugee admissions. (See Table 4.3.)

GAINING ENTRY INTO THE UNITED STATES

Processing Priority System

The United States has established three priority categories for admitting refugees. Table 4.4 lists the 2007 refugee ceilings by region and priority categories. Besides the three priority categories, refugees already in the approval process from the previous year are counted as "approved pipeline from fiscal year 2006."

PRIORITY 1: INDIVIDUAL REFERRALS. This category is available to individuals with compelling protection needs or those for whom no other durable solution exists and who are identified and referred to the program by the UNHCR, a U.S. embassy, or a designated nongovernmental organization (NGO). This processing priority is available to people of any nationality.

PRIORITY 2: GROUP REFERRALS. This category is used for groups of special humanitarian concern to the United States that are designated for resettlement processing. It includes specific groups (which can be defined by their particular nationalities, clans, ethnicities, religions, location, or a combination of such characteristics) identified by the State Department in consultation with U.S. Citizenship and Immigration Services (USCIS), NGOs, the UNHCR, and other experts.

Priority 2 groups processed outside their countries of origin include Burmese in the Tham Hin Refugee Camp, Iranian religious minorities (primarily in Austria), certain Burundi refugees in Tanzania, Kunama in Ethiopia, Tibetans in Nepal, and Congolese Banyamulenge in Burundi.

TABLE 4.2

Median age and gender of refugee arrivals by country of origin, fiscal year 2005

Rank (# of arrivals)	Country of origin	Refugees admitted	Median age	% Females	% Males
1	Former Soviet Union	11,175	28.4	50.4%	49.6%
2	Somalia	10,405	21.1	48.4%	51.6%
3	Laos	8,517	20.1	50.5%	49.5%
4	Cuba	6,356	33	47.3%	52.7%
5	Liberia	4,289	21	55.1%	44.9%
6	Sudan	2,205	22.3	40.8%	59.2%
7	Vietnam	2,084	25.4	46.1%	53.9%
8	Iran	1,849	32.3	47.1%	52.9%
9	Ethiopia	1,665	25.2	47.6%	52.4%
10	Burma	1,447	24.7	45.1%	54.9%
11	Afghanistan	902	23.8	47.7%	52.3%
12	Sierra Leone	829	28.2	52.2%	47.8%
13	Democratic Republic of Congo	424	19.4	46.5%	53.5%
14	Eritrea	329	27.4	24.3%	75.7%
15	Colombia	323	25.1	51.4%	48.6%
16	Burundi	214	18.4	45.8%	54.2%
17	Iraq	198	27.8	39.9%	60.1%
18	Rwanda	183	22.6	50.8%	49.2%
19	Former Yugoslavia	138	30.9	52.2%	47.8%
20	Togo	72	23.6	50.0%	50.0%
	All other countries	209	24.8	47.4%	52.6%
Total		**53,813**	**24.0**	**48.9%**	**51.1%**

Notes: Former Soviet Union includes countries of Armenia, Azerbaijan, Belarus, Estonia, Georgia, Kazakhstan, Kyrgyzstan, Latvia, Lithuania, Moldova, Russia, Tajikistan, Turkmenistan, Ukraine, and Uzbekistan. Former Yugoslavia includes countries of Montenegro, Bosnia and Herzegovina, Croatia, Serbia, Slovenia, and Yugoslavia.

SOURCE: "Table IV. Median Age and Gender of Refugee Arrivals, FY2005," in *Proposed Refugee Admissions for Fiscal Year 2007: Report to Congress*, U.S. Department of State, U.S. Department of Homeland Security, U.S. Department of Health and Human Services, http://www.state.gov/documents/organization/74762.pdf (accessed December 30, 2006)

TABLE 4.3

Refugee arrivals by category of admission, fiscal years 2003–05

Category	2005		2004		2003	
	Number	Percent	Number	Percent	Number	Percent
Total	**53,813**	**100.0**	**52,868**	**100.0**	**28,422**	**100.0**
Principal applicant	18,252	33.9	17,835	33.7	10,483	36.9
Dependents						
Spouse	8,523	15.8	7,012	13.3	4,073	14.3
Parent	208	0.4	134	0.3	88	0.3
Child	25,006	46.5	25,677	48.6	12,721	44.8
Sibling	799	1.5	1,029	1.9	455	1.6
Other	1,025	1.9	1,181	2.2	602	2.1

SOURCE: Kelly Jefferys, "Table 2. Refugee Arrivals by Category of Admission: Fiscal Years 2003 to 2005," in *Annual Flow Report: Refugees and Asylees, 2005*, U.S. Department of Homeland Security, Office of Immigration Statistics, May 2006, http://www.dhs.gov/xlibrary/assets/statistics/publications/Refugee_Asylee_5.pdf (accessed January 3, 2007)

The program is expected to continue to expand and include new Priority 2 groups.

PRIORITY 3: FAMILY REUNIFICATION CASES. This category is used for spouses, unmarried children under twenty-one, parents of people admitted to the United States as refugees or granted asylum, or people who were lawful permanent residents or U.S. citizens and were initially admitted to the United States as refugees or granted asylum. In FY2007 Priority 3 eligibility was extended to nationals of particular countries based on the UNHCR's annual assessment of refugees in need of resettlement, prospective or ongoing repatriation efforts, and U.S. foreign policy interests. For FY2007 the president recommended the following as Priority 3 countries: Afghanistan, Burma, Burundi, Colombia, Congo (Brazzaville), Cuba, Democratic People's Republic of Korea, Democratic Republic of Congo, Eritrea, Ethiopia, Haiti, Iran, Iraq, Rwanda, Somalia, Sudan, and Uzbekistan.

United States Responds to Special Needs

In October 2006 the State Department announced that, at the request of the UNHCR, the United States would offer permanent resettlement to approximately ten thousand refugees from Burundi beginning in FY2007 (October 17, 2006, http://usinfo.state.gov/). Tom Casey, the State Department spokesperson, described the plight of the Burundian refugees as "a long-standing issue." He noted that only in 2006 did the UNHCR ask the United States and other countries to resettle them. The group of Burundian refugees fled in 1972 from the Tutsi-dominated government's ethnic killings directed against the country's Hutu population. They had been living in refugee camps in western Tanzania. Many had been displaced multiple times, and the majority had spent their lives in exile. More than 315,000 Burundian refugees had been able to return home since 2002, but because of a critical

TABLE 4.4

Regional ceilings by priority, proposed fiscal year 2007

Africa	
Approved pipeline from fiscal year 2006	6,000
Priority 1 individual referrals	2,500
Priority 2 groups	6,000
Priority 3 family reunification refugees	7,500
Total proposed:	**22,000**
East Asia	
Approved pipeline from fiscal year 2006	1,600
Priority 1 individual referrals	300
Priority 2 groups	9,000
Priority 3 family reunification refugees	100
Total proposed:	**11,000**
Europe/Central Asia	
Approved pipeline from fiscal year 2006	3,500
Priority 1 individual referrals	350
Priority 2 groups	2,500
Priority 3 family reunification refugees	150
Total proposed:	**6,500**
Latin America/Caribbean	
Approved pipeline from fiscal year 2006	1,850
Priority 1 individual referrals	100
Priority 2 groups	3,000
Priority 3 family reunification refugees	50
Total proposed:	**5,000**
Near East/South Asia	
Approved pipeline from FY 2006	200
Priority 1 individual referrals	2,200
Priority 2 groups	3,000
Priority 3 family reunification refugees	100
Total proposed:	**5,500**
Subtotal, regional ceilings	50,000
Unallocated reserve	20,000
Total proposed ceiling	**70,000**

SOURCE: "Table II. Proposed FY2007 Regional Ceilings by Priority," in *Proposed Refugees Admissions for Fiscal Year 2007: Report to Congress*, U.S. Department of State, U.S. Department of Homeland Security, U.S. Department of Health and Human Services, http://www.state.gov/documents/organization/74762.pdf (accessed December 30, 2006)

shortage of land, the group remaining in the western Tanzanian camps was seen as being unlikely to return. Casey said the refugees would be brought to the United States over the next two years and would be eligible to apply for U.S. citizenship. Since 1975 the United States has offered more than 2.6 million refugees a permanent home as part of its ongoing refugee resettlement program according to Casey.

SEEKING ASYLUM

Like a refugee, an asylee is someone who wants refuge in another country. The only difference is the location of the alien when he or she applies for refuge: a refugee is outside the United States when applying for refuge, whereas an asylee is already in the United States, perhaps on an expired tourist visa or at a port of entry. Just like a refugee applying for entrance into the country, an asylee seeks the protection of the United States because of persecution or a well-founded fear of persecution.

Countries of origin differ between refugees and asylees in any given year. (See Table 4.5.) In 2003 the total refugee admissions (28,422) nearly matched granted asylums (28,684). In 2004, however, refugee admissions rose to 52,868, whereas granted asylums dipped to 27,169. The greatest number of refugees admitted in 2003 came from the Ukraine, and Somalia produced the most refugees admitted in both 2004 and 2005. Other major sources of refugees were Liberia (2003 and 2004), Laos (2004 and 2005), Cuba (2005), and Russia (2005). From 2003 to 2005 China produced the most asylum seekers, followed by Colombia and Haiti. Only two countries, Russia and Ethiopia, appear in the top ten source lists for both refugees and asylees.

Asylees in the United States include sailors who jumped ship while their boat was docked in a U.S. port, athletes who asked for asylum while participating in a sports event, and women who based their claim on a fear of being compelled to undergo a coercive population-control procedure such as abortion or sterilization. Any alien physically present in the United States or at a port of entry can request asylum in the United States. It is irrelevant whether the person is a legal or illegal alien. Like refugees, asylum applicants do not count against the worldwide annual U.S. limitation of immigrants.

In the fact sheet "Asylum Protection in the United States" (April 28, 2005, http://www.usdoj.gov/eoir/press/05/AsylumProtectionFactsheetQAApr05.htm), the U.S. Department of Justice notes that certain individuals are barred from obtaining asylum, including those who:

- Have firmly resettled in another country prior to arriving in the United States

- Have ordered, incited, assisted, or otherwise participated in the persecution of any person on account of race, religion, nationality, membership in a particular social group, or political opinion

- Were convicted of a particularly serious crime (includes aggravated felonies)

- Committed a serious nonpolitical crime outside the United States

- Pose a danger to the security of the United States

- Are members or representatives of a foreign terrorist organization

- Have engaged in or incited terrorist activity

Filing Claims

Asylum seekers must apply for asylum within one year from the date of last arrival in the United States. If the application is filed past the one-year mark, asylum seekers must show changed circumstances that materially affect their eligibility or extraordinary circumstances that delayed filing. They must also show that they filed within

TABLE 4.5

Refugee arrivals and persons granted asylum, by country of origin, fiscal years 2003–05

[Refugee arrivals ranked by 2005 country of origin]

Country	2005		2004		2003	
	Number	Percent	Number	Percent	Number	Percent
Total	**53,813**	**100.0**	**52,868**	**100.0**	**28,422**	**100.0**
Somalia	10,405	19.3	13,331	25.2	1,993	7.0
Laos	8,517	15.8	6,005	11.4	13	—
Cuba	6,361	11.8	2,958	5.6	303	1.1
Russia	5,982	11.1	1,446	2.7	1,394	4.9
Liberia	4,289	8.0	7,140	13.5	2,957	10.4
Ukraine	2,889	5.4	3,482	6.6	5,065	17.8
Sudan	2,205	4.1	3,500	6.6	2,140	7.5
Vietnam	2,079	3.9	1,007	1.9	1,472	5.2
Iran	1,856	3.4	1,787	3.4	2,471	8.7
Ethiopia	1,665	3.1	2,710	5.1	1,704	6.0
Other	7,565	14.1	9,502	18.0	8,910	31.3

[Persons granted asylum ranked by 2005 country of origin]

Country	Number	Percent	Number	Percent	Number	Percent
Total	**25,257**	**100.0**	**27,169**	**100.0**	**28,684**	**100.0**
China	5,225	20.7	4,302	15.8	5,999	20.9
Colombia	3,375	13.4	4,368	16.1	4,561	15.9
Haiti	2,962	11.7	2,319	8.5	1,728	6.0
Venezuela	1,114	4.4	1,255	4.6	350	1.2
Ethiopia	728	2.9	1,010	3.7	808	2.8
Albania	695	2.8	899	3.3	964	3.4
Cameroon	647	2.6	863	3.2	998	3.5
Russia	488	1.9	552	2.0	668	2.3
Indonesia	469	1.9	528	1.9	581	2.0
Armenia	426	1.7	545	2.0	867	3.0
Other	9,128	36.1	10,528	38.8	11,160	38.9

— Figure rounds to 0.0.

SOURCE: Kelly Jefferys, "Table 3. Refugee Arrivals by Country of Origin: Fiscal Years 2003 to 2005," and "Table 6. Persons Granted Asylum by Country of Origin: Fiscal Years 2003 to 2005," in *Annual Flow Report: Refugees and Asylees, 2005,* U.S. Department of Homeland Security, Office of Immigration Statistics, May 2006, http://www.dhs.gov/xlibrary/assets/statistics/publications/Refugee_Asylee_5.pdf (accessed January 3, 2007)

a reasonable amount of time given these circumstances. The Justice Department identifies two types of asylum claims: affirmative and defensive. Aliens in the United States can apply for asylum by filing an Application for Asylum (Form I-589) with the U.S. Citizenship and Immigration Services. Initiating this process is called an affirmative asylum claim. Aliens who have been placed in removal proceedings and who are in immigration court can request asylum through the Executive Office of Immigration Review. This last-resort effort is called a defensive asylum claim.

Expedited Removal

In *Immigration Enforcement Actions: 2005* (November 2006, http://www.dhs.gov/xlibrary/assets/statistics/yearbook/2005/Enforcement_AR_05.pdf), Mary Dougherty, Denise Wilson, and Amy Wu report that the 72,911 expedited removals in 2005 accounted for 35% of all formal removals. Aliens already in the country without authorization and those who attempted entry by fraud, misrepresentation, or without documents accounted for 71% of expedited removals. Nineteen percent of removals were related to criminal charges.

Under the expedited removal provisions of the 1996 Illegal Immigration Reform and Immigrant Responsibility Act, any alien subject to expedited removal because of fraud, misrepresentation, or a lack of valid documents must be questioned by an immigration officer regarding the fear of persecution at home. Aliens who express such a fear are detained until an asylum officer can determine the credibility of the fear. Aliens found to have a credible fear are referred to an immigration judge for a final determination and are generally released until their cases are heard. In some cases an alien is detained while his or her case is pending before an immigration judge. If the fear is deemed not credible, the alien is refused admission and removed.

Critics charge that the expedited removal process denies aliens a fair chance to fully present their asylum claims, places unprecedented authority in the hands of asylum officers, is conducted so quickly that mistakes are inevitable, limits an alien's right to review of a deportation order, and results in the wrongful expulsion of individuals with legitimate fears of persecution. An alien who is deported under the expedited removal process is barred from returning to the United States for five years.

According to Daniel Gilbert, in "Immigration Appeals Pile Up" (*Potomac News*, June 19, 2006), increased immigration enforcement in the mid-1990s led to a backlog of asylum claims. Appeals of decisions by the Board of Immigration increased from 1,723 in 2000 to 12,349 in 2005. For example, the median time for resolving an appeal in Ninth Circuit courts rose to more than sixteen months.

Nina Bernstein reports in the *New York Times* that 218 immigration judges in 53 immigration courts nationwide handle 350,000 asylum cases annually ("In New York Immigration Court, Asylum Roulette," October 8, 2006). Bernstein notes allegations of vast disparity in decisions "like 90 percent of asylum cases granted by one judge and 9 percent [by another judge] down the hall." Concerning asylum cases, "the wrong decision can be a death sentence. In others, banishment hangs in the balance, with the prospect of families split up or swept into harm's way." Judges face challenges, including understanding changing conditions in distant lands and asylum seekers speaking 227 different languages who are "vulnerable to an interpreter's mistake as small as pronouncing 'rebels' like 'robbers.'" According to Bernstein, in April 2006 the chief judge of the Court of Appeals for the Second Circuit urged the Senate Judiciary Committee to double the number of immigration judges.

Affirmative and Defensive Asylum Claims

Figure 4.1 shows refugee admissions from 1990 through 2005, and Figure 4.2 shows affirmative and defensive asylum claims for the same period. The pattern of asylum claims is almost the reverse of refugee admissions. The volume of asylum claims in the early 1990s was less than five thousand, perhaps because so many people were being admitted as refugees in that period. Defensive asylum claims increased steadily from less than three thousand in 1994 to a high of more than thirteen thousand in 2003. Affirmative claims rose dramatically from four thousand in 1991 to eighteen thousand in 1996, dipped in 1997 and 1998, then hit a peak of more than twenty-eight thousand in 2001.

Affirmative and defensive asylum claims differ by countries of origin. Table 4.6 compares affirmative and defensive data from 2003 to 2005. In all three years studied Haitian and Colombian asylees were granted more affirmative claims than defensive claims, whereas Chinese asylees were granted more defensive than affirmative claims. In 2005, 2,309 Haitians received asylum affirmatively and 653 defensively. In the same year 3,008 Chinese were granted defensive asylum and 2,217 were granted affirmative asylum. From 2003 to 2005 there were nearly twice the number of affirmative asylees from Colombia as defensive asylees.

How Many Asylees?

Thousands of people apply for asylum in the United States every year, but under the Immigration Act of 1990,

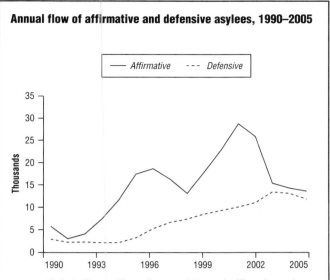

FIGURE 4.2

Annual flow of affirmative and defensive asylees, 1990–2005

SOURCE: Kelly Jefferys, "Figure 2. Annual Flow of Affirmative and Defensive Asylees: 1990 to 2005," in *Annual Flow Report: Refugees and Asylees, 2005*, U.S. Department of Homeland Security, Office of Immigration Statistics, May 2006, http://www.dhs.gov/xlibrary/assets/statistics/publications/Refugee_Asylee_5.pdf (accessed January 3, 2007)

only ten thousand asylees per year can be granted lawful permanent resident (LPR) status. Moreover, LPR status cannot be granted until the asylee has been in the country for one year. The REAL ID Act of 2005 removed the ten-thousand-per-year limit on asylee adjustments of status to LPR. Whereas the total number of LPRs granted rose from 946,142 in 2004 to 1,122,373 in 2005, the number of asylees granted LPR status tripled from 10,217 to 30,286. (See Table 4.7.)

Critics charge that many people seek asylum in the United States to avoid dismal economic conditions at home rather than the legitimate reasons to seek asylum under U.S. law—to escape political or religious persecution or because of a well-founded fear of physical harm or death. In addition, some illegal aliens try to obtain the legal right to work by filing for asylum.

Criteria for Granting Asylum

Under the Immigration and Nationality Act, as amended, a person can be granted asylum only if he or she establishes a well-founded fear of persecution on account of one of five protected grounds: race, religion, nationality, membership in a particular social group, or political opinion. Some people charge that the United States constantly changes its definition of what constitutes "membership in a particular social group" to accommodate the growing number of asylum seekers. The Refugee Act of 1980 defined a social group as comprising people who all "share a common characteristic that is either immutable [not susceptible to change], or should not be

TABLE 4.6

Persons granted asylum affirmatively and defensively, by country of origin, fiscal years 2003–05

[Persons granted asylum affirmatively ranked by 2005 country of origin]

Country	2005 Number	2005 Percent	2004 Number	2004 Percent	2003 Number	2003 Percent
Total	**13,520**	**100.0**	**14,207**	**100.0**	**15,310**	**100.0**
Haiti	2,309	17.1	1,786	12.6	1,162	7.6
Colombia	2,225	16.5	2,898	20.4	2,971	19.4
China	2,217	16.4	900	6.3	2,398	15.7
Venezuela	961	7.1	1,198	8.4	315	2.1
Ethiopia	464	3.4	752	5.3	569	3.7
Cameroon	384	2.8	593	4.2	812	5.3
Guatemala	253	1.9	204	1.4	155	1.0
Russia	236	1.7	231	1.6	287	1.9
Nepal	231	1.7	162	1.1	143	0.9
Zimbabwe	204	1.5	239	1.7	193	1.3
Other	4,036	29.9	5,244	36.9	6,305	41.2

[Persons granted asylum defensively ranked by 2005 country of origin]

Country	2005 Number	2005 Percent	2004 Number	2004 Percent	2003 Number	2003 Percent
Total	**11,737**	**100.0**	**12,962**	**100.0**	**13,374**	**100.0**
China	3,008	25.6	3,402	26.2	3,601	26.9
Colombia	1,150	9.8	1,470	11.3	1,590	11.9
Haiti	653	5.6	533	4.1	566	4.2
Albania	608	5.2	724	5.6	717	5.4
Indonesia	374	3.2	421	3.2	366	2.7
India	310	2.6	450	3.5	595	4.4
Armenia	268	2.3	299	2.3	412	3.1
Ethiopia	264	2.2	258	2.0	239	1.8
Cameroon	263	2.2	270	2.1	186	1.4
Guinea	257	2.2	258	2.0	155	1.2
Other	4,582	39.0	4,877	37.6	4,947	37.0

SOURCE: Kelly Jefferys, "Table 7. Persons Granted Asylum Affirmatively by Country of Origin: Fiscal Years 2003 to 2005," and "Table 8. Persons Granted Asylum Defensively by Country of Origin: Fiscal Years 2003 to 2005," in *Annual Flow Report: Refugees and Asylees, 2005*, U.S. Department of Homeland Security, Office of Immigration Statistics, May 2006, http://www.dhs.gov/xlibrary/assets/statistics/publications/Refugee_Asylee_5.pdf (accessed January 3, 2007)

TABLE 4.7

Refugees, asylees, and other persons granted legal permanent resident (LPR) status, 2004–05

	2004 Number	2004 Percent	2005 Number	2005 Percent
Total LPRs	**946,142**	**100.0%**	**1,122,373**	**100.0%**
Refugees	61,013	6.4%	112,676	10.0%
Asylees	10,217	1.1%	30,286	2.7%
All other LPRs	874,912	92.5%	979,411	87.3%

SOURCE: Adapted from "Table 2. Persons Obtaining Legal Permanent Resident Status by Region and Selected Country of Last Residence: Fiscal Years 1820 to 2005," and "Table 7. Persons Obtaining Legal Permanent Resident Status by Type and Detailed Class of Admission: Fiscal Year 2005," in *2005 Yearbook of Immigration Statistics*, U.S. Department of Homeland Security, Office of Immigration Statistics, November 2006, http://www.dhs.gov/xlibrary/assets/statistics/yearbook/2005/OIS_2005_Yearbook.pdf (accessed January 4, 2007)

required to change because it is fundamental to their individual identities and consciences."

Those who believe the term should be interpreted broadly argue that the intent of the law is to provide a catch-all to include all the types of persecution that can occur. Those with a narrow view see the law as a means of identifying and protecting individuals from known forms of harm, not in anticipation of future types of abuse.

Persecution Based on Gender and Sexual Orientation

As the United States and the world became more aware of persecution based on gender and sexual orientation, victims came to be considered members of a social group. In *Guidelines on International Protection: Gender-Related Persecution within the Context of Article 1A(2) of the 1951 Convention and/or Its 1967 Protocol Relating to the Status of Refugees* (May 7, 2002, http://www.unhcr.org/publ/PUBL/3d58ddef4.pdf), the UNHCR issues the formal statement in that countries "are free to adopt the interpretation that women asylum seekers who face harsh or inhuman treatment due to their having transgressed the social mores of the society in which they live may be considered as 'a particular social group.'"

In 1994 nineteen-year-old Fauziya Kasinga fled her native Togo to escape genital mutilation. When she arrived in the United States, she asked for asylum and was held in a detention center for sixteen months waiting for her case to be heard by the Board of Immigration Appeals. On June 13, 1996, the board ruled in her favor in *In re Fauziya Kasinga* (A 73 479 695); she became the first individual granted asylum on the basis of gender persecution.

On August 24, 2000, the U.S. Court of Appeals for the Ninth Circuit, in *Hernandez-Montiel v. INS* (No. 98-70582), ruled that "gay men with female sexual identities" constitute a "particular social group" eligible for asylum and withholding of deportation.

VICTIMS OF TRAFFICKING AND VIOLENCE

The *Attorney General's Report to Congress on U.S. Government Activities to Combat Trafficking in Persons Fiscal Year 2005* (June 2006, http://www.usdoj.gov/ag/annualreports/tr2005/agreporthumantraficing2005.pdf) estimates that 600,000 to 800,000 people are trafficked across international borders each year and 14,500 to 17,500 victims may be trafficked into the United States annually. Many more are trafficked within their own national borders for a variety of purposes, including forced labor, bonded labor, sexual servitude, and involuntary servitude.

In the United States the Trafficking Victims Protection Act of 2000 (TVPA) makes victims of severe forms of trafficking eligible for benefits and services to the same extent as refugees. In addition, the law attempts to identify and prosecute traffickers. The Trafficking Victims Protection Reauthorization Act of 2003 mandates informational awareness campaigns and created a new civil action provision that allows victims to sue their traffickers in federal district court. It also requires an annual report to Congress on the results of U.S. government activities to combat trafficking. The Trafficking Victims Protection Reauthorization Act of 2006 appropriated over $361 million in funding through FY2007. The act also amended the Violent Crime Control and Law Enforcement Act of 1994 to include foreign offenses in the sexually violent offender registration program and expanded efforts to combat trafficking.

Trafficking victims in the United States are eligible for Continued Presence (CP) or T (nonimmigrant visa) status. CP authorizes the victim to remain in the United States as a potential witness in the investigation and prosecution of traffickers. Victims who are over age eighteen and have complied with reasonable requests for assistance in the investigation and prosecution of acts of trafficking may apply for a T visa. The T visa allows the victim to remain in the United States for three years and then apply for lawful permanent residence. The U.S. attorney general reports that there were 160 requests for CP status in FY2005. Two requests were withdrawn and the remaining 158 were awarded CP status. The requesting victims came from twenty-nine countries, with the highest number of victims coming from Korea, Peru, and Honduras. In addition, ninety-two extensions of existing CP status were granted. A total of 229 people applied for T visas in 2005. Of these, 112 were approved and 213 denied (170 denials were from one trafficking case and the applicants did not meet the TVPA definition of trafficking victims). There were also 124 applications for T visas by victims' family members; all but 18 were approved.

Monitoring Foreign Governments

The TVPA requires the State Department to monitor the efforts of foreign governments to eliminate trafficking. The State Department identifies governments in full compliance with TVPA (Tier I), governments in compliance with minimum standards of TVPA (Tier II), governments that have shown positive efforts toward minimum compliance (Tier II Watch List), and those countries that have not taken serious action to stop trafficking (Tier III). (See Table 4.8.)

VICTIMS OF TORTURE

The Torture Victims Relief Act of 1998 provides federal funds to help support treatment centers for refugees and asylees who are victims of torture in their home country. In his testimony before the House Committee on International Relations, Wade F. Horn of the U.S. Department of Health and Human Services (HHS) stated that at the end of FY2004 organizations providing services reported that 6,600 victims of torture received services, including mental health, medical, legal assistance, and other kinds of social services (June 23, 2005, http://www.foreignaffairs.house.gov/archives/109/21978.pdf).

REFUGEE ADJUSTMENT TO LIFE IN THE UNITED STATES

Table 4.9 lists the number of refugees resettled in FY2005 by state. More than one-third (35%) of all refugees were initially settled in three states: California (13.9%), Minnesota (11.8%), and Florida (8.9%).

According to Table 4.10, the U.S. government expected to spend $852.9 million on processing and resettling refugees in FY2007. The bulk of this budget—$614.9 million—supported the Office of Refugee Resettlement (ORR) under the HHS. The ORR administers programs to assist refugees and asylees in adjusting to life in the United States. The U.S. resettlement program is designed to function as a public-private partnership, with NGOs playing a key role. Through the Reception and Placement Program refugees are welcomed on arrival and provided essential services (housing, clothing, food, and referrals to medical and social services) during the first thirty days in the United States. During this initial period the resettlement agencies also link refugees to longer-term resettlement and integration programs funded by the ORR.

TABLE 4.8

Tier placement of countries, 2006

Tier 1

Australia	France	Malawi	South Korea
Austria	Germany	Morocco	Spain
Belgium	Hong Kong	The Netherlands	Sweden
Canada	Ireland	New Zealand	Switzerland
Colombia	Italy	Norway	United Kingdom
Denmark	Lithuania	Poland	
Finland	Luxembourg	Singapore	

Tier 2

Afghanistan	East Timor	Latvia	Rwanda
Albania	Ecuador	Lebanon	Senegal
Angola	El Salvador	Macedonia	Serbia-
Azerbaijan	Estonia	Madagascar	Montenegro
Bangladesh	Ethiopia	Mali	Sierra Leone
Belarus	Gabon	Malta	Slovak Republic
Benin	The Gambia	Mauritius	Slovenia
Bosnia/Herz.	Georgia	Moldova	Sri Lanka
Bulgaria	Ghana	Mongolia	Suriname
Burkina Faso	Greece	Mozambique	Tajikistan
Burundi	Guatemala	Nepal	Tanzania
Cameroon	Guinea	Nicaragua	Thailand
Chad	Guinea-Bissau	Niger	Tunisia
Chile	Guyana	Nigeria	Turkey
Congo (DRC)	Honduras	Pakistan	Uganda
Costa Rica	Hungary	Panama	Ukraine
Côte d'Ivoire	Japan	Paraguay	Uruguay
Croatia	Jordan	Philippines	Vietnam
Czech Republic	Kazakhstan	Portugal	Yemen
Dominican Rep.	Kyrgyz Republic	Romania	Zambia

Tier 2 watch list

Algeria	China (PRC)	Jamaica	Oman
Argentina	Cyprus	Kenya	Peru
Armenia	Djibouti	Kuwait	Qatar
Bahrain	Egypt	Libya	Russia
Bolivia	Equatorial Guinea	Macau	South Africa
Brazil	India	Malaysia	Taiwan
Cambodia	Indonesia	Mauritania	Togo
Central African Rep.	Israel	Mexico	United Arab Emirates

Tier 3

Belize	Iran	Saudi Arabia	Uzbekistan
Burma	Laos	Sudan	Venezuela
Cuba	North Korea	Syria	Zimbabwe

SOURCE: "Tier Placements," in *Trafficking in Persons Report, 2006*, U.S. Department of State, June 2006, http://www.state.gov/documents/organization/66086.pdf (accessed January 2, 2007)

The State Department makes funds available for the transportation of refugees resettled in the United States. The cost of transportation is provided to refugees in the form of a loan. Refugees are responsible for repaying these loans over time, beginning six months after their arrival.

Some of the NGOs recruit church groups and volunteers from local communities to provide a variety of services and to contribute clothing and household furnishings to meet the needs of arriving refugees. In addition, they often become mentors and friends of the refugees, providing orientation to community services, offering supportive services such as tutoring children after school,

TABLE 4.9

Refugee arrivals by state of initial settlement, fiscal year 2005

State	Refugee arrivals	Amerasian arrivals	Total arrivals	Percent of total arrivals to U.S.
Alabama	102	0	102	0.19%
Alaska	80	0	80	0.15%
Arizona	1,872	0	1,872	3.48%
Arkansas	12	0	12	0.02%
California	7,505	11	7,516	13.97%
Colorado	901	0	901	1.67%
Connecticut	526	0	526	0.98%
Delaware	19	0	19	0.04%
District of Columbia	42	4	46	0.09%
Florida	4,793	0	4,793	8.91%
Georgia	1,870	0	1,870	3.47%
Guam	5	0	5	0.01%
Hawaii	25	0	25	0.05%
Idaho	534	0	534	0.99%
Illinois	1,463	0	1,463	2.72%
Indiana	493	0	493	0.92%
Iowa	361	4	365	0.68%
Kansas	145	9	154	0.29%
Kentucky	774	5	779	1.45%
Louisiana	205	0	205	0.38%
Maine	151	0	151	0.28%
Maryland	734	3	737	1.37%
Massachusetts	1,279	6	1,285	2.39%
Michigan	866	4	870	1.62%
Minnesota	6,357	0	6,357	11.81%
Missouri	987	0	987	1.83%
Montana	5	0	5	0.01%
Nebraska	225	0	225	0.42%
Nevada	385	0	385	0.72%
New Hampshire	311	0	311	0.58%
New Jersey	713	0	713	1.32%
New Mexico	81	0	81	0.15%
New York	2,561	7	2,568	4.77%
North Carolina	1,259	14	1,273	2.37%
North Dakota	228	0	228	0.42%
Ohio	1,560	0	1,560	2.90%
Oklahoma	136	0	136	0.25%
Oregon	1,024	0	1,024	1.90%
Pennsylvania	1,521	0	1,521	2.83%
Puerto Rico	8	0	8	0.01%
Rhode Island	283	0	283	0.53%
South Carolina	105	0	105	0.20%
South Dakota	214	0	214	0.40%
Tennessee	869	0	869	1.61%
Texas	3,243	2	3,245	6.03%
Utah	753	0	753	1.40%
Vermont	182	0	182	0.34%
Virginia	1,276	0	1,276	2.37%
Washington	2,841	6	2,847	5.29%
West Virginia	3	0	3	0.01%
Wisconsin	1,851	0	1,851	3.44%
Total	**53,738**	**75**	**53,813**	**100.0%**

Note: Arrival figures do not reflect secondary migration.

SOURCE: "Table VI. Refugee Arrivals by State of Initial Resettlement, Fiscal Year 2005," in *Proposed Refugees Admissions for Fiscal Year 2007: Report to Congress*, U.S. Department of State, U.S. Department of Homeland Security, U.S. Department of Health and Human Services, http://www.state.gov/documents/organization/74762.pdf (accessed December 30, 2006)

and teaching families how to shop and handle other essential functions of living in the community.

Mutual Assistance Associations, many of which have national networks, provide opportunities for refugees to meet their countrymen who are already settled in the

TABLE 4.10

U.S. government costs for refugee resettlement, estimated fiscal year 2006 and budget request, fiscal year 2007

[Dollars in millions.]

Agency	Estimated funding FY 2006 (by activity)	Estimated funding FY 2007 (by activity)
Department of Homeland Security United States Citizenship and Immigration Services Refugee processing	$12.1	$15.3
Department of State Bureau of Population, Refugee, and Migration Refugee admissions	$165.5[a]	$222.7
Department of Health and Human Services Administration for Children and Families, Office of Refugee Resettlement (ORR) Refugee resettlement	$569.8[b]	$614.9[b]
Total	**$747.4**	**$852.9**

[a]Includes $4 million in recoveries from prior FY.
[b]Does not include costs associated with the Transitional Assistance for Needy Families (TANF), Medicaid, or SSI programs. ORR's refugee benefits and services are also provided to asylees, Cuban and Haitian entrants, certain Amerasians from Vietnam, victims of a severe form of trafficking who have received certification or eligibility letters from ORR, and certain family members who are accompanying or following to join victims of severe forms of trafficking, and some victims of torture. None of these additional groups is included in the refugee admissions ceiling.

SOURCE: "Table VIII. Estimated Costs of Refugee Processing, Movement, and Resettlement FY 2006 Estimate and FY 2007 Budget Request ($Millions)," in *Proposed Refugee Admissions for Fiscal Year 2007: Report to Congress*, U.S. Department of State, U.S. Department of Homeland Security, U.S. Department of Health and Human Services, http://www.state.gov/documents/organization/74762.pdf (accessed December 30, 2006)

United States. These associations also help refugees connect with their ethnic culture through holiday and religious celebrations.

Benefits to Assist Transition

Ongoing benefits for the newly arrived refugees include transitional cash assistance, health benefits, and a wide variety of social services, which are provided through grants from the Office of Refugee Resettlement. English-language training is a basic service offered to all refugees. The primary focus is preparation for employment through skills training, job development, orientation to the workplace, and job counseling. Early employment leads not only to early economic self-sufficiency for the family but also helps establish the family in their new country and community. Special attention is paid to ensure that women have equal access to training and services leading to job placement. Other services include family strengthening, youth and elderly services, adjustment counseling, and mental health services.

Support for Elderly and Disabled Refugees

Refugees who are elderly or disabled receive benefits from the Social Security Administration, the same as U.S. citizens. However, changes by Congress in the late 1990s limit the eligibility of noncitizens to their first seven years in the United States. Time limits for noncitizens do not apply once they become U.S. citizens. The refugee program offers citizenship classes to assist refugees who want to study for the citizenship test.

UNACCOMPANIED MINOR CHILDREN

Each year thousands of children enter the United States illegally and unaccompanied by a parent or guardian; some of them are sent away by parents who fear for their safety in war-torn regions of the world. Beginning in 1984 the U.S. Immigration and Naturalization Service (INS, now the USCIS) refused to release these children to anyone other than a parent or legal guardian. As a result, children whose parents were not in the United States were detained for months or years while immigration authorities decided what to do with them. In 1985 the National Center for Youth Law filed a class action lawsuit in which it challenged INS policies governing the release of children and the conditions of confinement of those who were not released.

Following the 1993 U.S. Supreme Court ruling in *Flores v. Reno* (507 U.S. 292), the INS pledged to improve conditions for children in its custody. However, in *Why Am I Here? Children in Immigration Detention* (June 18, 2003, http://www.amnestyusa.org/refugee/pdfs/children_detention.pdf), Amnesty International charges that more than five thousand children who enter the country illegally and alone are being locked up each year, and some of them are "shackled, strip-searched, or subject to physical or verbal abuse." As of March 1, 2003, the Homeland Security Act transferred responsibility for the care and custody of these children to the Office of Refugee Resettlement.

Unaccompanied Children Seeking Asylum

Jacqueline Bhabha and Susan Schmidt address the plight of child refugees arriving in the United States in *Seeking Asylum Alone: Unaccompanied and Separated Children and Refugee Protection in the U.S.* (June 2006, http://www.humanrights.harvard.edu/conference/Seeking_Asylum_Alone_US_Report.pdf). They find it difficult to identify the actual number of unaccompanied children entering the United States each year because records of many agencies do not specify ages of arriving aliens. Bhabha and Schmidt note that the ORR reported 6,200 unaccompanied alien children in its custody during FY2004. Central American countries were the primary sources of unaccompanied children in ORR custody, with nearly one-third (30%) coming from Honduras. (See Table 4.11.)

Bhabha and Schmidt report that unaccompanied children face an increased risk of military recruitment, sexual

TABLE 4.11

Top countries of origin for children in Office of Refugee Resettlement (ORR) custody, fiscal year 2004

Honduras	30%
El Salvador	26%
Guatemala	20%
Mexico	10%
Brazil	3%
China	2%
Ecuador	2%
Nicaragua	.82%
Costa Rica	.47%
Other	5.71%

SOURCE: Reproduced from Jacqueline Bhabha and Susan Schmidt, "2.b. Top 9 Countries of Origin for Children in ORR Custody in FY 2004," in *Seeking Asylum Alone: Unaccompanied and Separated Children and Refugee Protection in the U.S.*, Cambridge, MA: University Committee on Human Rights Studies, Harvard University, June 2006, http://www.humanrights.harvard.edu/conference/Seeking_Asylum_Alone_US_Report.pdf (accessed December 29, 2006)

violence, deprivation, exploitation, and abuse. Concerns identified by Bhabha and Schmidt include the need to separate children from adults in detention facilities, providing legal counsel to assist children in articulating their claims for asylum, and establishing a more child-focused approach to children seeking asylum. According to Bhabha and Schmidt, applicants with legal representation are six times more likely to be granted asylum than those appearing without an attorney. They note an overall decline in rates of approval for asylum applications by children from 63% in 1999 to 31% in 2003. The 2003 approval rate for children was slightly higher than the 29% total approval rate for all asylum applications. Bhabha and Schmidt also identify vast differences in approval rates for children among the eight USCIS asylum offices—a high of 49% in Arlington, Virginia, compared with a low of 17% in the Chicago Asylum Office.

Children without parents in the United States who are granted asylum are eligible for the Specialized Refugee Foster Care Program, which is coordinated by the Lutheran Immigration and Refugee Service and the U.S. Conference of Catholic Bishops. Benefits include financial support for housing, food, clothing, and other necessities; case management by a social worker; medical care; independent living skills training; education and English as a second language; tutoring and mentoring; job skills training and career counseling; mental health services; ongoing family tracing; cultural activities and recreation; special education where needed; and legal assistance.

Debra Fergus, a child welfare supervisor for a Catholic Charities foster care program in Phoenix, Arizona, believes time spent in foster care is good for young asylum seekers. According to Fergus, it often takes several months in foster care before the children open up and tell their stories: "The majority of the kids have witnessed death. ... Whether they're trafficking victims is very difficult to determine. ... They're ashamed of what happened, they're scared, they've been threatened" (Patricia Zapor, "Minors Who Cross U.S. Border Hit a Muddle of Legal Issues, Options," Catholic News Service, October 31, 2006).

Bhabha and Schmidt advocate legislation to improve treatment of children seeking asylum. The Child Status Protection Act of 2002 increased the benefits eligibility age from eighteen to twenty-one and essentially froze a child's age at the date of application. This prevented the child from passing the maximum age and becoming ineligible for benefits because of bureaucratic delays in application processing. In January 2005 Senator Dianne Feinstein (D-CA) introduced the Unaccompanied Alien Child Protection Act of 2005 (S.119). The bill passed the Senate in December 2005, but by the end of 2006 it was still in committee with the U.S. House of Representatives. Similar legislation was introduced in both 2001 and 2003 without success. The proposed legislation was intended to prohibit placing such children in adult detention facilities or facilities housing delinquent children; prohibit the unreasonable use of restraints, solitary confinement, and strip searches; provide for appointing qualified and trained guardians for such children; and require guidelines be developed to ensure the children received appropriate legal counsel.

Angelina Jolie, an actress, UNHCR goodwill ambassador, and advocate for the protection of unaccompanied alien children, launched the National Center for Refugee and Immigrant Children in March 2005 in Washington, D.C. The center's focus is providing better access to free legal counsel for children who arrive alone in the United States and are fleeing persecution. In December 2006 the center (http://www.refugees.org/uploadedFiles/Participate/National_Center/NovDecember.pdf) reported receiving over 1,550 requests in the previous 18 months. More than 1,350 children had received assistance with change of venue, social service referrals, and information on continuances. A total of 480 children had been matched with pro bono (services offered for free) attorneys across the country.

CHAPTER 5
ILLEGAL ALIENS

BARRIERS TO LEGAL IMMIGRATION: TIME AND MONEY

According to Stuart Anderson and David Miller, in *Legal Immigrants: Waiting Forever* (May 2006, http://www.competeamerica.org/resource/h1b_glance/NFAP_Study.pdf), "those who 'play by the rules' are likely to wait many years" to enter the United States legally. The word is out around the world that there are jobs in the United States. Even low-paying jobs by U.S. standards far exceed what workers can earn in many parts of the world, if jobs were available in their impoverished countries. Many aliens who enter the United States accept high risk and sometimes great expense for a chance at jobs sooner rather than later. Their families often follow.

Long Waiting Time for Legal Entry Documents

The annual limit on the number of U.S. employment-based legal admissions is well below the number requested by potential immigrants seeking jobs. This has created backlogs in some categories. Anderson and Miller indicate that wait times in 2006 for new employer-sponsored skilled workers and professionals to receive green cards exceeded five years. The demand for "Other Worker" green cards exceeded the established annual limits to such an extent that the State Department set cutoff dates and only processed applications received before that date. This resulted in visas for Other Worker applicants as being "unavailable" for part of the year. (See Table 5.1.) Highly educated workers with specialty skills from China and India had been so heavily recruited that wait times ranged from one to three years. Anderson and Miller note that a worker being sponsored by a U.S. employer goes into a state of "limbo" while waiting for a green card. With no knowledge of when the card will arrive, the worker cannot make firm plans, secure housing, or travel freely; in most cases the worker cannot even change jobs in his or her home country.

There are no quotas for U.S. citizens sponsoring a spouse, minor children, or parents for legal entry, but annual limits do apply to siblings and adult children. According to Anderson and Miller, the waiting time for adult children of a U.S. citizen ranges from six to fifteen years. (See Table 5.2.) Siblings of a U.S. citizen can wait as long as twenty-two years. Waiting times are similarly long for spouses and minor children of legal permanent residents.

Obtaining a nonimmigrant visa is no simple task either. In May 2006 foreign nationals seeking a business or tourist visa waited as long as 169 days in Mumbai, India, for the required in-person interview at a U.S. consular office. (See Table 5.3.) Wait times varied dramatically by country. In May 2006 Vietnamese nationals could get an interview in 1 day at the U.S. consulate in Hanoi, whereas Mexico City visa seekers waited 122 days—an improvement from over 160 days in January 2006.

Cost of a U.S. Visa

Foreign visitors or immigrants who want to travel to the United States pay a variety of fees to obtain visas. Fees for visa services are collected by the U.S. Department of State's Bureau of Consular Affairs. Fees for services related to immigration status are collected by the U.S. Citizenship and Immigration Services (USCIS).

COMING TO THE UNITED STATES TEMPORARILY—TEMPORARY NONIMMIGRANT VISA SERVICES. Visas are classified by type of nonimmigrant visitor. A foreign government official has an A visa, and a student has an F visa. (See Table 5.4.) The State Department charges visa issuance fees based on reciprocity (what another country charges a U.S. citizen for a similar type of visa). For example, most countries welcome tourists and the money they spend, so they charge them no visa fees. Most U.S. B visas—temporary visitors for business or pleasure—have no fee. Yemen is one of the few countries

TABLE 5.1

Wait time for employment-based immigrants, June 2006

	China	India	Mexico	Philippines	All other countries
Priority workers (1st preference)	1 year wait (processing applications before July 2005)	1 year wait (processing applications before January 2006)	Numbers immediately available to qualified applicants	Numbers immediately available to qualified applicants	Numbers immediately available to qualified applicants
Advanced degree holders and persons of exceptional ability (2nd preference)	2 year wait (processing applications before July 2004)	3 year wait (processing applications before January 2003)	Numbers immediately available to qualified applicants	Numbers immediately available to qualified applicants	Numbers immediately available to qualified applicants
Skilled workers and professionals (3rd preference)	5 year wait (processing applications before July 2001)	5 year wait (processing applications before April 2001)	5 year wait (processing applications before April 2001)	5 year wait (processing applications before July 2001)	5 year wait (processing applications before July 2001)
Other workers (3rd preference)	Unavailable	Unavailable	Unavailable	Unavailable	Unavailable

Note: The relatively small number of those in the schedule A workers, certain special immigrants, and employment creation immigrants categories do not experience backlogs and are not included on the chart. Once a number/visa is available processing can take from 2 months at an overseas post to longer periods with U.S. Citizenship and Immigration Services. Of the 10,000 slots in the other workers category, 5,000 are available to be used for certain qualified Central Americans under legislation passed by Congress in 1997.

SOURCE: Stuart Anderson and David Miller, "Table 1. Wait Times for Employment-Based Immigrants," in *Legal Immigrants: Waiting Forever,* National Foundation for American Policy, May 2006, http://www.nfap.com/researchactivities/studies/NFAPStudyLegalImmigrantsWaitingForever052206.pdf (accessed January 6, 2007)

TABLE 5.2

Wait time for family-sponsored immigrants

[In years]

	China	India	Mexico	Philippines	All other countries
Unmarried adult children of U.S. citizens (1st preference) 23,400 a year	6 year wait (processing applications before April 2001)	6 year wait (processing applications before April 2001)	13 year wait (processing applications received before January 1992)	14 year wait (processing applications received before September 1991)	6 year wait (processing applications before April 2001)
Spouses and minor children of permanent residents (2nd Preference-A) 87,934 a year*	5 year wait (processing applications before April 2001)	5 year wait (processing applications before April 2001)	7 year wait (processing applications received before July 1999)	5 year wait (processing applications before April 2001)	5 year wait (processing applications before April 2001)
Unmarried adult children of permanent residents (2nd preference-B) 26,266 a year	9 year wait (processing applications before August 1996)	9 year wait (processing applications before August 1996)	14 year wait (processing applications before October 1991)	9 year wait (processing applications before July 1996)	9 year wait (processing applications before August 1996)
Married adult children of U.S. citizens (3rd preference) 23,400 a year	7 year wait (processing applications before August 1998)	7 year wait (processing applications before August 1988)	11 year wait (processing applications before March 1993)	15 year wait (processing applications before July 1988)	7 year wait (processing applications before August 1998)
Siblings of U.S. citizens (4th preference) 65,000 a year	11 year wait (processing applications before March 1995)	12 year wait (processing applications before August 1994)	12 year wait (processing applications before August 1993)	22 year wait (processing applications before November 1983)	11 year wait (processing applications before March 1995)

*The spouses and minor and adult children of permanent residents category is 114,200 annually "plus the number (if any) by which the worldwide family preference level exceeds 226,000". 75% of spouses and minor children of lawful permanent residents are exempt from the per-country limit.

SOURCE: Stuart Anderson and David Miller, "Table 4. Wait Time in Years for Family-Sponsored Immigrants," in *Legal Immigrants: Waiting Forever*, National Foundation for American Policy, May 2006, http://www.nfap.com/researchactivities/studies/NFAPStudyLegalImmigrantsWaitingForever052206.pdf (accessed January 6, 2007)

that charges a visa fee to U.S. business or pleasure visitors, including travelers and airline crew members passing through on the way to another country. Thus, the State Department charges reciprocal visa fees of $30 for these classifications of people from Yemen to enter the United States. The State Department's Visa Reciprocity Tables (March 12, 2007, http://travel.state.gov/visa/reciprocity/index.htm) identify reciprocal visa fees and special requirements by country.

In "Fees for Visa Services" (March 2005, http://travel.state.gov/visa/temp/types/types_1263.html), the State Department discusses the charges and other fees for processing visas and related documents. Examples of common fees are:

TABLE 5.3

Wait times for visa interviews at key consular posts

[In days]

City as of:	Visit or visa		Student/exchange visitor		Other non-immigrant visas	
	5/6/2006	1/10/2006	5/6/2006	1/10/2006	5/6/2006	1/10/2006
Beijing	14	34	2	6	2	27
Bogota	6	10	1	1	1	1
Brasilia	35	48	5	13	35	48
Calcutta	114	91	9	14	14	91
Caracas	37	32	7	7	7	7
Chennai	58	114	2	73	163	114
Hanoi	1	1	1	1	1	1
Managua	2	21	1	7	2	21
Manila	38	27	4	1	45	27
Mexico City	122	160	9	18	9	18
Moscow	21	7	10	7	10	7
Mumbai (Bombay)	169	98	10	20	18	98
New Dehli	98	40	14	4	14	50
Nogales	23	1	Same day	Same day	23	1
San Salvador	2	10	1	1	2	1
Seoul	3	3	3	3	3	3
Shanghai	31	31	1	3	2	1
Taipei	8	10	1	1	8	10
Tel Aviv	70	24	2	5	2	24
Warsaw	2	2	1	2	1	2

SOURCE: Stuart Anderson and David Miller, "Table 6. Wait Times in Days for Visa Interview Times at Key Consular Posts," in *Legal Immigrants: Waiting Forever*, National Foundation for American Policy, May 2006, http://www.nfap.com/researchactivities/studies/NFAPStudyLegalImmigrantsWaitingForever 052206.pdf (accessed January 6, 2007)

TABLE 5.4

U.S. nonimmigrant visa classifications

Category	Description
A	Foreign government officials
B	Temporary visitors for business or pleasure
C	Aliens in transit (airplane passenger passing through to another country)
D	Crew members (airplanes, ships)
E	Treaty traders and treaty investors
F	Academic students
G	Foreign government officials to international organizations
H	Temporary workers
I	Foreign media representatives
J	Exchange visitors
K	Fiance of a U.S. citizen
L	Intracompany transferee
M	Vocational and language students
N	Parent or child of certain "special immigrants"
NAFTA	North American Free Trade Agreement representatives
NATO	North Atlantic Treaty Organization representatives
O	Workers with extraordinary ability
P	Athletes and entertainers
Q	International cultural exchange visitors
R	Religious workers
S	Witness or informant of criminal organization or terrorism
T	Victims of severe forms of trafficking in persons
U	Victims of certain crimes
V	Nonimmigrant spouse of child of a U.S. permanent resident
TPS	Temporary protected status

SOURCE: Adapted from "Immigration Classification and Visa Categories," U.S. Citizenship and Immigration Services, http://www.uscis.gov/portal/site/ uscis (accessed January 22, 2007)

- Nonimmigrant visa application processing fee, Form DS-156 (nonrefundable): $100

- Border crossing card–10 year (age 15 and over) non-refundable: $100

- Border crossing card (under age 15) for Mexican citizen if parent or guardian has or is applying for a border-crossing card (nonrefundable): $13

COMING TO THE UNITED STATES PERMANENTLY— IMMIGRANT SERVICES. The USCIS, in "Immigration Forms" (2007, http://www.uscis.gov/), provides a complete list of immigration-related forms and fees. A few examples of fees are:

- Form I-130, petition to classify status of alien relative for issuance of immigrant visa: $190

- Form I-600, petition to classify an orphan as an immediate relative: $545

- Form I-485, application to register permanent residence or alien status (green card): $325

- Form N-400, application for naturalization: $330

FEES FUND THE USCIS BUDGET. Fees charged for immigrant services are intended to fund much of the expense of USCIS services. In fiscal year (FY) 2005 the USCIS collected over $1.5 billion in fees. (See Figure 5.1.) The forms generating the greatest shares of annual revenue ($184 million each) were the N-400 Naturalization (Citizenship)

FIGURE 5.1

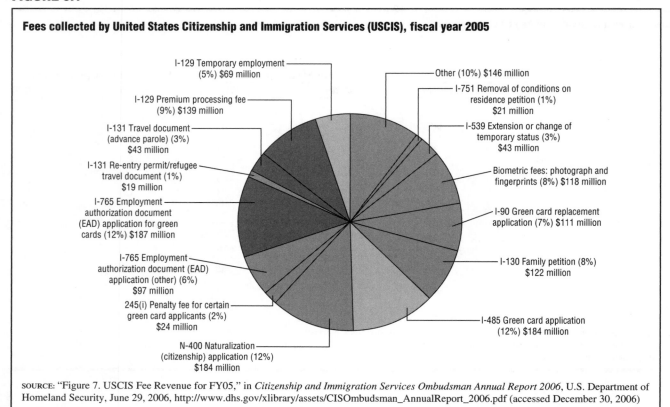

Fees collected by United States Citizenship and Immigration Services (USCIS), fiscal year 2005

I-129 Temporary employment (5%) $69 million

I-129 Premium processing fee (9%) $139 million

I-131 Travel document (advance parole) (3%) $43 million

I-131 Re-entry permit/refugee travel document (1%) $19 million

I-765 Employment authorization document (EAD) application for green cards (12%) $187 million

I-765 Employment authorization document (EAD) application (other) (6%) $97 million

245(i) Penalty fee for certain green card applicants (2%) $24 million

N-400 Naturalization (citizenship) application (12%) $184 million

Other (10%) $146 million

I-751 Removal of conditions on residence petition (1%) $21 million

I-539 Extension or change of temporary status (3%) $43 million

Biometric fees: photograph and fingerprints (8%) $118 million

I-90 Green card replacement application (7%) $111 million

I-130 Family petition (8%) $122 million

I-485 Green card application (12%) $184 million

SOURCE: "Figure 7. USCIS Fee Revenue for FY05," in *Citizenship and Immigration Services Ombudsman Annual Report 2006*, U.S. Department of Homeland Security, June 29, 2006, http://www.dhs.gov/xlibrary/assets/CISOmbudsman_AnnualReport_2006.pdf (accessed December 30, 2006)

Application and the I-485 Green Card Application. These two applications accounted for nearly one-fourth (24%) of documents processed by the USCIS in 2005.

In the *Citizenship and Immigration Services Ombudsman Annual Report 2006* (June 2006, http://www.dhs.gov/xlibrary/assets/CISOmbudsman_AnnualReport_2006.pdf), the U.S. Department of Homeland Security (DHS) suggests that some of the delays in the USCIS document processing generated additional revenue to the organization. For example, delays in green card processing caused the USCIS to issue interim Employment Authorization Documents (EADs) to waiting applicants. EAD fees represented 12% of the USCIS fee revenue in FY2005. (See Figure 5.1.) An EAD allows a green card applicant to obtain a Social Security number, a driver's license, and credit. Generally, the EAD gives the impression that the person has legal status in the United States when the status has not yet been determined. The DHS estimates that thousands of applicants who were ultimately found to be ineligible for a green card were issued EADs.

USCIS FEE INCREASE. The Migration Information Source notes in its December 2006 *Policy Beat* that the USCIS planned to raise fees in 2007 for immigration benefits, including green cards, work permits, and naturalization. Even though immigrant advocates argue that raising fees will present a further barrier to citizenship for

working-class immigrants, the USCIS defends increased fees as necessary to decrease backlogs in the system.

WHO IS AN ILLEGAL ALIEN?

The term *illegal alien* is used in legislation and by the U.S. Border Patrol to describe a person who is not legally authorized to live in the United States. Illegal aliens are also known as immigrants, migrants, or workers who are unauthorized, undocumented, or paperless. People often assume that the term *illegal alien* refers specifically to Mexicans who have crossed the U.S.-Mexican border. Although Mexicans account for a large share of the unauthorized entrants to the United States, illegal aliens can come from anywhere in the world.

An illegal alien is defined as a person who is not a U.S. citizen and who is in the United States in violation of U.S. immigration laws. An illegal alien could be one of the following:

- An undocumented alien who entered the United States without a visa, often between land ports of entry

- A person who entered the United States using fraudulent documentation

- A person who entered the United States legally with a temporary visa and then stayed beyond the time allowed (this person is often called a nonimmigrant overstay or a visa overstay)

- A legal permanent resident who committed a crime after entry, became subject to an order of deportation, but failed to depart

HOW MANY ILLEGAL ALIENS ARE THERE?

Because illegal aliens do not readily identify themselves for fear of deportation, it is almost impossible to determine how many illegal aliens are in the United States. Various sources estimate between two million and twelve million, but these estimates are little more than educated guesses and are often politically influenced. The wide variance among the estimates is an indication of their unreliability. Furthermore, the number of illegal aliens varies somewhat between the winter and summer months based on availability of agricultural work.

Estimates of the Illegal Alien Population Vary

According to the Congressional Budget Office, in *The Role of Immigrants in the U.S. Labor Market* (November 2005, http://www.cbo.gov/ftpdocs/68xx/doc6853/11-10-Immigration.pdf), government estimates, based on data from the U.S. Bureau of the Census and various federal agencies, counted 10 million U.S. illegal aliens in 2004, with 6.3 million of these in the workforce. In *The Underground Labor Force Is Rising to the Surface* (January 3, 2005, http://www.firecoalition.com/docs/bear%20stearns%20study.pdf), Robert Justich and Betty Ng of Bear Stearns Asset Management dispute estimates of the illegal alien population that were based on Census Bureau counts. They suggest that the Census Bureau accounted for only half of the illegal alien population. They project that the 2004 illegal alien population was as great as twenty million. Justich and Ng arrive at this figure using increases in school enrollments, foreign remittances (money sent by foreign workers to their families back home), border crossings, and housing permits.

In *Immigrants at Mid-decade: A Snapshot of America's Foreign-Born Population in 2005* (December 2005, http://www.cis.org/articles/2005/back1405.pdf), Steven A. Camerota of the Center for Immigration Studies pegs the total illegal population in 2005 at 9.6 to 9.8 million. Researchers debate the accuracy of Census Bureau counts in the Current Population Survey, noting that other research indicates roughly 10% of the illegal population was not counted. This would raise the illegal population to nearly eleven million in March 2005.

Jeffrey S. Passel of the Pew Hispanic Center in *Size and Characteristics of the Unauthorized Migrant Population in the U.S.* (March 7, 2006, http://pewhispanic.org/files/reports/61.pdf) estimates the unauthorized population at 11.5 to 12 million in 2006. Passel indicates that in 2005 Mexican nationals comprised 56% of the illegal immigrant population and that immigrants from Latin

FIGURE 5.2

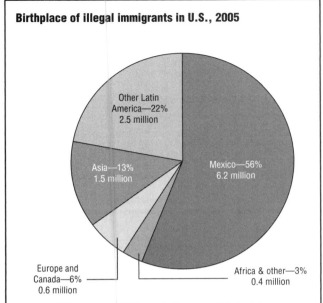

Birthplace of illegal immigrants in U.S., 2005

SOURCE: Jeffrey S. Passel, "Figure 4. Country of Birth of the Unauthorized Migrant Population: March 2005," in *The Size and Characteristics of the Unauthorized Migrant Population in the U.S.*, Pew Hispanic Center, March 7, 2006, http://pewhispanic.org/files/reports/61.pdf (accessed December 13, 2006). © 2006 Pew Hispanic Center, a Pew Research Center project, www.pewhispanic.org.

American countries represented another 22%. (See Figure 5.2.) In the fact sheet "Modes of Entry for the Unauthorized Migrant Population" (May 22, 2005, http://pewhispanic.org/files/factsheets/19.pdf), the Pew Hispanic Center estimates that half of all illegal aliens living in the United States originally entered the country legally through a port of entry such as an airport or border crossing point. They came on visas or border crossing cards (good for frequent short visits and commuting back and forth to work) and simply did not leave. This group totaled an estimated 4.5 to 6 million people. (See Table 5.5.)

MONITORING WHO COMES AND GOES

Following the terrorist attacks of September 11, 2001 (9/11), it became apparent that some or all of the perpetrators had entered the United States legally and that many had overstayed their allotted time with no notice taken by the U.S. Immigration and Naturalization Service (INS, now the USCIS) or any other enforcement agency. On March 1, 2003, the INS and the U.S. Customs Service were folded into the newly created Department of Homeland Security. Within the DHS the new U.S. Customs and Border Protection (CBP) agency oversaw the movement of goods and people into the United States, and the U.S. Immigration and Customs Enforcement (ICE) was responsible for enforcing immigration laws within the United States. On March 17, 2004, Asa Hutchinson

TABLE 5.5

Modes of entry for the unauthorized migrant population, 2006

Entered legally with inspection	Non-immigrant visa overstayers	4 to 5.5 million
	Border crossing card violators	250,000 to 500,000
	Sub-total legal entries	**4.5 to 6 million**
Entered illegally without inspection	Evaded the immigration inspectors and border patrol	6 to 7 million
Estimated total unauthorized population in 2006		11.5 to 12 million

Note: Estimates based on the March 2005 Current Population Survey (CPS) and Department of Homeland Security reports.

SOURCE: "Modes of Entry for the Unauthorized Migrant Population," in Fact Sheet, Pew Hispanic Center, May 22, 2006, http://pewhispanic.org/files/factsheets/19.pdf (accessed January 15, 2007). © 2006 Pew Hispanic Center, a Pew Research Center project, www.pewhispanic.org.

(http://www.globalsecurity.org/security/library/congress/2004_h/040317-hutchinson.doc), the undersecretary for border and transportation security, addressed the challenges of border control before the Subcommittee on Infrastructure and Border Security of the House Select Committee on Homeland Security. Five hundred million nonimmigrant visitors enter the United States annually. Ports of entry into the United States stretch across 7,500 miles of land border with Mexico and Canada and 95,000 miles of shoreline and navigable rivers. Among more than three hundred air, land, and sea ports of entry, conditions and venues vary considerably, from air and sea ports in metropolitan New York City with dozens of employees to a two-person land entry point in North Dakota.

Nonimmigrant Overstays

Despite congressional initiatives to track foreign visitors after the 1993 World Trade Center bombing, and again after 9/11, by 2006 the United States was not able to determine whether temporary foreign visitors had actually left the country. Section 110 of the Illegal Immigration Reform and Immigrant Responsibility Act of 1996 (IIRIRA) mandated that the INS develop an automated system to track the entry and exit of all noncitizens entering or leaving all ports of entry, including land borders and sea ports. The INS, the Canadian government, and the airline industry, among others, opposed Section 110. According to the INS, it lacked the resources to put in place such an integrated system. The Canadian government claimed that filling out the entry form (Form I-94) and having it checked by INS inspectors would cause large backups at the border. The airlines considered Section 110 an additional reporting burden.

A PAPER TRACKING SYSTEM. The I-94 form had long been the primary tracking document for nonimmigrant visitors entering the United States with a visa. (See Figure 5.3.) This form, which was still in use in 2007, has two specific perforated sections to it. The top section provides arrival information. The bottom section is a departure coupon that should be returned to U.S. officials when exiting the United States. Many visitors lose the form or simply fail to return it on departure. Some visitors leave by different ports from where they enter, creating either a challenge for matching paper stubs or a data entry workload. Thus, immigration officials lose track of who actually remains in the country as visa overstays.

US-VISIT—AN ELECTRONIC TRACKING SYSTEM. On June 15, 2000, Congress passed the Immigration and Naturalization Service Data Management Improvement Act to amend Section 110 of the IIRIRA. It required implementation of an electronic system—U.S. Visitor and Immigrant Status Indicator Technology (US-VISIT)—using available data to identify lawfully admitted nonimmigrants who might have overstayed their visits. The proposed system would scan visitors' fingerprints and check them against databases of known terrorists and criminals. It would also scan passports and record entries and departures. The system was to be operational at all ports of entry by December 31, 2005. In FY2004 a total of 335.3 million people entered the United States through land ports of entry. (See Figure 5.4.) Even though US-VISIT processed 42.2% of the 75.1 million international travelers arriving at airports that year, it processed just 1.4% of people arriving at land ports of entry. These numbers included U.S. citizens who were not subject to US-VISIT processing. According to the DHS, in "US-VISIT: Current Ports of Entry" (November 27, 2006, http://www.dhs.gov/xtrvlsec/programs/editorial_0685.shtm), US-VISIT biometric entry procedures were in place at 116 airports, 15 seaports, and in the secondary inspection areas of 154 of 170 land ports of entry as of November 2006. However, pilot programs for exit procedures were in operation at just twelve airports and two seaports.

US-VISIT EXIT SYSTEM PROBLEMS. In *Border Security: US-VISIT Program Faces Strategic, Operational, and Technological Challenges at Land Ports of Entry* (December 2006, http://www.gao.gov/new.items/d07248.pdf), the Government Accountability Office reports that "for various reasons, a biometric US-VISIT exit capability cannot now be implemented without incurring a major impact on land POE [port of entry] facilities. An interim nonbiometric exit technology being tested ... does not meet the statutory requirement for a biometric exit capability and cannot ensure that visitors who enter the country are those who leave. ... US-VISIT officials stated that they believe a biometrically based solution that does not require those exiting the country to stop for processing, that minimizes the need for major facility changes, and that can [be] used to definitively match a visitor's entry and exit will be available in 5 to 10 years. In the interim, it remains unclear how officials plan to proceed." Appropriations for this border security

FIGURE 5.3

Form I-94

DEPARTMENT OF HOMELAND SECURITY
U.S. Customs and Border Protection

OMB No. 1651-0111

Admission Number

Welcome to the United States

I-94 Arrival/Departure Record - Instructions

This form must be completed by all persons except U.S. Citizens, returning resident aliens, aliens with immigrant visas, and Canadian Citizens visiting or in transit.

Type or print legibly with pen in ALL CAPITAL LETTERS. Use English. Do not write on the back of this form.

This form is in two parts. Please complete both the Arrival Record (Items 1 through 13) and the Departure Record (Items 14 through 17).

When all items are completed, present this form to the CBP Officer.

Item 7 - If you are entering the United States by land, enter **LAND** in this space. If you are entering the United States by ship, enter **SEA** in this space.

CBP Form I-94 (10/04)

Admission Number

OMB No. 1651-0111

Arrival Record

1. Family Name
2. First (Given) Name
3. Birth Date (Day/Mo/Yr)
4. Country of Citizenship
5. Sex (Male or Female)
6. Passport Number
7. Airline and Flight Number
8. Country Where You Live
9. City Where You Boarded
10. City Where Visa was Issued
11. Date Issued (Day/Mo/Yr)
12. Address While in the United States (Number and Street)
13. City and State

CBP Form I-94 (10/04)

Departure Number

OMB No. 1651-0111

**I-94
Departure Record**

14. Family Name
15. First (Given) Name
16. Birth Date (Day/Mo/Yr)
17. Country of Citizenship

CBP Form I-94 (10/04)

See Other Side

STAPLE HERE

FIGURE 5.3

Form I-94

This Side For Government Use Only
Primary Inspection

Applicant's Name

Date Referred _____ Time _____ Insp. # _____

Reason Referred

☐ 212A ☐☐ ☐ PP ☐ Visa ☐ Parole ☐ SLB ☐ TWOV

☐ Other

Secondary Inspection

End Secondary Time _____ Insp. # _____

Disposition

18. Occupation
19. Waivers
20. CIS A Number
A -
21. CIS FCO
22. Petition Number
23. Program Number
24. ☐ Bond
25. ☐ Prospective Student

26. Itinerary/Comments

27. TWOV Ticket Number

Warning A nonimmigrant who accepts unauthorized employment is subject to deportation.
Important - Retain this permit in your possession; *you must surrender it when you leave the U.S.* Failure to do so may delay your entry into the U.S. in the future. You are authorized to stay in the U.S. only until the date written on this form.To remain past this date, without permission from Department of Homeland Security authorities, is a violation of the law.
Surrender this permit when you leave the U.S.:
  - By sea or air, to the transportation line;
  - Across the Canadian border, to a Canadian Official;
  - Across the Mexican border, to a U.S. Official.
Students planning to reenter the U.S. within 30 days to return to the same school, see "Arrival-Departure" on page 2 of Form 1-20 **prior to surrendering this permit.**

Record of Changes

Port: **Departure Record**
Date:
Carrier:
Flight # / Ship Name:

SOURCE: Form I-94, U.S. Customs and Border Protection, http://www.cbp.gov/xp/cgov/travel/id_visa/i-94_instructions/filling_out_i94.xml (accessed January 18, 2007)

FIGURE 5.4

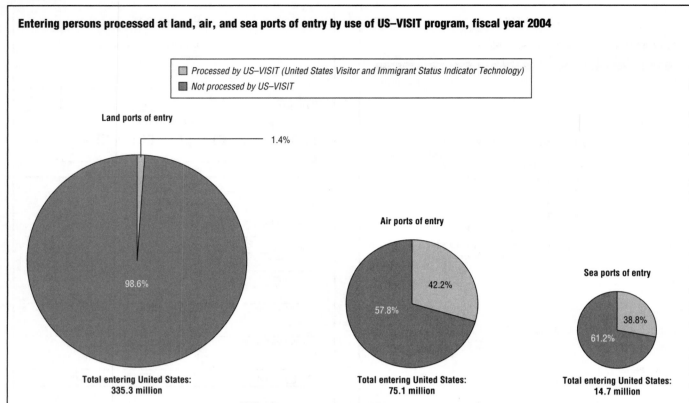

Entering persons processed at land, air, and sea ports of entry by use of US–VISIT program, fiscal year 2004

☐ Processed by US–VISIT (United States Visitor and Immigrant Status Indicator Technology)
■ Not processed by US–VISIT

Land ports of entry

1.4%

98.6%

Total entering United States:
335.3 million

Air ports of entry

42.2%

57.8%

Total entering United States:
75.1 million

Sea ports of entry

38.8%

61.2%

Total entering United States:
14.7 million

Note: Persons processed by US–VISIT may include foreign nationals who were also issued an I-94 valid for multiple entries and who have re-entered multiple times. Total entering the U.S. includes U.S. citizens who may have re-entered the country multiple times and foreign nationals, including those not issued I-94s, such as Canadian citizens and Mexicans with BCCs, and those issued multiple entry I-94s who also may have re-entered multiple times. U.S. citizens do not fall within the statutory scope of US–VISIT and therefore are exempt from US–VISIT screening.

SOURCE: "Figure 1. Persons Processed under US–VISIT as a Percentage of All Border Crossings at Land, Air and Sea Ports of Entry, Fiscal Year 2004," in *Border Security: US–VISIT Program Faces Strategic, Operational, and Technological Challenges at Land Ports of Entry*, U.S. Government Accountability Office, GAO-07-248, December 2006, http://www.gao.gov/new.items/d07248.pdf (accessed January 22, 2007)

TABLE 5.6

US-VISIT appropriations, fiscal years 2003–07

[In millions of dollars]

Budget activity	2003 appropriated	2004 appropriated	2005 appropriated	2006 appropriated	2007 appropriated
US-VISIT	$362	$328	$340	$337	$362

Note: Starting in fiscal year 2004, funding for the US-VISIT (United States Visitor and Immigration Status Indicator Technology) program has been appropriated on a "no-year" basis, meaning that there is no time limit on the spending of appropriated funds; funds that remain unexpended at the end of a fiscal year are carried over into the next fiscal year.

SOURCE: "Table 2. US-VISIT Appropriations Enacted, Fiscal Years 2003 through 2007 (in Millions of Dollars)," in *Border Security: US-VISIT Program Faces Strategic, Operational, and Technological Challenges at Land Ports of Entry*, U.S. Government Accountability Office, GAO-07-248, December 2006, http://www.gao.gov/new.items/d07248.pdf (accessed January 22, 2007)

program over five fiscal years totaled $1.7 billion through 2007. (See Table 5.6.)

Visa Waiver Program

According to the press release "Vast Majority of Visa Waiver Countries Meet Security Upgrade to e-Passports" (October 26, 2006, http://www.dhs.gov/xnews/releases/ pr_1161876358429.shtm), the DHS reports that each year approximately fifteen million people travel to the United States without a visa to stay ninety days or less for business or pleasure. Citizens of any of the twenty-seven countries participating in the Visa Waiver Program (VWP) can enter the United States on a passport issued by their country of citizenship. Representatives of the foreign press, radio, film, journalists, or other information media cannot use the visa waiver when traveling for professional pursuits.

NEW REQUIREMENTS FOR PASSPORTS. In the Enhanced Border Security and Visa Entry Reform Act of 2002, as amended, Congress mandated machine-readable, biometric passports would be required for all VWP travelers by October 26, 2006. Children would no longer be able to travel on their parents' passports. This change required VWP countries to certify that they had programs in place to issue their citizens machine-readable passports that incorporated biometric identifiers and complied with standards established by the International Civil Aviation Organization.

The new passports are identified by an international e-Passport logo on the cover and contain a secure contactless chip with the passport holder's biographic information and a biometric identifier. Biometric data are measurable physical characteristics or personal behavioral traits used to recognize the identity or verify the claimed identity of an enrollee. Among the features that can be measured are face, fingerprints, hand geometry, handwriting, iris, retina, vein, and voice. The size of the passport and photograph, and the arrangement of data fields, especially the two lines of data, have to be exact to be read by an Optical Character Reader. The DHS states in the October 26, 2006, press release that twenty-four of the twenty-seven VWP countries have met the requirements for issuing e-Passports.

TRACKING SECURITY RISKS. The National Security Entry-Exit Registration System was launched in 2003 to track nonimmigrant visitors coming from designated countries and others who meet a combination of intelligence-based criteria that identify them as potential security risks. State Department offices in foreign countries identify such people when issuing visas. These individuals are required to register on arrival at a port of entry, participate in an interview with the Bureau of Citizenship and Immigration before being allowed into the country, and report any change of address, employment, or educational institution while in the country. They are also required to register on departure and are restricted to using certain designated ports of entry/departure. This system focuses only on the preidentified security risk visitors.

BORDERS ON THE WATER

The U.S. Coast Guard is responsible for preventing unauthorized people from entering the United States by water. The Coast Guard reports in "USCG Migrant Interdictions" (April 19, 2007, http://www.uscg.mil/hq/g-o/g-opl/amio/FlowStats/currentstats.html) that in FY2006 it intercepted 7,886 illegal entry attempts, which it refers to as "alien migrant interdictions." Most aliens attempting to enter the country by water came from Central America and the Car-

ibbean. The largest share of 2006 interdictions, 2,810 or 36%, came from Cuba. The United States has long maintained a unique "wet-foot, dry-foot" policy toward Cuban migrants. A Cuban who reaches U.S. land is allowed to apply for asylum, but those captured in the water are returned to Cuba.

In 2005 the Coast Guard caught and returned 2,712 Cuban migrants. However, according to Alan Gomez, in "More Cubans Take Trip to USA, Using Alternate Routes" (*USA Today*, November 15, 2006), the Department of Homeland Security reports that twice as many (6,356) Cubans reached land that year. When rumors of Fidel Castro's declining health surfaced, the Coast Guard began seeing an upsurge in Cubans attempting to enter the United States. The Coast Guard reports that during FY2002 it intercepted 666 Cubans who were trying to enter the United States illegally by sea; by FY2006 the number had increased 322% to 2,810, as noted above.

U.S. BORDER PATROL

The U.S. Border Patrol, the mobile, uniformed law enforcement arm of the Customs and Border Protection agency, is responsible for the detection and apprehension of illegal aliens and smugglers of aliens at or near U.S. land borders.

Southwest Border

The biggest illegal entry problems occur along the nearly two-thousand-mile U.S.-Mexican border. The CBP (2007, http://apps.cbp.gov/bwt/index.asp) reports that the four states bordering Mexico—Texas, New Mexico, Arizona, and California—have thirty-six ports of entry. According to the U.S. Mexico Border Health Commission (January 2004, http://www.paho.org/English/DD/PIN/sv_border.ppt#290,5,Region), 6.4 million Mexican nationals reside in the Mexican municipalities along the southwestern border.

A FENCE TO CONTROL ENTRY. The United States began using barrier fencing in the 1990s to deter illegal entry and drug smuggling, particularly to prevent vehicle entry. Blas Nuñez-Nito and Stephen Viña of the Congressional Research Service report in *Border Security: Barriers along the U.S. International Border* (December 12, 2006, http://www.fas.org/sgp/crs/homesec/RL33659.pdf) that the fourteen-mile fence at San Diego, the nation's busiest border port of entry, was the first constructed. It was strengthened by increased Border Patrol staffing. Nuñez-Nito and Viña indicate that increased enforcement in San Diego had "little impact on overall apprehensions" of illegal entrants. The border barrier simply shifted illegal traffic to more remote areas. The Border Patrol reports the same number of apprehensions in 2004 (1.2 million) as it had in 1992. The difference is that the bulk of the apprehensions shifted from San Diego in 1992 to Tucson and Yuma, Arizona, in 2004.

According to Nuñez-Nito and Viña, an unintended consequence of this shift in migration paths was an increase in migrant deaths. The 1990s annual average of 200 deaths during attempted border crossings rose to 472 in 2005. Nuñez-Nito and Viña also report increased crime in the more remote border areas.

A 150-mile stretch of fence was added in conjunction with the National Park Service near Yuma, and the Secure Fence Act of 2006 directed the Department of Homeland Security to build an additional 850 miles of border fence. Nuñez-Nito and Viña note the proliferation of tunnels that have been dug under border fences. One tunnel discovered under the fourteen-mile-long San Diego fence was built of reinforced concrete, suggesting a sophisticated smuggling operation. The Border Patrol reports that fencing is most effective in urban areas, where populated neighborhoods are only a short distance away for border crossers; in areas of open land, agents prefer to see as far as possible without obstructions.

A DANGEROUS JOURNEY. Some illegal aliens drown while trying to swim across the Rio Grande, which forms the border between Texas and Mexico. Others fall prey to border bandits, who steal from them and injure or kill them. Others die from exposure in the desert or as a result of negligence on the part of smugglers paid to take them into the United States. Some have perished because the smugglers' trucks were poorly ventilated. In 2004 Tucson's *Arizona Daily Star* newspaper established a searchable database (http://regulus.azstarnet.com/borderdeaths/search.php) of deaths occurring on the U.S.-Mexican border as recorded by the medical examiners in four Arizona counties: Pima, Santa Cruz, Cochise, and Yuma. The total death count for FY2006 was 206. Using information supplied by the Mexican secretary of foreign relations, Arizona medical examiners, and local law enforcement, the paper creates the online database, which can be used by relatives searching for missing family members who left to cross the border and were never heard from again.

MORE THAN MEXICANS USE THE BORDER AS A GATEWAY TO THE UNITED STATES. The U.S.-Mexican border offers an illegal crossing point for people from all over the world. According to Joel Millman and Gina Chon, in "Lost in Translation: Iraq's Injured 'Terps'" (*Wall Street Journal*, January 18, 2007), an Iraqi national explained that he hoped to hire a smuggler to take him from the Middle East to Tijuana, Mexico, and across the border into San Diego. The man knew others who had made the journey and joined a growing Iraqi community in southern California. The man was one of many Iraqi interpreters injured while working for the U.S. military.

Millman and Chon indicate that interpreter jobs are attractive because they pay $1,050 per month (three times the pay of an Iraqi police officer) plus extra pay for duty in particularly hazardous areas. Injured interpreters are treated in a hospital in Jordan, but Jordan does not want to keep them as refugees. They cannot go home; considered enemy collaborators, their presence would endanger their families. Medical care for their injuries is covered by the employer (a government contractor). According to Millman and Chon, injury-compensation packages (to cover future income loss because of the severity of injury) range from $20,000 to $200,000—enough to pay travel expenses and a smuggler for a new but illegal life in the United States.

In 2005 Congress approved a special immigration program to admit fifty interpreters per year from Iraq and Afghanistan (combined) who completed at least one year's service with U.S. troops. The application for immigration requires high-level recommendations, which is difficult to obtain for interpreters who rarely meet anyone above the rank of lieutenant or captain. A DHS spokesperson told Millman and Chon that an interpreter who fears persecution if he or she returns to Iraq can apply for refugee admission. There were 5,500 slots in 2007 for refugees from Iraq, Afghanistan, Iran, Saudi Arabia, India, Pakistan, and other countries in the Near East and South Asia, plus 20,000 undesignated reserve slots not tied to a particular area. Millman and Chon contacted Assistant Secretary of State Ellen Sauerbrey, who said just 466 Iraqis had been admitted to the United States as refugees since the 2003 U.S.-British invasion.

Northern Border

According to the International Boundary Commission, the U.S./Canadian border stretches 5,525 miles over land and waterways, including the portion between Alaska and Canada. Border security assessments following the September 11 terrorist attacks highlighted the vulnerability of the northern border and prompted U.S. Immigration and Customs Enforcement to increase staff. According to the fact sheet "Securing the Northern Border" (August 14, 2006, http://www.ice.gov/pi/news/factsheets/securing_northern_borders.htm), in 2001, 340 agents guarded the U.S.-Canadian border and not all crossing points were guarded full time. By 2006 the number of agents had nearly tripled to 980. Furthermore, the number of CBP inspectors increased from 1,615 to 3,391 between 2001 and 2006.

IDENTIFICATION OF THOSE WHO ENTER. The Intelligence Reform and Terrorism Prevention Act of 2004 required the DHS and the State Department to implement a plan requiring all travelers, U.S. citizens, and foreign nationals to present a passport or other identity and citizenship documents when entering the United States.

Previously U.S. citizens could enter and return from certain nearby countries such as Canada and Mexico without a passport. The proposed plan was called the Western Hemisphere Travel Initiative. Beginning on January 23, 2007, all people, including U.S. citizens, traveling by air between the United States and Canada, Mexico, Central and South America, the Caribbean, and Bermuda were required to present a valid passport, Air NEXUS card, U.S. Coast Guard Merchant Mariner Document, or an Alien Registration Card. As early as January 1, 2008, the requirements will be expanded to include arrivals by land or sea (including ferries).

According to the article "Passport Rules Worry Canada, Border States" (Associated Press, January 18, 2007), only seventy-three million U.S. citizens (less than one-third of all citizens) currently hold valid passports. The cost of a new passport—$97 for an adult and $82 for a child—might be prohibitive for some citizens. As a result, U.S. and Canadian officials began discussing border crossing cards, which are already in use on the U.S.-Mexican border, as an alternative. Canadian officials are concerned about delays and clogged traffic at U.S.-Canadian border crossings. Affected counties that have enjoyed easy access for international tourists worry about revenue losses.

U.S. AND CANADIAN OPINIONS ABOUT THE BORDER. In "Survey of U.S. Border State Voters and Canadians about New Border Regulations" (February 2006, http://www.citywindsor.ca/DisplayAttach.asp?AttachID=5082), Zogby International surveyed a sample of Americans and Canadians living in states or territories near the U.S.-Canadian border about the impending changes in border crossing procedures. Even though a greater number of Americans cross into Canada per year, Canadians report crossing the border more frequently (48% of Canadians enter the United States "a few times per year," compared with 17% of Americans entering Canada as often).

Vacationing is the most frequent reason for 56% of Americans and 44% of Canadians to cross the border. Shopping/entertainment and visiting relatives are the next most frequent reasons for border crossing. Canadians are more likely to stay a week in the United States, whereas Americans are more likely to stay two or three days in Canada. The people surveyed support border security concerns, but 68% of Americans and 70% of Canadians think there is no need for a border crossing ID; they believe a driver's license should be sufficient. A majority on both sides—68% of Americans and 54% of Canadians—say they are unlikely to purchase an ID card.

According to a Zogby poll released on January 19, 2007 (http://www.zogby.com/news/ReadNews.dbm?ID=1239), most Americans welcome the new passport rules. A 76% majority believe a valid passport should be required for all travelers entering the United States from Canada or Mex-

ico. The new passport requirements will make no difference in travel plans for 85% of Americans traveling to Canada and 86% traveling to Mexico.

MEXICO'S UNIQUE RELATIONSHIP WITH THE UNITED STATES

In no other place in the world does a nation as wealthy as the United States share a border with a nation as poor as Mexico. Huge disparities exist between the rich and poor people of Mexico, so it is understandable that Mexico's poor are attracted to the United States.

An Open Border

Before the twentieth century Mexicans moved easily back and forth across completely open borders to work in the mines, on the ranches, and on the railroad. Even though just 734 Mexicans immigrated between 1890 and 1899, 31,188 came between 1900 and 1909. (See Table 1.1 in Chapter 1.) The flow of immigrants to the United States from Mexico soared to 185,334 between 1910 and 1919 and reached 498,945 between 1920 and 1929.

A large amount of illegal immigration also occurred. Some historians estimate that during the 1920s there might have been more illegal Mexican aliens than legal immigrants. The need for Mexican labor was so great in the United States that in 1918 the commissioner-general of immigration exempted Mexicans from meeting most immigration conditions, such as head taxes (small amounts paid to come into the country) and literacy requirements.

First Illegal Alien "Problem"

The increase in the number of illegal aliens from Mexico led to the creation of the U.S. Border Patrol in 1924. The United States had maintained a small force of mounted guards to deter alien smuggling, but this force was inadequate to stop large numbers of illegal aliens. The efforts of the Border Patrol contributed to a sharp increase in the number of aliens deported during the 1920s and 1930s.

In 1929 administrative control along the U.S.-Mexican border was significantly tightened as the Great Depression led many Americans to blame the nation's unemployment on the illegal aliens. Consequently, thousands of Mexicans—both legal immigrants and illegal aliens—were repatriated (sent back to Mexico). According to David Spener, in *Mexican Migration to the United States, 1882–1992: A Long Twentieth Century of Coyotaje* the Mexican-born population in the United States declined from 639,000 in 1930 to 377,000 in 1940 (Center for Comparative Immigration Studies, October 2005, http://www.ccis-ucsd.org/publications/wrkg124.pdf).

Bracero Program

World War II brought the country out of the Great Depression. Industry expanded and drew rural laborers into the cities. Other workers were drafted and went off to war. Once more, the United States needed laborers, especially farm workers, and the nation again turned to Mexico. In "Bracero Program" (June 6, 2001, http://www.tsha.utexas.edu/handbook/online/articles/BB/omb1.html), Fred L. Koestler notes that the Bracero Program was a negotiated treaty between the United States and Mexico, permitting the entry of Mexican farm workers on a temporary basis under contract to U.S. employers. The entire program lasted from 1942 to 1964 and involved approximately 4.5 million Mexican workers.

North American Free Trade Agreement

In December 1993 the North American Free Trade Agreement (NAFTA) was passed to eliminate trade and investment barriers among the United States, Canada, and Mexico over a fifteen-year period. NAFTA was intended to promote economic growth in each country so that, in the long run, the number of illegal immigrants seeking to enter the United States for work would diminish. One of NAFTA's provisions facilitated temporary entry on a reciprocal basis among the three countries. It established procedures for Canadian and Mexican citizens who were professional businesspeople to temporarily enter the United States to render services for pay. President Bill Clinton claimed that more jobs on both sides of the southwestern border meant more income for Mexican nationals, which would help reduce the number of undocumented aliens entering the United States.

IMPACT OF ILLEGAL IMMIGRATION ON COUNTIES ALONG THE SOUTHWESTERN BORDER

Front Line—Twenty-four U.S. Counties on the Border

The US/Mexico Border Counties Coalition (USMBCC) commissioned a study of the economic condition of the twenty-four U.S. counties that are contiguous with Mexico. The resulting report, *At the Cross Roads: US/Mexico Border Counties in Transition* (March 2006, http://www.bordercounties.org/index.asp?Type=B_BASIC&SEC={62E35327-57C7-4978-A39A-36A8E00387B6}), was based on research conducted by the Institute for Policy and Economic Development. The report addressed the question: "If these 24 counties were the 51st state, how would they compare with the rest of the nation?"

The USMBCC notes that prosperous San Diego County in California is an anomaly among the border counties. Even though it shares many of the border problems, its per capita income is greater than the combined incomes of the other twenty-four border counties. For this reason, San Diego County data are omitted, unless otherwise noted, in the data reported in this chapter.

POPULATION. Figure 5.5 maps the twenty-four U.S. border counties located in California, Arizona, New Mexico, and Texas, and the adjoining states of Mexico. According to the USMBCC, these border counties collectively experienced a 29.3% growth rate from 1990 to reach a population of 6.7 million residents in 2006. The border counties were home to 5% of the nation's foreign-born residents, and nearly 72% of the foreign-born living in the border counties were from Mexico.

EMPLOYMENT. The USMBCC notes that from 1993 to 2003 total full-time and part-time jobs increased by nearly 800,000 in the border counties. However, half the job gains were in San Diego County and another quarter of new jobs were in Pima and El Paso counties. San Diego County claimed 52.3% of total jobs along the border and 60.7% of all wages and salaries. By contrast, the unemployment rate in twenty-two of the twenty-four border counties was double the national average. Nine border counties had unemployment rates more than 10%. Except for San Diego County, the border counties lacked private industry jobs in the high-paying professional, scientific, and technical sectors. Many border counties had high employment in health services because of state and federal assistance programs and growing retiree services in areas such as Pima and Doña Ana counties. Retail businesses were important to the border economy with many Mexican residents crossing the border to shop.

Between 1993 and 2003 the USMBCC indicates that the total personal income in the border counties increased 41.4%, compared with 29.3% in the other counties within the four states. However, more than 21% of personal income in the border counties (not including San Diego) came from transfer receipts, such as government assistance. When compared with the fifty states, the border counties (including San Diego) would have ranked thirty-first in per capita income in 1970. (See Table 5.7.) By 2003 these counties (including San Diego) would have dropped to thirty-ninth among the states. Without San Diego the border counties would have been dead last by 1990.

The USMBCC notes that from 1990 to 2006 crime rates in border counties dropped 30%. Property crimes dropped 40% and violent crime rates were among the lowest in the nation. The region also boasted low housing costs. These factors offer potential for attracting industries seeking affordable housing for staff relocation as well as industries serving retirees seeking warm climates with affordable housing.

HEALTH AND HEALTH CARE. Table 5.8 offers some of the key findings by the USMBCC. Ten of the twenty-six findings relate to health issues.

Health issues are of significant concern in the border counties, where much of the population lacks health insurance and access to health care facilities. The USMBCC

FIGURE 5.5

Twenty-four U.S. counties bordering Mexico

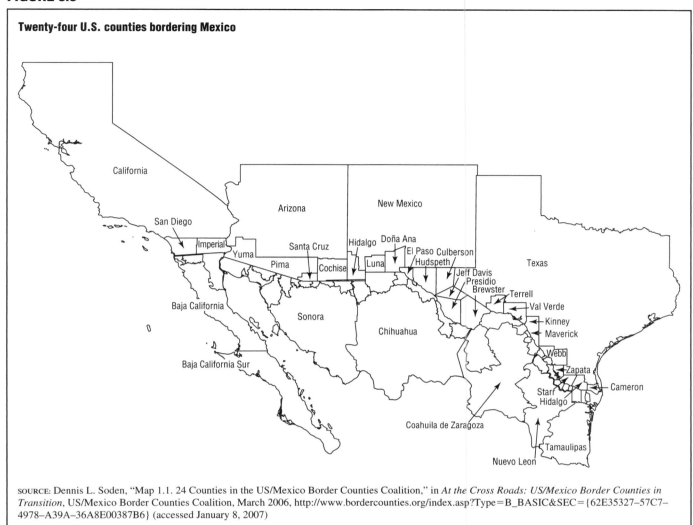

SOURCE: Dennis L. Soden, "Map 1.1. 24 Counties in the US/Mexico Border Counties Coalition," in *At the Cross Roads: US/Mexico Border Counties in Transition*, US/Mexico Border Counties Coalition, March 2006, http://www.bordercounties.org/index.asp?Type=B_BASIC&SEC={62E35327–57C7–4978–A39A–36A8E00387B6} (accessed January 8, 2007)

states that, according to the American Hospital Association, the $800 million in uncompensated care provided by hospitals in the twenty-four border counties was approximately 3% of annual uncompensated care in all U.S. hospitals. The USMBCC also cites the National Association of Counties, which stated that undocumented immigrants account for nearly 25% of uncompensated costs incurred by border county hospitals. According to the USMBCC, a large migrating population between the United States and Mexico relies heavily on public and charity health programs. As this significant "segment of the population moves back and forth across the U.S.-Mexico border, they become transfer agents of contagions and potential illnesses."

The acquired immunodeficiency syndrome (AIDS) rate per 100,000 population in the combined border counties was 16.1, which was higher than the national rate of 15.2. (See Table 5.9.) However, in Pima County the rate was 34.7 per 100,000 population and in San Diego County it was 20.2. Twelve of the twenty-four

border counties reported rates above the nationwide rate of 2.6 per 100,000 population for hepatitis A. The hepatitis A rate in Maverick County, Texas, was 11.2 and in Santa Cruz County, Arizona, 7.4. The tuberculosis rate of 10.4 for the combined border counties was more than double the national rate of 5.1 cases per 100,000 population. In Starr County, Texas, the 34.8 tuberculosis rate was nearly seven times higher than the nationwide rate.

Besides communicable diseases, border counties experience higher than average rates of adult diabetes, a condition that affects Hispanics more than all other ethnic groups. In Imperial County, California, the diabetes rate of 11.2 per 100 population was almost double the national rate of 6.7 per 100. (See Table 5.10.) According to the USMBCC, the border counties as a fifty-first state would rank fifth for diabetes-related deaths. Border counties also reported higher than average rates of asthma. The national rate was 7.7 cases per 10,000 population. In

TABLE 5.7

Per capita income rankings by state, 2003, 1990, and 1970

[In dollars]

	2003			1990			1970	
1	Connecticut	42,972	1	Connecticut	37,312	1	Alaska	24,959
2	New Jersey	39,577	2	New Jersey	34,593	2	Hawaii	24,157
3	Massachusetts	39,504	3	New York	33,116	3	Connecticut	24,081
4	Maryland	37,446	4	Massachusetts	32,440	4	Nevada	23,408
5	New York	36,112	5	Maryland	32,171	5	New York	23,114
6	New Hampshire	35,140	6	Alaska	32,104	6	New Jersey	22,862
7	Colorado	34,561	7	Hawaii	31,234	7	California	22,810
8	Delaware	34,199	8	California	30,462	8	Delaware	21,800
9	Minnesota	34,031	9	Delaware	30,158	9	Illinois	21,672
10	Virginia	33,730	10	Illinois	29,316	10	Maryland	21,615
11	California	33,415	11	New Hampshire	28,877	11	Massachusetts	21,260
12	Washington	33,254	12	Virginia	28,788	12	Michigan	19,908
13	Alaska	33,213	13	Nevada	28,643	13	Washington	19,875
14	Illinois	32,965	14	Rhode Island	28,165	14	Rhode Island	19,462
15	Wyoming	32,433	15	Minnesota	28,003	15	Ohio	19,377
16	Rhode Island	32,038	16	Washington	27,966	16	Pennsylvania	19,306
17	Pennsylvania	31,911	17	Pennsylvania	27,715	17	Colorado	19,197
18	Nevada	31,910	18	Colorado	27,558	18	Minnesota	19,154
19	Michigan	31,178	19	Florida	27,542	19	Florida	18,988
20	Vermont	30,888	20	Michigan	26,638	20	Wisconsin	18,869
21	Wisconsin	30,685	21	Ohio	26,386	21	Oregon	18,609
22	Hawaii	30,441	22	Kansas	25,460	22	Wyoming	18,514
23	Nebraska	30,179	23	Wisconsin	25,442	23	New Hampshire	18,428
24	Ohio	30,129	24	Oregon	25,355	24	Iowa	18,329
25	Florida	30,098	25	Wyoming	25,343	25	Missouri	18,258
26	Missouri	29,464	26	Nebraska	25,317	26	Arizona	18,187
27	Kansas	29,438	27	Vermont	25,166	27	Kansas	18,106
28	Maine	29,164	28	Missouri	24,815	28	Nebraska	17,983
29	Texas	29,074	29	Georgia	24,782	29	Virginia	17,968
30	Georgia	29,000	30	Indiana	24,624	30	Indiana	17,935
31	North Dakota	28,922	31	Texas	24,525	31	**Border counties**	**17,791**
32	South Dakota	28,856	32	Iowa	24,480	**32**	Texas	17,229
33	Indiana	28,838	33	Maine	24,462	33	Vermont	17,153
34	Oregon	28,734	34	North Carolina	24,279	34	Montana	17,124
35	Tennessee	28,641	35	Arizona	23,940	35	Idaho	16,693
36	Iowa	28,340	36	Tennessee	23,499	36	Oklahoma	16,479
37	North Carolina	28,071	**37**	**Border counties**	**23,220**	37	Maine	16,176
38	Arizona	27,232	38	Oklahoma	22,788	38	Utah	16,072
39	**Border counties**	**27,012**	39	South Dakota	22,767	39	Georgia	16,019
40	Oklahoma	26,719	40	North Dakota	22,445	40	North Carolina	15,493
41	Kentucky	26,575	41	South Carolina	22,376	41	South Dakota	15,484
42	Alabama	26,505	42	Idaho	22,136	42	North Dakota	15,318
43	Louisiana	26,312	43	Alabama	22,135	43	New Mexico	15,118
44	South Carolina	26,144	44	Montana	21,748	44	Tennessee	15,033
45	Idaho	25,902	45	Kentucky	21,732	45	Kentucky	15,014
46	Utah	25,407	46	Louisiana	21,361	46	West Virginia	14,739
47	Montana	25,406	47	New Mexico	21,010	47	Louisiana	14,654
48	New Mexico	24,995	48	Utah	20,995	48	South Carolina	14,469
49	West Virginia	24,542	49	West Virginia	20,403		**Border counties w/out San Diego**	**14,138**
50	Arkansas	24,384	50	Arkansas	20,357	49	Alabama	14,023
51	Mississippi	23,466	51	Mississippi	18,427	50	Arkansas	13,411
	Border counties w/out San Diego	**20,039**		**Border counties w/out San Diego**	**17,530**	51	Mississippi	12,411

SOURCE: Dennis L. Soden, "Table 4.1. 2003, 1990, and 1970 U.S. State Per Capita Income Rankings (Adjusted for Inflation, in 2003 Real Dollars)," in *At the Cross Roads: US/Mexico Border Counties in Transition*, US/Mexico Border Counties Coalition, March 2006, http://www.bordercounties.org/index .asp?Type=B_BASIC&SEC={62E35327–57C7–4978–A39A–36A8E00387B6} (accessed January 8, 2007). Data from Regional Economic Information System (REIS).

large border towns such as Brownsville and El Paso, Texas, asthma rates were greater than 22 per 10,000.

DISASTERS PRESENT SPECIAL CHALLENGES TO ILLEGAL ALIENS
Undocumented Families of 9/11 Victims

According to Lisa J. Adams, in "Kin Struggle for Proof of Foreign 9/11 Victims" (*Denver Post*, September 24, 2004), an estimated 500 people from 91 foreign countries were among the approximately 3,000 people who died in 9/11. In New York City, some of the victims were undocumented workers employed in the World Trade Center. From the more than 7,000 claims filed with the September 11th Victim Compensation Fund, survivors of some 250 foreigners qualified for compensation. Fund administrators estimated about 50 of the 250 were undocumented.

TABLE 5.8

If the 24 U.S. counties bordering Mexico were the 51st state, how would they compare to the rest of the nation?

1st in federal crimes, primarily due to drug and immigration arrests by federal agencies
2nd in incidence of tuberculosis
2nd in percentage of population under age 18
2nd in unemployment (5th with San Diego County included)
3rd in deaths due to hepatitis
3rd in concentration of Hispanics
4th in military employment
5th in diabetes-related deaths
7th in incidence of adult diabetes
10th in employment of federal civilians
12th in government and government enterprise employment
12th in incidence of AIDS
13th in population
16th in violent crime
22nd in allocation of federal highway planning and construction expenditures
22nd in home ownership
29th in receipt of total federal government expenditures
37th in low birth weight babies
39th in infant mortality
42nd in percent of teen pregnancy
45th in home affordability (37th with San Diego County included)
46th in percentage of adults with four-year college degree (27th with San Diego County included)
50th in insurance coverage for adults and children
51st in percent of population that has completed high school (50th with San Diego)
51st in per capita income (40th with San Diego County included)
51st in number of health care professionals

Note: San Diego County is a major metropolitan area and an anomaly to the other 23 border counties in many respects.

SOURCE: Adapted from Dennis L. Soden, "One Page Report Highlights," in *At the Cross Roads: US/Mexico Border Counties in Transition*, US/Mexico Border Counties Coalition, March 2006, http://www.bordercounties.org/index.asp?Type=B_BASIC&SEC={62E35327–57C7–4978–A39A–36A8E00387B6} (accessed January 8, 2007)

TABLE 5.9

Reported rates of AIDS, hepatitis A, and tuberculosis cases by border county, 1999–2003

	AIDS rate per 100,000	Hepatitis A rate per 100,000	Tuberculosis rate 100,000
United States (2003)	15.2	2.6	5.1
Border counties	16.1	*	10.4
Arizona (2003)	28.0	4.7	5.3
Cochise	13.9	3.4	0.0
Pima	34.7	2.5	2.7
Santa Cruz	14.9	7.4	5.0
Yuma	17.5	3.6	14.6
California (1999–2001)	16.3	2.0	9.8
Imperial	2.9	3.0	19.2
San Diego	20.2	2.2	10.5
New Mexico (2000–2002)	4.9	3.9	3.0
Dona Ana	5.9	2.6	6.1
Hidalgo	0.0	1.5	0.0
Luna	2.7	2.2	0.0
Texas (2001)	14.0	1.6	7.7
Brewster	11.2	1.0	11.2
Cameron	11.3	3.7	16.0
Culberson	0.0	2.7	0.0
El Paso	17.6	3.8	9.7
Hidalgo	8.8	3.2	12.5
Hudspeth	0.0	.9	0.0
Jeff Davis	0.0	.9	0.0
Kinney	0.0	1.3	0.0
Maverick	12.4	11.2	22.7
Presidio	0.0	1.7	0.0
Starr	3.7	4.4	34.8
Terrell	0.0	0.0	0.0
Val Verde	2.2	4.2	19.8
Webb	5.0	5.3	15.4
Zapata	0.0	2.2	15.9

*A complete data base to calculate this value is not available.

SOURCE: Dennis L. Soden, "Table 9.7. 1999–2003 Reported Rates of AIDS, HEPA, and TB Cases by County," in *At the Cross Roads: US/Mexico Border Counties in Transition*, US/Mexico Border Counties Coalition, March 2006, http://www.bordercounties.org/index.asp?Type=B_BASIC&SEC={62E35327–57C7–4978–A39A–36A8E00387B6} (accessed January 8, 2007)

Although fund administrators took great pains to ensure that undocumented immigrants who came forward would not be reported to immigration authorities, many families of illegal aliens decided it was not worth the risk. In the *Final Report of the Special Master for the September 11th Victim Compensation Fund of 2001* (September 6, 2005, http://www.usdoj.gov/final_report.pdf), Kenneth R. Feinberg indicates that the stakes were high. The average settlement was about $1.3 million per claim.

For families of illegal aliens who did make a claim, seeking compensation or just a death certificate ranged from difficult to impossible. Illegal aliens often used fake names and shared housing, so they had no rent receipts or utility bills in their names. Many were paid in cash for their work. Without a paycheck stub, Social Security number, tax records, money transfer receipts, or an employer who would verify the deceased as an employee, grieving families were unable to prove that their relatives worked at the World Trade Center. Adams reports that of approximately sixteen undocumented Mexican victims, only five families were able to prove the person died in 9/11 and qualify for compensation. In the end, a total of eleven survivors of illegal aliens received awards.

ILLEGAL AND AFRAID TO SPEND THE MONEY. Nearly five years later, Cara Buckley interviewed three recipients of money from the 9/11 fund—undocumented spouses of undocumented workers who were 9/11 victims—and published the interviews in "With Millions in 9/11 Payments, Bereaved Can't Buy Green Cards" (*New York Times*, September 3, 2006). The millions these survivors received did not change their immigration status, and they continue to live in fear of deportation. Furthermore, they are reluctant to buy a house or a new car because they fear calling attention to themselves. An unidentified widow from Ecuador told Buckley, "I can't dream very high, because I have no papers."

Undocumented Workers in Post-Katrina New Orleans

Hurricane Katrina struck the U.S. Gulf Coast region on August 29, 2005. A storm surge broke three levees and flooded much of New Orleans, Louisiana. As the nation

TABLE 5.10

Diabetes rates by border county, 2001–03

	Adult diabetes	Rate per 100 persons over 18
United States (2002)	14,055,189	6.7
All border counties	322,685	7.0
Arizona (2001)	257,942	6.6
Arizona border counties	60,858	7.0
Cochise	6,355	7.3
Pima	44,235	7.0
Santa Cruz	1,746	6.7
Yuma	8,522	7.3
California (2003)	1,702,615	6.6
California border counties	144,302	6.3
Imperial	11,466	11.2
San Diego	132,837	6.1
New Mexico (2002)	120,555	8.9
New Mexico border counties	14,392	9.6
Dona Ana	12,409	9.7
Hidalgo	344	9.1
Luna	1,639	9.1
Texas (2001)	1,055,002	6.9
Texas border counties	103,133	7.7
Brewster	479	6.9
Cameron	17,531	7.7
Culberson	154	7.4
El Paso	36,151	7.7
Hidalgo	29,618	7.8
Hudspeth	169	7.5
Jeff Davis	114	6.7
Kinney	177	7.0
Maverick	2,422	7.9
Presidio	386	7.7
Starr	2,763	8.0
Terrell	56	6.9
Val Verde	2,334	7.5
Webb	10,141	8.0
Zapata	638	7.7

SOURCE: Dennis L. Soden, "Table 9.5. 2001–2003 Diabetes Rates by County," in *At the Cross Roads: US/Mexico Border Counties in Transition*, US/Mexico Border Counties Coalition, March 2006, http://www.border counties.org/index.asp?Type=B_BASIC&SEC={62E35327–57C7–4978–A39A–36A8E00387B6} (accessed January 8, 2007)

realized the magnitude of the disaster, contractors from all over the country began setting up operations in Louisiana to obtain federal reconstruction grants that would aid the cleanup effort. However, a majority of the residents had evacuated the city and were living in temporary shelters, many in other states, so workers were scarce.

Because so many New Orleans residents lost all identity documents, the Department of Homeland Security suspended for forty-five days the requirement that government contractors verify the identity and work eligibility of employees hired for the massive demolition and cleanup that was necessary before rebuilding began. To further support local employment, the U.S. Department of Labor offered a two-month reprieve from the prevailing wage standards of the Davis Bacon Act required for federally funded construction projects. Thousands of eager job seekers poured into the area anticipating high pay and plentiful overtime. Many were foreign born, and many were undocumented.

In March 2006 Laurel E. Fletcher and a team of colleagues from the University of California, Berkeley, and Tulane University conducted interviews to study construction workers in post-Katrina New Orleans, focusing particularly on the differences between documented and undocumented workers. The resulting report, *Rebuilding after Katrina: A Population-Based Study of Labor and Human Rights in New Orleans* (June 2006, http://www.hrcberkeley.org/download/report_katrina.pdf), provides a unique portrait of the types of challenges and abuses undocumented workers can suffer.

The 2000 census counted a total of 484,674 people in Orleans Parish. In September 2006, one year after the hurricane, the Louisiana Department of Health and Hospitals surveyed the population and published its findings in *Louisiana Health and Population Survey: Expanded Preliminary Results: Orleans Parish* (October 6, 2006, http://popest.org/files/PopEst_ExpanPrelim_Report _Orleans_100606.pdf). The survey found roughly 187,500 residents, a total population decrease of 61%.

UNSKILLED, UNEDUCATED, AND UNDOCUMENTED. Fletcher and her colleagues report in *Rebuilding after Katrina* that 25% of the workforce in New Orleans were undocumented (illegal aliens). The main countries of origin for undocumented workers were Mexico (43%), Honduras (32%), Nicaragua (9%), and El Salvador (8%). The undocumented workers were generally younger and had far less education than documented workers. In the comparison of educational levels, Figure 5.6 shows that 45% of undocumented workers had a sixth-grade education or less, compared with 4% of documented workers.

The researchers found that most undocumented workers did not live in the New Orleans area before the hurricane; 77% had been in the area less than six months, when the survey was conducted in March 2006. (See Figure 5.7.) By contrast, more than half (56%) of documented workers had been in the area more than five years. Just 36% of documented workers had arrived in the past six months seeking jobs. As reported in *Rebuilding after Katrina*, the majority (87%) of the undocumented workers had been living elsewhere in the United States before coming to New Orleans; 41% came from Texas and another 10% came from Florida.

LIVING CONDITIONS. According to Fletcher and her colleagues, both documented and undocumented workers shared houses or apartments, typically with five other people. Two percent of undocumented workers lived in cars or at the construction site. Ten percent of undocumented workers reported that they lived without access to a bathroom with a shower, running water, electricity, and a kitchen. Just 7% of documented workers had no kitchen facilities and 3% lived without electricity.

FIGURE 5.6

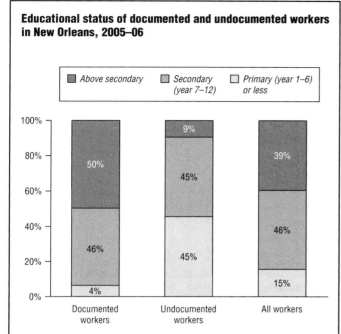

Educational status of documented and undocumented workers in New Orleans, 2005–06

Above secondary | Secondary (year 7–12) | Primary (year 1–6) or less

SOURCE: Laurel E. Fletcher, Phuong Pham, Eric Stover, and Patrick Vinck, "Figure 2. Educational Status of Construction Workers in New Orleans," in *Rebuilding after Katrina: A Population-Based Study of Labor and Human Rights in New Orleans*, International Human Rights Law Clinic, Human Rights Center, Payson Center for International Development and Technology Transfer, June 2006, http://www.payson .tulane.edu/katrina/katrina_report_final.pdf (accessed January 15, 2007)

FIGURE 5.7

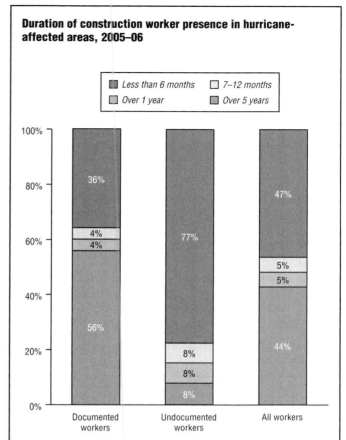

Duration of construction worker presence in hurricane-affected areas, 2005–06

Less than 6 months | 7–12 months | Over 1 year | Over 5 years

SOURCE: Laurel E. Fletcher, Phuong Pham, Eric Stover, and Patrick Vinck, "Figure 3. Duration of Presence of Construction Workers in Hurricane-Affected Areas," in *Rebuilding after Katrina: A Population-Based Study of Labor and Human Rights in New Orleans*, International Human Rights Law Clinic, Human Rights Center, Payson Center for International Development and Technology Transfer, June 2006, http://www.payson.tulane.edu/katrina/katrina_report_final.pdf (accessed January 15, 2007)

PAY DIFFERENCE BETWEEN DOCUMENTED AND UNDOCUMENTED. Before coming to New Orleans 79% of documented workers and 58% of undocumented workers had jobs, according to *Rebuilding after Katrina*. In New Orleans undocumented workers performed jobs with higher associated risks. Of workers performing roofing repairs, 43% were undocumented, compared with 12% documented. (See Figure 5.8.) Of workers installing sheet rock, 24% were undocumented, compared with 9% documented.

Fletcher and her collaborators note that all workers reported averaging nine and a half hours of work, six days per week. Documented workers reported earning an average of $16.50 per hour, compared with an average of $10 per hour for undocumented workers. The researchers found the same relative wage difference between documented and undocumented workers performing the same jobs. Thirty-four percent of undocumented workers reported receiving less total pay than expected on payday, compared with 16% of documented workers. Roughly two-thirds of documented (69%) and undocumented (64%) workers reported they did not receive extra compensation for working more than forty hours per week. When extra compensation was provided, undocumented workers more often received their regular hourly rate for additional hours worked, whereas documented workers received one and one-half times their normal pay rate. Of those who reported receiving overtime pay, 74% of documented workers and 20% of undocumented workers received one and one-half times their normal pay rate. (See Figure 5.9.)

HAZARDOUS WORK. *Rebuilding after Katrina* also indicated a general lack of adequate protective equipment issued to workers. Just 22% of all construction workers and 13% of undocumented workers reported having hard hats. Less than half of all construction workers surveyed had face masks to protect them from breathing contaminated materials and goggles to protect their eyes from debris—46% of documented and 42% of undocumented workers had face masks; and 51% of documented and 32% of undocumented workers had goggles. Not even half of either group had gloves.

FIGURE 5.8

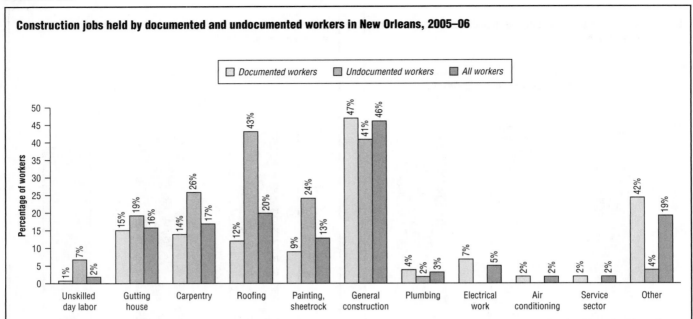

Construction jobs held by documented and undocumented workers in New Orleans, 2005–06

□ Documented workers ■ Undocumented workers ■ All workers

SOURCE: Laurel E. Fletcher, Phuong Pham, Eric Stover, and Patrick Vinck, "Figure 5. Construction Jobs of Workers in New Orleans," in *Rebuilding after Katrina: A Population-Based Study of Labor and Human Rights in New Orleans*, International Human Rights Law Clinic, Human Rights Center, Payson Center for International Development and Technology Transfer, June 2006, http://www.payson.tulane.edu/katrina/katrina_report_final.pdf (accessed January 15, 2007)

FIGURE 5.9

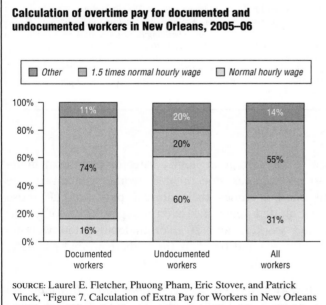

Calculation of overtime pay for documented and undocumented workers in New Orleans, 2005–06

■ Other ■ 1.5 times normal hourly wage □ Normal hourly wage

SOURCE: Laurel E. Fletcher, Phuong Pham, Eric Stover, and Patrick Vinck, "Figure 7. Calculation of Extra Pay for Workers in New Orleans (2)," in *Rebuilding after Katrina: A Population-Based Study of Labor and Human Rights in New Orleans*, International Human Rights Law Clinic, Human Rights Center, Payson Center for International Development and Technology Transfer, June 2006, http://www.payson.tulane.edu/katrina/katrina_report_final.pdf (accessed January 15, 2007)

Post-disaster cleanup and construction often exposed workers to polluted water, spilled chemicals, downed electrical lines, mold-infested buildings, and asbestos. New Orleans workers interviewed by Fletcher et al. reported working with harmful substances and in dangerous conditions. Fewer undocumented workers (21%) reported working with harmful substances. However, the researchers note that the undocumented workers may not have known what substances they were being exposed to. Among undocumented workers, just 38% reported being informed about risks related to mold, 36% to asbestos, and 19% to unsafe buildings. (See Figure 5.10.) By contrast, 67% of documented workers said they had been informed about mold.

HEALTH CONCERNS. Fletcher and her associates asked workers if they had experienced any of fifteen health problems. The top five symptoms reported were colds/flu, coughs, cuts/bruises, recurring headaches, and eye infections. Undocumented workers reported more colds and flu (49%), compared with documented workers (36%). (See Table 5.11.) Differences may relate to general health, living conditions, and access to medications. According to *Rebuilding after Katrina*, 83% of documented workers said they had access to medicine when needed, compared with 38% of undocumented workers. Thirty-seven percent of documented workers said they had some type of health insurance; 20% said they relied on free clinics. All undocumented workers said the only health care they received was through mobile clinics and health services provided by charitable organizations.

FIGURE 5.10

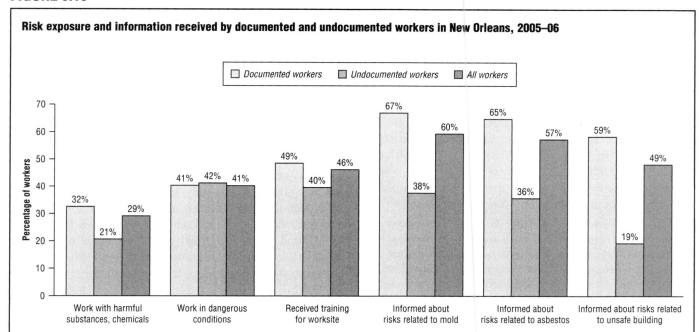

Risk exposure and information received by documented and undocumented workers in New Orleans, 2005–06

SOURCE: Laurel E. Fletcher, Phuong Pham, Eric Stover, and Patrick Vinck, "Figure 9. Worker Risk Exposure and Information (% Workers)," in *Rebuilding after Katrina: A Population-Based Study of Labor and Human Rights in New Orleans*, International Human Rights Law Clinic, Human Rights Center, Payson Center for International Development and Technology Transfer, June 2006, http://www.payson.tulane.edu/katrina/katrina_report_final.pdf (accessed January 15, 2007)

TABLE 5.11

Reported health problems among documented and undocumented workers in New Orleans, 2005–06

	Documented workers (n=155)	Undocumented workers (n=53)	All workers (n=208)
Cold/flu	36%	49%	39%
Cough	34%	32%	34%
Cuts/bruises*	38%	17%	33%
Recurring headache*	17%	42%	24%
Eye infections (red/watery)	20%	25%	21%
Difficulty breathing	17%	9%	15%
Hypertension	13%	4%	11%
Depression	9%	17%	11%
Skin rashes, swelling	10%	8%	9%
Difficulty remembering	9%	8%	9%
Broken/sprained limbs	8%	6%	7%
Nose bleeds*	4%	15%	7%
Diarrhea	7%	0%	5%
Head injuries	5%	2%	4%
Diabetes	5%	0%	3%
Asthma attack	4%	2%	3%
Burns	2%	0%	1%

*Indicates health symptoms for which there is a statistically significant difference among documented and undocumented workers. n=sample size.

SOURCE: Laurel E. Fletcher, Phuong Pham, Eric Stover, and Patrick Vinck, "Table 3. Reported Health Problems among Workers in New Orleans," in *Rebuilding after Katrina: A Population-Based Study of Labor and Human Rights in New Orleans*, International Human Rights Law Clinic, Human Rights Center, Payson Center for International Development and Technology Transfer, June 2006, http://www.payson.tulane.edu/katrina/katrina_report_final.pdf (accessed January 15, 2007)

ILLEGAL ALIENS AND CRIME

In "Information on Certain Illegal Aliens Arrested in the United States" (2005, Government Accountability Office, http://www.gao.gov/new.items/d05646r.pdf), researchers studied "55,322 aliens [who] had entered the country illegally and were still illegally in the country at the time of their incarceration in federal and state prison or local jail during fiscal year 2003." Among the findings presented were number of arrests, types of crimes committed, and location of the crimes. The researchers learned that "[the imprisoned illegal aliens] were arrested at least a total of 459,614 times, averaging about 8 offenses per illegal alien. Ninety-seven percent had more than 1 arrest. About 38 percent had between 2 and 5 arrests, 32 percent had between 6 and 10 arrests, and 26 percent had over 11 arrests. Eighty-one percent of all arrests occurred after 1990." The GAO also noted that not all arrests were prosecuted; of those that were prosecuted, not all led to a conviction.

The GAO further reports that the total number of alleged criminal offenses covered in the arrests numbered 691,890. Drugs (24%) topped the list of offenses, followed by immigration violations (21%), traffic violations (8%), assault (7%), obstruction of justice (7%), burglary (6%), larceny/theft (5%), and fraud/forgery/counterfeiting (4%). Weapons violations and motor vehicle theft registered 3% apiece, while sex offenses, robbery, and stolen property numbered 2% each. Murder was cited in only 1% of the offenses. The state with the most arrests of illegal aliens was California (58%), followed by Texas (14%) and Arizona (8%).

DO ILLEGAL ALIENS TAKE JOBS FROM LOW-SKILLED U.S. WORKERS?

An Example from the Post-Katrina Cleanup

During hearings before the House Committee on the Judiciary's Subcommittee on Immigration, Border Security, and Claims, Phyllis Schlafly (July 18, 2006, http://frwebgate .access.gpo.gov/cgi-bin/getdoc.cgi?dbname=109_house _hearings&docid=f:28781.pdf) presented an example of U.S. workers being replaced by foreign workers:

> An employment service in Mobile, Alabama, received an "urgent request" this year to fill 270 job openings from contractors who were hired to rebuild and clear areas of Alabama devastated by Hurricane Katrina. The agency immediately sent 70 laborers and construction workers to three job sites. After two weeks on the job, the men were fired by employers who told them "the Mexicans had arrived" and were willing to work for lower wages. The Americans had been promised $10 an hour, but the employers preferred Mexicans who would work for less. Employment agency manager Linda Swope told the *Washington Times*, "When they told the guys they would not be needed, they actually cried . . . and we cried with them. This is a shame."

> Ms. Swope said that employment agencies throughout Alabama, Louisiana and Mississippi all face similar problems because an estimated 30,000 men from Mexico and Central and South America, many in crowded buses and trucks, came into those three states after Hurricane Katrina, willing to work for less than whatever was paid to American citizens.

Immigrant Labor in Georgia

According to Evan Pérez and Corey Dade in "Reversal of Fortune: An Immigration Raid Aids Blacks—For a Time" (*Wall Street Journal*, January 17, 2007), raids by federal immigration agents on Labor Day 2006 left Crider Inc., a chicken processing plant in Stillmore, Georgia, short 75% of its 900-person workforce. Agents removed about 120 workers. Panic sent many more workers into hiding to avoid the same fate. Immigration officials had approached Crider management in May 2006 alleging that 700 workers were suspected of using false documents to secure employment. The company cooperated, resulting in two employees being arrested as part of a document mill operation that sold fake green cards and other documents. A number of employees who could not prove legal work status were released.

To replace the missing workers after the Labor Day raid, Crider announced increased wages starting at $7 to $9 per hour—more than a dollar above what many immigrant workers had received. The company also offered free transportation from nearby towns and free rooms in a company-owned dormitory. Local officials reported that Crider recruited workers through the state-funded employment office, a particularly important job placement source for low-skilled native workers.

According to Pérez and Dade, "the sudden reversal of economic fortunes in Stillmore underscores some of the most complex aspects of the pitched debate over immigration: Do illegal immigrants take jobs from low-skilled American workers? The answer in Stillmore initially appeared to be yes."

HISPANIC IMMIGRANT INFLUX IN GEORGIA. Pérez and Dade assert that NAFTA had a negative impact on many Mexican farmers, prompting a surge of illegal immigration. U.S. immigration crackdowns made crossing the border more treacherous, so migrant workers began to settle in the United States. The South was soon home to over one-third of the nation's Hispanics. Pérez and Dade note that, according to U.S. census estimates, the Hispanic immigrant population in Georgia tripled during the 1990s to over 435,000. In 2005 the 625,000 Hispanics in Georgia comprised 7% of the state's population. As native-born workers left the Crider plant for better pay or better working conditions than plucking, gutting, and packing chickens, most were replaced by Hispanic immigrants, many illegal. Wages hovered just above the U.S. minimum wage of $5.15 per hour.

In the months after the raid, Crider hired hundreds of native-born workers from surrounding communities. Most were African-American, and many had been unable or unwilling to follow jobs when other companies left small rural towns for urban areas. The Crider plant struggled with high turnover, lower productivity, and pay disputes with the new employees. The native-born workers were more likely than the immigrant workers to assert their rights as workers—to complain about unsafe working conditions and demand breaks and overtime compensation.

IMMIGRANT LABOR OR INCREASED PRICES IN THE GROCERY STORE? The question of gaining productivity in unappealing jobs with low-cost foreign workers or increasing production costs with employee native workers is the subject of "Collateral Damage in the Immigration War" (*Denver Post*, January 19, 2007) by Linda Chavez, the president of the Center for Equal Opportunity in Washington, D.C. Chavez suggests that Crider's use of more expensive and less productive native workers would force the company to either increase costs to consumers or go out of business. "Magnify this problem by the thousands and you can see the impact on the U.S. economy [of eliminating foreign workers]," Chavez states. She indicates that anti-immigration proponents boast they would rather pay more for food than have illegal aliens take jobs from U.S. workers. Chavez asks, "But are they willing to pay companies' actual costs, which in the Georgia case more than quadrupled? [Or] would they rather these jobs simply disappear altogether, striking devastating blows to many local economies?"

CHAPTER 6
THE COST OF IMMIGRATION

WEIGHING THE COSTS AND BENEFITS OF IMMIGRATION

Immigration is a hotly contested issue. Immigration supporters contend that immigrants contribute considerable sums of money to the public coffers and that, in an aging society, immigration is the only hope for a secure economic future. By contrast, immigration opponents argue that immigrants cost taxpayers far more than they contribute.

According to the Center for Immigration Studies (CIS), in "Costs" (December 17, 2006, http://www.cis.org/topics/costs.html), the National Research Council estimates the annual net fiscal impact of immigration to be between $11 billion and $22 billion per year, "with most government expenditures on immigrants coming from state and local coffers, while most taxes paid by immigrants go to the federal treasury." Because immigrants are disproportionately low skilled, they earn lower wages and pay a lower level of taxes. The CIS notes that their relative poverty and higher fertility rate causes them to use more government services.

FEDERAL SPENDING FOR IMMIGRATION
Immigrants and Public Assistance

In *Immigrants at Mid-decade: A Snapshot of America's Foreign-Born Population in 2005* (December 2005, http://www.cis.org/articles/2005/back1405.pdf), Steven A. Camerota of the Center for Immigration Studies states that "immigration accounts for most of [the] increase in the uninsured" population in the United States. He cites Census Bureau reports that the total population without health insurance grew by 12.4 million between 1989 and 2004. Much of this growth in uninsured population has been attributed to reduced availability of employer-sponsored insurance because of escalating costs. Camerota reports that 8.3 million immigrants who arrived during or after 1990 do not have health insurance. He further estimates that nearly 700,000 children born to these post-1990 immi-

grants lack insurance. Thus, the roughly nine million new immigrants and their U.S.-born children account for 73% of the growth in the nation's uninsured population. Table 6.1 shows that Central American countries produced the highest percentages of uninsured immigrants. More than half of the immigrants in the United States from three countries—Guatemala (58%), Mexico (53.8%), and Honduras (50.4%)—lacked insurance. The greatest number of uninsured immigrants (5.8 million) came from Mexico.

MEDICAID. According to Camerota, 17.4% of immigrants and their U.S.-born children under age eighteen were enrolled in Medicaid in 2004, compared with 12% of natives and their children. He arrives at these figures with the last two sets of data at the bottom of Table 6.1. For example, subtracting 29.3% "Immigrants and Their US-Born Children [Uninsured]" from 46.7% "Immigrants and Their US-born Children Uninsured or on Medicaid" leaves 17.4% of all immigrants and their U.S.-born children using Medicaid insurance benefits.

ALL PUBLIC ASSISTANCE PROGRAMS. Camerota also evaluates use of public assistance programs by immigrants. Table 6.2 shows the share of U.S. households in which at least one member of the household received public assistance (including Temporary Assistance to Needy Families and state-administered general assistance programs); Supplemental Security Income (SSI) for low-income elderly and disabled people; food stamps; Medicaid health insurance for those with low incomes; subsidized or government-owned housing; or Women, Infants, and Children nutrition program services. Information is reported for the entire household based on whether the head of household is a native or an immigrant. This means U.S.-born children of immigrants are counted with the immigrant household. Besides comparing all native households to all immigrant households, Camerota compares immigrants by period of arrival in the United States.

TABLE 6.1

Immigrants without health insurance, by country of origin, 2004

Country	Number uninsured (in thousands)	Percent uninsured
Guatemala	316	58.0%
Mexico	5,812	53.8%
Honduras	191	50.4%
El Salvador	507	45.2%
Ecuador	151	44.5%
Haiti	243	42.6%
Brazil	139	39.2%
Peru	122	37.0%
Colombia	149	31.1%
Dominican Republic	212	30.5%
Cuba	243	25.6%
Jamaica	154	25.4%
Poland	126	24.2%
Vietnam	240	24.1%
Korea	149	22.1%
China	397	21.7%
Iran	56	16.9%
India	232	16.4%
Russia	89	14.3%
Philippines	211	13.8%
Italy	42	10.7%
Great Britain	55	9.3%
Japan	32	9.1%
Canada	55	8.2%
Germany	25	4.8%
All immigrants	11,858	33.8%
All natives	33,962	13.3%
Immigrants 18 and older	10,781	33.8%
Natives 18 and older	36,771	14.4%
Children (under 18) of immigrant mothers[a]	2,849	19.6%
Children (under 18) of native mothers[a]	5,420	9.1%
Immigrants and their US-born children[a]	13,629	29.3%
Natives and their children[b]	32,191	13.2%
Immigrants and their U.S.-born children uninsured or on Medicaid[a]	21,639	46.7%
Natives and their children uninsured or on Medicaid[b]	61,639	25.2%

[a]Includes all children of immigrant mothers under age 18, including those born in the United States.
[b]Includes the children of native mothers under 18. The U.S.-born children of immigrant mothers are not included.

SOURCE: Steven A. Camarota, "Table 11. Immigrants without Health Insurance," in *Immigrants at Mid-Decade: A Snapshot of America's Foreign-Born Population in 2005*, Center for Immigration Studies, December 2005, http://www.cis.org/articles/2005/back1405.html (accessed January 9, 2007)

In Camerota's analysis, if "welfare" only means cash assistance programs (public assistance, SSI, food stamps, and public or subsidized housing), then immigrant use was roughly the same as natives. However, he notes that "some may reasonably argue that because immigration is supposed to benefit the United States, our admission criteria should, with the exception of refugees, select only those immigrants who are self-sufficient. ... From the point of view of taxpayers, immigrant use of Medicaid is the most problematic because that program costs more than the combined total for the other five programs" identified in Table 6.2. Medicaid was used by 24.2% of immigrant households, compared with 14.8% of native households.

NEW DOCUMENTATION REQUIREMENTS MAY AFFECT CITIZENS. The Deficit Reduction Act of 2005 requires people applying for or renewing Medicaid coverage to provide documentation of U.S. citizenship. These new requirements were implemented to address concerns that illegal aliens are receiving Medicaid benefits for which they are not eligible. Primary evidence of citizenship is a U.S. passport, Certificate of Naturalization or Certificate of Citizenship, and in some cases state driver's licenses that meet the same documentation requirements for issue. Documentation such as a birth certificate, hospital records, insurance records, and so on have to be accompanied by an identity document. Some groups are excluded from this requirement, such as people already receiving Social Security Disability Insurance and children in foster care.

The Kaiser Commission on Medicaid and the Uninsured, in the fact sheet "Citizenship Documentation Requirements in Medicaid" (January 2007, http://www.kff.org/medicaid/upload/7533-02.pdf), expresses concern that obtaining passports and birth certificates to enroll in Medicaid can be costly and time consuming for low-income people. The Kaiser Commission identifies Native Americans; people with disabilities who do not receive Medicaid, SSI, or Social Security Disability Insurance; the homeless; and Hurricane Katrina victims as groups particularly likely to have difficulty obtaining the required documents to prove their eligibility for Medicaid. An additional change requires that a U.S.-born child of an ineligible immigrant mother cannot obtain Medicaid benefits, other than emergency care at birth, until an application with citizenship documentation has been filed on behalf of the child. The Kaiser Commission believes that this change will discourage the mothers from applying and the infants will not receive routine medical care.

Since implementation of the new documentation requirements, the Kaiser Commission reports that some states have experienced declining enrollments in the State Children's Health Insurance Program, a program available to low-income children who do not qualify for Medicaid. Child welfare advocates are concerned that difficulty in obtaining required documentation will delay or prevent vulnerable children from receiving needed health care.

EARNED INCOME TAX CREDITS. The Earned Income Tax Credit (EITC) is for low-income workers. People eligible to receive the EITC pay no federal income tax and instead receive cash assistance from the government based on their earnings and family size. Camerota notes that the figures for the EITC are probably overstated because the Census Bureau estimated the numbers based on income and family size. (See Table 6.2.) According to Camerota, with an annual cost of over $30 billion, the EITC is the nation's largest means-tested cash assistance program for workers with low incomes. In 2005, 15.8% percent of native households qualified for the credit, compared with 30% of immigrant households.

TABLE 6.2

Use of welfare programs and the earned income tax credit (EITC) for native and immigrant households, by period of arrival in the U.S., selected years pre-1980–2005

	Native households	All immigrant households	Year of entry[a]			
			Pre–1980 immigrant households	1980–89 immigrant households	1990–99 immigrant households	2000–05 immigrant households
Public assisstance[b]	1.5%	1.8%	1.9%	2.3%	2.0%	1.9%
Supplemental Security Income	4.0%	4.4%	6.0%	4.5%	3.9%	1.6%
Food stamps	6.3%	7.0%	5.3%	7.0%	9.3%	5.9%
Public or subsidized housing	4.1%	4.9%	4.0%	5.5%	5.0%	5.3%
Medicaid	14.8%	24.2%	18.7%	27.5%	29.1%	20.6%
WIC	2.7%	6.6%	2.1%	6.3%	10.5%	8.6%
Using any of above programs	18.2%	28.6%	21.5%	31.7%	34.1%	26.9%
EITC eligibility	15.8%	30.0%	17.1%	35.2%	36.8%	36.5%

[a]Based on the year the household head said he or she came to the United States to stay.
[b]Includes TANF and state general assistance programs.

SOURCE: Steven A. Camarota, "Table 12. Use of Welfare Programs and EITC for Immigrant- and Native-Headed Households (Percent)," in *Immigrants at Mid-Decade: A Snapshot of America's Foreign-Born Population in 2005,* Center for Immigration Studies, December 2005, http://www.cis.org/articles/2005/back1405. (accessed January 9, 2007)

Table 6.3 shows that in 2004 and 2005 immigrants from the Dominican Republic had the highest use of welfare programs in general (57.2%) and the highest use of food stamps (19.4%), subsidized housing (17.8%), and Medicaid (49.7%). Immigrants from Russia had the highest use of SSI (15.4%). The EITC was used by nearly half of immigrants from Mexico (49.9%) and Guatemala (49.5%). Slightly less than twice the share of immigrant households (30.1%) used welfare programs, compared with native households (16%).

IMPLICATIONS OF IMMIGRANT WELFARE USE FOR STATES. More than one-third of immigrant households in Arizona (37.3%), California (35%), and New York (34.5%) used some type of welfare program. (See Table 6.4.) For state governments, Medicaid is a particular concern because half to two-thirds of the program's costs are borne by state taxpayers. Arizona and Texas had the greatest share of immigrants and their foreign-born children using Medicaid—63.2% and 61.3%, respectively.

SOCIAL SECURITY AND IMMIGRANT EARNINGS

According to Eduardo Porter, in "Illegal Immigrants Are Bolstering Social Security with Billions" (*New York Times*, April 5, 2005), "Immigrant workers in the United States are now providing the [Social Security] system with a subsidy of as much as $7 billion a year." His report is based on Social Security taxes, which are deducted from employee paychecks, matched by employers, and held in the Social Security Administration's (SSA) Earnings Suspense File (ESF). These are wage credits for which Social Security numbers and employee names do not match SSA records. Mismatches often result from typographical errors in employer annual wage reports or in omissions, such as an employee's failure to notify the SSA of a name change because of marriage. However, taxes paid by illegal aliens using false Social Security numbers (numbers never issued) or stolen numbers also end up in the ESF.

In *Social Security Benefits for Noncitizens: Current Policy and Legislation* (July 22, 2004, http://hutchison .senate.gov/RL32004.pdf), Dawn Nuschler and Alison Siskin of the Congressional Research Service report the total ESF at $421 billion at the end of fiscal year (FY) 2003. In his testimony before the House Committee on Ways and Means, Subcommittee on Social Security, Deputy Commissioner of Social Security James B. Lockhart III (February 16, 2006, http://www.ssa.gov/legislation/testimony_021606.html) reported that the $7.2 billion in payroll taxes credited to the ESF in tax year 2003 represented 1.3% of total 2003 Social Security taxes paid. According to Lockhart, 2003 was the most recent year for which data were available. Lockhart and Porter both appear to be using 2003 ESF data, but there is no clear definition of what share of the 2003 ESF actually came from illegal workers.

Porter cites a U.S. Government Accountability Office (GAO) audit of the ESF concerning the earnings reported under false Social Security numbers. The audit identified one hundred employers filing the most earnings reports with false numbers between 1997 and 2001. More than half of such employers were located in three states with large immigrant populations: California, Texas, and Illinois. About 17% of these employers were restaurants, 10% construction companies, and 7% farm operations.

Totalization Agreements

Nuschler and Siskin report that most jobs in the United States are subject to Social Security tax. Noncitizens

TABLE 6.3

Immigrant households using welfare programs and EITC by country of birth, 2004 and 2005

Country of birth	Any	Public assistance	SSI	Food stamps	Subsidized housing	Medicaid	WIC	EITC
Dominican Republic	57.2%	5.0%	12.2%	19.4%	17.8%	49.7%	9.4%	40.1%
Mexico	43.4%	2.8%	2.7%	11.1%	4.6%	37.3%	16.1%	49.9%
Russia	39.8%	1.2%	15.4%	15.4%	13.4%	35.0%	0.8%	12.5%
Honduras	37.5%	3.9%	7.2%	3.2%	6.6%	31.6%	5.3%	42.4%
Guatemala	35.7%	0.5%	3.9%	4.3%	2.9%	29.5%	11.6%	49.5%
Haiti	35.3%	4.7%	4.2%	7.4%	7.4%	26.5%	7.0%	40.6%
Cuba	33.0%	2.1%	9.9%	13.7%	8.7%	27.3%	1.7%	17.2%
Vietnam	31.8%	2.0%	6.3%	7.0%	6.5%	27.3%	3.0%	28.4%
Jamaica	31.3%	5.9%	6.9%	9.7%	5.6%	26.0%	4.9%	33.2%
Colombia	29.7%	2.7%	3.2%	7.6%	5.9%	29.2%	3.8%	29.1%
El Salvador	29.7%	1.2%	4.1%	3.6%	2.7%	26.5%	8.8%	42.3%
Ecuador	23.1%	0.0%	1.5%	3.1%	2.3%	22.3%	4.6%	19.2%
Iran	21.9%	1.5%	12.4%	2.2%	8.0%	19.0%	0.0%	19.2%
Brazil	21.9%	0.0%	3.1%	6.3%	4.7%	16.4%	2.3%	26.8%
Peru	20.6%	0.0%	3.1%	3.1%	3.8%	15.3%	3.1%	30.8%
China	18.5%	0.3%	4.8%	1.6%	2.9%	15.8%	1.2%	22.5%
Korea	17.4%	0.7%	4.3%	2.5%	7.6%	13.0%	2.5%	13.1%
Philippines	15.6%	0.3%	6.1%	0.7%	2.4%	13.8%	1.4%	18.1%
Japan	13.4%	0.0%	0.0%	2.0%	2.7%	11.4%	1.3%	16.8%
Canada	12.2%	0.3%	2.7%	3.0%	2.4%	9.9%	0.6%	7.1%
Poland	10.8%	1.1%	1.1%	1.8%	2.5%	9.0%	0.7%	9.7%
Great Britain	10.8%	2.2%	2.2%	4.1%	2.9%	9.2%	1.6%	13.6%
Germany	9.1%	0.6%	3.6%	1.3%	1.3%	8.7%	0.0%	11.7%
India	7.9%	0.0%	0.8%	1.8%	1.3%	6.4%	0.3%	15.4%
Italy	3.4%	0.0%	1.1%	1.1%	0.6%	2.2%	0.0%	4.7%
All immigrants	28.6%	1.8%	4.4%	7.0%	4.9%	24.2%	6.6%	30.0%
All natives	18.2%	1.5%	4.0%	6.3%	4.1%	14.8%	2.7%	15.8%
Immigrant households w/children*	40.5%	3.1%	2.7%	10.7%	5.0%	23.7%	13.0%	44.0%
Native households w/children*	27.0%	3.4%	2.6%	9.8%	4.6%	35.7%	7.4%	27.9%
Refugee-sending countries	30.7%	1.8%	8.6%	9.7%	8.3%	25.5%	2.6%	20.3%
Non-refugee-sending countries	28.2%	1.8%	3.7%	6.6%	4.3%	24.0%	7.2%	31.4%
Immigrant households w/65+ head	30.1%	0.3%	12.3%	8.4%	9.9%	25.9%	0.7%	7.5%
Native households w/65+ head	16.0%	0.4%	4.1%	3.6%	4.9%	11.6%	0.8%	6.2%

*Households with children under 18.
Notes: SSI=Supplemental Security Income. WIC is Women, Infants and Children. EITC is Earned Income Tax Credit.

SOURCE: Steven A. Camarota, "Table 13. Percent Using Welfare Programs and EITC by Household-Headed Country of Birth," in *Immigrants at Mid-Decade: A Snapshot of America's Foreign-Born Population in 2005*, Center for Immigration Studies, December 2005, http://www.cis.org/articles/2005/back1405.html (accessed January 9, 2007)

performing Social Security–covered work must pay Social Security payroll taxes. This includes legal temporary workers and those working without authorization. Nuschler and Siskin note some exceptions. For example, the work of aliens under certain visa categories (e.g., H2A agricultural workers) is not covered by Social Security. Generally, the work of citizens of a country with which the United States has a totalization agreement is not covered if they work in the United States for less than five years. A totalization agreement coordinates the payment of Social Security taxes and benefits for workers who divide their careers between two countries.

In June 2004 U.S. and Mexican representatives signed a totalization agreement. According to the SSA, in "The U.S.-Mexico Totalization Agreement" (January 2007, http://www.numbersusa.com/hottopic/totalization.htm), totalization with Mexico relieves U.S. citizens working for U.S. companies in Mexico from paying Social Security taxes to both countries. The agreement also removes the double-taxation requirement for Mexican citizens working for Mexican companies in the United States. Employers and their employees in both countries contribute to either the U.S. or Mexican Social Security systems, but not both. By SSA estimates, approximately three thousand U.S. workers and their employers will share tax savings of $140 million over the first five years of the agreement. However, according to Nuschler and Siskin, the SSA also estimates the agreement will cost about $105 million in annual benefits paid during the first five years of the agreement. Nuschler and Siskin state the GAO reported in 2003 that "'the cost of a totalization agreement with Mexico is highly uncertain' because of the large number of unauthorized immigrants from Mexico estimated to be living in the United States."

Opponents of the totalization agreement argue that Mexican workers who cross the border and work illegally in the United States will be able to collect U.S. Social Security benefits. They also believe that an amnesty

TABLE 6.4

Top states ranked by immigrant households using welfare programsª, 2005

[In thousands]

| | Use of major welfare program | | | | Uninsured | | | | Uninsured or on Medicaid | | | |
| State | Immigrant-headed households | | Native-headed households | | Immigrants and their children[b] | | Natives and their children[c] | | Immigrants and their children[b] | | Natives and their children[c] | |
	Percent	Number	Percent	Number	Percent	Number	Percent	Number	Percent	Number	Percent	Number
Arizona	37.3%	137	16.0%	291	36.9%	449	11.9%	540	63.2%	770	24.8%	1,129
California	35.0%	1,369	17.5%	1,561	27.5%	3,742	13.3%	2,969	50.1%	6,919	26.6%	5,912
New York	34.5%	609	22.6%	1,283	20.2%	995	12.1%	1,709	44.3%	2,182	27.3%	3,959
Texas	30.6%	419	18.0%	1,229	45.2%	2,096	19.7%	3,487	61.3%	2,942	90.6%	5,416
Massachusetts	28.9%	110	20.6%	426	19.4%	211	10.2%	537	37.4%	409	23.1%	1,218
Georgia	27.2%	84	19.0%	596	39.9%	409	14.4%	1,104	56.9%	583	28.5%	2,187
Maryland	25.2%	71	12.5%	230	32.9%	319	10.8%	497	42.3%	403	10.6%	956
Florida	24.5%	334	14.6%	832	33.7%	1,369	15.7%	2,111	47.6%	1,932	26.4%	3,541
North Carolina	22.0%	50	18.8%	584	40.9%	297	13.3%	1,025	49.4%	359	25.5%	1,962
New Jersey	19.9%	138	13.7%	349	28.5%	590	11.1%	732	38.8%	902	18.7%	1,232
Colorado	18.7%	34	11.5%	185	40.0%	249	13.3%	519	47.4%	295	20.1%	786
Illinois	17.5%	106	14.1%	606	25.2%	485	12.0%	1,279	35.8%	689	21.3%	2,274
Virginia	13.7%	37	14.3%	369	26.5%	246	12.8%	915	29.4%	279	20.8%	1,330
Nation	28.8%	4,135	18.2%	17,957	29.3%	13,629	13.2%	32,191	46.7%	21,696	25.2%	61,639

[a]Includes use of any of the following: Temporary Assistance for Needy Families (TANF), general assistance, Supplemental Security Income (SSI), food stamps, public/subsidized housing, Women, Infants and Children or Medicaid.
[b]Include all children of immigrant mothers under age 18, including those born in the United States.
[c]Includes only the children on native mothers under 18. The U.S.-born children of immigrants are not included.

SOURCE: Steven A. Camarota, "Table 18. Welfare Usage and Insurance Coverage by State, Ranked by Immigrant Welfare Use (in Thousands)," in *Immigrants at Mid-Decade: A Snapshot of America's Foreign-Born Population in 2005*, Center for Immigration Studies, December 2005, http://www.cis.org/articles/2005/back1405.html (accessed January 9, 2007)

could give illegal workers credit for Social Security taxes paid during years of illegal work.

EXISTING U.S. TOTALIZATION AGREEMENTS. According to the SSA (March 2, 2007, http://www.ssa.gov/international/status.html), the United States has totalization agreements in effect with twenty-one countries. Table 6.5 details the number and types of U.S. Social Security monthly benefit payments made to citizens of foreign countries under totalization agreements. Between 1996 and 2005 the total number of payments increased from 59,455 to 112,910.

U.S. Department of Homeland Security Budget

The government's focus on border security measures since the terrorist attacks of September 11, 2001, dramatically increased immigration-related costs. The largest segments of the 2007 U.S. Department of Homeland Security's (DHS) $42.7 billion budget were focused on monitoring and limiting who enters the country. (See Table 6.6.) The U.S. Coast Guard received $8.2 billion of the total budget, the U.S. Customs and Border Patrol, $7.8 billion, and the Transportation Security Administration, $6.3 billion. The $4.7 billion allotted to the U.S. Immigration and Customs Enforcement (ICE) agency was 11% of the overall 2007 budget, but it represented the largest increase (21%) over the 2006 budget.

According to the DHS, in *Budget-in-Brief Fiscal Year 2007* (2007, http://www.dhs.gov/xlibrary/assets/

Budget_BIB-FY2007.pdf), the second priority listed in its budget was strengthening border security and reforming immigration processes as part of a Secure Border Initiative. This included "establishing a Temporary Worker Program." The addition of fifteen hundred new agents would bring the border patrol to nearly fourteen thousand agents. About $100 million was targeted to electronic border surveillance and response. Another $400 million would be used to increase to 27,500 the number of detention beds for aliens apprehended.

U.S. Aid for Refugees

U.S. refugee policy has been based on the premise that the care of refugees and other conflict victims, as well as the pursuit of permanent solutions for refugee crises, are shared international responsibilities. The more refugees assisted in their home regions, the fewer that might ultimately require resettlement outside those regions. Following this philosophy, the U.S. Department of State annually contributes to overseas assistance funds administered by international organizations and nongovernmental organizations that carry out relief services.

The FY2007 State Department budget request for the Emergency Refugee and Migration Assistance program was $832.9 million. (See Figure 6.1.) Overseas aid to refugees accounted for 65% of the budget, whereas 27% was targeted for refugees admitted to the United States.

TABLE 6.5

Social Security benefits paid under U.S. totalization agreements, by country and type of benefit, selected years 1983–2005

Year and country	Total	Retired workers	Disabled workers	Wives and husbands	Widow(er)s	Children
			Number			
1983	1,541	970	97	266	109	99
1984	2,717	1,664	254	435	202	162
1985	7,857	4,773	404	1,730	578	372
1990	27,662	17,432	1,609	5,801	2,078	742
1995	54,806	35,925	2,428	10,974	4,431	1,048
1996	59,455	39,085	2,514	11,917	4,893	1,046
1997	63,842	42,163	2,662	12,583	5,342	1,092
1998	68,748	45,632	2,708	13,376	5,926	1,106
1999	74,933	50,018	2,749	14,421	6,636	1,109
2000	82,404	55,398	2,687	15,806	7,302	1,211
2001	88,770	59,713	2,859	17,013	7,917	1,268
2002	94,350	63,418	2,992	18,032	8,585	1,323
2003	99,728	67,055	2,986	19,171	9,190	1,326
2004	106,096	71,782	2,826	20,308	9,835	1,345
2005	112,910	76,590	2,974	21,554	10,443	1,349
Australia	901	659	53	157	18	14
Austria	1,035	760	63	143	46	23
Belgium	663	466	5	121	59	12
Canada	44,513	27,977	1,396	9,338	5,326	476
Chile	72	55		14	*	*
Finland	233	169	10	41	8	5
France	3,875	2,781	39	691	303	61
Germany	17,890	13,363	598	2,711	1,006	212
Greece	2,921	2,004	134	535	197	51
Ireland	1,470	1,040	32	271	101	26
Italy	8,545	5,478	111	1,634	1,203	119
Korea	9	7	*	*	*	*
Luxembourg	47	27	5	*	4	*
Netherlands	2,352	1,661	9	502	150	30
Norway	3,590	2,326	96	729	401	38
Portugal	1,868	1,212	114	294	216	32
Spain	2,190	1,370	77	453	245	45
Sweden	1,782	1,322	33	332	69	26
Switzerland	3,653	2,670	36	733	174	40
United Kingdom	15,301	11,243	163	2,844	914	137

*Not shown to avoid disclosure of information regarding particular individuals.

SOURCE: Adapted from "Table 5.M1. Number of Beneficiaries and Average Monthly Benefit under U.S. Totalization Agreements, by Country and Type of Benefit, December 1983–2005, Selected Years," in *Annual Statistical Supplement, 2006*, U.S. Social Security Administration, http://www.ssa.gov/policy/docs/statcomps/supplement/2006/5m.html (accessed January 13, 2007)

STATE SPENDING ON IMMIGRATION

Cost to States for Incarcerating Criminal Aliens

The DHS's Bureau of Justice Administration oversees the State Criminal Alien Assistance Program (SCAAP), in conjunction with ICE. SCAAP provides federal payments to states and localities that incurred correctional officer salary costs for incarcerating undocumented criminal aliens. These funds apply to aliens with at least one felony or two misdemeanor convictions for violations of state or local law who are incarcerated for at least four consecutive days during the reporting period. SCAAP covers only a share of corrections staff salaries related to the incarceration of criminal aliens. Other expenses, such as feeding, clothing, and providing medical attention to the prisoners, are not included in this federal reimbursement program.

The Bureau of Justice Assistance (2007, http://www.ojp.usdoj.gov/BJA/grant/scaap.html) reports that FY2006 awards totaled $376 million, an increase of 31% over $287 million awarded in FY2005. Because the funding formula did not change, the increased awards represented a combination of more localities applying for reimbursement and a greater number of prisoner days attributed to criminal aliens. According to the Federation for American Immigration Reform, in "Immigration's Impact on the U.S." (January 2007, http://www.fairus.org/site/PageServer?pagename=research_research9605), the $287 million SCAAP awards for FY2005 represented just 33.5% of actual salary costs incurred by states and localities in housing illegal aliens.

Financial Impact of Undocumented Immigrants in Texas

In *Undocumented Immigrants in Texas: A Financial Analysis of the Impact to the State Budget and Economy* (December 2006, http://www.cpa.state.tx.us/specialrpt/

TABLE 6.6

U.S. Department of Homeland Security budget by organization, fiscal year 2007

[Gross discretionary and mandatory, fees, trust funds]

	FY 2005 revised enacted $000	FY 2006 revised enacted $000	FY 2007 President's budget $000	FY 2007 +/– FY 2006 enacted $000	FY 2007 +/– FY 2006 enacted %
Departmental operations	$527,257	$559,230	$674,791	$115,561	21%
Counter-Terrorism Fund	8,000	1,980	—	(1,980)	–100%
Office of Screening Coordination and Operations	—	3,960	3,960	—	—
Office of the Inspector General	82,317	82,187	96,185	13,998	17%
US–VISIT	340,000	336,600	399,494	62,894	19%
U.S. Customer & Border Protection (CBP)	6,344,398	7,109,875	7,846,681	736,806	10%
U.S. Immigration & Customs Enforcement (ICE)	3,127,078	3,866,443	4,696,932	830,489	21%
Transportation Security Administration (TSA)	6,068,275	6,167,014	6,299,462	132,448	2%
Preparedness Directorate	—	678,395	669,980	(8,415)	–1%
Preparedness: Office of Grants & Training	—	3,352,437	2,750,009	(602,428)	–18%
Analysis and operations	—	252,940	298,663	45,723	18%
Federal Emergency Management Agency (FEMA)	5,038,256	4,834,744	5,326,882	492,138	10%
U.S. Citizenship & Immigration Services (CIS)	1,775,000	1,887,850	1,985,990	98,140	5%
U.S. Secret Service (USSS)	1,385,758	1,399,889	1,465,103	65,214	5%
U.S. Coast Guard (USCG)	7,558,560	8,193,797	8,422,075	228,278	3%
Federal Law Enforcement Training Center (FLETC)	222,357	279,534	244,556	(34,978)	–13%
Service & Technology (S&T) Directorate	1,115,450	1,487,075	1,002,271	(484,804)	–33%
Domestic Nuclear Detection Office (DNDO)	—	—	535,788	535,788	—
Legacy Department of Homeland Security organizations					
Bureau of Transportation Statistics Under Secretary	9,617	—	—	—	—
Information Analysis & Infrastructure Protection Directorate	887,108	—	—	—	—
State & Local Government Coordination & Preparedness	3,984,846	—	—	—	—
Total:	**$38,474,277**	**$40,493,950**	**$42,718,822**	**$2,224,872**	**5%**
Less rescission of prior year carryover funds:	(104,760)	(148,603)	(16,000)	132,603	–89%
Adjusted total budget authority:	$38,369,517	$40,345,347	$42,702,822	$2,357,475	6%
Bioshield:	$2,507,776	—	—	—	—
Supplemental:	$67,329,867	$(23,076,917)	—	—	—

Notes: The following offices are less than one percent of the total budget authority and are not reflected in the chart above: Office of the Inspector General, and Screening Coordination and Operations. The fiscal year 2007 proposed rescission of prior year unobligated balances is from the Counter-Terrorism Fund and is not reflected against the total budget authority shown in the chart above.

SOURCE: "Total Budget Authority by Organization," and "FY2007 Percent of Total Budget Authority by Organization $42,718,822,000," in *Budget-in-Brief Fiscal Year 2007*, U.S. Department of Homeland Security, http://www.dhs.gov/xlibrary/assets/Budget_BIB-FY2007.pdf (accessed January 10, 2007)

FIGURE 6.1

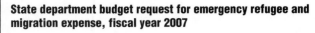

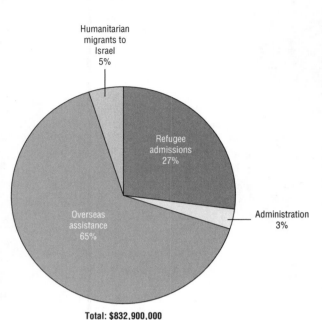

State department budget request for emergency refugee and migration expense, fiscal year 2007

Humanitarian migrants to Israel 5%

Refugee admissions 27%

Overseas assistance 65%

Administration 3%

Total: $832,900,000

SOURCE: Adapted from "FY 2007 Budget Request Total: $832,900,000," in *Emergency Refugee and Migration Assistance: Fiscal Year 2007*, U.S. Department of State, Bureau of Population, Refugees, and Migration, http://www.state.gov/g/prm/rls/rpt/2006/66292.htm (accessed January 5, 2007)

TABLE 6.7

Availability of major federal government programs to illegal aliens

Unavailable	Available
Medicare	K–12 education
Medicaid	Emergency medical care
Cash assistance (TANF-welfare)	Children with special health care needs
Children's Health Insurance Program (CHIP)	Substance abuse services
Food stamps	Mental health services
Supplemental Security Income (SSI)	Immunizations
Public housing assistance	Women and children's health services
Job opportunities for low income individuals	Public health
Child care and development	EMS

Notes: TANF is Temporary Assistance for Needy Families. EMS is emergency medical service(s).

SOURCE: Carole Keeton Strayhorn, "Exhibit 1. Major Government-Sponsored Programs and their Availability to Undocumented Immigrants," in *Undocumented Immigrants in Texas: A Financial Analysis of the Impact to the State Budget and Economy*, Texas Comptroller of Public Accounts, December 2006, http://www.window.state.tx.us/specialrpt/undocumented/undocumented.pdf (accessed January 6, 2007)

undocumented/undocumented.pdf), Carole Keeton Strayhorn indicates that state revenue generated by the estimated 1.4 million illegal aliens living in Texas exceeded the cost of state services they received in FY2005. Strayhorn notes that her findings are contrary to two other studies on costs to states: *The Cost of Illegal Immigration to Texans* (April 2005, http://www.fairus.org/site/DocServer/texas_costs. pdf?docID=301) by Jack Martin and Ira Mehlman and *Costs of Federally Mandated Services to Undocumented Immigrants in Colorado* (June 30, 2006, http://www.thebell.org/PUBS/IssBrf/2006/06ImmigCosts.pdf) by Rich Jones and Robin Baker. These studies find state costs for illegal aliens exceeded revenues generated by the illegal aliens. According to Strayhorn, these two studies do not accurately represent costs of illegal aliens because they include data for legal permanent residents, citizen children of illegal alien parents, and expenses paid from other than state funds.

Strayhorn focuses on state-funded services to "undocumented immigrants" living in Texas. In many cases funding is determined by federal restrictions on state spending. The government-sponsored programs listed as "available" to undocumented immigrants are in Table 6.7, such as K–12 education or emergency medical care, generated a cost to the state when used. Because Texas

does not have a state income tax, Strayhorn suggests it is easier to identify undocumented immigrants' share of consumption taxes that all residents pay.

EDUCATION COSTS. Using data from the GAO and the Texas Education Agency, Strayhorn estimates that 135,013 undocumented students attended Texas public schools in the 2004–05 academic year and cost the state $957 million. Strayhorn notes that Martin and Mehlman have a much higher estimate of $1.7 billion for the 2003–04 Texas academic year because they include federal funds.

In 2001 the Texas Legislature made provisions to allow certain noncitizen residents to be classified as Texas residents for in-state college tuition. In 2005 the legislature made residency requirements for in-state tuition uniform for all students regardless of legal status. As a result, the number of noncitizen students enrolled with in-state tuition increased tenfold, from 393 in 2001 to 3,792 in 2004. (See Table 6.8.) During this period the average per student cost of state funding decreased. Strayhorn notes that not all noncitizen students in this report were undocumented. For example, noncitizen children of ambassadors and diplomats living in the state might qualify for in-state tuition and thus be counted in the report. Strayhorn estimates the state's cost for undocumented students receiving in-state tuition at $11.2 million.

HEALTH CARE COSTS. Health care for undocumented immigrants was a major expense shared by private, local, state, and federal entities. Table 6.9 identifies major types of health care expenses paid by Texas in 2005. The largest share (30% of all health care costs for undocumented immigrants) was $38.7 million in emergency Medicaid. Medicaid provides health care to low-income families, pregnant women, elderly people, people with

TABLE 6.8

Cost of noncitizen college students classified as Texas residents for tuition, 2001 and 2004

	Fall 2001 avg. state cost per student	Fall 2001 resident students	Fall 2001 total	Fall 2004 avg. state cost per student	Fall 2004 resident students	Fall 2004 total
Universities	$5,366	64	$343,424	$4,816	747	$3,597,552
Health related institutions	$31,693	29	$919,097	$25,237	16	$403,792
Community colleges	$2,627	300	$788,100	$2,239	2,894	$6,479,666
Technical colleges		0		$5,509	120	$661,080
State colleges		0		$4,265	15	$63,975
Total		**393**	**$2,050,621**		**3,792**	**$11,206,065**

SOURCE: Carole Keeton Strayhorn, "Exhibit 5. Cost to State of Non-Citizen College Student Classified as Texas Residents," in *Undocumented Immigrants in Texas: A Financial Analysis of the Impact to the State Budget and Economy*, Texas Comptroller of Public Accounts, December 2006, http://www.window.state.tx.us/specialrpt/undocumented/undocumented.pdf (accessed January 6, 2007). Data from Texas Higher Education Coordinating Board and the University of Texas System.

TABLE 6.9

Texas state health care costs for illegal aliens, fiscal year 2005

Service area	General revenue	Percent of expenditures on undocumented immigrants	Undocumented immigrant costs
Emergency Medicaid[a]	$129,153,257	30.0%	$38,745,977
CSHCN[b]	$9,111,352	78.9%	$7,189,280
Substance abuse	$17,305,929	1.7%	$287,651
Mental health	$225,650,365	1.7%	$3,750,650
Immunizations	$26,906,780	0.1%	$33,143
Women/school	$21,901,933	3.1%	$674,463
Public health	$64,300,000	6.1%	$3,937,888
EMS[c]	$55,156,810	6.1%	$3,377,937
Total	**$549,486,426**	**10.6%**	**$57,996,990**

[a]Program type 30 (foreign-born: 30% undocumented)
[b]CSHCN is children with special health care needs.
[c]EMS is emergency medical service(s).

SOURCE: Carole Keeton Strayhorn, "Exhibit 10. State Healthcare Costs Associated with Undocumented Immigrants Fiscal 2005," in *Undocumented Immigrants in Texas: A Financial Analysis of the Impact to the State Budget and Economy*, Texas Comptroller of Public Accounts, December 2006, http://www.window.state.tx.us/specialrpt/undocumented/undocumented.pdf (accessed January 6, 2007). Data from Texas Health and Human Services Commission and Carole Keeton Strayhorn, Texas Comptroller of Public Accounts.

disabilities, and dependent children who meet income and assets limitations. In the case of a medical emergency that may threaten an individual's life (including labor and childbirth), Medicaid is available to people who otherwise qualify regardless of immigration status. The estimated $57.9 million total cost of services for undocumented immigrants comprised 10.6% of Texas's health care expenditures in FY2005.

REVENUES. Strayhorn identifies revenue sources from undocumented immigrants in Texas as consumption taxes (general merchandise, motor vehicles, gasoline, alcoholic beverages, cigarettes and tobacco, and hotels), lottery proceeds, utility taxes, court costs and fees, other revenue (including higher education tuition, state park fees, and fireworks taxes), and school property taxes. Table 6.10 provides estimates of these state revenues and the share paid by undocumented immigrants. By this calculation undocumented immigrants contributed about 3.3% of Texas state revenues in FY2005.

ECONOMIC IMPACT. Table 6.11 tallies the costs of undocumented immigrants in Texas and the revenues they generated in FY2005, according to Strayhorn in *Undocumented Immigrants in Texas*. The result was a net $424.7 million positive impact on the state of Texas. Strayhorn notes, however, that undocumented immigrants had an estimated negative impact of $928.9 million on local governments and hospitals.

Cost of Undocumented Immigrants to Colorado

Jones and Baker note in *Costs of Federally Mandated Services to Undocumented Immigrants in Colorado* that "while there is a small deficit, it is clear ... that undocumented immigrants are not bankrupting state and local government" in Colorado. Jones and Baker examine the cost of federally mandated services provided to Colorado's undocumented immigrants during fiscal years 2005 and 2006. The $224.9 million expense came from the three major categories used by Strayhorn: K–12 education, emergency medical care, and incarceration. They do not include in-state tuition expenses for higher education. According to Jones and Baker, a March 2006 report by Defend Colorado Now, an organization they characterized as "proponents of a proposed constitutional amendment to deny nonfederally mandated, non-emergency government services to undocumented immigrants in Colorado," estimated the costs of these services at over $1 billion. Jones and Baker note that a May 2006 *Issue Brief* by the Colorado Legislative Council placed the cost of these services considerably lower at $218 million.

Key differences among these studies are the data sources and methods used to determine how many undocumented residents are in a state and what services they

TABLE 6.10

Estimated Texas state revenue from illegal aliens, fiscal year 2005

Revenue source	Total revenue for selected taxes and fees	Estimated revenue from undocumented immigrants	Percent of total
Major consumption taxes and fees	$23,798.7	$866.7	3.6%
Lottery	$1,584.1	$60.9	3.8%
Utilities-related	$664.0	$19.5	2.9%
Court costs and fees	$337.9	$20.6	6.1%
All other revenue	$1,640.5	$31.2	1.9%
State revenue subtotal	$28,025.1	$999.0	3.6%
School property tax	$20,194.9	$582.1	2.9%
Total estimated revenue	**$48,220.0**	**$1,581.1**	**3.3%**

Note: Amounts may not add due to rounding.

SOURCE: Carole Keeton Strayhorn, "Exhibit 17. Estimated Revenue from Undocumented Immigrants Fiscal 2005 (in Millions)," in *Undocumented Immigrants in Texas: A Financial Analysis of the Impact to the State Budget and Economy*, Texas Comptroller of Public Accounts, December 2006, http://www.window.state.tx.us/specialrpt/undocumented/undocumented.pdf (accessed January 6, 2007). Data from Carole Keeton Strayhorn, Texas Comptroller of Public Accounts.

TABLE 6.11

Illegal aliens' costs, revenues, and economic impact for state of Texas, fiscal year 2005

Costs	
Education	−$967.8
Healthcare	−$58.0
Incarceration	−$130.6
Total	**−$1,156.4**
Revenues	
State revenue	$999.0
School property tax	$582.1
Total	**$1,581.1**
Net impact to state	$424.7

SOURCE: Carole Keeton Strayhorn, "Exhibit 18. State Costs, Revenues and Economic Impact to Texas of Undocumented Immigrants Fiscal Year 2005 (in Millions)," in *Undocumented Immigrants in Texas: A Financial Analysis of the Impact to the State Budget and Economy*, Texas Comptroller of Public Accounts, December 2006, http://www.window.state.tx.us/specialrpt/undocumented/undocumented.pdf (accessed January 6, 2007). Data from Carole Keeton Strayhorn, Texas Comptroller of Public Accounts.

used. Both Jones and Baker and Strayhorn rely on 2005 estimates of the nation's undocumented population developed by Jeffrey S. Passel of the Pew Hispanic Center in *Size and Characteristics of the Unauthorized Migrant Population in the U.S.* (March 7, 2006, http://pewhispanic.org/files/reports/61.pdf). Jones and Baker estimate that 28,480 school-age undocumented children in Colorado cost the state $175.6 million. Furthermore, they tally $31.3 million in emergency medical care that, like Strayhorn, includes legal permanent residents and other authorized foreign nationals.

Jones and Baker estimate that 250,000 undocumented immigrants in Colorado paid $159 million to $194 million in state and local taxes, which covered 70% to 86% of their estimated $224.9 million in expenses to the state for federally mandated services.

COST OF IMMIGRATION CONTROL LEGISLATION. In 2005 Colorado voters approved a ban on state spending on illegal immigrants except as required by the federal government. Mark P. Couch notes in "Pricey Immigration Law" (*Denver Post*, January 25, 2007) that state departments acknowledged spending about $2 million in 2006 to comply with the law. No departments reported a cost savings.

REMITTANCES—THE FLOW OF MONEY OUT OF THE UNITED STATES TO LATIN AMERICA

In "Consulates in U.S. Hit the Road to Help Far-Flung Paisanos" (*Wall Street Journal*, November 29, 2006), Joel Millman describes efforts by Latin American governments to help migrants continue working in the United States. At stake was some $50 billion in remittances—money migrant workers send to support family members back home. Millman states that "for El Salvador, Haiti and Nicaragua, such remittances are their largest source of hard currency." The income is so important to the economies of Latin American countries that diplomatic teams at consulates in the United States are taking their services to their constituents.

Millman describes a visit by members of El Salvador's San Francisco, California, consulate to the remote island of Kodiak, Alaska, where an estimated six hundred Salvadoran nationals worked in the fishing and canning industries. Among other services, the consul staff helped fifty Salvadoran nationals complete applications for Temporary Protected Status that would allow them to stay permanently in the United States. In another example cited by Millman, members of the Mexican consulate set up an assembly line of laptop computers, digital cameras, and fingerprint scanners to renew passports and produce identification documents for Mexican nationals during a trip to Anchorage, Alaska.

Identification Documents

Some foreign governments, including Mexico, issue consular ID cards to their citizens living abroad. According to Katherine Gigliotti and Ann Morse in *The ABCs of IDs for Immigrants in the United States* (December 2004, http://www.ncsl.org/print/immig/immigrantid05.pdf), the ID cards provide no proof of legal immigration status in the United States but help consuls keep track of their citizens for tax and census purposes. Mexican nationals can obtain a Certificate of Consular Registration—the Matrícula Consular—only by appearing in person at one of their country's forty-five consular offices in the United

States (or a traveling office) and providing documentation of their identification and Mexican birth.

Consul officials have persuaded many banks to accept consul IDs in lieu of Social Security cards so foreign nationals can open U.S. bank accounts. According to Millman, the consuls cited concern for migrant safety. Most migrants have no secure place to keep large amounts of money, and keeping cash in their wallets or in their homes makes them targets for theft.

Transmitting Remittances

The effectiveness of such consular campaigns can be seen in migrants' increased use of banks or credit unions to transmit remittances to their families back home. The Inter-American Development Bank (IADB) reports in *Sending Money Home: Leveraging the Development Impact of Remittances* (2006, http://www.iadb.org/news/docs/remittances _EN.pdf) that from 2004 to 2006 remittances sent through banks rose from 8% to 19%. Sixty-three percent of migrants used commercial money transmitters in 2006, whereas 8% still entrusted cash remittances to friends or acquaintances traveling back to their homeland. (See Figure 6.2.)

Value of Remittances to Families Back Home

In *Remittances 2005: Promoting Financial Democracy* (March 2006, http://www.iadb.org/am/2006/doc/ StatisticalComparisons.pdf), the IADB states that "one out of every ten persons around the globe is directly involved with remittances." The IADB estimates that 125 million economic migrants (those who migrate seeking jobs as distinguished from refugees, students, and so on) sent financial support to 500 million family members back home in 2005. Latin America and the Caribbean (LAC) was the largest region receiving remittances. In 2005 about 75% of remittances to LAC were sent from the United States. Other significant sources were western Europe, Japan (primarily to Brazil and Peru), and Canada (primarily to Jamaica and Haiti).

International remittances doubled between 2000 and 2005 to an estimated total of $167 billion, according to the World Bank in *Global Economic Prospects: Economic Implications of Remittances and Migration* (2006, http:// www-wds.worldbank.org). The World Bank suggests that the true amount of remittances is even greater because money is often sent in cash or not reported in the receiving country.

IMMIGRANT PROFILES AND OPINIONS. According to the IADB, in the *Public Opinion Research Study of Latin American Remittance Senders in the United States* (October 18, 2006, http://idbdocs.iadb.org/wsdocs/getdocument.aspx? docnum=826095), over half (55%) of the migrants did not have jobs before they left their homeland. (See Figure 6.3.) Thirty percent earned less than $200 per month, and the average monthly wage for the group surveyed was $150.

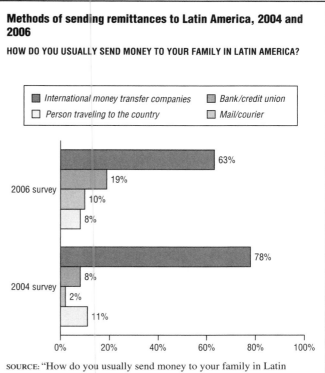

FIGURE 6.2

Methods of sending remittances to Latin America, 2004 and 2006

HOW DO YOU USUALLY SEND MONEY TO YOUR FAMILY IN LATIN AMERICA?

- ■ International money transfer companies
- □ Person traveling to the country
- ■ Bank/credit union
- ■ Mail/courier

2006 survey: 63%, 19%, 10%, 8%

2004 survey: 78%, 8%, 2%, 11%

SOURCE: "How do you usually send money to your family in Latin America?" in *Public Opinion Research Study of Latin American Remittance Senders in the United States*, Inter-American Development Bank, Office of the Multilateral Investment Fund, October 18, 2006, http://idbdocs.iadb.org/wsdocs/getdocument.aspx?docnum=826095 (accessed December 4, 2006)

Within a month after arriving in the United States, more than half of the migrants surveyed had found jobs. The majority (65%) earned $500 or more per month at their first U.S. job. (See Figure 6.4.) The average monthly wage of these new migrants was $900. More than half (61%) of migrants surveyed sent money home each month. (See Figure 6.5.) The average remittance was $300 per month.

DOLLARS FLOW SOUTH. The volume of remittance dollars appears to support the argument of immigration opponents that when people move north by the millions, money moves south by the billions. The IADB suggests that $45 billion in remittances were sent to Latin America in 2006. Figure 6.6 shows the total estimated remittances sent to Latin America by state in 2006. California migrants sent home $13.2 million, more than double the $5.2 million sent from Texas. The smallest amount of remittances—$9 million—came from Vermont.

How Much Money Stays in the States?

In *Sending Money Home*, the IADB calculates the combined annual incomes of the estimated 12.6 million Latin American migrants in the United States at more than $500 billion. Less than 10% of these wages left the United States as remittances in 2006. The remainder was

FIGURE 6.3

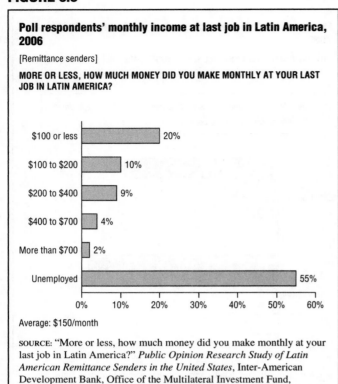

Poll respondents' monthly income at last job in Latin America, 2006

[Remittance senders]

MORE OR LESS, HOW MUCH MONEY DID YOU MAKE MONTHLY AT YOUR LAST JOB IN LATIN AMERICA?

Average: $150/month

SOURCE: "More or less, how much money did you make monthly at your last job in Latin America?" *Public Opinion Research Study of Latin American Remittance Senders in the United States*, Inter-American Development Bank, Office of the Multilateral Investment Fund, October 18, 2006, http://idbdocs.iadb.org/wsdocs/getdocument.aspx?docnum=826095 (accessed December 4, 2006)

FIGURE 6.4

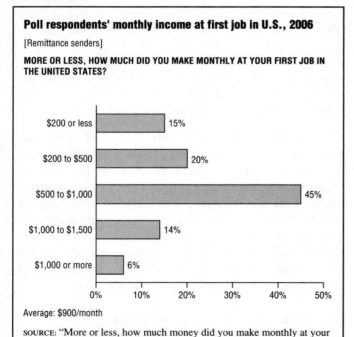

Poll respondents' monthly income at first job in U.S., 2006

[Remittance senders]

MORE OR LESS, HOW MUCH DID YOU MAKE MONTHLY AT YOUR FIRST JOB IN THE UNITED STATES?

Average: $900/month

SOURCE: "More or less, how much money did you make monthly at your first job in the United States?" *Public Opinion Research Study of Latin American Remittance Senders in the United States*, Inter-American Development Bank, Office of the Multilateral Investment Fund, October 18, 2006, http://idbdocs.iadb.org/wsdocs/getdocument.aspx?docnum=826095 (accessed December 4, 2006)

FIGURE 6.5

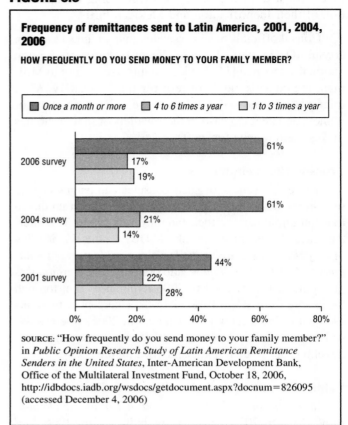

Frequency of remittances sent to Latin America, 2001, 2004, 2006

HOW FREQUENTLY DO YOU SEND MONEY TO YOUR FAMILY MEMBER?

SOURCE: "How frequently do you send money to your family member?" in *Public Opinion Research Study of Latin American Remittance Senders in the United States*, Inter-American Development Bank, Office of the Multilateral Investment Fund, October 18, 2006, http://idbdocs.iadb.org/wsdocs/getdocument.aspx?docnum=826095 (accessed December 4, 2006)

spent in the states and towns where the migrants lived. For example, the IADB estimates that migrants in Texas sent home $5.2 billion in remittances but contributed $52.8 billion to local economies. (See Table 6.12.)

NATIVE AND IMMIGRANT COMPETITION FOR JOBS

In "Cost of Illegal Immigration May Be Less Than Meets the Eye" (*New York Times*, April 16, 2006), Eduardo Porter considers the impact of illegal immigrants on U.S. workers. He reports that the immigrants who poured into California over the past twenty-five years competed for jobs with the least educated among the native population: high school dropouts. Between 1980 and 2004 wages of high school dropouts in California fell 17%. However, Porter cautions readers not to jump to conclusions. In Ohio, a state relatively free of illegal immigrants according to Porter, high school dropout wages declined 31% during the same period.

Porter cites the work of two Harvard economists, George J. Borjas and Lawrence F. Katz, that drew attention to the impact of immigrants on U.S. workers. In 2005 Borjas and Katz estimated that illegal Mexican immigrants who arrived between 1980 and 2000 had reduced the wages of U.S. high school dropouts by

FIGURE 6.6

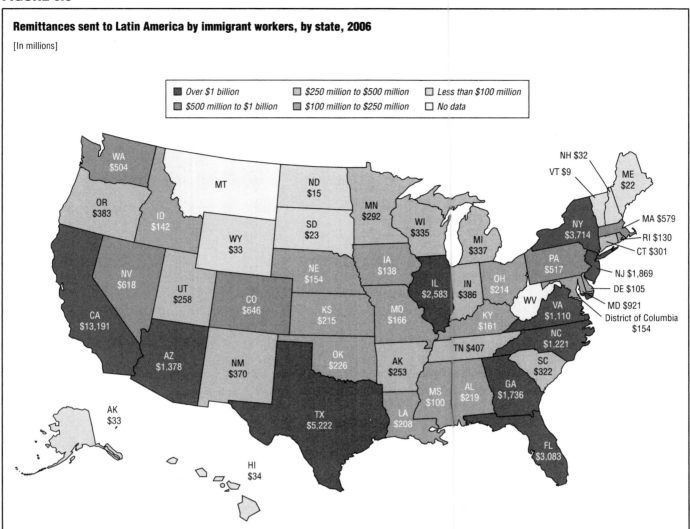

Remittances sent to Latin America by immigrant workers, by state, 2006

[In millions]

- ■ Over $1 billion
- ▨ $500 million to $1 billion
- ▢ $250 million to $500 million
- ▨ $100 million to $250 million
- ▢ Less than $100 million
- □ No data

SOURCE: "Total Money Sent: Remittances to Latin America from the US—2006 (in Millions)," in *Public Opinion Research Study of Latin American Remittance Senders in the United States*, Inter-American Development Bank, Office of the Multilateral Investment Fund, October 18, 2006, http://idbdocs .iadb.org/wsdocs/getdocument.aspx?docnum=826095 (accessed December 4, 2006).

8.2% percent. Porter notes that factors other than immigration affected low-skilled jobs available to dropouts.

Fewer Dropouts and More College Degrees

During the last quarter-century education levels in the United States increased and high school dropout rates fell. The total dropout rate in 2004 was 10.3%, compared with 14.6% in 1972. (See Table 6.13.) Dropout rates for African-American students declined more dramatically during that period, from 21.3% to 11.8%. Porter suggests that increased educational levels further reduced the number of dropouts competing for low-skilled jobs. According to "Special Report: Inequality in America" (*The Economist*, June 15, 2006), the share of U.S. workers with college degrees rose from 20% in 1980 to 30% by 2005.

Technology and Outsourcing

Between 1980 and 2005 technology revolutionized the workplace. Many routine jobs were automated— replaced by more efficient computerized machines. As the number of routine jobs declined, the need for workers with specialized education and computer skills increased. Employers found that some jobs could be done more cheaply in other countries where workers could be paid lower wages. However, many low-skilled jobs such as cleaning, food preparation and delivery, or construction still required onsite workers.

Porter suggests that the availability of low-wage immigrant workers helped new businesses start and existing businesses expand. He cites as an example the Nebraska poultry industry, where an influx of low-wage workers allowed companies to invest in new equipment and create new jobs.

TABLE 6.12

Remittances from the United States to Latin America, 2006

[Estimated dollars in millions]

State	LAC-born adults*	Percent that send regularly	Remittances	Percent increase since 2004	Contribution to local economy
California	5,829,226	63%	13,191	37%	133,365
Texas	2,832,784	47%	5,222	64%	52,792
New York	1,444,224	77%	3,714	4%	37,547
Florida	1,370,345	70%	3,083	26%	31,171
Illinois	935,656	73%	2,583	69%	26,110
New Jersey	712,207	79%	1,869	36%	18,898
Georgia	465,786	85%	1,736	83%	17,555
Arizona	701,863	57%	1,378	127%	13,930
North Carolina	376,272	84%	1,221	47%	12,340
Virginia	318,436	88%	1,110	89%	11,219
Maryland	264,193	88%	921	84%	9,308
Colorado	328,960	57%	646	19%	6,529
Nevada	314,722	57%	618	38%	6,246
Massachusetts	307,158	74%	579	10%	5,849
Pennsylvania	148,452	88%	517	187%	5,230
Washington	233,272	70%	504	43%	5,092
Tennessee	140,611	78%	407	151%	4,113
Indiana	147,652	68%	386	103%	3,906
Oregon	177,190	70%	383	75%	3,868
New Mexico	188,698	57%	370	260%	3,745
Michigan	125,709	71%	337	75%	3,404
Wisconsin	125,174	71%	335	121%	3,389
South Carolina	111,211	78%	322	117%	3,253
Connecticut	159,753	74%	301	133%	3,042
Minnesota	108,912	71%	292	98%	2,949
Utah	131,650	57%	258	58%	2,613
Arkansas	87,573	78%	253	122%	2,562
Oklahoma	115,340	57%	226	45%	2,289
Alabama	75,654	78%	219	47%	2,213
Kansas	81,999	68%	215	128%	2,169
Ohio	79,881	71%	214	98%	2,163
Louisiana	71,861	78%	208	241%	2,102
Missouri	63,392	68%	166	58%	1,677
Kentucky	55,501	78%	161	203%	1,623
D.C.	44,148	88%	154	64%	1,555
Nebraska	58,748	68%	154	92%	1,554
Idaho	65,752	70%	142	48%	1,435
Iowa	52,690	68%	138	100%	1,394
Rhode Island	69,279	74%	130	n/a	1,319
Delaware	30,240	88%	105	n/a	1,065
Mississippi	34,428	78%	100	n/a	1,007
Hawaii	15,974	70%	34	n/a	349
Wyoming	15,244	70%	33	n/a	333
Alaska	15,184	70%	33	n/a	331
New Hampshire	16,998	74%	32	n/a	324
South Dakota	8,795	68%	23	n/a	233
Maine	11,530	74%	22	n/a	220
North Dakota	5,821	68%	15	n/a	154
Vermont	4,969	74%	9	n/a	95
Total 48 states and D.C.	**17,228,349**	**73%**	**45,276**	**51%**	**457,746**

*LAC is Latin America and Caribbean.
Note: No data are available for West Virginia and Montana.

SOURCE: "Remittances 2006: United States to Latin America (Estimated $ in Millions)," in *Sending Money Home: Leveraging the Development Impact of Remittances*, Inter-American Development Bank, Multilateral Investment Fund, 2006, http://www.iadb.org/news/docs/remittances_EN.pdf (accessed December 4, 2006)

TABLE 6.13

Dropout rates for 16- to 24-year-olds by race/ethnicity, October 1972–2004

[In percent]

Year	Total	Race/ethnicity		
		White	Black	Hispanic
1972	14.6	12.3	21.3	34.3
1973	14.1	11.6	22.2	33.5
1974	14.3	11.9	21.2	33.0
1975	13.9	11.4	22.9	29.2
1976	14.1	12.0	20.5	31.4
1977	14.1	11.9	19.8	33.0
1978	14.2	11.9	20.2	33.3
1979	14.6	12.0	21.1	33.8
1980	14.1	11.4	19.1	35.2
1981	13.9	11.4	18.4	33.2
1982	13.9	11.4	18.4	31.7
1983	13.7	11.2	18.0	31.6
1984	13.1	11.0	15.5	29.8
1985	12.6	10.4	15.2	27.6
1986	12.2	9.7	14.2	30.1
1987	12.7	10.4	14.1	28.6
1988	12.9	9.6	14.5	35.8
1989	12.6	9.4	13.9	33.0
1990	12.1	9.0	13.2	32.4
1991	12.5	8.9	13.6	35.3
1992	11.0	7.7	13.7	29.4
1993	11.0	7.9	13.6	27.5
1994	11.5	7.7	12.6	30.0
1995	12.0	8.6	12.1	30.0
1996	11.1	7.3	13.0	29.4
1997	11.0	7.6	13.4	25.3
1998	11.8	7.7	13.8	29.5
1999	11.2	7.3	12.6	28.6
2000	10.9	6.9	13.1	27.8
2001	10.7	7.3	10.9	27.0
2002	10.5	6.5	11.3	25.7
2003	9.9	6.3	10.9	23.5
2004	10.3	6.8	11.8	23.8

SOURCE: "Table 26-1. Status Dropout Rates of 16-through 24-Year-Olds, by Race/Ethnicity: October 1972–2004," in *Student Effort and Educational Progress*, U.S. Department of Education, National Center for Education Statistics, November 13, 2006, http://nces.ed.gov/programs/coe/2006/section3/table.asp?tableID=481 (accessed January 11, 2007)

Immigrant Impact on Native Wages

The Congressional Budget Office (CBO) states in *The Role of Immigrants in the U.S. Labor Market* (November 2005, http://www.cbo.gov/ftpdocs/68xx/doc6853/11-10-Immigration.pdf) that "with the projected slowdown in the growth of the native workforce as the baby-boom generation reaches retirement age, immigrants are likely to hold an even greater share of jobs in the future." Between 1994 and 2004 the native workforce grew 7%, whereas the foreign-born workforce grew 66%. The CBO indicates that "the presence of an increasing number of immigrant workers clearly reduces overall earnings growth ... simply because foreign-born workers earn less than native workers ... [which] lowers the average earnings of the U.S. workforce as a whole." However, the CBO notes that the increased presence of foreign-born workers can distort earnings growth particularly among workers at lower educational levels. Table 6.14 compares average weekly earnings of all male workers (both foreign and native born) to that of native-born male workers at four educational levels. Average wages of all workers with no high school diploma grew just 2.3% between 1994 and 2004.

TABLE 6.14

Earnings growth for native and immigrant men by educational level, 1994–2004

	2004		1994 to 2004
	Number employed (thousands)	Average weekly earnings (dollars)	Real earnings growth (percentage change)
Foreign- and native-born men			
No diploma	6,340	515	2.3
High school diploma	17,690	730	4.3
Some college	15,035	860	6.2
Bachelor's degree	19,240	1,290	11.9
Total	**58,300**	**920**	**10.1**
Native-born men			
No diploma	3,160	575	5.4
High school diploma	15,265	750	5.8
Some college	13,590	870	6.8
Bachelor's degree	16,315	1,310	12.4
Total	**48,330**	**960**	**12.0**

Note: Data are for full-time workers ages 25 to 64.

SOURCE: "Average Weekly Earnings of Foreign-and Native-Born Men, by Educational Attainment, 1994 to 2004," in *The Role of Immigrants in the U.S. Labor Market*, Congressional Budget Office, November 2005, http://www.cbo.gov/ftpdocs/68xx/doc6853/11-10-Immigration.pdf (accessed January 11, 2007)

FIGURE 6.7

Occupations of first- and second-generation immigrants and native-born workers in California, 2004

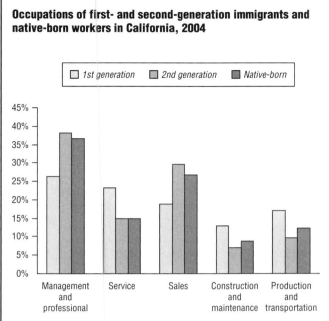

SOURCE: "Workers by Major Occupation: Generation Grouping," in *The Impact of Immigration on the California Economy*, Center for Continuing Study of the California Economy, September 2005, http://www.labor.ca.gov/panel/impactimmcaecon.pdf (accessed January 11, 2007)

However, wages of native-born workers with no high school diploma grew 5.4% in that period. The differences in wage growth narrowed as educational levels increased.

The CBO states that various studies across many local markets find little if any adverse effect on native workers. In particular the CBO cites David Card's "Is the New Immigration Really So Bad?" (August 2005, http://www.phil.frb.org/econ/conf/immigration/card.pdf), in which he studied the effect of immigrant workers on native workers in three hundred metropolitan areas. Card, an economist at the University of California, Berkeley, concluded, "Although immigration has a strong effect on relative supplies of different skill groups, local labor market outcomes of low skilled natives are not much affected by these relative supply shocks." Critics argue that foreign-born workers go where the job opportunities are best. Had foreign-born workers not arrived, workers already present in a community might have enjoyed greater benefits.

Finally, the CBO notes that the long-term impact of immigration on the U.S. workforce will include the children of current immigrants. With many of these children educated in the United States, their work-related characteristics are more likely to resemble those of native-born workers. For example, the Center for the Continuing Study of the California Economy, in *The Impact of Immigration on the California Economy* (September 2005, http://www.labor.ca.gov/panel/impactimmcaecon.pdf), reveals that children of immigrants (second-generation workers) have occupational profiles similar to native-born workers. In 2004 a greater percentage of second-generation workers (39%) were found in management and professional occupations than native workers (37%). (See Figure 6.7.) Immigrant workers (first-generation) represented only 26% of this occupational group. On the other end of the scale, second-generation workers had the lowest representation in construction occupations.

CHAPTER 7
THE IMPACT OF IMMIGRATION ON THE UNITED STATES IN THE TWENTY-FIRST CENTURY

CHANGING AMERICA

The history professor Alan Kraut states in Michael Bowman's "From Colonial Times, Immigrants Have Changed, Invigorated the United States" (*Voice of America*, May 3, 2005):

Newcomers have contributed to the heterogeneity of American culture and the richness, the texture of American life. Whether we are talking about a young George Gershwin coming out of the teeming lower Eastside or modern day Latino musicians or young Asian playwrights, there is no question about it. Our culture has always fed upon newcomers, who have brought with them cultural traditions and added their traditions to ours. . . . Today's immigrants, whether they are coming from Latin America or Southeast Asia, have a great deal in common with those who have come from Italy, Poland, Russia, Ireland, other countries in the past. They are coming for economic reasons and economic opportunities, or they are coming to escape oppressive political regimes. But they are certainly coming for very similar reasons.

Kraut compares the experiences of some Hispanic immigrants with poor Irish Catholics who arrived in large numbers in the mid-1800s. The Irish had to struggle for both an economic foothold and broader societal acceptance. Kraut concludes that "despite being a nation of immigrants and their offspring, established communities have not always been welcoming to new arrivals."

What Will the United States Look Like in Another Fifty Years?

Bowman notes that Fred Hollmann, a demographer for the U.S. Bureau of the Census, predicts a historic shift in the population:

The non-Hispanic white population is not going to continue to be a majority population, as it is now . . . this group [will drop] below 50% sometime in the 2050s. The Hispanic population, we suspect, will become an increasingly large portion [of U.S. population], but at

the same time the Hispanic population will be increasingly a native population—a smaller proportion of it will be recent immigrants, or even immigrants at all. The Asian population will continue to grow quite rapidly. It is still a relatively small proportion of the population, and yet, we see trends that are showing increases in migration from these areas.

American Views on Immigration

The Pew Research Center for the People and the Press and the Pew Hispanic Center, in *America's Immigration Quandary* (March 30, 2006, http://pewhispanic.org/files/reports/63.pdf), state, "The American public views today's immigrants with a mix of admiration and concern. Overall impressions of recent migrants to the U.S. from Latin American and Asian nations are generally positive, and nearly half of the public believes immigrants today are just as willing to assimilate as those of two centuries ago. Still, majorities express the view that new immigrants do not learn English fast enough and pluralities believe that most immigrants today are here illegally."

According to the Pew study, American attitudes toward Latin American immigrants improved dramatically between 1997 and 2006. Just 63% of survey respondents in 1997 believed immigrants from Latin America work very hard, and 55% said Latino immigrants often go on welfare. Responding to the same survey choices in a 2006 survey, 80% said Latinos work very hard, and 37% saw Latinos as frequent welfare users. Nationwide, 49% said they often came in contact with people who speak little or no English, a dramatic increase from 28% in a 1997 survey.

The Pew study finds that exposure to immigrants influenced American attitudes. Native-born Americans who lived in areas with few immigrants did not see immigration as a problem in their local communities. However, they were more likely to view immigrants as a burden to

TABLE 7.1

Public opinion on how attitudes toward immigration relate to experience with foreign-born people, 2006

	Concentration of foreign-born in area*		
	High	Med	Low
The growing number of newcomers to the US ...	%	%	%
Threaten traditional American customs and values	47	46	60
Strengthen American society	48	48	33
Mixed/don't know	5	6	7
	100	100	100
Immigrants from Latin America ...			
Have strong family values	**87**	80	76
Often go on welfare	29	34	**43**
Increase crime	30	26	**40**
Legal immigration should be decreased	37	39	**52**
Immigration problem in your community			
Very big	**33**	19	10
Moderately big	21	21	18
Small/none	44	57	68
Don't know	2	3	4
	100	100	100

*Percent foreign-born in respondent's zip code, based on national survey only. Analysis limited to those whose parents were U.S.-born.

SOURCE: "Immigration: Where You Live And How You Feel," in *America's Immigration Quandary*, The Pew Research Center for the People & The Press, Pew Hispanic Center, March 30, 2006, http://people-press.org/reports/pdf/274.pdf (accessed January 19, 2007)

TABLE 7.2

Public opinion about Latin and Asian immigrants, 1993, 1997, and 2006

PERCENT SAYING EACH CHARACTERISTIC APPLIES TO ...

	1993	1997	2006	Change 93–06
Immigrants from Latin American countries	%	%	%	
Work very hard	65	63	80	+15
Have strong family values	72	75	80	+8
Keep to themselves	—	—	45	
Do very well in school	42	29	41	−1
Often end up on welfare	60	55	37	−23
Significantly increase crime	62	43	33	−29
Immigrants from Asian countries				
Work very hard	74	77	82	+8
Have strong family values	77	73	79	+2
Do very well in school	74	69	75	+1
Keep to themselves	—	—	49	
Significantly increase crime	43	28	19	−24
Often end up on welfare	38	27	17	−21

SOURCE: "Impressions of Latin and Asian Immigrants Grow More Positive," in *America's Immigration Quandary*, The Pew Research Center for the People & The Press, Pew Hispanic Center, March 30, 2006, http://people-press.org/reports/pdf/274.pdf (accessed January 19, 2007)

the nation and a threat to American customs. They also held more negative opinions of Hispanics. Sixty percent of respondents living in areas with low concentrations of foreign-born people saw immigrants as a threat and believed that immigrants from Latin America often go on welfare (43%) and increase crime (40%). (See Table 7.1.) By contrast, only 47% of respondents who lived in areas with high foreign-born populations saw immigrants as a threat. Just 29% believed Latin American immigrants were on welfare, and 30% believed they increased crime. Attitudes also changed over time. The Pew study finds that impressions of both Latin American and Asian immigrants have become significantly more favorable since the 1990s. Just 37% of total 2006 survey respondents thought Latin American immigrants ended up on welfare, compared with 60% in 1993. (See Table 7.2.) Images of Asian immigrants as increasing crime dropped from 43% in 1993 to 19% in 2006.

LATIN AMERICAN IMPACT
Expanding Influence of Spanish Language

The Census Bureau reports in *Statistical Abstract of the United States: 2007* (2006, http://www.census.gov/prod/2006pubs/07statab/pop.pdf) that 49.6 million people living in the United States in 2004 spoke a language other than English at home. Spanish was predominant in 61%

of these homes. (See Figure 7.1.) The next largest single language group was the 5% who spoke Chinese at home.

By 2006 a dramatic rise in Spanish-language marketing and bilingual services added to American concerns about assimilation of the growing Spanish-speaking population. In "Marketing en Español" (*Denver Post*, December 24, 2006, http://www.denverpost.com/business/ci_4894232), Elizabeth Aguilera reports that the estimated $750 billion annual spending power of the Spanish-speaking population is "captivating corporate America." She estimates spending on Spanish-language marketing by the five hundred largest print and television advertisers in the United States had increased 42% since 2003. Using Wal-Mart as an example of businesses that cater to the Spanish-speaking population, Aguilera reports the national retailer had implemented signage in several languages to make stores user-friendly. It also added services such as low-cost payroll check cashing and money transfers that are particularly attractive to Spanish-speaking immigrant shoppers.

Radio, television, and print media sought to tap the Spanish-speaking market. Sandra Yin reports in "Look Who's Tuned In—Overview of Spanish-Language Radio Broadcasting Market" (*American Demographics*, October 1, 2002) that in 2001 the 603 Spanish-language radio stations in the United States represented just 5.6% of all commercial stations. However, this represented an 82% increase in just ten years. In *Hispanic Radio Today: How America Listens to Radio* (2005, http://www.arbitron

FIGURE 7.1

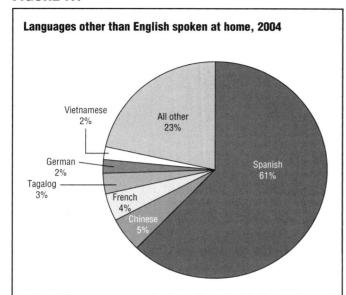

Languages other than English spoken at home, 2004

Vietnamese 2%
German 2%
Tagalog 3%
French 4%
Chinese 5%
All other 23%
Spanish 61%

Notes: Data based on persons age 5 and older. Spanish includes Spanish Creole and French includes French Creole, Patois, and Cajun.

SOURCE: Adapted from "Table 51. Languages Spoken at Home by Language: 2004," in *Statistical Abstract of the United States: 2007*, U.S. Census Bureau, http://www.census.gov/prod/2006pubs/07statab/pop.pdf (accessed December 21, 2006)

.com/downloads/hispanicradiotoday05.pdf), Arbitron indicates that 750 of the more than 13,800 U.S. radio stations broadcast in Spanish.

WILL IMMIGRANTS WHO DO NOT SPEAK ENGLISH ASSIMILATE? According to Aguilera, critics contend that Spanish-focused advertising makes it easier for illegal immigrants to survive in the United States and weakens efforts to get legal immigrants to assimilate and learn English. U.S. Representative Tom Tancredo, a leading spokesperson for tougher immigration laws, believes that marketing in Spanish "is causing a problem. It makes it easier for people to be here without assimilating." Tancredo accuses companies that do business in Spanish of accommodating the deficiencies of people who lack adequate English skills.

Barbara Schoetzau reports in "New US Immigrants Creating Different Assimilation Patterns" (*Voice of America*, May 2, 2005) that Anthony Orum, a specialist in immigration issues and trends at the University of Illinois, cites studies showing noticeable differences in recent patterns of assimilation. Most strikingly, unlike earlier groups, many recent immigrants have abandoned inner cites and resettled in suburban ethnic enclaves, where they are able to survive without learning English well.

Anxiety about the growing use of Spanish and bilingual services is evidenced by efforts in some states and cities to adopt English as the official language. In "English as Official Language Gains Support at Local Level"

(*USA Today*, November 17, 2006), Oren Dorell notes that many states have designated English the official language for conducting business. One such law, Arizona's Proposition 103, passed by a three-to-one ratio in the 2006 elections. An Associated Press exit poll estimated 48% of Hispanic voters supported the measure. The Pew Hispanic Center, in the fact sheet "Hispanic Attitudes toward Learning English" (June 7, 2006, http://pewhispanic.org/files/factsheets/20.pdf), finds that in 2006, 57% of Hispanics believed "immigrants have to speak English to be a part of American society." Dorell notes that Lydia Guzman of the Phoenix Coalition for Latino Political Action opposes the new English-only law. Guzman believes that many Arizona Hispanics have lived in the United States for generations, do not speak Spanish, and thus do not appreciate the language struggles of new immigrants. Further expressing their frustration with illegal immigration, Arizona voters also passed a law mandating that all public school education be conducted in English; students not fluent in English are placed in intensive English programs for one year while continuing with other academic subjects.

Mary Kent and Robert Lalasz, in "In the News: Speaking English in the United States" (Population Reference Bureau, June 2006, http://www.prb.org/Articles/2006/IntheNewsSpeakingEnglishintheUnitedStates.aspx), discuss the studies by the researchers Rubén G. Rumbaut and Alejandro Portes. Rumbaut and Portes argue that young immigrants (aged five to seventeen) adapt to English quickly because it is the dominant language of popular youth media from video to the Internet. When they studied second-generation (born in the United States) immigrant students in the Miami and San Diego school systems, they found that 99% spoke fluent English by age seventeen, and less than one-third remained fluent in the language of their parents.

INFLUENCE OF COMPUTERS AND THE INTERNET ON EDUCATION AND LANGUAGE. The study *Crossing the Divide: Immigrant Youth and Digital Disparity in California* (Center for Justice, Tolerance, and Community, September 2006, http://cjtc.ucsc.edu/docs/digital.pdf) by Robert W. Fairlie et al. raises concerns about the lack of access to computers in education and language acquisition of immigrant youth. Nationwide in 2003, 53.9% of immigrant children had access to a computer at home, compared with 75% of native-born children. (See Figure 7.2.) Asian immigrant youth were the exception; they had greater home access to computers, Internet, and high-speed Internet than any other group, including native-born Asian youth. Immigrant families from the Philippines had the greatest rate of home computer availability (82.6%), whereas families from India had the greatest rate of home Internet (77.3%) and high-speed Internet access (42.4%). (See Table 7.3.) Families from Mexico, by far the largest

FIGURE 7.2

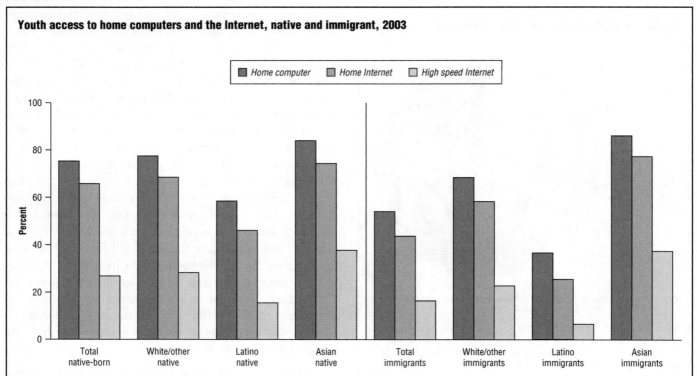

Youth access to home computers and the Internet, native and immigrant, 2003

Legend: ■ Home computer ■ Home Internet □ High speed Internet

Categories (left to right): Total native-born, White/other native, Latino native, Asian native, Total immigrants, White/other immigrants, Latino immigrants, Asian immigrants

SOURCE: Robert W. Fairlie, Rebecca A. London, Rachel Rosner, and Manuel Pastor, "Exhibit 3.5. Percent of U.S. Youth Ages 5–25 with Access to Home Computers and the Internet," in *Crossing the Divide: Immigrant Youth and Digital Disparity in California*, Center for Justice, Tolerance, and Community, Community Technology Foundation of California, September 2006, http://cjtc.ucsc.edu/docs/digital.pdf (accessed January 26, 2007)

TABLE 7.3

Home technology access rates for 20 largest immigrant groups, 2003

Country of origin	Percent with home computer	Percent with home Internet	Percent with high-speed Internet	Population in U.S.
Philippines	82.6%	75.3%	32.0%	1,460,380
India	79.9%	77.3%	42.4%	1,186,091
Korea	78.3%	72.0%	39.4%	815,622
England	76.7%	70.3%	36.4%	461,340
Canada	76.2%	70.7%	31.6%	678,589
China	73.3%	66.6%	35.2%	1,171,926
Vietnam	69.6%	56.0%	17.7%	870,960
Poland	65.9%	53.1%	16.0%	496,568
Germany	65.6%	58.8%	18.9%	581,777
Jamaica	64.9%	52.5%	15.5%	614,725
Russia	64.4%	51.9%	19.7%	460,766
Colombia	62.2%	57.9%	13.6%	579,560
Italy	54.8%	50.1%	18.6%	451,588
Haiti	51.7%	33.9%	13.7%	572,276
Dominican Republic	51.1%	42.4%	17.7%	695,399
Cuba	50.9%	39.8%	11.5%	967,051
El Salvador	50.6%	33.2%	11.7%	947,793
Mexico	33.5%	23.0%	5.9%	10,330,580
Guatemala	31.3%	20.4%	8.3%	591,873
Honduras	22.6%	19.9%	6.7%	398,976

SOURCE: Robert W. Fairlie, Rebecca A. London, Rachel Rosner, and Manuel Pastor, "Exhibit 3.8. Home Technology Access Rates for 20 Largest Immigrant Groups in the United States," in *Crossing the Divide: Immigrant Youth and Digital Disparity in California*, Center for Justice, Tolerance, and Community, Community Technology Foundation of California, September 2006, http://cjtc.ucsc.edu/docs/digital.pdf (accessed January 26, 2007)

immigrant population group, fell among the lowest three groups for home computer availability (33.5%) and Internet access (23%). Fairlie and his collaborators note that Spanish-speaking households are least likely to have home computers and Internet access. According to the authors of *Crossing the Divide*, other research finds high school graduation rates are six to eight percentage points higher for students with home computer access. Researchers speculate that students with home computers have less idle time to become involved in disruptive or dangerous behaviors.

MEXICAN INFLUENCE. The U.S. Library of Congress (LOC), in *Immigration: Mexican* (April 20, 2005, http://memory.loc.gov/learn/features/immig/mexican.html), notes that Mexican-Americans now live in all regions of the country and can be found in most professions and trades. The greatest impact of Mexican immigration may be its contribution to the growing Latin American influence on the everyday life of all Americans. The nation's clothing, music, architecture, literature, and food have all been influenced by growing Latin and Mexican-American populations. According to the LOC, American English has been most profoundly affected by the influx of Spanish-speaking immigrants from Mexico and other nations. More people in the United States speak Spanish than ever before, and many find it a great advantage to speak more than one language. Mexican immigrants and their descendants now make up a significant portion of the U.S. population and have become an influential social and cultural group in the United States.

Immigration Energizes the Catholic Church

In "Nuevo Catholics" (*New York Times Magazine*, December 24, 2006), David Rieff describes Sunday Mass at St. Thomas the Apostle Church in downtown Los Angeles—eight packed services, seven in Spanish. The Hispanic influence on this Californian church might be expected because the state has a long history of immigration from Latin America and has the largest immigrant population of any U.S. state. However, Rieff suggests that Hispanic immigrants are leading a nationwide resurgence of the Catholic Church. In Smyrna, Georgia, where Hispanic immigration was a recent phenomenon, one Catholic church offered three out of seven Sunday masses in Spanish.

Rieff states, "Today, more than 40 percent of the Hispanics residing in the United States, legally and illegally, are foreign-born, and the fate of the American Catholic Church has become inextricably intertwined with the fate of these immigrants and their descendants." He cites statistics on the decline of the American church in the latter half of the twentieth century. Between 1958 and 2000 attendance at Mass fell from 74% of self-identified Catholics to 25%. By 2002 just 786 Catholic high schools remained from a national peak of 1,556 in 1965. During the same period the number of seminarians preparing for the priesthood fell from 49,000 to 4,700.

In 2002 an estimated twenty-five million Hispanics represented 39% of the Catholic population in the United States and, since 1960, they accounted for 71% of new Catholics in the nation. Rieff notes that new priests appointed in the archdiocese of Los Angeles are required to have adequate bilingual skills to say Mass and take confessions in Spanish or in another language of local immigrant populations. Tagalog and Vietnamese are in particular demand in the central Los Angeles area.

Rieff indicates that Mass has become less formal, reflecting the intimate, family-oriented style of the Latin American church. Monsignor David O'Connell of another Los Angeles Catholic church tells Rieff, "For many immigrants, the church is the mediating institution they trust the most, in which they feel they already have a foothold and are treated with respect." Priests, O'Connell explains, spend much of their time acting as go-betweens for the immigrant community, including illegal aliens, and local authorities.

NEW YORK CITY—IMMIGRATION MICROCOSM

In 1992 the New York City Department of City Planning prepared a detailed analysis of the city's immigration patterns during the 1980s. The information proved so valuable that the Planning Department continued to study the city's immigration patterns and publish periodic reports. The fourth such study, *The Newest New Yorkers, 2000: Immigrant New York in the New Millennium* (http://home2 .nyc.gov/html/dcp/html/census/nny.shtml), was released in October 2004.

The report notes that after 1950 most U.S. cities in the Northeast and Midwest experienced population declines. The thriving postwar economy made houses affordable; subsequently, many families moved to new homes in the suburbs. New shopping and business centers followed, resulting in economic changes and job losses for established urban areas. Even though New York experienced similar suburban flight, a steady influx of immigrants replenished the city's population. In 2000 New York City's population totaled approximately 8 million, of which 2.9 million were foreign-born residents, the greatest number of immigrants in the city's history.

Foreign-Born in the New York City Workforce

Given that the foreign born accounted for 43% of all workers in New York City in 2000, according to *The Newest New Yorkers*, immigrants were a vital part of the city's labor force. They represented 64% of manufacturing workers and 58% of construction workers. More than one-third of foreign-born workers in manufacturing were employed in textile and apparel-producing industries. Immigrants represented more than half (54%) of all workers in accommodation, food, and other services—23,800 were employed in private households. The city's hospitals, home healthcare businesses, nursing facilities, schools, colleges, and universities employed 311,300 foreign-born workers.

A number of entrepreneurial foreign-born residents established their own businesses. Many imported and sold goods from their home countries to other immigrants and tourists. Ethnic restaurants have long been an attraction of the city's neighborhoods, and each new wave of immigrants added different scents and flavors that attracted city dwellers and visitors alike.

New York City's Population

The Newest New Yorkers concludes that "the post-1965 flow of immigrants to New York mitigated catastrophic population losses in the 1970s, stabilized the city's population in the 1980s, helped the city reach a new population peak in 2000, and continues to play a crucial role in the city's population growth."

IMMIGRANT ENTREPRENEURS CONTRIBUTE TO THE U.S. ECONOMY
Venture Capital–Financed Immigrant Entrepreneurs

According to Stuart Anderson and Michaela Platzer in *American Made: The Impact of Immigrant Entrepreneurs*

TABLE 7.4

Percentage of immigrant-founded, venture-backed public companies, by year established, selected years 1980–2005

Year founded	Immigrant-founded	Native-founded	Total	Immigrant-founded percent of all U.S. venture-backed public companies
Prior to 1980	8	115	123	7%
1980–1989	48	198	246	20%
1990–2005	88	268	356	25%

SOURCE: Stuart Anderson and Michaela Platzer, "Percentage of Immigrant-Founded Venture-Backed Public Companies by Year Established," in *American Made: The Impact of Immigrant Entrepreneurs and Professionals on U.S. Competitiveness*, National Venture Capital Association, November 15, 2006, http://www.nvca.org/pdf/AmericanMade_study.pdf (accessed December 7, 2006). Data from Thomson Financial.

TABLE 7.5

Immigrant-founded, venture-backed public companies, by industry, 2005

Industry	Number of companies	Employment	Percent of immigrant-founded firms by industry
High-tech manufacturing	60	282,442	42%
Information technology	34	48,794	24%
Life sciences*	30	18,660	21%
Professional, scientific, and technical services	6	17,317	4%
Other services	5	14,919	3%
Other manufacturing	5	13,177	3%
Finance and insurance	2	8,872	1%
E-commerce	2	234	1%
Total	**144**	**404,415**	**100%**

*Life sciences includes research and production of medical equipment and pharmaceuticals and medical services delivery.
Note: Employment reflects 2005 worldwide total.

SOURCE: Stuart Anderson and Michaela Platzer, "Immigrant-Founded Venture-Backed U.S. Public Companies by Industry," in *American Made: The Impact of Immigrant Entrepreneurs and Professionals on U.S. Competitiveness*, National Venture Capital Association, November 15, 2006, http://www.nvca.org/pdf/AmericanMade_study.pdf (accessed December 7, 2006). Data from Hoover's.

and Professionals on U.S. Competitiveness (November 15, 2006, http://www.nvca.org/pdf/AmericanMade_study.pdf), immigrant entrepreneurs and foreign-born professionals, scientists, and engineers have made significant contributions to the U.S. economy. Between 1990 and 2005 immigrants founded 25% of all venture-capital-financed businesses that went public. (See Table 7.4.) In 2005 these companies, founded by immigrants and publicly traded on the U.S. stock exchanges, employed an estimated 220,000 people in the United States and generated more than $130 billion in revenues.

Venture capitalists finance start-up businesses that demonstrate strong potential for rapid and profitable growth. Venture capitalists expect to wait for return on their investment, unlike other lenders that require regular principal and interest payments. With part ownership in a business, the venture capitalist encourages putting profits back into growth of the business and expects a huge return on investment when the company goes public. Private companies choose to become public companies by selling company stock to the general public. The company enters the public arena with an initial public offering of stock.

IMMIGRANT-FOUNDED PUBLIC COMPANIES. Anderson and Platzer note that immigrant-founded companies go public more quickly—6.8 years is the average time from founding to initial public offering date, compared with 9.3 years for companies with U.S.-born founders. Furthermore, in 2005 the majority of immigrant-founded public companies were in high-tech manufacturing (42%), information technology (24%), and life sciences (21%) industries. (See Table 7.5.) Together, the 144 immigrant-founded public companies identified by Anderson and Platzer employed more than 400,000 people worldwide.

India was the leading source country for immigrant entrepreneurs who founded these companies—22% from India, 12% from Israel, and 11% from Taiwan. Other company founders came from Canada, France, the United

Kingdom, Germany, Australia, China, Iran, and two dozen additional countries.

IMMIGRANT-FOUNDED PRIVATE COMPANIES. Anderson and Platzer also examine venture-backed private companies. Information about public companies is found in public records, but private companies are not required to publish financial information; Anderson and Platzer note that private company data used in their report is limited to the 342 companies that responded to their survey. This was only a small percentage of the more than 5,400 venture-backed private firms in the United States as of January 1, 2006, as reported by Ernst & Young in *Ernst & Young/Dow Jones VentureOne Annual Venture Insight Study* (March 28, 2006, http://www.ey.com/GLOBAL/content.nsf/International/Strategic_Growth_Markets_-_Annual_Venture_Insight_Study_2006).

FOREIGN STUDENTS WHO STUDIED IN THE UNITED STATES AND LATER FOUNDED U.S. BUSINESSES. Though small, the sample of private venture-backed companies responding to Anderson and Platzer provides some insight into immigrant entrepreneurs. Of responding businesses, 47% were started by immigrants. Forty-six percent of the immigrant founders came to the United States as students, and half of these students started their companies within twelve years of entering the United States. Sixty-nine percent of the founders became U.S. citizens. These start-up companies had an average of 123 employees. Forty percent reported annual revenues less than $1 million, and 4% had annual revenues exceeding $100 million.

FIGURE 7.3

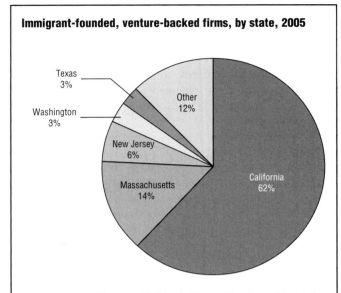

Immigrant-founded, venture-backed firms, by state, 2005

- Texas 3%
- Washington 3%
- New Jersey 6%
- Massachusetts 14%
- Other 12%
- California 62%

SOURCE: Stuart Anderson and Michaela Platzer, "Immigrant-Founded Venture-Backed Firms by State," in *American Made: The Impact of Immigrant Entrepreneurs and Professionals on U.S. Competitiveness*, National Venture Capital Association, November 15, 2006, http://www.nvca.org/pdf/AmericanMade_study.pdf (accessed December 7, 2006). Data from Thomson Financial.

Public or private, California was home to the majority (62%) of headquarters for immigrant-founded venture-backed businesses in 2005. (See Figure 7.3.) This is due in part to the concentration of high-tech firms in the Silicon Valley.

Immigrant Women—Fastest Growing Group of Business Owners

According to Susan C. Pearce, in "Today's Immigrant Woman Entrepreneur" (*Immigration Policy in Focus*, January 2005, http://www.ailf.org/ipc/ipf011705.asp), immigrant women comprised one of the fastest growing groups of business owners in the United States. Immigrant women were more likely than nonimmigrant women to own their own business. Pearce cites the 2000 census, which reveals that 8.3% of all employed immigrant women were business owners, compared with 6.2% of employed native-born women. Between 1990 and 2000 the number of immigrant women business owners increased nearly 190%. According to Pearce, "Immigrant women entrepreneurs represent a potential source of continued new business growth that brings a broad range of international skills to the work force."

U.S. SCHOOLS EDUCATING FOREIGN STUDENTS

Allan E. Goodman, the president and chief executive officer of the Institute of International Education, addressed the cultural and economic benefits of welcoming foreign students to U.S. college campuses in a statement before the Senate Foreign Relations Committee on October 6, 2004 (http://www.senate.gov/~foreign/testimony/2004/GoodmanTestimony041006.pdf):

> Educational exchange programs ... are the best investment that America can make in reducing misunderstanding of our culture, our people and our policies. An educational experience in America pays dividends to our nation's public diplomacy over many years. ... Foreign students ... come into the classroom with a very different worldview from American students. Raised in a different culture with a different history, they enrich the classroom discussion and share their global perspectives with American classmates, many of whom may never have the opportunity to study or travel abroad. ... For the vast majority [of U.S. students] who will never study abroad, academic dialog with foreign students on U.S. campuses may well be their only training opportunity before entering careers which will almost certainly be global, whether in business, government, academia, or the not-for-profit sector.

Foreign Student Enrollment

Enrollments by international students at U.S. colleges and universities increased steadily between the 1959–60 academic year, when 48,486 foreign students attended U.S. academic institutions, and 2002, when 586,323 foreign students were enrolled. By 2006 the number had declined by 21,557 students, although total enrollments in U.S. colleges and universities had increased by about 1.7 million U.S. students. In the press release "New Enrollment of Foreign Students in the U.S. Climbs in 2005/06" (November 13, 2006, http://opendoors.iienetwork.org/?p=89251), Goodman reports an 8% increase in new international students enrolling for the first time in the fall semester of 2005. He notes, "America's colleges and universities have begun to see positive results from their proactive efforts to recruit international students and make them feel welcome on campus. With several thousand campuses able to host international students (ten times as many as any of the other leading host countries), the U.S. has a huge untapped capacity to meet the growing worldwide demand for higher education."

According to the Institute of International Education in *Open Doors 2006* (November 13, 2006, http://opendoors.iienetwork.org/), the top school of choice for international students in 2005–06 was the University of Southern California, with 6,881 foreign students enrolled. Columbia, Purdue, and New York universities and the University of Texas at Austin each enrolled more than 5,000 foreign students. Schools in California (75,385 students) and New York (64,283) attracted nearly 25% of the total 564,766 foreign students counted in the survey. Whereas some states saw significant increases in international students, such as Indiana (6.4%) and North Carolina (5.3%), other states saw foreign student enrollments decline, such as in Virginia (−6.4%) and Maryland (−4.1%). (See Table 7.6.) India was the leading country

TABLE 7.6

States with the most international students, 2004–05 and 2005–06 academic years

Rank	State	2004–05	2005–06	% Change
1	California	75,032	75,385	0.5
2	New York	61,944	64,283	3.8
3	Texas	47,367	46,869	−1.1
4	Massachusetts	27,985	28,007	0.1
5	Florida	26,264	26,058	−0.8
6	Illinois	25,021	25,116	0.4
7	Pennsylvania	22,773	22,418	−1.6
8	Michigan	20,879	20,827	−0.3
9	Ohio	17,952	18,002	0.3
10	Indiana	13,149	13,992	6.4
11	Maryland	13,439	12,887	−4.1
12	New Jersey	12,571	12,779	1.7
13	Georgia	12,111	11,921	−1.6
14	Virginia	12,501	11,701	−6.4
15	Washington	10,674	11,234	5.2
16	Missouri	9,540	9,641	1.1
17	Arizona	10,011	9,617	−3.9
18	North Carolina	9,029	9,507	5.3
19	Minnesota	8,491	8,709	2.6
20	Oklahoma	8,454	8,149	−3.6

SOURCE: "States with the Most International Students, 2004/05 & 2005/06," in *Open Doors 2006 Fast Facts*, Institute of International Education (IIE), 2006, http://opendoors.iienetwork.org/file_depot/0-10000000/0-10000/3390/folder/50084/Open+Doors+2006_FastFacts.pdf (accessed January 27, 2007)

of origin for international students in both the 2004–05 and 2005–06 academic years, even though the number of students from India dropped nearly 5% in 2005–06.

The top fields of study for international students in 2005–06 were business and management (17.9%) and engineering (15.7%). (See Table 7.7.) Enrollment in optional practical training—internships related to the

major field of study—was a new trend for international students, increasing 46.1% from the 2004–05 academic year to 2005–06. In his statement before the Senate Foreign Relations Committee, Goodman noted that foreign students have become an important source of graduate-level teaching and research assistants in U.S. universities, particularly in science and engineering fields, because not enough U.S. students apply to fill the available positions.

Foreign Students Contribute to the U.S. Economy

"Educational exchange [is] one of the leading American service export industries, according to the U.S. Department of Commerce," Goodman told the Senate Foreign Relations Committee. The *Open Doors 2006* survey notes that for the 2005–06 academic year, the 564,766 foreign students enrolled in U.S. colleges and universities contributed nearly $13.5 billion to the U.S. economy. A majority of international students (63.4%) reported that they and/or their families provided primary funding for their 2005–06 educational expenses. (See Table 7.8.) U.S. colleges and universities were the other major source of funds for 25.9% of foreign students through scholarships, grants, loans, and assistantships.

In calculating foreign student contributions to the U.S. economy, any U.S. financial aid was subtracted from the total tuition and living expenses paid by the students. Expenses for students' dependents were added. Just 11.3% of international students were married, and most of these students (85%) brought their families with them to the United States. (See Table 7.9.) An estimated 63,786 spouses and 38,224 children accompanied these enrolled foreign students. Living expenses paid by students for

TABLE 7.7

Fields of study for international students, 2004–05 and 2005–06 academic years

Field of study	2004–05 int'l students	2005–06 int'l students	2005–06 % of total	% change
Business & management	100,079	100,881	17.9	0.8
Engineering	92,952	88,460	15.7	−4.8
Other*	59,700	59,404	10.5	−0.5
Physical & life sciences	49,499	50,168	8.9	1.4
Social sciences	46,085	46,132	8.2	0.1
Mathematics & computer sciences	50,747	45,518	8.1	−10.3
Optional practical training	28,432	41,535	7.4	46.1
Fine & applied arts	28,063	29,509	5.2	5.2
Health professions	26,301	27,124	4.8	3.1
Undeclared	27,982	17,888	3.2	−36.1
Intensive English language	16,133	17,239	3.1	6.9
Education	15,697	16,546	2.9	5.4
Humanities	15,850	16,480	2.9	4.0
Agriculture	7,519	7,883	1.4	4.8
Total	**565,039**	**564,766**	**100.0**	**−0.05**

*"Other" mainly includes liberal/general studies, communications & journalism, multi/interdisciplinary studies, and law.

SOURCE: "Fields of Study of International Students, 2004/05 & 2005/06," in *Open Doors 2006 Fast Facts*, Institute of International Education (IIE), 2006, http://opendoors.iienetwork.org/file_depot/0-10000000/0-10000/3390/folder/50084/Open+Doors+2006_FastFacts.pdf (accessed January 27, 2007)

TABLE 7.8

Primary source of funding for international students, 2005–06 academic year

Primary source of funds	2005–06 int'l students	2005–06 % of total
Personal & family	358,318	63.4
U.S. college or university	146,211	25.9
Home government/university	14,476	2.6
U.S. government	2,501	0.4
U.S. private sponsor	8,367	1.5
Foreign private sponsor	8,661	1.5
International organization	1,326	0.2
Current employment	21,745	3.9
Other sources	3,161	0.6
Total	**564,766**	**100.0**

SOURCE: "Primary Source of Funding of International Students, 2005/06," in *Open Doors 2006 Fast Facts*, Institute of International Education (IIE), 2006, http://opendoors.iienetwork.org/file_depot/0-10000000/0-10000/3390/folder/50084/Open+Doors+2006_FastFacts.pdf (accessed January 27, 2007)

these family members were estimated at $432 million annually. California and New York, the states with the greatest number of foreign students, received the greatest economic benefits from international students—$2.1 billion and $1.8 billion, respectively.

Foreign Student Visas Tracked by SEVIS

The U.S. Immigration and Customs Enforcement agency uses the Student and Exchange Visitors Program (SEVIS) to monitor foreign students who have been issued visas to attend U.S. schools. SEVIS (March 31, 2006, http://www.ice.gov/sevis/numbers/student/level_ of_education.htm) reports that in 2006 a total of 611,581 foreign students were in the United States. Even though most discussion of foreign students focuses on colleges and universities, SEVIS notes 3.8% of foreign students attended primary and secondary schools. Another 9.9% chose language schools, and 4.6% attended vocational schools.

The numbers of students reported by SEVIS differ from those reported in the *Open Doors* survey for several reasons. SEVIS tallies visas issued to people reporting active student status on March 31, 2006; numbers in *Open Doors* are based on survey data reported by about one thousand participating colleges and universities for the 2005–06 academic year. SEVIS reports foreign students at all grade levels; *Open Doors* focuses only on college- and university-level foreign students. Even though SEVIS reports people in two student visa categories (F-Academic and M-Vocational), colleges and universities include students holding J-Exchange Visitor visas and other visa categories. For example, a person with a work visa might enroll for part-time education. This person would be counted by *Open Doors* but not by SEVIS. SEVIS reports that in 2006, 40.9% of international students were in graduate-level programs. Schools reporting to *Open Doors* counted 46% of international students in graduate-level programs. (See Table 7.10.) These different percents are due to the reporting times and the 5.4% of graduate students on J visas in the *Open Doors* survey.

Sources of Foreign Students

According to SEVIS, the majority (58%) of 2006 foreign students came from Asia. (See Figure 7.4.) Students

TABLE 7.9

Economic impact of international students in U.S., 2005–06 academic year

Total number of foreign students:	**564,766**

Part 1: Net contribution to U.S. economy by foreign students (2005–06)

Contribution from tuition and fees to U.S. economy:	$9,444,000,000
Contribution from living expenses:	$10,079,000,000
Total contribution by foreign students:	$19,522,000,000
Less U.S. support of 33.1%	−$6,463,000,000
Plus dependents' living expenses:	+$432,000,000
Net contribution to U.S. economy by foreign students and their families:	**$13,491,000,000**

Part 2: Contribution to U.S. economy by foreign students' dependents (2005–06)

Spouses' contribution		**Children's contribution**	
Percent of married students:	11.3%	Number of couples in the U.S.:	63,786
Percent of spouses in the U.S.:	85.0%	Number of children per couple:	0.6
Number of spouses in the U.S.:	63,786	Number of children in the U.S.:	38,224
Additional expenses for a spouse: (% of student living expenses)	25.0%	Additional expenses for a child: (% of student living expenses)	20.0%
Spouses' contribution:	$292,000,000	Children's contribution:	$140,000,000
Net contribution to U.S. economy by foreign students' dependents:			**$432,000,000**

SOURCE: Adapted from "Economic Impact of International Students," in *Open Doors 2006*, Institute of International Education (IIE), 2006, http://opendoors.iienetwork.org/file_depot/0-10000000/0-10000/3390/folder/50084/OD+2006+Econ+Analysis+USA.pdf (accessed January 27, 2007)

TABLE 7.10

International college students in U.S. by academic level and visa type, 2005–06 academic year

	Undergraduate	Graduate	Other	Total
Total international students	**236,342**	**259,717**	**68,707**	**564,766**
Percent of all students	41.8%	46.0%	12.2%	
Percent of level by type of visa:				
F: Academic	85.5%	88.0%	85.0%	86.6%
J: Exchange visitor	3.2%	5.4%	10.8%	5.1%
M: Vocational	0.0%	0.0%	0.2%	0.0%
Other	11.1%	6.6%	4.0%	8.2%

SOURCE: Adapted from "Personal & Academic Characteristics of International Students by Academic Level, 2005/06," in *Open Doors 2006*, Institute of International Education (IIE), 2006, http://opendoors.iienetwork.org/?p=89208 (accessed January 27, 2007)

FIGURE 7.4

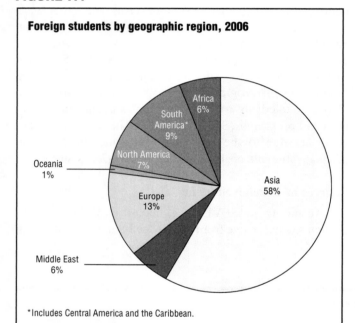

Foreign students by geographic region, 2006

*Includes Central America and the Caribbean.

SOURCE: Adapted from "Students by Geographic Region," in *SEVIS by the Numbers*, U.S. Immigration and Customs Enforcement, March 31, 2006, http://www.ice.gov/sevis/numbers/student/geographic.htm (accessed December 14, 2006)

from North America (7%) and South America (9%), including Central America and the Caribbean, accounted for just 16% of all foreign students. South Korean students brought the greatest number of dependents—34,380. (See Table 7.11.) Students from Pakistan, Russia, Israel, and Egypt also brought high numbers of dependents per student.

PUBLIC OPINION ON IMMIGRATION
Burden or Blessing?

In *A Portrait of "Generation Next"* (January 9, 2007, http://people-press.org/reports/pdf/300.pdf), the

TABLE 7.11

Top 20 countries of citizenship for foreign students in the U.S., 2006

Rank	Country	Active student rank	Dependents
1	South Korea	1	34,380
2	China	3	14,588
3	Japan	4	6,615
4	India	2	6,371
5	Taiwan	5	2,876
6	Israel*	35	2,379
7	Mexico	7	2,241
8	Saudi Arabia	18	2,201
9	Canada	6	2,192
10	Brazil	10	1,893
11	Turkey	8	1,810
12	Pakistan*	23	1,287
13	Kenya	13	1,239
14	Germany	14	1,231
15	Nepal	15	1,185
16	Russia*	27	1,164
17	Egypt*	62	1,149
18	Poland	17	1,149
19	Colombia	19	1,118
20	France	20	1,094

*Not in top 20 countries of citizenship of active students.

SOURCE: "Top 20 Countries of Citizenship by Number of Student Dependents," in *SEVIS by the Numbers*, U.S. Immigration and Customs Enforcement, March 31, 2006, http://www.ice.gov/sevis/numbers/student/dependents.htm (accessed December 14, 2006)

Pew Research Center for the People and the Press finds the American public evenly divided on the impact of immigration: 41% of total respondents see immigrants as a blessing for their hard work and talents, and another 41% consider immigrants a burden because they take jobs, housing, and health care benefits from citizens.

In comparing attitudes toward immigration over a five-year period, researchers in the Pew study *America's Immigration Quandary* find that the public remains divided on views of the overall effect of immigration. In September 2000, 50% of respondents said, "Immigrants today strengthen the U.S. with their hard work and talents." (See Table 7.12.) In March 2006, 52% of respondents said, "Immigrants today are a burden because they take jobs [and] housing." Perhaps the key change in five years is that fewer people were undecided. In 2000, 12% of respondents could not choose between immigrants as a burden or blessing (responded "don't know"). By 2006, only 7% were undecided.

ATTITUDES DIFFER BY AGE GROUP. According to *Portrait of "Generation Next,"* views on immigration differ by age groups. Even though the report was designed as a profile of the eighteen- to twenty-five-year-old group, responses to survey questions were compared by four age groups: Generation Next (born between 1981 and 1988), Generation X (1966–80), baby boomers (1946–64), and seniors (born before 1946).

TABLE 7.12

Public opinion about immigration concerns, 2000, 2005, and 2006

	Sept 2000	Dec 2005	Mar 2006
Immigrants today...	%	%	%
Are a burden because they take jobs, housing	38	44	52
Strengthen the US with their hard work & talents	50	45	41
Don't know	12	11	7
	100	100	100

SOURCE: "Increasing Immigration Worries," in *America's Immigration Quandary*, The Pew Research Center for the People & The Press, The Pew Hispanic Center, March 30, 2006, http://people-press.org/reports/pdf/274.pdf (accessed January 19, 2007)

TABLE 7.13

Public opinion on immigrants, 2004 and 2007

	Age			
	18–25	26–40	41–60	61+
	%	%	%	%
Immigrants today...[a]				
Strengthen the country with their hard work and talents	52	39	44	30
Are a burden because they take jobs, housing, health care	38	33	43	50
Neither/both equally	6	24	10	15
Don't know	4	4	3	5
	100	100	100	100
Growing number of immigrants[b]				
Strengthens American society	67	57	47	38
Threatens our customs and values	30	35	44	45
Neither/both equally	1	3	3	4
Don't know	2	5	6	13
	100	100	100	100

[a]2006 gen next survey.
[b]Pew 2004 typology survey.

SOURCE: "Gen Next and Immigration," in *A Portrait of "Generation Next,"* The Pew Research Center for the People & The Press, January 9, 2007, http://people-press.org/reports/pdf/300.pdf (accessed January 19, 2007)

Among Generation Next, 52% counted immigrants as a blessing, compared with just 30% of seniors (over age sixty-one). (See Table 7.13.) When considering the impact of the surging numbers of new immigrants, 67% of Generation Next thought immigrants strengthened American society, whereas 45% of seniors regarded immigrants as a threat to American customs and values.

ATTITUDES VARY BY REGION. In *America's Immigration Quandary*, Pew researchers find no consensus on the level of immigration problems or solutions. The study of Americans' attitudes toward immigration was based on a nationwide random survey of two thousand adults plus surveys of eight hundred people conducted in each of five metropolitan statistical areas: Phoenix, Arizona; Las Vegas, Nevada; Chicago; Raleigh-Durham, South Carolina; and Washington, D.C. The five metro-

politan areas surveyed were chosen for their different histories of immigration combined with significant recent growth in foreign-born population. Chicago has a long history of immigration. Phoenix is a principal gateway for illegal immigrants from the southwestern border. Las Vegas has experienced significant growth and an influx of Hispanic population. Raleigh-Durham is a site of new Hispanic concentrations in areas of the South that previously had not experienced major immigration growth. Washington, D.C., is an economically thriving area with a majority African-American population.

HOW IMPORTANT IS THE IMMIGRATION PROBLEM? Survey respondents were asked to identify the most important problems facing their local communities. Immigration topped the list only in Phoenix. (See Table 7.14.) However, it ranked among the top four issues—along with traffic congestion, employment availability, and crime—in all five metropolitan areas and in nationwide responses. When asked about problems facing the nation, immigration fell in line behind health care, terrorism, crime, and corrupt politicians. According to the Pew report, immigration was of greatest concern to senior citizens, those with a high school education or less, and white evangelical Protestants.

The public was divided in a variety of ways when asked to choose whether immigrants were a burden because they take jobs, housing, and health care, or strengthen the country with their hard work and talents. Figure 7.5 reveals that even though 52% of all respondents said immigrants were a burden, 64% of Hispanics, 53% of eighteen- to twenty-nine-year-olds, 56% of college graduates, 48% of people with excellent to good finances, and 50% of people living in the West saw immigrants as strengthening the nation.

Most people overestimated the size of the foreign-born population and the relative sizes of the legal and illegal immigrant populations. When asked whether most immigrants were in the United States legally or illegally, 44% said there were more illegals and another 8% thought the numbers were nearly equal. (See Table 7.15.) Respondents in Phoenix estimated 60% of the immigrant population to be illegal. According to Jeffrey S. Passel in *Size and Characteristics of the Unauthorized Migrant Population in the U.S.* (March 7, 2006, http://pewhispanic.org/files/reports/61.pdf), in 2005, 30% of the foreign-born population was unauthorized.

DO IMMIGRANTS TAKE JOBS FROM AMERICANS? The majority (65%) of respondents in the Pew survey said immigrants took jobs Americans did not want, compared with 24% who said immigrants took jobs away from Americans. (See Table 7.16.) About 16% of the people surveyed believed they or a family member had either

TABLE 7.14

Public opinion on how immigration ranks as a local and national problem, 2006

[Percent rating each a "very big problem" for their community]

Nationwide	Phoenix	Las Vegas
33 Jobs availability	**55 Immigration**	53 Traffic congestion
26 Traffic congestion	49 Traffic congestion	**36 Immigration**
21 Immigration	42 Pollution	34 Education
20 Crime	27 Crime	33 Crime
20 Public education	25 Education	23 Pollution
15 Pollution	21 Jobs availability	16 Jobs availability

Raleigh-Durham	Washington DC	Chicago
29 Traffic congestion	60 Traffic congestion	27 Jobs availability
26 Immigration	**21 Immigration**	27 Traffic congestion
22 Jobs availability	20 Crime	20 Crime
18 Crime	18 Education	**19 Immigration**
17 Education	16 Jobs availability	19 Education
11 Pollution	15 Pollution	18 Pollution

[Percent rating each a "very big problem" for the country based on national survey]

	%
Health care system	55
Terrorism	50
Crime	47
Corrupt politicians	46
Immigration	**42**
Environmental pollution	39
Availability of jobs	37

SOURCE: "How Immigration Ranks as a Local Problem," and "Rating National Problems," in *America's Immigration Quandary*, The Pew Research Center for the People & The Press, Pew Hispanic Center, March 30, 2006, http://people-press.org/reports/pdf/274.pdf (accessed January 19, 2007)

lost a job or not obtained a job because the employer hired an immigrant instead.

DO IMMIGRANTS AFFECT SOCIAL SERVICES? According to a majority (62%) of national respondents, immigrants did not have much impact on the quality of local government services. (See Table 7.17.) However, a significant share of respondents in Phoenix (41%), Raleigh-Durham (36%), and Las Vegas (34%) thought local services were worse because of immigrants. More than half of all respondents, except those in the Washington, D.C., metropolitan area, believed that immigrants did not pay their fare share of taxes. Additionally, 67% of respondents said illegal immigrants should not be eligible for local or state social services. However, a majority (71%) did favor educating children of illegal immigrants in public schools.

Use of social services by U.S.-born children of immigrants is a major cost concern. According to the U.S. Constitution, anyone born in the United States is automatically a U.S. citizen regardless of the parents' immigration status. A substantial minority (42%) of respondents in the 2006 Pew survey wanted to change the Constitution to require parents to be legal U.S. residents for a newborn child to be a citizen.

FIGURE 7.5

Public opinion of immigrants as a burden or a means of strengthening our country, by demographic characteristics 2006

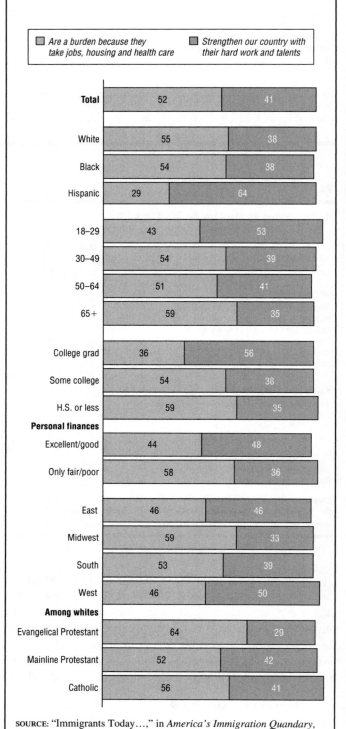

SOURCE: "Immigrants Today…," in *America's Immigration Quandary*, The Pew Research Center for the People & The Press, Pew Hispanic Center, March 30, 2006, http://people-press.org/reports/pdf/274.pdf (accessed January 19, 2007)

SHOULD ILLEGALS STAY OR GO? In 2006, 53% of Americans surveyed thought illegal immigrants should be required to go home, according to Pew researchers in

TABLE 7.15

Public opinion on whether most immigrants are here legally or illegally, 2006

	Legally	Illegally	Think no. is equal	Don't know
National	39	44	8	9=100
Phoenix	26	60	8	6=100
Las Vegas	27	54	7	12=100
Chicago	39	42	9	10=100
Raleigh-Durham	34	51	6	9=100
Washington DC	43	40	6	11=100

SOURCE: "Are Most Immigrants Here Legally or Illegally?" in *America's Immigration Quandary*, The Pew Research Center for the People & The Press, Pew Hispanic Center, March 30, 2006, http://people-press.org/reports/pdf/274.pdf (accessed January 19, 2007)

TABLE 7.16

Public opinion about immigrants taking jobs Americans don't want or taking jobs away from Americans, 2006

	National
Immigrants take jobs …	**%**
That Americans don't want	65
Away from American citizens	24
Both/don't know	11
	100
Self or family member lost job to immigrant worker?	
Yes	16
No	81
Don't know	3
	100

SOURCE: "Immigrants' Impact on Jobs," in *America's Immigration Quandary*, The Pew Research Center for the People & The Press, Pew Hispanic Center, March 30, 2006, http://people-press.org/reports/pdf/274.pdf (accessed January 19, 2007)

America's Immigration Quandary, whereas 40% favored allowing them to stay. Half (49%) of national respondents saw penalizing employers who hire illegal immigrants as the best way to reduce illegal immigration. (See Table 7.18.) Just 9% thought building border fences was a solution. Responses varied slightly by where people lived as seen in the separate surveys of the five metropolitan areas. Among survey respondents in Chicago, 43% favored penalizing employers, and 36% viewed increased border patrol as the best deterrent to illegal immigration.

The 2006 Pew report identifies proposals for a temporary guest worker program as the immigration issue that most divides the nation. Opinion was almost evenly divided among those who favored allowing some illegal immigrants to remain in the United States under a guest worker program (32%), those who said illegal immigrants already in the country should be allowed to stay permanently (32%), and those who said illegal immigrants should be sent home (27%).

Two-thirds (66%) said they would support creation of a government database of everyone eligible to work—both citizens and legal immigrants—and requiring all employers to verify eligibility before hiring someone for any kind of work. Three-quarters (76%) would support a national identity card for everyone who worked. Support for these two measures was strong across all demographic groups, including recent immigrants and Hispanics.

Competing with the World for Workers

In *The State of American Business 2007* (2007, http://www.uschamber.com/publications/reports/sab.htm), Thomas J. Donahue of the U.S. Chamber of Commerce reports that 30% of U.S. high school students do not graduate, and

TABLE 7.17

Public opinion about immigrants' impact on local government services and taxes, 2006

	National	Phoenix	Las Vegas	Chicago	Raleigh Durham	Washington DC
Effect of immigrants on local services	%	%	%	%	%	%
Better	7	10	8	7	7	11
Worse	26	41	34	22	36	25
No difference/none	62	43	52	65	52	55
Don't know	5	6	6	6	5	9
	100	100	100	100	100	100
Do most recent immigrants pay their fair share of taxes?						
Yes	33	33	38	36	29	41
No	56	57	51	56	62	46
Don't know	11	10	11	8	9	13
	100	100	100	100	100	100

SOURCE: "Immigrants, Local Services and Taxes," in *America's Immigration Quandary*, The Pew Research Center for the People & The Press, Pew Hispanic Center, March 30, 2006, http://people-press.org/reports/pdf/274.pdf (accessed January 19, 2007)

TABLE 7.18

Public opinion on the best way to reduce illegal immigration from Mexico, 2006

	National	Phoenix	Las Vegas	Chicago	Raleigh Durham	Washington DC
	%	%	%	%	%	%
Penalize employers	49	45	46	43	52	50
Increase border patrol	33	32	31	36	31	30
Build more fences	9	10	10	9	7	7
Don't know	9	13	13	12	10	13
	100	100	100	100	100	100

SOURCE: "Best Way to Reduce Illegal Immigration from Mexico," in *America's Immigration Quandary*, The Pew Research Center for the People & The Press, Pew Hispanic Center, March 30, 2006, http://people-press.org/reports/pdf/274.pdf (accessed January 19, 2007)

TABLE 7.19

Public opinion on issues related to immigration that are of the biggest concern, October 2006

WHICH OF THE FOLLOWING ISSUES RELATED TO IMMIGRATION WOULD YOU SAY IS YOUR BIGGEST CONCERN?

27%	Burden on taxpayers, such as health care and schools
14%	Immigrants' failure to assimilate or become part of American culture
13%	Compromised national security
10%	Loss of American jobs to immigrants
7%	Increased crime and drug activity
5%	Overcrowding of U.S. cities and towns
11%	All of the above
7%	None of the above

SOURCE: Adapted from *The Public's View of Immigration: A Comprehensive Survey and Analysis*, Center for Immigration Studies, November 2006, http://www.cis.org/articles/2006/back906.html (accessed December 20, 2006)

40% of students enrolling in college have to take remedial courses. He estimates the nation's economy generated nearly 3 million new jobs in 2006 and about 6.3 million since the end of 2003. He projects 2007 job gains to average about 130,000 per month. Using engineers as an example of the types of skilled workers needed by U.S. companies, Donahue estimates the United States is producing 140,000 graduates per year in engineering, compared with 350,000 in Asia. Donahue warns that unless such workforce issues as education and immigration restrictions are addressed promptly, companies will be left with only one choice: taking their business outside the United States. To stay competitive in a global economy, Donahue states that U.S. companies need a ready supply of skilled workers and higher educational standards.

AMNESTY. In "The Public's View of Immigration: A Comprehensive Survey and Analysis" (November 2006, http://www.cis.org/articles/2006/back906.pdf), the Center for Immigration Studies indicates that in October 2006 eight out of ten people believed amnesty would only encourage more illegals to cross U.S. borders. Sixty-eight percent of respondents believed the number of immigrants in the United States is too high, regardless of legal status. The majority (73%) said the government has done too little enforcement, and seven out of ten believed that increased enforcement is preferable to legalizing current illegal residents. Forty-five percent strongly held the opinion that employers are bypassing Americans to fill low-wage jobs with immigrants who will work for even lower wages. By a margin of more than two to one (62% to 29%), respondents rejected news media coverage about immigrants as mostly "human-interest fluff that largely ignores or omits information about the downside of a steady stream of people entering this country illegally." Immigration's additional burden on taxpayers for items such as health care and schools was the greatest concern of survey respondents. (See Table 7.19.)

The Pew report *Portrait of "Generation Next"* notes that in exit polls from the November 2006 midterm elections, voters were asked whether illegal immigrants in the United States should be given a chance to apply for legal status or be deported. A clear majority (70%) of eighteen- to twenty-five-year-olds favored an option for legalization, whereas less than 60% of voters over age thirty said illegal immigrants should be allowed to stay.

CHAPTER 8

MORE LIBERAL POLICIES WILL SOLVE THE PROBLEM OF ILLEGAL IMMIGRATION

HONORABLE ALAN K. SIMPSON, FORMER U.S. SENATOR FROM THE STATE OF WYOMING, PREPARED STATEMENT SUBMITTED FOR THE HEARING BEFORE THE COMMITTEE ON THE JUDICIARY, U.S. HOUSE OF REPRESENTATIVES, 109TH CONGRESS, SECOND SESSION, SEPTEMBER 1, 2006

Mr. Chairman, and Members of the Committee, thank you for your invitation to share my thoughts with you on the lessons of the Immigration Reform and Control Act of 1986 (IRCA), and how they may apply to the current immigration reform debate—and impasse—currently taking place in Congress. ...

I believe there are three principal lessons to be learned from IRCA:

1. a more secure employment verification system was lacking in IRCA ... and this remains the critical problem that must be fixed if illegal immigration is ever going to be deterred;

2. "amnesty" may yet be justified in some certain circumstances, but it should not take effect until a credible body of policy-makers determines that effective enforcement measures are in effect; and

3. guestworker programs may be necessary, but Congress should never repeat the mistakes of the Special Agricultural Worker (SAW) program when addressing shortages in U.S. pools of unskilled labor.

Let me discuss each point in detail.

Secure Worker Verification

It should always be illegal for a U.S. employer "knowingly" to hire an unauthorized alien. There was a clear consensus on this point in 1986, and that consensus remains today. A crucial corollary to this policy, however, is that U.S. employers should be allowed to actually "know" when they might be "knowingly" hiring an illegal alien.

In other words, the burden of a more secure worker verification system should be placed squarely on the federal government, and not on U.S. employers. ...

[However,] there was no political consensus in 1986 for a more secure document, or a secure database, or any other proposal on which U.S. employers could rely. As a result, the employer sanctions regime became easily defeated by high-quality, low-cost fraudulent documents that "on their face appear genuine." For nearly twenty years, all factions agreed that employment in the U.S. was the principal magnet that drew illegal immigrants to the United States, yet there was insufficient political support for—and nearly hysterical and emotional warnings not to address—the one most glaring loophole in employer sanctions: the widespread availability of counterfeit documents. ...

Lesson Number One from IRCA therefore is that immigration reform legislation must establish a truly secure worker verification for all U.S. workers and all U.S. employers. ... Indeed, the most significant political "shift of winds" I have witnessed in the intervening twenty years is that there now seems to be a political consensus for establishment of a secure worker verification system. That is a real change in national politics, and an indication of just how serious the problem of illegal immigration has become. ...

Amnesty Triggered by Effective Enforcement Measures

IRCA provided legal status to nearly three million people who had resided unlawfully in our country since January 1, 1982. The bipartisan sponsors of IRCA described it as a responsible "trade-off" for the establishment of employer sanctions and the definitive declaration that the United States was fully opposed to unauthorized immigration. I well recall describing the program as being for "one-time only," and as "an extraordinary act of grace." I meant that then, and

I respectfully encourage this Committee to again consider those words now. Amnesty is indeed extraordinarily generous, and fully within the discretion of the Congress to bestow or to withhold. The question today is: should amnesty be granted once again? I believe the answer is, "Yes, in limited situations and for practical reasons, *but only* after all of the effective enforcement measures are in place."

"Experts" estimate the current illegal population in the U.S. at eleven million. The number itself is staggering. The maximum number estimate in 1986 was six million. Clearly, the problem has become much worse in twenty years, not better. But an enormous practical problem remains about how to realistically deal with this population. Perhaps a secure worker verification system could encourage them to leave—over time. This then is even more reason for ensuring that any worker verification system must be truly secure. . . .

Guestworker Programs

Guestworker issues haunted IRCA for two Congresses and proved to be one of the thorniest political and policy challenges that we faced. I can honestly say that IRCA's resolution of the issue—creation of the Special Agricultural Worker or "SAW" program—was a real mistake. The SAW program was a political compromise that was made necessary in order to enact the legislation. . . . In order to satisfy employer interests who were seeking a large pool of unskilled labor, the terms of the program were overly generous (a mere ninety days of "labor in agriculture" qualified an unauthorized alien for the SAW program). In order to satisfy organized labor and immigrants' rights organizations, the status provided to the "guestworkers" had to be permanent (reportedly to avoid employer exploitation), not temporary. As a result, over 1.3 million people obtained permanent residence under the SAW program, and the vast majority of them then promptly exited agricultural labor—if they had ever even worked at that in the first place. You can bet the need for unskilled labor then arose again in short order. . . .

IRCA's lesson on guestworkers therefore is to make certain that the terms of the program are dictated by sound practical policy, and not by coalition politics. First, Congress should determine that guestworkers are indeed necessary. There is a serious argument today that they are critically needed, given the current demographic trends which project a large pool of aging workers and a shrinking pool of younger workers. Still, that alone is not enough. Perhaps there are some unskilled jobs that should be mechanized or outsourced, and today is the right moment for the great entrepreneurs in our America to figure out just how to do so. I would suspect, however, that there will always remain jobs which cannot be mechanized or outsourced, and the diminishing pool of younger Americans will not fill them. In that situation, a guestworker program may well prove to be a rational response.

Second, careful thought should be given to the form of the guestworker program. If the SAW program is any lesson at all, it is surely inefficient and ultimately futile to grant permanent residence to a group of foreign nationals in the hope that they will perform unskilled labor that most Americans today will avoid. If the guestworker program is honestly intended to address labor shortages, then a temporary status that is linked to *specific* employers or *specific* industries (with appropriate protections against abusive employers), is the proper policy choice.

COUNCILWOMAN ANN E. MICHALSKI, CITY COUNCIL OF DUBUQUE, IOWA, HEARING BEFORE THE COMMITTEE ON THE JUDICIARY, U.S. HOUSE OF REPRESENTATIVES, 109TH CONGRESS, SECOND SESSION, SEPTEMBER 1, 2006

Some media voices have questioned why [immigration] hearings should be held in Dubuque, Iowa. While not as immediately impacted as cities along our Nation's northern and southern borders, these comments betray a lack of understanding of the true dimensions of the challenge. . . . Dubuque, like every city in the United States, is a city of immigrants. Founded by a French fur trader in the eighteenth century, we have lived under five flags through the years, ultimately being incorporated as Iowa's oldest city. In the course of the nineteenth century, our population soon became primarily Irish and German and remained so until our very recent past. Studies done up to the late twentieth century indicated that Dubuque's population was uniquely homogeneous with very few diverse populations. Since the 1990's, this profile has gradually changed, even though our population remains predominantly European, even western European. But we have welcomed significant numbers of new citizens. This has presented our community with both challenge and opportunity.

These changes in our population, while significant, have been relatively undramatic. There is not a perception that large numbers of undocumented immigrants have come here, though the assumption must be made that we do have such persons. Several religious and civic groups, notably, the Archdiocesan Office for Immigration, a program for Marshallese Islanders by several Pentecostal church groups and the Iowa State University Extension Diversity Center and the two school districts, have managed to keep pace with the challenge. Thanks to these efforts, the problem of immigration has not yet become a crisis and can be appreciated from a more long range economic, political and philosophical point of view.

So from this rather lofty stance, it's possible for us to posit a number of local realities:

Like immigrants everywhere, our new Dubuque residents come here for a simple reason. They want a better life for themselves and their families.

Second, the employment situation in Dubuque is currently very strong with a wide range of varied job opportunities. Businesses, however, still feel the need for a growing supply of workers with a strong work ethic and a willingness to accept a lower rate of pay. In short, we need good workers to keep our economic surge going.

Third, we must assume that some of our new inhabitants have illegally crossed our borders. We can tell this by the degree of anxiety they express in certain situations and by their reluctance to participate in some aspects of community life.

Even given this barrier, our Hispanic residents are becoming part of our community and we find their presence enriching.

We do see areas of potential, even immediate concern. And we believe this is best addressed by a comprehensive approach, including tighter, enforceable border security; tighter, enforceable and enforced employment regulations; assistance for localities most heavily impacted by large numbers of both legal and illegal immigrants; and a pathway to citizenship which rewards those who enter the country legally and penalizes those who do not, without destroying their hopes for the future. . . .

We are convinced that when immigrants are admitted through a well-regulated system, they strengthen our country by creating economic opportunities, increasing America's scientific and cultural resources, strengthening our ties with other nations, fulfilling humanitarian commitments, and perhaps most important, supporting family ties and family values. All this is necessary to build strong communities.

RICARDO PARRA, MIDWEST COUNCIL OF LA RAZA, HEARING BEFORE THE COMMITTEE OF THE JUDICIARY, U.S. HOUSE OF REPRESENTATIVES, EVANSVILLE, INDIANA, AUGUST 29, 2006

The immigration system is broken and needs to be fixed. . . . [Congress] ignored the need to look at national security interests, economic interests in a changing global economy. They have ignored the need to build an immigration system that is tough, efficient, fair, and also compassionate. . . .

I believe that border security alone is not enough. Border security must fit within a process of comprehensive reform (i.e. interior and employer enforcement, legalization, and guest workers); enforcement only is insufficient.

Earlier in June, 500-plus economists . . . indicated immigration was an economic plus, saying, "the gains from immigration outweigh the losses."

Immigrant labor is needed to fill jobs in the U.S. that an older, more educated American workforce is not willing to fill, especially at the low wages and poor working conditions many unscrupulous employers offer. Currently, there are approximately nine million undocumented workers in the U.S. filling important gaps in the labor market. There is substantial evidence that their presence in the labor force creates jobs and strengthens local economies. . . .

The costs of education and social welfare systems are not unreasonable or unbearable.

When it comes to education [of immigrants,] this is an investment in not only human capital, but people who will be integrated into this society and be stakeholders.

Undocumented immigrants pay taxes in a number of ways, including income and sales tax. The majority of undocumented immigrants pay income taxes using Individual Taxpayer Identification Numbers (ITINs) or false Social Security numbers. All immigrants, regardless of status, will pay on average $80,000 per capita more in taxes than they use in government services over their lifetime. The Social Security system reaps the biggest windfall from taxes paid by immigrants; the Social Security Administration reports that it holds approximately $420 billion from the earnings of immigrants who are not in a position to claim benefits. . . .

To enforce our immigration laws we need to make them enforceable. Our broken immigration system is a complex problem that needs a comprehensive overhaul. We've been implementing piecemeal measures for twenty years, which have made the system more complex, but not more controlled. "Seal the borders" is a sound bite. "Enforce our laws" is a sound bite. Comprehensive reform is a solution, and only by changing our laws to meet economic need and family ties will we be able to restore control and order to the system.

People smuggling has become big business. Fake document merchants have plenty of customers. Unscrupulous employers have a large pool of exploitable workers. Families stay separated for years. Hundreds die in the desert each year. There are twelve million undocumented immigrants—and counting—and Americans all across the U.S. are angry at the government's failure. In light of all this, calls for more of the same do not make sense. Illegal immigration happens because we have jobs or loved ones on this side of the border, and an insufficient number of legal visas for these workers and family members. . . .

We need to bring well-intentioned immigrants through the legal system. When the vast majority of current illegal flow is happening legally, our enforcement resources will be better trained on the smugglers and fake documents rings, the drug runners and violent criminals, and the terrorists who might manipulate our system. . . . A path to legal status for the current undocumented population is integral to enhance national security. Once the good people come forward for registration and criminal background checks, the people who cannot and do not will be isolated.

STEVEN A. CAMAROTA, DIRECTOR OF RESEARCH, CENTER FOR IMMIGRATION STUDIES, HEARING BEFORE THE COMMITTEE OF THE JUDICIARY, U.S. HOUSE OF REPRESENTATIVES, AUGUST 29, 2006

Over the last three decades, socio-economic conditions, especially in the developing world, in conjunction with U.S. immigration policy, have caused twenty-five million people to leave their homelands and emigrate legally to the United States. . . . The Immigration and Naturalization Service estimates that the illegal alien population grows by 400,000 to 500,000 each year. The current influx has caused an enormous growth in the immigrant population, from 9.6 million in 1970 (4.8% of the population) to 35 million (12.1% of the population) today.

. . . The impact on the overall economy is actually very small. . . . And these effects are even smaller when one focuses only on illegal aliens, who comprise one-fourth to one-third of all immigrants. While the impact on the economy as a whole may be tiny, the effect on some Americans, particularly workers at the bottom of [the] labor market may be quite large. These workers are especially vulnerable to immigrant competition because wages for these jobs are already low and immigrants are heavily concentrated in less-skilled and lower-paying jobs. . . .

. . . Its short- and long-term impact demographically on the share of the population that is of working age is also very small. It probably makes more sense for policymakers to focus on the winners and losers from immigration. The big losers are natives working in low-skilled low-wage jobs. Of course, technological change and increased trade also have reduced the labor market opportunities for low-wage workers in the United States. But immigration is different because it is a discretionary policy that can be altered. On the other hand, immigrants are the big winners, as are owners of capital and skilled workers, but their gains are tiny relative to their income.

. . . Arguments for or against immigration are as much political and moral as they are economic. The latest research indicates that we can reduce immigration secure in the knowledge that it will not harm the economy. Doing so makes sense if we are very concerned about low-wage and less-skilled workers in the United States. On the other hand, if one places a high priority on helping unskilled workers in other countries, then allowing in a large number of such workers should continue. Of course, only an infinitesimal proportion of the world's poor could ever come to this country even under the most open immigration policy one might imagine. Those who support the current high level of unskilled legal and illegal immigration should at least do so with an understanding that those American workers harmed by the policies they favor are already the poorest and most vulnerable.

MARGARET D. STOCK, ASSOCIATE PROFESSOR OF LAW, U.S. MILITARY ACADEMY, WEST POINT, NEW YORK, BEFORE THE SENATE COMMITTEE ON THE JUDICIARY, SUBCOMMITTEE ON IMMIGRATION, BORDER SECURITY, AND CITIZENSHIP AND THE SUBCOMMITTEE ON TERRORISM, TECHNOLOGY, AND HOMELAND SECURITY, IN WASHINGTON, D.C., MAY 17, 2005

We best enhance our security by enhancing our intelligence capacity. National security is most effectively enhanced by improving the mechanisms for identifying actual terrorists, not by implementing harsher immigration laws or blindly treating all foreigners as potential terrorists. Policies and practices that fail to properly distinguish between terrorists and legitimate foreign travelers are ineffective security tools that waste limited resources, damage the U.S. economy, alienate those groups whose cooperation the U.S. government needs to prevent terrorism, and foster a false sense of security by promoting the illusion that we are reducing the threat of terrorism. Reforming our immigration laws will help us to identify those who seek to enter our country or are already residing here. . . .

We need to make our borders our last line of defense. The physical borders of the United States should be our last line of defense because terrorism does not spring up at our borders. In fact, we need to re-conceptualize how we think about our "borders," because in our modern world they really start at our consulates abroad. . . .

Our economic prosperity depends on the free movement of people and goods. We must be careful not to create an environment conducive to terrorists and criminals at our ports-of-entry as we seek to secure our borders in a way that does not trump cross-border facilitation. We need to adopt a "virtual border" approach that recognizes the importance of the continued flow of people and goods, and underscores that effective border management needs to take place away from our physical borders. I would only add that comprehensively reforming our immigration laws is the other component that is necessary for our borders to work and work well because such reform helps identify the people who present themselves at our ports-of-entry, thereby making legality the norm.

. . . Because all nineteen of the September 11th terrorists were foreigners, some observers have been quick to blame our vulnerability to terrorist attacks on lax immigration laws. While such a response was predictable, it was misguided and has inevitably resulted in overreaction. Calls to impose a "moratorium" on immigration, halt the issuance of student visas, close the borders with Canada and Mexico, eliminate the Diversity

Lottery visa program, draft harsher immigration laws, and similar types of proposals reflect a serious misunderstanding of the relationship between immigration policy and national security.

Although the attacks of September 11th revealed serious management and resource deficiencies in the bureaucracies that administer our borders, U.S. immigration laws in and of themselves did not increase our vulnerability to attack. In fact, U.S. immigration laws already are among the toughest in the world and have long provided the federal government with broad powers to prevent anti-American terrorists from entering or residing in the United States. A careful analysis of the September 11th attacks reveals that deficiencies in U.S. intelligence collection and information sharing, not immigration laws, prevented the terrorists' plans from being discovered.

FRANK SHARRY, EXECUTIVE DIRECTOR, NATIONAL IMMIGRATION FORUM, TESTIMONY BEFORE THE SENATE COMMITTEE ON THE JUDICIARY, OCTOBER 18, 2005

The evidence of the system's dysfunction is all around us: young men and women die gruesome deaths in southwestern deserts as they attempt to enter the U.S. in search of work; fake document merchants and criminal smugglers turn huge profits in networks that one day might be exploited not by those seeking work in our economy but by those seeking to attack our nation; local community tensions simmer and sometimes explode as housing gets stretched, schools experience change, and language differences emerge; immigrant families remain divided for years, even decades, by restrictive admissions policies and inefficient processing; immigrant workers afraid of being discovered and deported are subject to abuse and exploitation by unscrupulous employers seeking to gain an unfair advantage over law-abiding competitors; meanwhile, public frustration mounts as the federal government seems incapable of mobilizing the political leadership and enacting the policy changes to fix the system once and for all. ...

Fixing the broken immigration system requires sizing up its complexity and its dimensions. The numbers tell part of the story. Some eleven million undocumented immigrants now live and work in the United States. That means that almost one-third of all the immigrants in America lives here without government authorization. Fourteen million people, including some five million kids, live in households headed by an undocumented immigrant. One out of twenty workers in the nation's labor force is living and working here illegally. Two-thirds of them have arrived in the last decade. More than half are from Mexico. More than 80% are from Latin America and the Caribbean. America's backyard is showing up on America's front porch.

Illegal immigration is no longer a niche issue affecting a handful of gateway states and cities. It has gone nationwide. Consider the five states with the fastest growing populations of undocumented immigrants: North Carolina, Utah, Colorado, Arizona, and Idaho. In fact, a wide swath of the nation's heartland, from the old South stretching up through the Mountain states to the Northwest, is undergoing a remarkable demographic transformation with little to no recent experience to draw on to respond to it.

Moreover, most new undocumented immigrants appear to be here to stay. The vast majority no longer fit the stereotype of the migrant male on his own here to do temporary work before returning home. Today, 70% live with spouses and/or children. And only 3% work in agriculture. The vast majority are employed in year-round service sector jobs. After all, the jobs are plentiful. More than half the new jobs created in the American economy require hard work, not multiple diplomas. Meanwhile, young native-born workers are smaller in number, better educated than ever, and more interested in office work than manual labor. Consequently, much of the nation's demand for housekeepers, childcare workers, landscapers, protein processors, busboys, cooks, janitors, drywallers, and construction workers is met by a steady flow of some 500,000 undocumented migrants who enter and settle in America each year.

... Since the U.S. has a legal immigration system, why don't these workers from Mexico and elsewhere simply wait in line and enter with legal visas? Answer: what legal visas? There are virtually none available for these workers. While the labor market demands an estimated 500,000 full-time low-skilled service jobs a year, our immigration laws supply just 5,000 permanent visas for workers to fill these jobs. And this tiny category is so backlogged it has been rendered useless. As the Immigration Policy Center recently pointed out, of the other fifteen immigrant visa categories available for employment and training, only two are available to industries that require little or no formal training. These two categories (H2A and H2B) are small and seasonal. In addition to the enormous mismatch between labor market realities and our government's immigration policy, our family visa lines are so backlogged that it can take a decade for spouses to be reunited, legally. Not surprisingly, many stop waiting and cross the border illegally in order to reunite with their loved ones.

What to do? Some argue that the solution is to simply enforce the laws we already have on the books. And while we certainly need tighter, more targeted, and more effective enforcement as part of a comprehensive overhaul, the fact is that over the past two decades the "enforcement only" approach has failed miserably. As another of this hearing's witnesses, Princeton professor

Douglas Massey, recently documented, since 1986 the border patrol budget has increased ten-fold in value. This beefing up of border enforcement has been augmented by tough restrictions on immigrant access to employment, public services, and due process protections.

And yet this unprecedented increase in enforcement has coincided with an unprecedented increase in illegal immigration.

Why hasn't "enforcement only" worked to stem illegal immigration? Because our current approach to immigration and border security policy fails to recognize that the United States has an increasingly integrated labor market with Latin America. In much the same way that we used to see workers from rural areas in the South migrate to the urban North to fill manufacturing jobs, we now see workers from rural areas south of the border migrating to all areas of the U.S. to fill service jobs. Our failure to account for this fact of life leads to a failure of policy. Instead of building a workable regulatory regime to govern what is essentially a market-driven labor migration, we keep legal channels severely restricted and then wonder why workers and their families have nowhere to go but into the clutches of a migration black market dominated by smugglers, fake document merchants, and unscrupulous employers.

Dan Griswold of the Cato Institute sums it up this way: "Demand for low-skilled labor continues to grow in the United States while the domestic supply of suitable workers inexorably declines—yet U.S. immigration law contains virtually no legal channel through which low-skilled immigrant workers can enter the country to fill that gap. The result is an illegal flow of workers characterized by more permanent and less circular migration, smuggling, document fraud, deaths at the border, artificially depressed wages, and threats to civil liberties." He adds, "American immigration laws are colliding with reality, and reality is winning."

Griswold is right. We will not be able to restore respect for the rule of law in our immigration system until we restore respect for the law of supply and demand. Instead of "enforcement only" or "enforcement first," we need an "enforcement plus" approach.

I recall the first time I came face to face with the reality of an integrated labor market and the futility of an "enforcement only" strategy. In the late 1990's I accompanied a delegation that visited Tixla ("Teesh-la"), a "sending community" located in Mexico. Most of its sons and daughters had left and migrated illegally to Chicago to fill available service jobs in construction, landscaping, hospitality, and childcare. Those left behind consisted mostly of women, children, and the elderly. The workers used to come back and forth, at least for visits, but this had mostly stopped due to the press of their multiple jobs up north and the risks associated with re-crossing the border illegally. The townspeople were proud to show us the new school and basketball court which had recently been built with pooled remittances. And there, right there in the middle of the basketball court, was a huge replica of the logo for the Chicago Bulls.

That's when it hit me. Tixla, a dusty, rural town south of Mexico City, is a bedroom community for Chicago. We may not think of it that way, but it is a twenty-first century fact. The town produces the workers needed to fill newly created service sector jobs in the Chicago area. There is plenty of work available just up the road, and these workers are willing to risk their lives to make the commute. . . .

Like so many other public policy debates, the highly charged immigration debate is often polarized and paralyzed by an "either/or" framework. The tit-for-tat goes something like this: you are either for immigrants or for control; you are either for higher levels or lower levels; you are either for closed borders or open borders; you are either for lax policies or tough policies. This narrow and lopsided framework is a trap that obscures realistic solutions.

What's needed is a "both/and" approach that recognizes the reality of an integrated labor market with Latin America and the legitimate U.S. demand for operational control of its borders in a post 9/11 world. Such an approach seeks to integrate seemingly contradictory elements into a comprehensive package; a package that combines expanded enforcement strategies and expanded legal channels for those entering the U.S. to work and join families and expanded pathways to legal status and citizenship for undocumented immigrants already living and working in the U.S. We need to change our immigration laws so that they are enforceable and enforce them effectively. . . .

The key to effective [immigration] enforcement is to augment our border enforcement efforts with a system that ensures that all workers hired in the United States are in our country legally. The [Secure America and Orderly Immigration Act of 2005] accomplishes this by building an electronic worker verification system . . . combined with tough sanctions for employers who attempt to end-run the new system. I predict that responsible employers will support it as long as the verification system is functional and the new system is combined with legal channels for workers here and those needed in the future. I predict that unscrupulous employers—those that benefit from the dysfunctional status quo—will oppose it.

The keys to making the admissions system realistic, controlled, and workable are a) to provide enough visas for the expected future flow of workers and families; and b) to avoid the exploitation and abuses of old-style guest worker programs. Secure America accomplishes the first by creating 400,000 worker visas a year and increasing family reunification visas so that the current illegal flow will be funneled into a legal one while being fair to those from around the world. It tackles the second by requiring employers to pay newly admitted workers the same wages as similarly situated workers, and by mostly de-linking workers' status from employer say-so. ...

The key to putting migration on legal footing once and for all is finding a way for the eleven million or so undocumented immigrants to come out of the shadows voluntarily and transition to legal status. Secure America addresses this controversial issue head on. It offers incentives for undocumented immigrants already here to come forward, register with the government, submit to criminal, security, and health screenings, pay a hefty fine, study English and civics, and clear up their taxes as a way to eventually earn permanent residency. Immigrants who meet these requirements can apply for permanent residence after six years, and become eligible for citizenship in eleven years at the earliest. And this component interacts with the family reunification provisions such that those waiting in the queue outside the U.S. secure permanent residence before those previously undocumented immigrants who obtain temporary status.

Immigration to America has worked throughout our history because newcomers have been encouraged to become new Americans. Secure America takes steps to renew this commitment by increasing English classes for adult immigrants, citizenship promotion and preparation, and the legal security immigrant workers need to move up the economic ladder. In fact, it's worth noting that when three million undocumented immigrants became legal immigrants some twenty years ago, their wages increased by 14% over five years—they were no longer afraid to speak up or change jobs—and their productivity increased dramatically—they studied English and improved their skills through training. The bill also deals with a longstanding and legitimate complaint from state and local governments by reimbursing costs related to health care and other public services.

The bill certainly has its faults and its critics. The immigration enforcement provisions are strong but will need to be strengthened if we are to ensure immigrant workers and families use widened legal channels and no others. Similarly, the bill aims to construct a temporary worker program that adequately protects both native and immigrant workers alike, but will probably need to be tweaked to fully realize this objective. After all, the goal of immigration reform should be nothing less than to restore the rule of law—both to our immigration system and to low-wage labor markets. And unfortunately, the bill does not adequately address the acknowledged long-term solution to the migration challenge: economic development in sending nations and communities. ...

Overall, though, the bill's premise is brilliant and its promise viable: take migration out of the black market and bring it under the rule of law; funnel the illegal flow into legal channels; increase the legality of the migration that is occurring, rather than increase the numbers of those who enter; get control of the flow so we get control of our border; bring undocumented immigrants out of the shadows and under the protection of our laws; know who is in our country and who is entering it; shift from repressing migration ineffectively to regulating migration intelligently; turn the broken status quo into a functioning, regulated system; drain the swamp of fake documents and criminal smugglers; vetted airport arrivals instead of deaths in the desert; families united rather than divided for decades; verification mechanisms that work and fake documents that don't; legal workers and an equal playing field for honest employers; equal labor rights for all rather than a race to the bottom for most.

... As a nation we seem poised to move beyond the old debate—characterized by simplistic and shallow prescriptions of the past, the non-solution, sound bite-driven "get tough and be done with it" approach. The nation is ready to take part in a new debate, one that takes all of the moving parts into full consideration and at the same time. The old debate suggests that we have to choose between being a nation of immigrants or a nation of laws. The new debate recognizes that the only way to be either is to be both.

STATEMENT OF LAURA W. MURPHY AND TIMOTHY H. EDGAR, AMERICAN CIVIL LIBERTIES UNION, HEARING BEFORE THE SUBCOMMITTEE ON IMMIGRATION, BORDER SECURITY, AND CLAIMS OF THE COMMITTEE ON THE JUDICIARY, HOUSE OF REPRESENTATIVES, 108TH CONGRESS, FIRST SESSION, MAY 8, 2003

When terrorists attacked the World Trade Center and the Pentagon on September 11, 2001, they attacked a nation of immigrants. Among those who died in the attacks were citizens of some twenty-six foreign countries. The attackers did not distinguish on the basis of citizenship or immigration status. Victims included United States citizens and permanent residents, temporary workers and visitors, and undocumented laborers.

Following these attacks, President Bush and Congress expressed solidarity with the Arab, Muslim, and South Asian immigrant communities and warned against singling out whole communities for the actions of the terrorists. Unfortunately, as we look back on the government's actions toward immigrants over the past twenty months, its actions are in sharp contrast to its words.

Even as the Department of Justice took swift and decisive action to stop hate crimes against Arabs, Muslims, and South Asians, it began a massive preventive detention campaign. This campaign has resulted in the secret detention and deportation of close to 1000 immigrants designated as "persons of interest" in its investigation of the attacks. Government officials now acknowledge that virtually all of the persons that it detained shortly after September 11 had no connection to terrorism. While the government told the public not to engage in ethnic stereotyping or to equate immigrants in general with terrorists, its own policies did precisely that.

Under new Department of Justice policies, immigrants today can be arrested and held in secret for a lengthy period without charge, denied release on bond without effective recourse, and have their appeals dismissed following cursory or no review. They can be subjected to special, discriminatory registration procedures involving fingerprinting and lengthy questioning concerning their religious and political views. An immigrant spouse who is abused by her husband must fear deportation if she calls the local police. Asylum-seekers fleeing repressive regimes like those of the Taliban or Saddam Hussein may face mandatory detention, without any consideration of their individual circumstances.

There is a better approach. Instead of automatically viewing non-citizens with inherent suspicion, America should focus its resources on investigating and apprehending those who intend to commit acts of terrorism. America puts itself at greater risk by alienating immigrant communities, making immigrants distrustful and fearful of government.

The government must stop equating immigration with terrorism. Stepping up border screenings in a smart way can be part of a policy to make the United States safer. ... Still, improving the "gatekeeper" function of immigration agencies is only one part, and not the most important one, of a balanced approach to national security that improves national security while respecting civil liberties. ...

Immigrants and new citizens make our country stronger, not weaker. They serve in our armed forces, as high-technology workers helping design the latest security technology, and as translators of critical intelligence information. They provide a bridge to world understanding, helping counter anti-American sentiment. If we isolate immigrants, we isolate ourselves—and make our country more vulnerable to terrorism.

Put simply, target terrorists, not immigrants. ...

Alienation of Immigrant Communities

Immigrants represent an extraordinary resource for the United States in its efforts to combat terrorism. Terrorism is a global problem that requires cooperation not just among governments, but among communities that increasingly straddle borders and cultures. Noting that an intelligence intercept warning of an impending terrorist attack that was received September 10, 2001 was not translated until September 12, Congress's own Joint Inquiry into the attacks of September 11, 2001, identified a critical need to hire more translators with knowledge of Arabic, Urdu, Farsi, and other foreign languages.

Likewise, to encourage cooperation in solving crime and terrorism, law enforcement officials have worked hard to win the trust of immigrant communities. Yet these efforts have been seriously undermined by a series of ham-handed policies likely to further alienate immigrants from the United States government. ...

Targeting immigrants comes at significant cost not only to basic fairness, it represents poor national security policy. ...

A Better Approach: Security and Liberty for a Nation of Immigrants

Designing immigration enforcement policy that remains true to our civil liberties and our values as a nation of immigrants while improving security is a challenge, but it is possible. First, we must recognize that immigration policy is simply one part of an overall strategy to reduce America's vulnerability to terrorism.

We should begin by recognizing the limits of immigration enforcement as a part of a counter-terrorism strategy. Immigration officials serve as gatekeepers, administering immigration laws that provide who may be admitted into the country and who may not. They cannot do their job without adequate intelligence.

The Joint Inquiry of the House and Senate intelligence committees into the September 11 attacks uncovered a number of serious, structural breakdowns in the intelligence agencies that may have contributed to the attacks. One vivid example is the failure of the CIA to share with the FBI or immigration agencies the names of two Al Qaeda members for a period of eighteen months—by which time they had already entered the United States, traveling under their own names. Immigration agencies cannot be saddled with the blame for this fiasco; they cannot arrest or keep out potential terrorists about whom they have no knowledge.

... These failures were not the result of civil liberties protections or checks and balances, but rather represented organizational failures which will take resources, including dollars and political will, to address. No border security policy can be effective without solving these intelligence problems. ...

Adequate resources for information technology. The immigration agencies have done an extraordinarily poor job of keeping basic records. Rather than saddle immigration offices with new responsibilities to collect information which they already maintain, such as through special registration, Congress should insist on fundamental record-keeping reforms that hold the immigration agencies accountable for keeping timely and accurate paperwork.

Improved information-sharing. Immigration agencies and the State Department must have adequate technology to access information maintained by law enforcement and intelligence agencies, to find out whether a particular individual is a criminal or a terrorist and should be kept out of the United States. Prior to September 11, 2001, not all consulates and immigration inspectors had real-time access to this information.

Put terrorism enforcement, not immigration enforcement, as the top priority. Where the FBI is conducting a terrorism investigation, immigration enforcement should take a back seat because the FBI's need to obtain the cooperation of potential witnesses and to track down leads to uncover possible terrorists is more important than deporting undocumented immigrants. The FBI should adopt a policy of not deporting those who are mere immigration violators but who are uncovered in a terrorism investigation, and make sure that policy is adequately publicized and enforced.

Reverse legal opinion claiming state and local law enforcement have immigration powers. For the same reason, the Department of Justice should revert to its previous opinion holding that state and local law enforcement lack authority to enforce immigration laws. State and local law enforcement must have the trust of their communities to ferret out crime and terrorism.

Abandon mandatory detention policies to free up scarce resources for those who are dangerous. Immigration detention space is limited and expensive, and continuing policies that prohibit release even of those noncitizens who show they are not dangerous and are not likely to flee simply forces the government to release others who may be dangerous.

Conclusion

By working together to find solutions to immigration enforcement that respect civil liberties and fundamental values, we can avoid the false choice between civil liberties and safety. By abandoning false solutions that target immigrants, not terrorists, America can remain safe, free, and true to its fundamental values as a nation of immigrants.

CHAPTER 9

STRICTER POLICIES WILL SOLVE THE PROBLEM
OF ILLEGAL IMMIGRATION

MICHAEL W. CUTLER, FORMER INSPECTOR, EXAMINER AND SPECIAL AGENT, IMMIGRATION AND NATURALIZATION SERVICE, HEARING BEFORE THE COMMITTEE ON THE JUDICIARY, U.S. HOUSE OF REPRESENTATIVES, 109TH CONGRESS, SECOND SESSION, SEPTEMBER 1, 2006

A nation's primary responsibility is to provide for the safety and security of its citizens and yet, for reasons I cannot begin to fathom, the members of the Senate who voted for S. 2611 are seemingly oblivious to the lessons that the disastrous amnesty of the Immigration Reform and Control Act of 1986 (IRCA) should have taught us. That piece of legislation led to the greatest influx of illegal aliens in the history of our nation. Fraud and a lack of integrity of the immigration system not only flooded our nation with illegal aliens who ran our borders, hoping that what had been billed as a "one time" amnesty would be repeated, but it also enabled a number of terrorists and many criminals to enter the United States and then embed themselves in the United States.

A notable example of such a terrorist can be found in a review of the facts concerning Mahmud Abouhalima, a citizen of Egypt who entered the United States on a tourist visa, overstayed his authorized period of admission and then applied for amnesty under the agricultural worker provisions of IRCA. He succeeded in obtaining resident alien status through this process. During a five year period he drove a cab and had his license suspended numerous times for violations of law and ultimately demonstrated his appreciation for our nation's generosity by participating in the first attack on the World Trade Center in 1993 that left six people dead, hundreds of people injured and an estimated one-half billion dollars in damage inflicted, on that iconic, ill-fated complex. ... The other terrorists who attacked our nation on subsequent attacks, including the attacks of September 11, 2001, similarly exploited our generosity, seeing in our nation's kindness, weakness, gaming the immigration system to enter our country and then, hide in plain sight, among us.

As I recall, when IRCA was proposed, one of the selling points was that along with amnesty for what was believed to have been a population of some 1.5 million illegal aliens would be a new approach to turn off what has been described as the "magnet" that draws the majority of illegal aliens into the United States in the first place, the prospect of securing employment in the United States. In order to accomplish this important goal, IRCA imposed penalties against those unscrupulous employers who knowingly hired illegal aliens. My former colleagues and I were pleased to see that under the employer sanctions of IRCA, the unscrupulous employers of illegal aliens would be made accountable, or so we thought. We were frustrated that we had seen all too many employers hire illegal aliens and treat them horrendously. They paid them sub-standard wages and created unsafe, indeed hazardous working conditions for the illegal aliens they hired, knowing full well that these aliens would not complain because they feared being reported to the INS [Immigration and Naturalization Service, now U.S. Citizenship and Immigration Services (USCIS)]. Meanwhile the employer would not face any penalty for his outrageous conduct. Finally, it seemed that the employer sanctions provisions of IRCA would discourage employers from hiring illegal aliens and would also make it less likely they would treat their employees as miserably as some of these employers did.

Of course, we now know that the relative handful of special agents who were assigned to conduct investigations of employers who hired illegal aliens made it unlikely that employers would face a significant risk of being caught violating these laws and that they would face an even smaller chance of being seriously fined. Furthermore, the way that the amnesty provisions of the law were enacted simply created a cottage industry of fraud document vendors who provided illegal aliens with counterfeit or altered identity documents and supporting documents to enable the illegal alien population to circumvent the immigration laws. Ultimately approximately 3.5 million illegal aliens emerged from the infamous shadows to participate in the amnesty program of 1986. I have never seen an explanation for the reason that more than twice as many aliens took advantage of the 1986 amnesty than was initially believed would but I believe that two factors came into play. It may well be that the number of illegal aliens in the country was underestimated. I also believe, however, that a large number of illegal aliens were able to gain entry into the United States long after the cutoff point and succeeded in making false claims that they had been present in the country for the requisite period of time.

To put this in perspective, I have read various estimates about the number of illegal aliens who are currently present in the United States. These estimates range from a low of twelve million to a high of twenty million. If, for argument sake, we figure on a number of fifteen million illegal aliens, or ten times the number that had been estimated prior to the amnesty of 1986, and if the same sort of under counting occurs, and if a comparable percentage of aliens succeed in racing into the United States and making . . . false claims that they had been here for the necessary period of time to be eligible to participate in the amnesty program that the Reid-Kennedy provisions would reward illegal aliens with, then we might expect some thirty-five million illegal aliens will ultimately participate in this insane program. Once they become citizens they would then be eligible to file applications to bring their family members to the United States, flooding our nation with tens of millions of additional new lawful immigrations while our nation's porous borders, visa waiver program and extreme lack of resources to enforce the immigration laws from within the interior of the United States would allow many millions of illegal aliens to continue to enter the United States in violation of law.

The utterly inept and incompetent USCIS, which is now unable to carry out its most basic missions with even a modicum of integrity would undoubtedly disintegrate. The system would simply implode, crushed by the burden of its vicious cycle of attempting to deal with an ever increasing spiral of rampant fraud thereby encouraging still more fraudulent applications to be filed. Terrorists would not find gaming this system the least bit challenging and our government will have become their unwitting ally, providing them with official identity documents in false names and then, ultimately, providing them with the keys to the kingdom by conferring resident aliens status and then, United States citizenship upon those who would destroy our nation and slaughter our citizens. . . .

America is at historic crossroads at this moment in time. Courageous decisions need to be made by our nation's leaders. If our nation fails to select the proper path, there will be no going back. If our nation decides to provide amnesty to millions of undocumented and illegal aliens, I fear that our national security will suffer irreparable harm as we aid and abet alien terrorists who seek to enter our country and embed themselves within it in preparation for the deadly attacks they would carry out. The priority must be clear, national security must be given the highest consideration and priority where the security of our nation's borders and the integrity of the immigration system are concerned.

VERNON M. BRIGGS JR., CORNELL UNIVERSITY, HEARING BEFORE THE COMMITTEE OF THE JUDICIARY, U.S. HOUSE OF REPRESENTATIVES, EVANSVILLE, INDIANA, AUGUST 29, 2006

Immigration reform is the domestic policy imperative of our time. The revival of the phenomenon of mass immigration from out of the nation's distant past was the accidental by-product of the passage of the Immigration Act of 1965. Immigration had been declining as a percentage of the population since 1914 and in absolute numbers since 1930. In 1965, only 4.4% of the population was foreign born—the lowest percentage in all of U.S. history and totaled 8.5 million people (the lowest absolute number since 1880). There was absolutely no intention in 1965 to increase the level of immigration. The post–World War "baby boom" was on the verge of pouring a tidal wave of new labor force entrants into the labor market in 1965 and would continue to do so for the next sixteen years. Instead, the stated goal of the 1965 legislation was to rid the immigration system of the overtly discriminatory admission system that had been in effect since 1924. But as subsequent events were to reveal, this legislation let the "Genie out of the jug." Without any warning to the people of the nation, the societal changing force of mass immigration was released on an unsuspecting American economy and its labor force. By 2005, the foreign-born population had soared to 35.5 million persons (or 12.1% of the population) and there were over 22 million workers in the labor force (or 14.7% of the labor force).

Clearly, the overarching conclusion from the experiences of the past forty-one years is that, when it comes to immigration reform, legislative changes should only be taken with great caution. While there is common agreement that the existing system requires major changes, the need for reforms should not be seen as an opportunity to introduce a myriad of dubious provisions—each of which has significant labor market implications—simply to placate the opportunistic pleadings of special interest groups.

Immigration is a policy-driven issue. Policy changes make a difference. Any changes should be to the benefit of the nation—especially the welfare of its existing labor force. ... For no matter how immigrants are admitted or by what means they enter the United States, most adult immigrants immediately join the labor force following their entry as do today many of their spouses and, eventually, most of their children. Immigration has economic consequences, which political leaders need to take into account when making any policy decisions. ...

The underlying reform issue that must be addressed before any others is illegal immigration. It makes no sense to debate remedies for deficiencies and/or additions to the extant immigration system when mass violations of whatever is enacted are tolerated year after year after year. The accumulated stock of illegal immigrants is believed to number between 11.5 to 12 million persons. The annual additional flow is estimated to be between 300,000 to 500,000 persons. Many believe these estimates are too low. Worse yet, these numbers exist despite the fact that over six million illegal immigrants have been allowed to legalize their status as the result of seven amnesties granted by the federal government since 1986. No other element of immigration reform has any claim of priority over the enactment of measures to end this scourge to effective policy implementation. The hemorrhage of illegal immigrants has not only made a mockery of the nation's immigration laws, it has seriously undermined the public's confidence in their own government's ability to secure its borders and control the nation's destiny. ...

... Because illegal immigrants tend to be disproportionately concentrated in certain segments of the nation's labor market, their direct impact is quite specific. The 2000 Census reported that 58% of the adult foreign-born population had only a high school diploma or less. Undoubtedly the educational attainment level of illegal immigrants is even worse than this bleak Census finding that is the product of our entire immigration system. Consequently, there is no doubt that most illegal immigrants are poorly educated, unskilled and often do not speak English. Of necessity, therefore, they seek employment in the low skilled occupations in a variety of industries. In the process, they artificially swell the labor supply in those occupations and industries and depress the wages of the low skilled American workers who also work in these sectors.

If permitted to compete for these jobs with American workers, the illegal immigrants will always win. This is because they will do anything to get the jobs—accept lower than prevailing wages; work longer hours; work under dangerous and hazardous working conditions; and live in crowded and sub-standard housing. They will accept conditions as they are and are less likely to report violations of prevailing laws pertaining to work standards, anti-discrimination and sexual harassment—even if they know these laws exist (which many do not). No American worker can successfully compete against them—nor should they—when the rules of the game are who will work the hardest, for the longest, and under the worst conditions.

As a consequence, the illegal immigrant worker becomes the "preferred worker" for employers. It is not that "American workers will not do certain jobs;" it is that they will not do the jobs under the same terms that illegal immigrants often will—nor should they. As for the illegal immigrants, they willingly work under these adverse conditions, because their orbit of comparison is with the conditions of work in their homelands. Literally, it does not matter how bad the working conditions are in the United States as they are invariably far better than they were where they come from. Sometimes it is simply the fact that it is possible to get a job at all that distinguishes the state of economic opportunity in the United States from their previous experiences in their countries of origin. ...

... There are more than thirty-four million low-wage workers in the U.S. labor force ... who are in the low skilled sector of the labor market. Overwhelmingly, most of these workers are American workers. ... Also, as the number of illegal immigrant workers has soared since ... 2000, 3.2 million native born persons of working age who had only a high school diploma or less have dropped-out of the labor force. Presumably, they have found it more rewarding to seek public benefits to support themselves or chosen to pursue illegal activities to support themselves. ... It is these low skilled American workers who bear most of the burden of competing for the jobs on the lower skill rungs of the nation's economic job ladder with illegal immigrants. ...

Massive numbers of illegal immigrants such as those now in the U.S. labor force—and the prospect that many more will continue to come until the magnet of finding jobs is turned-off—has opened wide the door for human exploitation. The literature is rampant with case studies and reports that document that the portion of the labor market where illegal immigrants work is infested with the use of extortion and brute force (by human smugglers which is a thriving criminal enterprise), human slavery (workers bound to human smugglers until their fees are paid off), wage kickbacks (to employers of illegal immigrants as well as to labor contractors), child labor, sexual harassment, job accidents (especially by illegal immigrants who cannot read safety warnings or who lie about their past work experiences and are injured or killed in jobs that they really do not know how to do), and the growth of "sweat shop" manufacturing.

Thus, there is nothing romantic about the nation's failure to enforce its immigration laws no matter how often or vocal pro-immigrant advocacy groups try to spin and to rationalize the issue. Indeed, the indifference paid by many of our national political leaders, the media, and many elite leaders of business, labor, religious, civil rights, and civil liberties groups to these exploitive conditions represents a decidedly seamy side ... of our democracy. ...

Illegal immigration is the primary issue that immigration reform must embrace. Not only is it a cause itself of significant harm to the economic well-being of the most needy members of the American populace, but it also adversely affects the broader society itself. Hence, there is little reason to believe that other policy reforms can be beneficial as long as the integrity of the entire system is in question. There are three steps that must be taken: 1. The employment sanctions system must be made to work. ... 2. Enforcement must become a reality. ... 3. There must be no amnesties—now or in the future—for those illegally in the United States.

PHYLLIS SCHLAFLY, HEARING BEFORE THE SUBCOMMITTEE ON IMMIGRATION, BORDER SECURITY, AND CLAIMS OF THE COMMITTEE ON THE JUDICIARY, U.S. HOUSE OF REPRESENTATIVES, 109TH CONGRESS, SECOND SESSION, JULY 18, 2006

Americans are basically a fair-minded people, and the continued entry of thousands of illegal aliens offends our ideals of fairness.

Failure to stop the entry of illegal aliens is unfair to those who don't have health insurance but see illegal aliens given costly treatment at U.S. hospitals for which U.S. taxpayers have to pay the bill. It is unfair to the legal immigrants who stand in line and wait their turn to comply with our laws. It is unfair to our friends in Arizona who are afraid to go out of their homes without a gun and a cell phone. It's unfair to small businessmen who are trying to run an honest business, pay their taxes and benefits to employees, but can't compete with their competitors whose costs are so much less because they hire illegal aliens in the underground economy. It is unfair to American children in public schools who see their classrooms flooded with kids who can't speak English and cause a gross decline in the quality of education. It's unfair to our own high school dropouts who need those low-wage jobs to start building a life.

Americans are basically a law-abiding people and they believe our government has betrayed us by its failure to enforce immigration law. Failure to stop the entry of illegal aliens is an offense against our fundamental belief that our nation respects the Rule of Law.

In addition to believing that failure to enforce the law is unfair and a betrayal, the American people have lost faith in the honesty of our leaders. Americans think we are being lied to ... by the Senate bill's use of the term "temporary guest workers." We know the President and the Senators are not telling the truth when they imply that guest workers will go home after a few years. The American people are thinking, we don't believe you—and worse, we don't believe that you believe what you are saying because the evidence is so overwhelming that guest workers do not go home. The Senate bill gives guest workers a path to citizenship after a few years and, anyway, it's obvious that those few years give plenty of time to produce an American-born anchor baby.

The American people also believe we are lied to by those who say we can't get border security unless we also have a guest-worker program and "amnesty lite." That's what they mean when they demand a "comprehensive" bill. But "comprehensive" has become a word as offensive as amnesty because we have figured out that it is just a cover for a plan to repeat the mistakes of the 1986 Immigration Reform and Control Act, known as Simpson-Mazzoli. That was truly a comprehensive law which combined amnesty with promises of border security and sanctions on employers who hired illegal aliens. The illegal aliens got their amnesty, but we did not get border security or employer sanctions. There was massive fraud, and the illegal population quadrupled.

The American people are not willing to be cheated again. ... When we hear the word "comprehensive," we believe that legalization and guest workers will be fully implemented, but that we will get nothing but pie-in-the-sky promises about border security and employment verification. ...

The Senate Bill Repeats the 1986 Mistakes

The Senate bill would give legal status and a path to citizenship (i.e., amnesty) to the eleven to twenty million aliens (workers, spouses and children) who entered our country illegally and have been using millions of fraudulent documents. They would then become recipients of our generous entitlements. The cost to the taxpayers of this monumental expansion of the welfare state would be at least $50 billion a year. U.S. taxpayers would be saddled with paying for the entitlements of these low-income families, including Medicaid, Social Security ... , Supplemental Security Income, Earned Income Tax Credit ... , the WIC program, food stamps, public and subsidized housing, Temporary Assistance to Needy Families, public schooling and school lunches, and federally funded legal representation. ...

"Comprehensive" Compromises Are Mistakes, Too

Faced with the American people demanding border security, we now hear some voices saying, okay, we'll package border security with legalization and guest worker, and we'll even promise to deal with border security *first*.

We don't believe them. We have to see proof that the border is closed to illegal aliens and to illegal drugs before we talk about anything else. These so-called compromise plans are heading down the same failed road as the Simpson-Mazzoli Act. . . .

Guest Worker Plans Are Immoral and Un-American

Even if a guest worker plan actually works the way it is promised, it would be immoral and un-American. . . . Inviting foreigners to come to America as guest workers is equivalent to sending the message: You people are only fit to do menial jobs that Americans think they are too good to do. We will let you come into our country for a few years to work low-paid jobs, but you have no hope of rising up the economic and social ladder, and we do not expect (or want) you to become Americans.

Inviting foreigners to come to America to do jobs that Americans think they are too good to do would create a subordinate underclass of unassimilated foreign workers, like the serf or peasant classes that exist in corrupt foreign countries such as Mexico or Saudi Arabia. That's not the kind of economy or social structure that made America a great nation. . . .

Border Security Is Essential and Must Come First

When is our government going to protect us from the crime, the drugs, the smuggling racket, destruction of property, and the endangerment to U.S. residents along our border and to our undermanned Border Patrol? . . .

Let's put border security in perspective. We currently have 37,000 U.S. troops guarding the 151-mile border between North and South Korea, but we have fewer than 12,000 agents to monitor 2,000 miles of our southern border. . . .

Illegal Immigration Is Affecting American Jobs

The American people know, even if our government doesn't seem to get it, that the vast influx of foreigners is costing Americans both jobs and good wages. We see this in unskilled entry-level jobs, needed by our own high school dropouts and college students, all the way up to skilled jobs needed by our engineers and computer specialists. . . .

. . . If every one of the illegal aliens in our country played hooky from his job, the overwhelming majority of those same types of jobs will be worked by millions of American citizens. All over the country, American citizens flip hamburgers in fast-food shops, wash dishes in restaurants, change sheets in hotels, mow lawns, trim shrubs, pick produce, drive taxis, replace roofs on houses, and do all kinds of construction work. Americans are quite willing to work unpleasant, menial, tiresome, and risky jobs, but not for Third World wages.

HEATHER MACDONALD, SENIOR FELLOW, MANHATTAN INSTITUTE FOR POLICY RESEARCH, HEARING BEFORE THE SUBCOMMITTEE ON IMMIGRATION, BORDER SECURITY, AND CLAIMS OF THE COMMITTEE ON THE JUDICIARY, U.S. HOUSE OF REPRESENTATIVES, 109TH CONGRESS, FIRST SESSION, APRIL 13, 2005

Sanctuary laws are a serious impediment to stemming gang violence and other crime. Moreover, they are a perfect symbol of this country's topsy-turvy stance towards illegal immigration.

Sanctuary laws, present in such cities as Los Angeles, New York, Chicago, Austin, Houston, and San Francisco, generally forbid local police officers from inquiring into a suspect's immigration status or reporting it to federal authorities. Such laws place a higher priority on protecting illegal aliens from deportation than on protecting legal immigrants and citizens from assault, rape, arson, and other crimes.

Let's say a Los Angeles police officer sees a member of Mara Salvatrucha hanging out at Hollywood and Vine. The gang member has previously been deported for aggravated assault; his mere presence back in the country following deportation is a federal felony. Under the prevailing understanding of Los Angeles's sanctuary law (special order 40), if that officer merely inquires into the gang-banger's immigration status, the officer will face departmental punishment.

To get the felon off the street, the cop has to wait until he has probable cause to arrest the gangbanger for a non-immigration crime, such as murder or robbery. It is by no means certain that that officer *will* successfully build a non-immigrant case against the gangster, however, since witnesses to gang crime often fear deadly retaliation if they cooperate with the police. Meanwhile, the gangbanger is free to prey on law-abiding members of his community, many of them immigrants themselves.

This is an extraordinarily inefficient way to reduce crime. If an officer has grounds for arresting a criminal now, it is perverse to ask him to wait until some later date when maybe, if he is lucky, he will have an additional ground for arrest.

Sanctuary laws violate everything we have learned about policing in the 1990s. Police departments across the country discovered that utilizing every law enforcement tool in their tool chest against criminals yielded enormous gains. Getting criminals off the streets for seemingly "minor" crimes such as turnstile jumping or graffiti saved lives. Gang crime, which exploded 50% from 1999 to 2002, is too serious a problem to ignore this lesson.

No one knows for certain the percentage of illegals in gangs, thanks in large part to sanctuary laws themselves. But various estimates exist:

- A confidential California Department of Justice study reported in 1995 that 60% of the 20,000-strong 18th Street Gang in southern California is illegal; police officers say the proportion is actually much greater. The bloody gang collaborates with the Mexican Mafia, the dominant force in California prisons, on complex drug-distribution schemes, extortion, and drive-by assassinations. It commits an assault or robbery every day in L.A. County. The gang has grown dramatically over the last two decades by recruiting recently arrived youngsters, most of them illegal, from Central America and Mexico. . . .

- Law enforcement officials estimate that 20% of gang members in San Diego County are illegal. . . .

- The leadership of the Columbia Lil' Cycos gang, which uses murder and racketeering to control the drug market around Los Angeles's MacArthur Park, was about 60% illegal in 2002. Francisco Martinez, a Mexican Mafia member and an illegal alien, controlled the gang from prison, while serving time for felonious reentry following deportation.

- In Los Angeles, 95% of all outstanding warrants for homicide in the first half of 2004 (which totaled 1,200 to 1,500) targeted illegal aliens. Up to two-thirds of all fugitive felony warrants (17,000) were for illegal aliens.

- The Los Angeles Police Department arrests about 2,500 criminally-convicted deportees annually. . . .

Though the numbers of illegal gang members remain elusive, the evidence for the destructive effects of sanctuary laws is incontrovertible. In 2002, for example, four illegal Mexicans, accompanied by one legal immigrant, abducted and brutally raped a forty-two-year-old mother of two near some railroad tracks in Queens, New York. The New York Police Department had already arrested three of the illegal aliens numerous times for such crimes as assault, attempted robbery, criminal trespass, illegal gun possession, and drug offenses. But pursuant to New York's sanctuary policy, the department had never notified the INS. . . .

In September 2003, the Miami police arrested a Honduran visa violator for seven vicious rapes. The previous year, Miami cops had had the suspect in custody for lewd and lascivious molestation. Pursuant to Miami's sanctuary law, however, the police had never checked his immigration status. Had they done so, they would have discovered his deportable status, and could have forestalled the rapes.

Cousins Aneceto and Jaime Reyes committed murder and a car-jacking, respectively, after returning to Los Angeles from Mexico following deportation. The Los Angeles police had encountered them before these most recent crimes, but had to wait for them to commit murder and a car-jacking before they could lay a finger on them for their immigration offenses. . . .

The Los Angeles Police Department began revisiting special order 40 last month. Its proposed revision merely underlines how perverse our attitudes towards illegal alien criminals remain.

Los Angeles's top brass propose to allow a Los Angeles officer who suspects that a criminal has previously been deported to contact his supervisor about the reentry felony. That supervisor would then contact ICE [U.S. Immigration Control and Enforcement]. ICE officials would next go before a federal judge to get an arrest warrant for the immigration felony. Then, with warrant in hand, the Los Angeles cop may finally arrest the felonious gangbanger—if he can still find him.

This burdensome procedure is preposterous. To arrest an American citizen for a crime, arrest warrants are rarely required; about 95% of arrests of citizens are warrantless. But in L.A., under the new rules, illegal criminals will have due process rights that citizens can only dream of: not just judicial review before they can be taken off the streets, but *federal* judicial review—the gold standard of all constitutional protections. Maybe home-grown criminals should renounce their citizenship and reenter the country illegally. It would be a constitutional windfall for them.

Other jurisdictions that are reconsidering their sanctuary laws are also proceeding with unnecessary timidity. The Orange County, California, sheriff plans to train a few deputies to use immigration laws only for special enforcement actions against sexual predators or gangs. . . . The Miami Police Department will join with ICE only on high-level gang cases.

These minor tinkerings all put unwise limitations on a vital law enforcement power. Local immigration enforcement power should not be limited to the felony of reentry following deportation. Nor should only a small subset of officers be authorized to use it. There are many illegal alien criminals who have not yet reentered following deportation, but who are just as dangerous to their communities. Every officer should have the power to enforce any immigration violation against a criminal suspect, not just immigration felonies.

Nothing demonstrates the necessity of this power better than ICE's March enforcement action against Mara Salvatrucha. Following the March round-up, ICE proudly displayed three of its trophy cases: the founding member of MS-13 in Hollywood, California, who had already been convicted for robbery and possession of a dangerous weapon; the leader of MS-13 in Long Branch, New Jersey, who had a prior criminal history of aggravated arson, weapons possession, grand larceny, and criminal possession of stolen property; and the founder of Port Washington, New York's, MS gang, who had a prior drug conviction.

ICE got all three of these leading gang bangers off the streets through what it calls administrative immigration violations, not felony immigration violations. Local officers in Hollywood, Long Branch, and Port Washington, as elsewhere, should have the power to use any type of immigration violation as well to get a thug (who may also prove to be a terrorist) off the street.

Immigration enforcement against criminals should also not wait upon a major federal-local gang initiative. The majority of opportunities to get criminals off the streets come from enforcing misdemeanors and quality of life offenses. While the police are waiting to make a major federal case against an illegal criminal, they are far more likely to have picked him up for a "petty" theft or an open-container offense. Officers should be empowered at every arrest or lawful stop to check someone's immigration status. If a suspect is committing an immigration offense, the officer should be empowered to arrest him immediately for that offense.

Jails and prisons should routinely check the immigration status of their prisoners. Such an initiative should not be dependent on the presence of an ICE officer stationed in a prison; there are simply not enough federal agents available to cover the relevant facilities. Moreover, ICE agents do not routinely visit local jails where misdemeanor offenders are held, yet those offenders may be as dangerous to the community as someone against whom a felony case has been made. Someone convicted of stealing a jacket today may be shooting a rival tomorrow. And many misdemeanor convicts in jails have been allowed to plead down from more serious felonies.

The standard argument for sanctuary laws is that they encourage illegal aliens to work with the police or seek government services. This argument is based on myth, not evidence. No illegal alien advocate has ever provided a shred of evidence that sanctuary laws actually accomplish their alleged ends. Nor has anyone shown that illegal aliens are even aware of sanctuary laws. The evidence for the destructive effects of sanctuary laws is clear, however.

The idea that sanctuary laws are "pro-immigrant" is perhaps the greatest myth of all. Keeping illegal criminals in the community subjects all immigrants to the thrall of crime and impedes economic growth in immigrant communities.

Obviously, the final prerequisite for ridding immigrant communities of illegal thugs is enough ICE detention space and deportation resources. But providing police officers with every lawful tool to fight crime is a crucial first step to protecting immigrant lives and should be the unanimous recommendation of the Subcommittee.

STATEMENT OF MICHAEL T. DOUGHERTY, DIRECTOR OF OPERATIONS, BUREAU OF IMMIGRATION AND CUSTOMS ENFORCEMENT (BICE), HEARING BEFORE THE SUBCOMMITTEE ON IMMIGRATION, BORDER SECURITY, AND CLAIMS OF THE COMMITTEE ON THE JUDICIARY, HOUSE OF REPRESENTATIVES, 108TH CONGRESS, FIRST SESSION, MAY 8, 2003

... We as a nation are proud of our globally celebrated—and unmatched—commitment to embracing those who come here legally to join us in building up America, and rightfully so. It is what makes our country great.

However, as the tragic events of September 11, 2001 made clear, those intent on tearing us down will try to take advantage of our generosity and openness by exploiting any mechanism that allows them access to the United States. The nineteen hijackers used our immigration system to gain access to the country in order to carry out the deadly attacks of September 11. While the horrific events of that date reinforced the vulnerabilities in our immigration system, operatives in prior terrorism cases have used fraudulent identities, visas, and travel documents to gain access to our country and further their operations. In the 1993 World Trade Center bombing, operatives arrived in the U.S. on student visas but never attended school here. What is also clear from this history is the incredibly powerful tool that immigration enforcement provides in addressing the vulnerabilities in our system that have been exploited by terrorists and other violent criminals. ...

Overview

... The investigation following the events of September 11, 2001, demonstrates how immigration authority and intelligence are critical to national security investigations. Immigration authority provided for the arrest and detention of Zacarias Moussaoui, the individual charged with complicity in the September 11th attacks, while the terrorism investigation was ongoing. Criminal immigration provisions allowed for the prosecution of associates of the September 11th hijackers who used fraudulent visas or documents or who applied for immigration benefits through fraud. The intelligence community relied on data produced by immigration databases and analyzed by the Intelligence Division to help track the hijackers and locate all their known places of residence and known associates in the U.S. and abroad. The Intelligence Division also provided data and analysis on travel patterns and document use by the hijackers. Finally, INS used its authorities to detain and remove aliens who came to the attention of law enforcement through leads related to the September 11th investigation, including known associates of the hijackers. Clearly immigration expertise and authority play a major role in such national security matters. ...

COUNTER-TERRORISM IMMIGRATION ENFORCEMENT

... A prime example of this national security focus is the initiative BICE launched on March 20, when agents began seeking out Iraqi nationals believed to be unlawfully in the United States. The joint effort, carried out with the FBI as part of Operation Liberty Shield, aimed to identify and collect information on individuals who might pose a threat to the safety and security of the American people. Approximately 2,000 interviews were conducted resulting in 92 arrests (84 on immigration violations and 8 on criminal charges) by BICE. The Iraqis targeted as part of this effort were identified using a range of intelligence criteria and based on screening of data from our immigration databases. Additionally, as part of Operation Liberty Shield, BICE detained arriving asylum applicants from Iraq and nations where al-Qaeda, al-Qaeda sympathizers, and other terrorist groups are known to have operated. This reasonable and prudent action allowed BICE agents to contact asylum seekers, determine the validity of claims, verify identities, and interview those detained in order to gather intelligence for potential threats and/or sources of information. Further, BICE led an initiative to review approximately 2,500 asylum files related to Iraqi nationals in order to exploit these files for potential threats and/or sources of information. Of the 2,629 reviewed, 619 cases have been referred for follow-up investigation by BICE and the FBI. ...

Absconder Apprehension Initiative

... Under this initiative, BICE tracks, apprehends, and removes violators of U.S. immigration law who had been ordered deported, but fled before the deportation order could be carried out. Careful analysis has determined there are in excess of 300,000 alien absconders with unexecuted final orders of removal including approximately 80,000 with criminal records. Moreover, historically, voluntary departures have not been tracked. BICE views the failure to track departures as a serious issue effecting national security. The affective implementation of the Entry-Exit system, now part of U.S. VISIT, under development will be part of the solution to confirm departures. ...

National Security Entry-Exit Registration System (NSEERS)

... Congress called for development of an integrated entry-exit system for arriving visitors. NSEERS is the first part of that system. NSEERS promotes several key national security objectives:

> Allows the United States to run the fingerprints of aliens seeking to enter the country or already present against a database of known terrorists and criminals;

> Enables the United States to determine whether such an alien has overstayed their visa status; and

Permits the United States to verify that an alien is complying with the terms of his visa status by living where he said he would live and by doing what he said he would do while in the United States, thus ensuring that he is not violating our immigration laws.

Since the implementation of NSEERS last September, more than 138,000 individuals from more than 151 countries have registered. BICE Special Agents are responsible for interviewing and processing registrants referred for investigation of possible immigration violations, criminal violations, or terrorism-related matters. To date, the program has resulted in the identification of 11 aliens linked to terrorism, the arrest of more than 120 criminal aliens, and the issuance of more than 12,000 notices to appear for removal proceedings.

Student and Exchange Visitor Information System (SEVIS)

Ensuring that foreign students comply with the terms of their visas is also vital to our nation's security. That is why the Congress mandated in 1996 the development of the Student and Exchange Visitor Information System (SEVIS), which was deployed under the legacy INS. This new Internet-based system, now part of U.S. VISIT and operated by BICE, maintains information that can be accessed electronically, making it a powerful tool for combating fraud and for ensuring that individuals comply with the terms of their visa. Student status violators are now referred to our Division of National Security Investigations where those leads are prioritized based upon factors such as criminal history and prior adverse immigration history. High priority leads are then referred to the appropriate field office for investigation. To date, 174 cases have been referred for field investigation resulting in 20 arrests. ...

Critical Infrastructure Protection Operations

Another priority within BICE is reflected through the creation of the Critical Infrastructure Protection Office which will focus its traditional immigration employment verification authorities on our nation's critical infrastructure or venues. The presence of workers who have presented fraudulent identification and employment authorization documents poses a significant security breach at our nation's critical infrastructure. Operation Tarmac, for example, was launched in recognition of the fact that illegal workers at airports may pose a serious security risk. It aims to ensure that people with access to secure areas at airports are properly documented and identified. Those without proper documentation are either prosecuted or removed. So far, more than 229,000 Employment Eligibility Verification Forms (Forms I-9) have been audited at more than 3,000 airport businesses. Nearly 1,000 unauthorized aliens have been arrested, with more than two-thirds of them being charged with criminal violations. Additionally, fines have been levied against employers for worksite violations. . . .

Anti-Smuggling Program

BICE's Anti-Smuggling Program aims to dismantle smuggling organizations with links to terrorism and others groups that pose a risk to our national security. Available information indicates terrorist organizations use human smuggling rings to move around the globe, which makes investigating and dismantling these organizations a vital part of our overall effort to enhance homeland security.

Focusing our anti-smuggling resources on domestic security led to the initiation of Operation Southern Focus in January 2002. This multi-jurisdictional operation targeted large-scale smuggling organizations specializing in the movement of U.S.-bound aliens from countries of concern. Many targets of Operation Southern Focus were believed to be responsible for smuggling hundreds of aliens into the country. Since the inception of this operation, nine major smugglers have been arrested and charged with alien smuggling violations, and significant alien smuggling pipelines have been severely disrupted. . . .

Conclusion

Deterring illegal migration and combating immigration-related crime have never been more critical to our national security. The men and women of BICE are tackling this challenging mission with diligence, determined to ensure that no duty is neglected even as they continue to adjust during this time of transition into the new Department. We are eager to work with you and the other members of Congress to provide the American people with the level of security they demand and deserve.

U.S. DEPARTMENT OF JUSTICE BROCHURE: FEDERAL PROTECTIONS AGAINST NATIONAL ORIGIN DISCRIMINATION

This brochure, which was issued in October 2000 and is reprinted virtually in its entirety below, is available on the U.S. Department of Justice Web site (http://www.usdoj.gov/crt/legalinfo/nordwg_brochure.html). The brochure is published in Arabic, Cambodian, Chinese, English, Farsi, French, Haitian Creole, Hindi, Hmong, Korean, Laotian, Punjabi, Russian, Spanish, Tagalog, Urdu, and Vietnamese.

INTRODUCTION

Federal laws prohibit discrimination based on a person's national origin, race, color, religion, disability, sex, and familial status. Laws prohibiting national origin discrimination make it illegal to discriminate because of a person's birthplace, ancestry, culture or language. This means people cannot be denied equal opportunity because they or their family are from another country, because they have a name or accent associated with a national origin group, because they participate in certain customs associated with a national origin group, or because they are married to or associate with people of a certain national origin.

The Department of Justice's Civil Rights Division is concerned that national origin discrimination may go unreported in the United States because victims of discrimination do not know their legal rights, or may be afraid to complain to the government. To address this problem, the Civil Rights Division has established a National Origin Working Group to help citizens and immigrants better understand and exercise their legal rights. . . .

CRIMINAL VIOLATIONS OF CIVIL RIGHTS

- A young man of South Asian descent is assaulted as he leaves a concert at a nightclub. The assailant, a member of a skinhead group, yells racial epithets as he beats the victim unconscious in the club's parking lot with fists and a pipe.

- At Ku Klux Klan meetings, a Klansman tells other members that Mexicans and Puerto Ricans should go "back where they came from." They burn a cross in the front yard of a young Hispanic couple in order to frighten them and force them to leave the neighborhood. Before burning the cross, the defendant displays a gun and gives one of his friends another gun in case the victims try to stop them.

- An American company recruits workers in a small Mexican town, promising them good work at high pay. The company smuggles the Mexicans to the United States in an empty tanker truck. When they finally arrive in the U.S., the workers are threatened, told that if they attempt to leave their factory they will be killed.

The Criminal Section of the Civil Rights Division prosecutes people who are accused of using force or violence to interfere with a person's federally protected rights because of that person's national origin. These rights include areas such as housing, employment, education, or use of public facilities. You can reach the Criminal Section at (202) 514-3204. . . .

DISABILITY RIGHTS

- An HMO that enrolls Medicaid patients tells a Mexican American woman with cerebral palsy to come back another day for an appointment while it provides immediate assistance to others.

This example may be a violation of federal laws that prohibit discrimination because of disability as well as laws that prohibit discrimination because of national origin. If you believe you have been discriminated against because you have a disability you may contact the Disability Rights Section at 1-800-514-0301 (voice) or 1-800-514-0383 (TTY). . . .

EDUCATION

- A child has difficulty speaking English, but her school does not provide her with the necessary assistance to help her learn English and other subjects.

- A majority Haitian school does not offer honors classes. Other schools in the district that do not have many Haitian students offer both honors and advanced placement courses.

These examples may be violations of federal law, which prohibits discrimination in education because of a person's national origin. The Division's Educational Opportunities Section enforces these laws in elementary and secondary schools as well as public colleges and universities. The Education Section's work addresses discrimination in all aspects of education, including assignment of students to schools and classes, transportation of students, hiring and placement of faculty and administrators, distribution of school resources, and provision of educational programs that assist limited English speaking students in learning English.

To file a complaint or for more information, contact the Education Section at (202) 514-4092. . . .

EMPLOYMENT

- A transit worker's supervisor makes frequent racial epithets against the worker because his family is from Iran. Last week, the boss put up a fake sign on the bulletin board telling everyone not to trust the worker because he is a terrorist.

- A woman who immigrated from Russia applies for a job as an accountant. The employer turns her down because she speaks with an accent even though she is able to perform the job requirements.

- A food processing company requires applicants who appear or sound foreign to show work authorization documents before allowing them to complete an employment application while native born Caucasian applicants are not required to show any documents before completing employment applications. Moreover, the documents of the ethnic employees are more closely scrutinized and more often rejected than the same types of documents shown by native born Caucasian employees.

These examples may be violations of the law that prohibits discrimination against an employee or job applicant because of his or her national origin. This means an employer cannot discipline, harass, fire, refuse to hire or promote a person because of his or her national origin.

If you believe an employer, labor organization or employment agency has discriminated against you because of your national origin, contact:

Equal Employment Opportunity Commission

1-800-669-4000

(Employers with fifteen or more employees)

Office of Special Counsel

1-800-255-7688

(Employers with four to fourteen employees)

Employment Litigation Section

(202) 514-3831

(State or local government employer with a pattern or practice of illegal discrimination)

In addition, an employer may violate federal law by requiring specific work authorization documents, such as a green card, or rejecting such documents only from applicants of certain national origins. For more information or to file a charge, contact the Division's Office of Special Counsel at the above address or toll-free number.

HOUSING

- A Native Hawaiian family is looking for an apartment. They are told by the rental agent that no apartments are available, even though apartments are available and are shown to white applicants.

- A realtor shows a Latino family houses only in Latino neighborhoods and refuses to show the family houses in white neighborhoods.

These examples may be violations of the federal Fair Housing Act. That law prohibits discrimination because of national origin, race, color, sex, religion, disability, or familial status (presence of children under eighteen) in housing. Individual complaints of discrimination may be reported to the Department of Housing and Urban Development (HUD) at 1-800-669-9777. If you believe there is a pattern or practice of discrimination, contact the Division's Housing and Civil Enforcement Section at (202) 514-4713.

LENDING

- A Latina woman is charged a higher interest rate and fees than white male customers who have similar financial histories and apply for the same type of loan.

This example may be a violation of federal laws that prohibit discrimination in lending because of national origin, race, color, sex, religion, disability and marital status or because any of a person's income comes from public assistance. If you believe you have been denied a loan because of your national origin or other protected reason, you may ask the lender for an explanation in writing of why your application was denied.

If the loan is for a home mortgage, home improvement, or other housing-related reasons, you may file a complaint with the Department of Housing and Urban Development at 1-800-669-9777. If the loan is for purposes other than housing (such as a car loan), you may file a complaint either with the Division's Housing and Civil Enforcement Section or with the lender's regulatory agency. If your experience was part of a pattern or practice of discrimination you may also call the Housing and Civil Enforcement Section at (202) 514-4713, to obtain more information about your rights or to file a complaint.

PUBLIC ACCOMMODATIONS

• In a restaurant, a group of Asian Americans waits for over an hour to be served, while white and Latino customers receive prompt service.

• Haitian American visitors to a hotel are told they must pay in cash rather than by credit card, are charged higher rates than other customers, and are not provided with the same amenities, such as towels and soap.

These examples may be violations of federal laws that prohibit discrimination because of national origin, race, color, or religion in places of public accommodation. Public accommodations include hotels, restaurants, and places of entertainment. If you believe you have been denied access to or equal enjoyment of a public accommodation where there is a pattern or practice of discrimination, contact the Housing and Civil Enforcement Section at (202) 514-4713. . . .

POLICE MISCONDUCT

• Police officers constantly pull over cars driven by Latinos, for certain traffic violations, but rarely pull over white drivers for the same violations.

• A police officer questioning a man of Vietnamese origin on the street gets angry when the man is unable to answer his questions because he does not speak English. The officer arrests the man for disorderly conduct.

These examples may be violations of the Equal Protection Clause of the United States Constitution. They may also be violations of the Omnibus Crime Control and Safe Streets Act of 1968. That law prohibits discrimination because of national origin, race, color, religion, or sex by a police department that gets federal funds through the U.S. Department of Justice. They may also violate Title VI of the Civil Rights Act of 1964, which prohibits discrimination by law enforcement agencies that receive any federal financial assistance, including asset forfeiture property.

Complaints of individual discrimination can be filed with the Coordination and Review Section . . . at 1-888-848-5306.

Complaints of individual discrimination may also be filed with the Office of Justice Programs . . . at (202) 307-0690.

The Special Litigation Section investigates and litigates complaints that a police department has a pattern or practice of discriminating on the basis of national origin. To file a complaint, contact the Special Litigation Section at (202) 514-6255. . . .

CIVIL RIGHTS OF INSTITUTIONALIZED PERSONS

• A jail will not translate disciplinary hearings for detainees who do not speak English.

• A state's psychiatric hospital has no means of providing treatment for people who do not speak English.

These examples may be violations of the Equal Protection Clause of the United States Constitution. The Special Litigation Section enforces the constitutional rights of people held in state or local government institutions, such as prisons, jails, juvenile correctional facilities, mental health facilities, developmental disability or mental retardation facilities, and nursing homes. If you are a resident of any such facility and you believe there is a pattern or practice of discrimination based on your national origin, contact the Special Litigation Section at (202) 514-6255. . . .

FEDERALLY ASSISTED PROGRAMS

• A local social services agency does not provide information or job training in Korean even though one-quarter of local residents speak only Korean.

• A hospital near the Texas/Mexico border dresses its security officers in clothes that look like INS uniforms to scare Latinos away from the emergency room. Latino patients are told to bring their own translators before they can see a doctor.

These examples may be violations of federal laws that prohibit discrimination because of national origin, race or color by recipients of federal funds. If you believe you have been discriminated against by a state or local government agency or an organization that receives funds from the federal government, you may file a complaint with the Division's Coordination and Review Section at 1-888-848-5306. . . . The Coordination and Review Section will refer the complaint to the federal funding agency that is primarily responsible for enforcing non-discrimination prohibitions applicable to its recipients.

VOTING

• Despite requests from voters in a large Spanish-speaking community, election officials refuse to provide election materials, including registration forms and sample ballots, in Spanish or to allow Spanish speakers to bring translators into the voting booth.

• A polling official requires a dark-skinned voter, who speaks with a foreign accent and has an unfamiliar last name, to provide proof of American citizenship, but does not require proof of citizenship from white voters.

The election officials' conduct may violate the federal laws prohibiting voting discrimination. The Voting Rights Acts do not specifically prohibit national origin discrimination. However, provisions of the Acts make it illegal to limit or deny the right to vote of any citizen not only because of race or color, but also because of membership in a language minority group. In addition, the Acts also require in certain jurisdictions that election materials and assistance be provided in languages other than English.

Additionally, Section 208 of the Voting Rights Act, allows voters, who need help because of blindness, disability or because they cannot read or write, to bring someone (other than an employer or union representative) to help. This means that a voter who needs help reading the ballot in English can bring a friend or family member to translate. In some places, election officials must provide information, such as voter registration and the ballot, in certain language(s) other than English. This can include interpreters to help voters vote.

If you believe that you have been discriminated against in voting or denied assistance in casting your ballot, you may contact the Division's Voting Section at 1-800-253-3931.

APPENDIX II
MAPS OF THE WORLD

NORTH AND CENTRAL AMERICA 140
SOUTH AMERICA AND THE CARIBBEAN 141
EUROPE AND RUSSIA 142
AFRICA 143
**EAST ASIA, SOUTH ASIA, AND THE MIDDLE
        EAST** 144
SOUTHEAST ASIA 145
OCEANIA 146

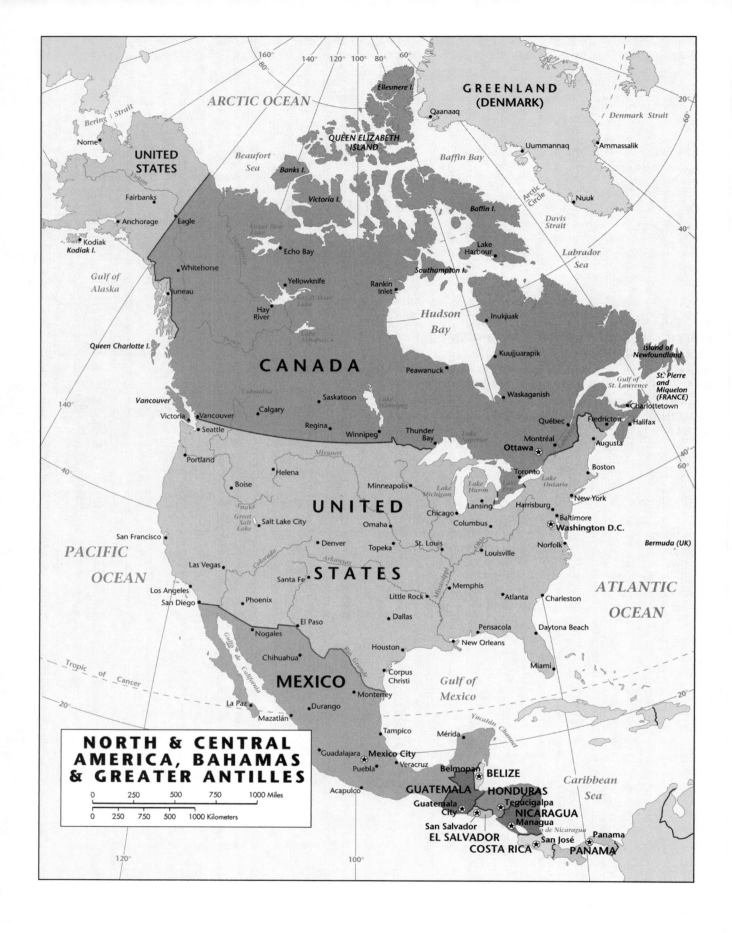

NORTH & CENTRAL AMERICA, BAHAMAS & GREATER ANTILLES

0   250   500   750   1000 Miles

0   250   750   500   1000 Kilometers

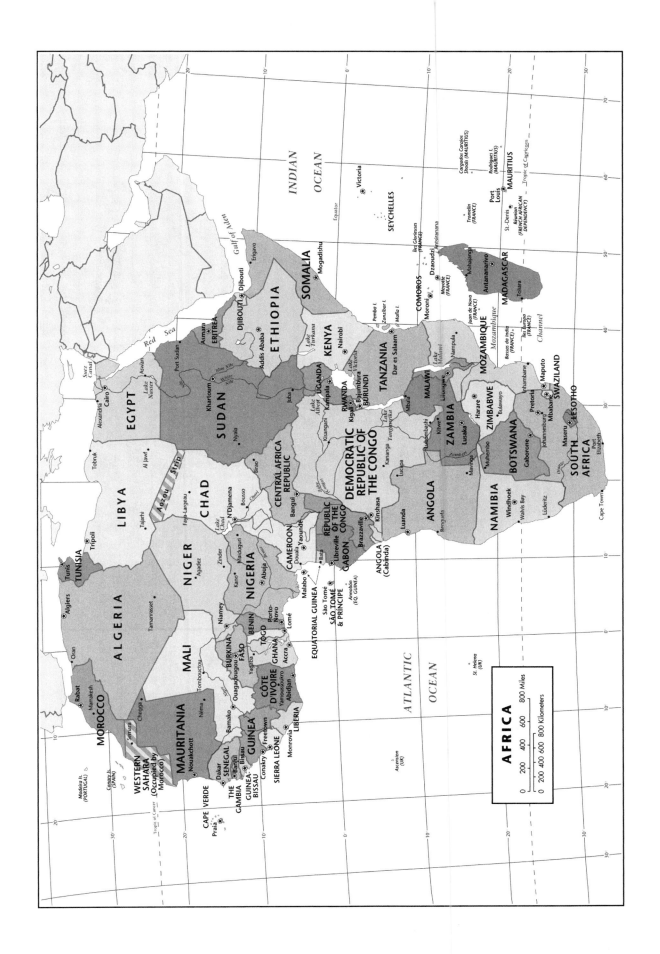

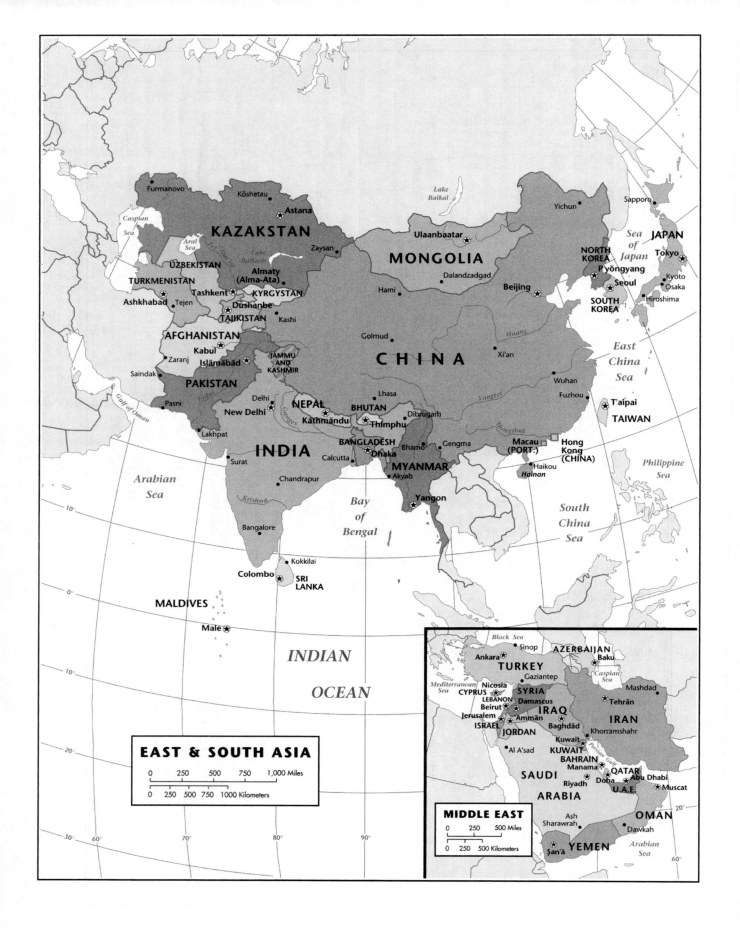

EAST & SOUTH ASIA

0   250   500   750   1,000 Miles

0   250   500 750   1000 Kilometers

MIDDLE EAST

0   250   500 Miles

0   250   500 Kilometers

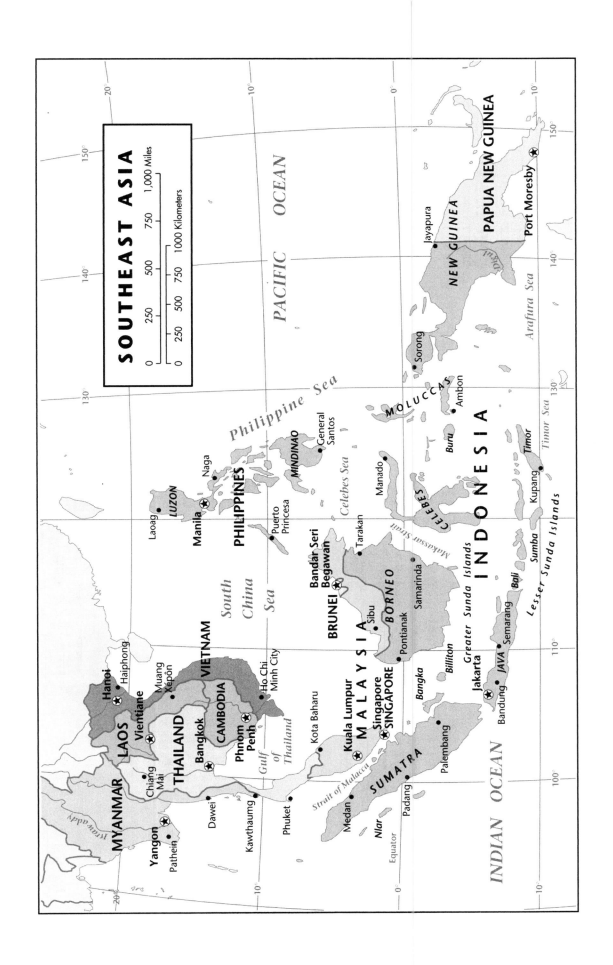

SOUTHEAST ASIA

1,000 Miles
0   250   500   750
0   250   500   750   1000 Kilometers

PACIFIC OCEAN

PAPUA NEW GUINEA
NEW GUINEA
Port Moresby
Jayapura
Sorong
Arafura Sea

MOLUCCAS
Ambon
Buru
INDONESIA
Timor Sea
Timor
Kupang
Lesser Sunda Islands
Sumba
Bali
Semarang
JAVA
Bandung
Jakarta
Billiton
Greater Sunda Islands
Bangka
Palembang
Manado
CELEBES
Makassar Strait
Celebes Sea
Tarakan
Samarinda
BORNEO
Pontianak
Sibu
BRUNEI
Bandar Seri Begawan
MALAYSIA
Singapore
SINGAPORE
Kuala Lumpur
Kota Baharu
SUMATRA
Medan
Niar
Padang
Equator
INDIAN OCEAN

Philippine Sea
PHILIPPINES
MINDANAO
General Santos
Naga
LUZON
Manila
Laoag
Puerto Princesa
South China Sea
Gulf of Thailand
Phuket
Kawthaumg
Dawei
Strait of Malacca

VIETNAM
Ho Chi Minh City
Muang Xépôn
Haiphong
Hanoi
LAOS
Vientiane
THAILAND
Bangkok
CAMBODIA
Phnom Penh
MYANMAR
Chiang Mai
Yangon
Pathein
Irrawaddy

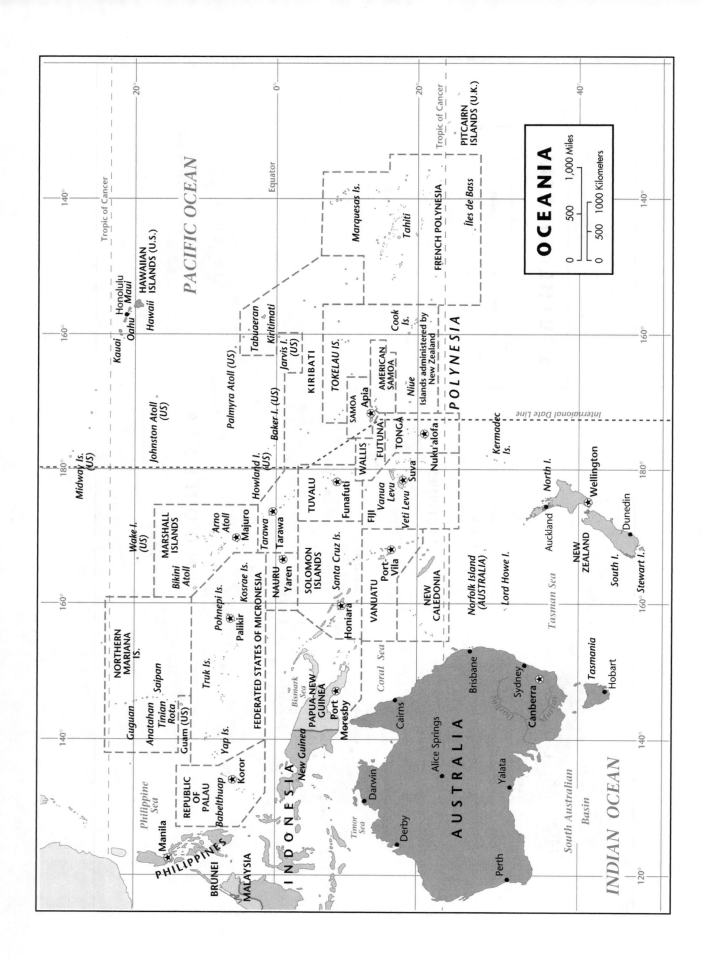

IMPORTANT NAMES
AND ADDRESSES

**American Civil Liberties Union
Immigrants' Rights Project**
125 Broad St., 18th Floor
New York, NY 10004
1-888-567-ACLU
URL: http://www.aclu.org/

Amnesty International USA
5 Penn Plaza
New York, NY 10001
(212) 807-8400
FAX: (212) 627-1451
E-mail: aimember@aiusa.org
URL: http://www.amnestyusa.org/

**Bureau of Population, Refugees,
and Migration
U.S. Department of State**
2201 C St. NW
Washington, DC 20520
(202) 647-8472
URL: http://www.state.gov/g/prm/

Cato Institute
1000 Massachusetts Ave. NW
Washington, DC 20001-5403
(202) 842-0200
FAX: (202) 842-3490
URL: http://www.cato.org/

Center for Immigration Studies
1522 K St. NW, Ste. 820
Washington, DC 20005-1202
(202) 466-8185
FAX: (202) 466-8076
E-mail: center@cis.org
URL: http://www.cis.org/

**Federation for American
Immigration Reform**
1666 Connecticut Ave. NW, Ste. 400
Washington, DC 20009
(202) 328-7004
FAX: (202) 387-3447
URL: http://www.fairus.org/

Human Rights Watch
350 Fifth Ave., 34th Floor
New York, NY 10118-3299
(212) 290-4700
FAX: (212) 736-1300
E-mail: hrwnyc@hrw.org
URL: http://www.hrw.org/

Institute of International Education
809 United Nations Plaza, 7th Floor
New York, NY 10017
(212) 984-5453
URL: http://www.iie.org/

**Lutheran Immigration and
Refugee Service**
700 Light St.
Baltimore, MD 21230
(410) 230-2700
FAX: (410) 230-2890
E-mail: lirs@lirs.org
URL: http://www.lirs.org/

**Mexican American Legal Defense and
Education Fund (MALDEF)**
634 S. Spring St.
Los Angeles, CA 90014
(213) 629-2512
URL: http://www.maldef.org/

Migration Policy Institute
1400 Sixteenth St. NW, Ste. 300
Washington, DC 20036
(202) 266-1940
FAX: (202) 266-1900
E-mail: info@migrationpolicy.org
URL: http://www.migrationpolicy.org/

**National Center for Refugee and
Immigrant Children
U.S. Committee for Refugees and
Immigrants**
1717 Massachusetts Ave. NW, Ste. 200
Washington, DC 20036
(202) 347-3507

FAX: (202) 347-3418
URL: http://www.refugees.org/

National Conference of State Legislatures
444 N. Capitol St. NW, Ste. 515
Washington, DC 20001
(202) 624-5400
FAX: (202) 737-1069
URL: http://www.ncsl.org/

National Council of La Raza
1126 Sixteenth St. NW
Washington, DC 20036
(202) 785-1670
FAX: (202) 776-1792
E-mail: comments@nclr.org
URL: http://www.nclr.org/

**National Foundation for
American Policy**
2111 Wilson Blvd., Ste. 700
Arlington, VA 22201
(703) 351-5042
E-mail: info@nfap.net
URL: http://www.nfap.net/

National Immigration Forum
50 F St. NW, Ste. 300
Washington, DC 20001
(202) 347-0040
FAX: (202) 347-0058
URL: http://www.immigrationforum.org/

**Office of Refugee Resettlement
Administration for Children and Families**
370 L'Enfant Promenade SW,
6th Floor/East
Washington, DC 20447
(202) 401-9246
FAX: (202) 401-5487
URL: http://www.acf.hhs.gov/programs/orr/

Pew Hispanic Center
1615 L St. NW, Ste. 700
Washington, DC 20036-5610
(202) 419-3600

FAX: (202) 419-3608
E-mail: info@pewhispanic.org
URL: http://www.pewhispanic.org/

Refugee Council USA
3211 Fourth St. NE
Washington, DC 20017-1194
(202) 541-5402
FAX: (202) 541-3468
URL: http://www.refugeecouncilusa.org/

**United Nations High Commissioner
for Refugees**
1775 K St. NW, Ste. 300
Washington, DC 20006
(202) 296-5191
FAX: (202) 296-5660
URL: http://www.unhcr.org/cgi-bin/texis/
vtx/home

Urban Institute
2100 M St. NW
Washington, DC 20037
(202) 833-7200
URL: http://www.urban.org/

U.S. Bureau of the Census
4600 Silver Hill Rd.
Washington, DC 20233
(301) 763-2422
URL: http://www.census.gov/

**U.S. Citizenship and Immigration
Services**
2675 Prosperity Ave.
Fairfax, VA 22031
1-800-375-5283
URL: http://www.uscis.gov/

**U.S. House of Representatives Committee
on the Judiciary
Subcommittee on Immigration, Border
Security, and Claims**
2138 Rayburn House Office Bldg.
Washington, DC 20515
(202) 225-3951
URL: http://www.house.gov/judiciary/
immigration.htm

**U.S. Senate Committee
on the Judiciary
Subcommittee on Immigration, Border
Security, and Citizenship**
224 Dirksen Senate Office Bldg.
Washington, DC 20510
(202) 224-7840
URL: http://judiciary.senate.gov/
subcommittees/immigration109.cfm

RESOURCES

The U.S. government provides most of the statistical information concerning immigration and naturalization. Much of the information comes from branches of the U.S. Department of Homeland Security (DHS). The primary source is the *Yearbook of Immigration Statistics* (2005, ongoing), an online publication of the U.S. Citizenship and Immigration Services (USCIS), which assumed the responsibilities of the U.S. Immigration and Naturalization Service in March 2003. The USCIS report *SEVIS by the Numbers* (2006) tracks the location and status of foreign students who attend U.S. schools. Other DHS reports providing valuable data include *Immigration Enforcement Actions: 2005* (November 2006), *Budget-in-Brief Fiscal Year 2007* (2007), and the *Citizenship and Immigration Services Ombudsman Annual Report 2006* (June 2006).

Because immigration affects so many areas, information on this topic also can be found in reports issued by government agencies outside the DHS. For example, the U.S. Department of Agriculture oversees and provides information on the Food Stamp Program. The Social Security Administration conducts the Basic Pilot Program and controls the Earnings Suspense File. The Centers for Disease Control and Prevention monitors health issues in such publications as *Reported Tuberculosis in the United States, 2005* (September 2006).

The U.S. Department of State details results of issued visas in the *Report of the VISA Office, 2005* (March 2007) and *FY2006 Performance and Accountability Report* (November 2006). Refugee admissions and future admission levels are provided in *Emergency Refugee and Migration Assistance: Fiscal Year 2007* (2006) and *Proposed Refugees Admissions for Fiscal Year 2007: Report to Congress* (2006). The Office of the United Nations High Commissioner for Refugees provides international data on asylum seekers in *Measuring Protection by Numbers, 2005* (November 2006).

The U.S. Department of Justice published "Asylum Protection in the United States" (April 2005), *Attorney General's Report to Congress on U.S. Government Activities to Combat Trafficking in Persons Fiscal Year 2005* (June 2006), and "Fact Sheet Regarding Post-9/11 Backlash Discrimination" (June 2002).

The Congressional Budget Office published "Cost Estimate H.R. 418" (February 2005) and *The Role of Immigrants in the U.S. Labor Market* (November 2005). The House Judiciary Committee provided *House Report 108-747—Security and Fairness Enhancement for America Act of 2003* (October 2004). The U.S. Bureau of the Census collects and distributes the nation's statistics in *Statistical Abstract of the United States, 2007* (2006).

The U.S. Government Accountability Office studies many aspects of immigration. Some of the reports used in this publication include *Welfare Reform: Many States Continue Some Federal or State Benefits for Immigrants* (July 1998), *Homeland Security: Justice Department's Project to Interview Aliens after September 11, 2001* (April 2003), and *Border Security: US-VISIT Program Faces Strategic, Operational, and Technological Challenges at Land Ports of Entry* (December 2006).

The Congressional Research Service (CRS) is a think tank that works exclusively for members and committees of Congress. CRS publications used in this book include *Social Security Benefits for Noncitizens: Current Policy and Legislation* (Dawn Nuschler and Alison Siskin, July 2004) and *Border Security: Barriers along the U.S. International Border* (Blas Nuñez-Nito and Stephen Viña, December 2006). The National Conference of State Legislatures published *The ABCs of IDs for Immigrants in the United States* (Katherine Gigliotti and Ann Morse, December 2004), "Immigrant Policy" (October 2006), and *The REAL ID Act: National Impact Analysis* (September 2006), jointly sponsored with the National Governors Association and the National Association of Motor

Vehicle Administrators. The U.S. Chamber of Commerce projects the economic future of the workplace in *The State of American Business 2007* (Thomas J. Donahue, 2007).

Organizations that support and oppose immigration have published extensive information on various immigration issues. Reports used in this book include the American Immigration Law Foundation's *U.S. Soldiers from around the World* (March 2003) and Amnesty International's *Why Am I Here? Children in Immigration Detention* (June 2003). Bear Stearns Asset Management produced *The Underground Labor Force Is Rising to the Surface* (Robert Justich and Betty Ng, January 2005). The Center for Immigration Studies published *Measuring the Fallout: The Cost of IRCA Amnesty after 10 Years* (David Simcox, May 1997) and "The Public's View of Immigration: A Comprehensive Survey and Analysis" (November 2006). Citizens against Government Waste issued the report *REAL ID: Big Brother Could Cost Big Money* (Angela French, October 2005). The Harvard University Committee on Human Rights published *Seeking Asylum Alone: Unaccompanied and Separated Children and Refugee Protection in the U.S.* (Jacqueline Bhabha and Susan Schmidt, June 2006). Human Rights Watch compiled "Above the Law: Executive Power after September 11 in the United States" (Allison Parker and Jamie Fellner, January 2004). The Institute of International Education provided detailed information about foreign students in U.S. colleges and universities in *Open Doors 2006* (November 2006). The Inter-American Development Bank studied the impact of money migrants send to their home countries to support family members in *Remittances 2005: Promoting Financial Democracy* (March 2006), *Sending Money Home: Leveraging the Development Impact of Remittances* (2006), and *Public Opinion Research Study of Latin American Remittance Senders in the United States* (October 2006). The Kaiser Commission on Medicaid and the Uninsured produced "Citizenship Documentation Requirements in Medicaid" (January 2007). The Pew Research Center for the People and the Press published *America's Immigration Quandary* (March 2006) and *A Portrait of "Generation Next"* (January 2007). The Pew Hispanic Center delivered results of its research in "Modes of Entry for the Unauthorized Migrant Population" (May 2005), *Size and Characteristics of the Unauthorized Migrant Population in the U.S.* (Jeffrey S. Passel, March 2006), *A Statistical Portrait of the Foreign Born at Mid-Decade* (October 2006), and "Hispanic Attitudes toward Learning English" (June 2006). An in-depth look at border issues was provided by the United States/Mexico Border

Counties Coalition in *At the Cross Roads: US/Mexico Border Counties in Transition* (March 2006). The Gale Group thanks these researchers for permission to reproduce their data and graphics.

The Newest New Yorkers, 2000: Immigrant New York in the New Millennium (October 2004), by the New York City Department of City Planning, is the latest in a quadrennial series of in-depth studies of changing demographic trends, costs, and contributions of the immigrant population of the city. The National Foundation for American Policy studied the impact of legal immigrants in *Legal Immigrants: Waiting Forever* (Stuart Anderson and David Miller, May 2006) and *Coming to America: Immigrants, Baseball, and the Contributions of Foreign-Born Players to America's Pastime* (Stuart Anderson and L. Brian Andrew, October 2006). The National Venture Capital Association considers the effects of immigrant entrepreneurs in *American Made: The Impact of Immigrant Entrepreneurs and Professionals on U.S. Competitiveness* (Stuart Anderson and Michaela Platzer, November 2006). The Refugee Council USA provides valuable information in *Material Support Backgrounder* (October 2005). The University of California at Berkley and Tulane University delivered an in-depth study of illegal immigrant workers in *Rebuilding after Katrina: A Population-Based Study of Labor and Human Rights in New Orleans* (Laurel E. Fletcher et al., June 2006). The Center for Justice, Tolerance, and Community at the University of California at Santa Cruz studied the importance of access to technology for all students in *Crossing the Divide: Immigrant Youth and Digital Disparity in California* (Robert W. Fairlie et al., September 2006). Economic impact studies on immigration were published by the Center for the Continuing Study of the California Economy, in *The Impact of Immigration on the California Economy* (September 2005), the Federation for American Immigration Reform, in *The Cost of Illegal Immigration to Texans* (Jack Martin and Ira Mehlman, April 2005), the Bell Policy Center, in *Costs of Federally Mandated Services to Undocumented Immigrants in Colorado* (Rich Jones and Robin Baker, June 2006), and the Texas Comptroller of Public Accounts, in *Undocumented Immigrants in Texas: A Financial Analysis of the Impact to the State Budget and Economy* (Carole Keeton Strayhorn, December 2006). Thomson Gale thanks all these organizations for permission to reproduce their data and graphics.

INDEX

Page references in italics refer to photographs. References with the letter t following them indicate the presence of a table. The letter f indicates a figure. If more than one table or figure appears on a particular page, the exact item number for the table or figure being referenced is provided.

A

The ABCs of IDs for Immigrants in the United States (Gigliotti and Morse), 94
Abouhalima, Mahmud, 125
"Above the Law: Executive Power after September 11 in the United States" (Parker and Fellner), 28
ACLU. *See* American Civil Liberties Union
Acquired immune deficiency syndrome (AIDS)
    aliens with, 50
    in border counties, 77
    rates of cases by border county, 79 (t5.9)
Act to Repeal the Chinese Exclusion Acts, to Establish Quotas, and for Other Purposes, 8
Active-duty military, 41
Adams, Lisa J., 78
Address, change of, 25
Addresses and names, 147–148
Adjustment of status, 35–36
Admissions
    annual refugee admissions limits, 54–55
    employment-based, 40
    immigrants admitted by class of admission, 39 (t3.12)
    quotas, 8, 10–12
    of refugees into U.S., 55–57
    regional ceilings by priority, 57t
    See also Immigration laws/policies
Adolescents. *See* Children; Youth
Adoption
    new arrivals by, 36, 38, 40

orphans adopted by U.S. citizens, 39 (t3.13)
top countries supplying orphans adopted by U.S. citizens, 40f
Adverse Effect Wage Rate (AEWR), 46 (t3.16)
Affirmative asylum claims, 59, 59f
Africa, map of, 143
African-Americans
    dropout rate decline for, 97
    first arrival in U.S., 1
    work in Georgia, 84
Age
    of foreign-born population, 34–35
    public opinion on immigration and, 110–111
    refugees arrivals by, 55, 56 (t4.2)
Agricultural Research, Extension, and Education Reform Act of 1998, 22
Aguilera, Elizabeth, 102, 103
AIDS. *See* Acquired immune deficiency syndrome
Al-Qaeda, 132
Alien Act, 2
Alien and Sedition Act of 1798, 2
Alien Enemies Act, 2
Alien registration, 11–12
Alien Registration Act of 1940 (Smith Act), 11–12
Alien registration number (A-number), 11
Alien Registration Receipt Card (Form I-151), 23–24
    See also Green card
Aliens
    excluded, by reason for exclusion, 10t
    expedited removal of, 58–59
    Illegal Immigration Reform and Immigrant Responsibility Act of 1996, 22–23
    Immigration Reform and Control Act of 1986 and, 15–16
    postwar immigration law, 12

refused entry, overview of, 49–50
refused entry, removal proceedings for, 50
refused entry for carrying communicable diseases, 50–52
removed by nationality, 51t
removed/reason for removal, 50t
    See also Illegal aliens
American Civil Liberties Union (ACLU)
    immigration law reform and, 121–123
    post-9/11 policies and, 28
    REAL ID Act of 2005 and, 26
American Hospital Association, 77
American Made: The Impact of Immigrant Entrepreneurs and Professionals in U.S. Competitiveness (Anderson and Platzer), 105–106
American Party, 2
America's Immigration Quandary (Pew Research Center for the People and the Press and Pew Hispanic Center)
    attitudes toward immigration, 111–113
    public opinion on immigration, 101–102, 110
Amnesty
    Alan K. Simpson on, 115–116
    flow of illegal aliens and, 125–126
    as IRCA mistake, 128
    public opinion on, 114
Amnesty International, 63
"Analysis: Maine Says 'No' to REAL ID Act" (Waterman), 26
Anderson, Stuart
    on immigrant businesses, 105–106
    on visas and baseball, 48–49
    on wait time for legal entry, 65
Andrew, L. Brian, 48–49
Anti-Smuggling Program, 133
Arizona
    immigrant welfare use in, 87
    legislation against illegal aliens in, 27
    Proposition 103, 103

Arizona Daily Star (newspaper), 74
Armed forces, 41
Arrests, of illegal aliens, 83
Articles of Confederation, 1
Ashcroft, et al., Detroit News, Inc., et al., v., 28
Ashcroft, John, 28
Asian immigrants
  access to computers/Internet, 103
  influx of, 8
  population shift and, 101
  public opinion on, 102, 102 (*t7.2*)
Asthma, 77–78
Asylees, 54, 57
Asylum
  affirmative/defensive asylum claims, 59
  asylees, annual flow of affirmative/ defensive, 59*f*
  children, unaccompanied, 63–64
  criteria for granting, 59–60
  definition of asylee, 54
  expedited removal, 58–59
  filing claims, 57–58
  number of asylees, 59
  parole authority and, 13
  persecution based on gender, sexual orientation, 60–61
  persons granted asylum affirmatively/ defensively, 60 (*t4.6*)
  refugee arrivals and persons granted asylum, 58*t*
  refugees, asylees, other persons granted legal permanent resident status, 60 (*t4.7*)
"Asylum Protection in the United States" (U.S. Department of Justice), 57
At the Cross Roads: US/Mexico Border Counties in Transition (US/Mexico Border Counties Coalition), 76–78
Attorney General's Report to Congress on U.S. Government Activities to Combat Trafficking in Persons Fiscal Year 2005 (U.S. Department of Justice), 61

B

Background checks, 24
Bahamas, map of, 140
Baker, Robin, 92, 93–94
Balanced Budget Act, 22
Baseball players
  in major leagues, foreign-born, 49*f*
  in major leagues, foreign-born, source country for, 50*f*
  salaries, foreign-born, 48*f*
  success, 49
  visas and, 48–49
Basic Naturalization Act of 1906, 9
Basic Pilot Program, 16
Battered brides, 20

Belluck, Pam, 40
Bernstein, Nina, 59
Bhabha, Jacqueline, 63–64
Bilingualism
  in Catholic Church, 105
  languages other than English spoken at home, 103*f*
  Spanish language, 102–103
Biometrics, 73
Birth certificates, 25
Birthplace, of illegal immigrants in U.S., 69*f*
Border. *See* U.S. border; U.S. Border Patrol
Border counties
  AIDS, hepatitis A, tuberculosis cases by border county, 79 (*t5.9*)
  diabetes rates by border county, 80*t*
  as fifty-first state, 79 (*t5.8*)
  illegal immigration, impact on counties along southwestern border, 76–78
  twenty-four U.S. counties bordering Mexico, 77*f*
Border Security: Barriers along the U.S. International Border (Nuñez-Nito and Viña), 73–74
Border Security: US-VISIT Program Faces Strategic, Operational, and Technological Challenges at Land Ports of Entry (U.S. Government Accountability Office), 70
Borjas, George J., 96
Bowman, Michael, 101
Bracero Program, 13, 76
Briggs, Vernon M., Jr., 126–128
Buckley, Cara, 79
Budget-in-Brief Fiscal Year 2007 (U.S. Department of Homeland Security), 89, 91*t*
Bureau of Immigration, 9
Bureau of Justice Assistance, 90
Burundi, refugees from, 56–57
Bury, David, 27
Bush, George W.
  Border Patrol and, 26
  Homeland Security Act of 2002, 24
  Intelligence Reform and Terrorism Prevention Act of 2004, 25
  naturalization of military personnel and, 41
Business
  immigrant-founded, venture-backed firms, by state, 107*f*
  immigrant-founded, venture-backed public companies, by industry, 106 (*t7.5*)
  immigrant-founded, venture-backed public companies, by year established, 106 (*t7.4*)
  venture capital-financed immigrant entrepreneurs, 105–107
  of women immigrants, 107

C

California
  foreign students in, 107, 109
  gangs in, 129–130
  gold rush, 8
  immigrant businesses in, 107
  immigrant welfare use in, 87
  legislation against illegal aliens, 27
  occupations of immigrants/native-born workers in, 99, 99*f*
  refugee settlement in, 61
Camarota, Steven A.
  on federal spending on immigration, 85–86
  on illegal alien population, 69
  on immigration policies, 118
Cambodia, refugees from, 13
Canada, 74–75
Card, David, 99
Caribbean immigrants, 11
Casey, Tom, 56–57
Catholic Church, 105
CBO. *See* Congressional Budget Office
CBP. *See* U.S. Customs and Border Patrol
Census Monograph I, 1922–1931 (U.S. Census Bureau), 10
Center for Immigration Statistics (CIS), 85, 114
Center for the Continuing Study of the California Economy, 99
Centers for Disease Control and Prevention, 51
Centers for Medicare and Medicaid Services (CMS), 22
Central America, map of, 140
Chavez, Linda, 84
Chicago Police Department, 30
"Chicago Police Videos Offer Insights into Various Faiths" (Kinzer), 30
Child Status Protection Act of 2002, 64
Children
  adopted, 36, 38, 40
  children in Office of Refugee Resettlement custody, top countries of origin for, 64*t*
  health insurance and, 85
  of immigrants, work of, 99
  living arrangements of, 32
  living arrangements of native/foreign-born by region of birth, 35 (*t3.7*)
  Medicaid for, 86
  orphans, top countries supplying, 40*f*
  orphans adopted by U.S. citizens, 39 (*t3.13*)
  refugees, percent of arrivals, 55
  refugees, unaccompanied children, 63–64
  top countries supplying orphans adopted by U.S. citizens, 40*f*
  U.S. citizenship of, 112

China, 38, 40

"China: Population May Peak under 'One-Child' Policy" (Sindelar), 38

"China Tightens Adoption Rules for Foreigners" (Belluck/Yardley), 40

Chinese Exclusion Act, 8, 10

Chinese immigrants
  asylum claims by, 59
  influx of, laws against, 8, 10

Chon, Gina, 74

CIS (Center for Immigration Statistics), 85, 114

Citizenship and Immigration Services Ombudsman Annual Report 2006 (U.S. Department of Homeland Security), 68

"Citizenship Documentation Requirements in Medicaid" (Kaiser Commission on Medicaid and the Uninsured), 86

Citizenship groups, immigrant, 43 (*f*3.6)

Civil rights
  detention/deportation of immigrants, 122, 123
  national origin discrimination, federal protections against, 135–138
  violations, post-9/11 policies, 28, 30

Civil Rights Act of 1964, 137

Civil Rights Division of the Department of Justice, 135–138

Civil War, U.S., 3

Clark, William, 2

Clinton, Bill, 76

CMS (Centers for Medicare and Medicaid Services), 22

Cohen, Felix S., 2

"Collateral Damage in the Immigration War"(Chavez), 84

College. *See* Education

Colombians, asylum claims by, 59

Colorado
  cost of undocumented immigrants to, 93–94
  legislation against illegal aliens, 27–28

Colorado Legislative Council, 93

Coming to America: Immigrants, Baseball, and the Contributions of Foreign-Born Players to America's Pastime (Anderson/Andrew), 48

Commission of Immigration, 7–8

Communicable diseases, alien entry and, 50–52

Communism, 12, 21

Computers
  home technology access rates for 20 largest immigrant groups, 104*t*
  influence on education/language, 103–104
  youth access to computers/Internet, 104*f*

Conditional immigrants
  marriage and, 20
  refugees as, 13

Congressional Budget Office (CBO)
  cost of REAL ID Act, 26
  on illegal alien population, 69
  information resources from, 149
  on role of immigrants in labor market, 98–99

Congressional Research Service (CRS), 149–150

Consul ID cards, 94–95

"Consulates in U.S. Hit the Road to Help Far-Flung Paisanos" (Millman), 94–95

Contact information, organizations, 147–148

Continued Presence (CP) status, 61

Conyers, John, 28

"Cost of Illegal Immigration May Be Less Than Meets the Eye" (Porter), 96–97

The Cost of Illegal Immigration to Texans (Martin and Mehlman), 92

Cost of immigration
  Department of Homeland Security budget by organization, 91*t*
  dropout rates for 16- to 24-year-olds by race/ethnicity, 98 (*t*6.13)
  earnings growth for native/immigrant men by educational level, 99*t*
  federal government programs, availability to illegal aliens, 92*t*
  federal spending for immigration, 85–87
  health insurance, immigrants without, 86*t*
  jobs, native and immigrant competition for, 96–99
  occupations of immigrants/native-born workers in California, 99*f*
  poll respondents' monthly income at first job in U.S., 96 (*f*6.4)
  poll respondents' monthly income at last job in Latin America, 96 (*f*6.3)
  REAL ID Act costs, 26
  refugee resettlement, 61, 63*t*
  remittances, 94–96
  remittances, methods for sending to Latin America, 95*f*
  remittances from U.S. to Latin America, 98 (*t*6.12)
  remittances sent to Latin America by immigrant workers, by state, 97*f*
  remittances sent to Latin America, frequency of, 96 (*f*6.5)
  Social Security, immigrant earnings and, 87–89
  Social Security benefits paid under U.S. totalization agreements, 90*t*
  State Department budget request for emergency refugee/migration expense, 92*f*
  state spending on immigration, 90, 92–94
  Texas, illegal aliens' costs, revenues, economic impact for, 94 (*t*6.11)
  Texas state health care costs for illegal aliens, 93 (*t*6.9)
  Texas state revenue from illegal aliens, 94 (*t*6.10)
  tuition costs for noncitizen college students in Texas, 93 (*t*6.8)
  USCIS fees, 68*f*
  visa costs, 65–68
  weighing costs/benefits, 85
  welfare programs, top states ranked by immigrant households using, 89*t*
  welfare programs/EITC, immigrant households using, 88*t*
  welfare programs/EITC use for native, immigrant households, 87t

"Costs" (Center for Immigration Statistics), 85

Costs of Federally Mandated Services to Undocumented Immigrants in Colorado (Jones and Baker), 92, 93–94

Court cases
  Detroit News, Inc., et al., v. Ashcroft, et al., 28
  Flores v. Reno, 63
  Henderson v. Mayor of the City of New York, 8
  Hernandez-Montiel v. INS, 61
  North Jersey Media Group, Inc.; New Jersey Law Journal v. John Ashcroft, Attorney General of the United States; Michael Creppy, Hon, 28
  Plyler v. Doe, 23, 27

CP (Continued Presence) status, 61

Creppy, Michael, 28

Crider Inc., 84

Crime
  in border counties, 76
  illegal aliens and, 83–84
  public opinion on immigrants, 102
  sanctuary laws and, 129–131

Critical Infrastructure Protection Office, 132–133

Crossing the Divide: Immigrant Youth and Digital Disparity in California (Fairlie et al.), 103–104

CRS (Congressional Research Service), 149–150

Cubans
  migrant interdictions, 73
  refugees, 13

Culture, 30

Cutler, Michael W., 125–126

D

Dade, Corey, 84

Deaths, migrant, 74

Defend Colorado Now, 93

Defensive asylum claims, 59, 59*f*

Deficit Reduction Act of 2005, 86

Department of Motor Vehicles (DMV), 26

Deportation
  of immigrants after 9/11, 122
  secret hearings, 28

Detention
    of child refugees, asylees, 63–64
    of immigrants after 9/11, 122
    mandatory detention policies, 123
Detroit News, Inc., et al., v. Ashcroft, et al., 28
DeWitt, John L., 12
DHS. *See* U.S. Department of Homeland Security
Diabetes, 77, 80*t*
Disability
    disabled refugees, support for, 63
    rights, 135
Disasters
    construction worker presence in hurricane-affected areas, 81 (*f*5.7)
    illegal aliens and, 78–82
    New Orleans, construction jobs held by documented/undocumented workers in, 82 (*f*5.8)
    New Orleans, educational status of documented/undocumented workers in, 81 (*f*5.6)
    New Orleans, health problems of documented/undocumented workers in, 83*t*
    New Orleans, overtime pay for documented/undocumented workers, 82 (*f*5.9)
    New Orleans, risk exposure/information received by workers in, 83*f*
Discrimination
    civil rights violations, 28, 30
    against immigrants after 9/11, 122
    national origin discrimination, federal protections against, 135–138
    9/11 backlash discrimination, 29*t*
Diseases
    AIDS, hepatitis A, tuberculosis cases by border county, 79 (*t*5.9)
    alien entry and, 50–52
    in border counties, 77
    diabetes rates by border county, 80*t*
Displaced Persons Act of 1948, 13, 53
Displaced persons (DPs), 12–13
"Diversity Visa Lottery 2007" (U.S. Department of State), 21
Diversity Visa Program, 20–21
Divorce, 32
DMV (Department of Motor Vehicles), 26
Doctorates, in science/engineering awarded to citizens/noncitizens, 48*t*
Documentation
    employment verification system, 115
    for Medicaid coverage, 86
    remittances and, 94–95
    See also Identification; specific documentation forms
Doe, Plyler v., 23, 27
Domestic Council Committee on Illegal Aliens, 13
Dominican Republic, immigrants from, 87

Donahue, Thomas J., 113–114
Dorell, Oren, 103
Dougherty, Mary, 58
Dougherty, Michael T., 131–133
DPs (displaced persons), 12–13
Driver's license, 25–26
Dropouts, high school
    competition with immigrants for jobs, 96–97
    dropout rates for 16- to 24-year-olds, 98 (*t*6.13)
Dubuque, Iowa, 116–117

E

E-Passport logo, 73
EADs (Employment Authorization Documents), 68
Earned Income Tax Credit (EITC)
    description of, 86
    welfare programs/EITC, immigrant households using, 88*t*
    welfare programs/EITC use for native, immigrant households, 87t
Earnings
    of documented/undocumented workers in New Orleans, 81
    earnings growth for native/immigrant men by educational level, 99*t*
    immigrant impact on native wages, 98–99
    overtime pay for documented/undocumented workers, 82 (*f*5.9)
    Social Security and, 87–89
    See also Income; Wages
Earnings Suspense File (ESF), 87
East Asia, map of, 144
Eastern European immigrants
    in early twentieth century, 9
    influx during 1880s, 5, 7
Economy
    financial impact of illegal aliens in Texas, 90, 92–93
    foreign students' contributions to, 108–109, 109 (*t*7.9)
    immigrant contributions to, 105–107
    immigrant-founded, venture-backed firms, by state, 107*f*
    immigrant-founded, venture-backed public companies, by industry, 106 (*t*7.5)
    immigrant-founded, venture-backed public companies, by year established, 106 (*t*7.4)
    impact of immigration on, 118
    international students, economic impact of, 109 (*t*7.9)
Edgar, Timothy H., 121–123
Education
    computers/Internet, influence on, 103–104

cost of noncitizen college student tuition, 92, 93 (*t*6.8)
    earnings growth for native/immigrant men by educational level, 99*t*
    in English language, 103
    foreign college students in U.S. by academic level, visa type, 110 (*t*7.10)
    of foreign students, 107–110
    foreign students, economic impact of, 109 (*t*7.9)
    foreign students, fields of study for, 108 (*t*7.7)
    foreign students, funding source for, 109 (*t*7.8)
    foreign students, states with most, 108 (*t*7.6)
    foreign students, top 20 countries of origin for, 110 (*t*7.11)
    foreign students by geographic area, 110*f*
    high school dropouts, 96–97, 98 (*t*6.13)
    literacy of immigrants, 43
    national origin discrimination, 136
    New Orleans, educational status of documented/undocumented workers in, 81 (*f*5.6)
EITC. *See* Earned Income Tax Credit
El Salvador, 94
Elderly, 63
Ellis Island, New York, 9
Emergency care, 22
"Emergency Health Services for Undocumented Aliens" (Centers for Medicare and Medicaid Services), 22
Employee
    eligibility for work, 16
    Employment Eligibility Verification form (Form I-9), 17–19
Employer
    earnings reported under false Social Security numbers, 87
    Employment Eligibility Verification form (Form I-9), 17–19
    employment verification system, 115
    sanctions, 16, 125–126
Employment
    of foreign-born population, 33–34
    impact of illegal immigration on border counties, 76
    industry of employment of native/foreign-born, 37 (*t*3.9)
    national origin discrimination, federal protections against, 136
    of native/foreign-born by region of birth, 37 (*t*3.9)
    state legislation against illegal aliens, 27–28
    of temporary workers, 45–48
    See also Work
Employment Authorization Documents (EADs), 68

Employment-based immigration
description of, 40
with Immigration Act of 1990, 20
wait time for, 65, 66 (t5.1)
Employment Eligibility Verification form (Form I-9)
example of, 17–19
requirement of, 16
Employment verification system, 115
Engineering, doctorate degrees awarded to citizens/noncitizens, 48t
English language, 42–43
Enhanced Border Security and Visa Entry Reform Act of 2002, 24, 73
Enrollment, foreign student, 107–108
Entry-exit system, 24
Equal Protection Clause, 137
ESF (Earnings Suspense File), 87
Ester, Karma, 20–21
Europe, map of, 142
Exclusion
IMMACT changes to, 21
immigrants denied entry, 10
quota laws, 10–11
Executive Order 9066, 12
Expedited removal
of asylees, 58–59
description of, 50

F

"Fact Sheet Regarding Post-9/11 Backlash Discrimination" (U.S. Department of Justice), 29t, 30
Fair Housing Act, 136
Fair Share Refugee Act of 1960, 54
Fairlie, Robert W., 103–104
Families
family reunification cases, 56
family-sponsored immigrants, wait time for, 66 (t5.2)
life of foreign-born population, 32
remittances, value to families back home, 95
size, native/foreign-born by region of birth, 34 (t3.5)
undocumented families of 9/11 victims, 78–79
Farm Security and Rural Investment Act of 2002, 22
Federal Bureau of Investigation (FBI), 123
Federal government
control over immigration, 9
Department of Homeland Security budget by organization, 91t
information resources from, 149–150
programs, availability to illegal aliens, 92t
programs, national origin discrimination and, 137
refugee resettlement costs, 61, 63t
role in immigration, development of, 7–8

spending for immigration, 85–87
State Department budget request for emergency refugee/migration expense, 92f
See also Immigration laws/policies
Federal Protections against National Origin Discrimination (U.S. Department of Justice), 135–138
Federal Trade Commission, 16
Fees
USCIS fees, 68f
for visa services, 65–68
Feinstein, Dianne, 64
Fellner, Jamie, 28
Felons, 1
Fence, at southwest border, 73–74
Fergus, Debra, 64
Fertility, of native/foreign-born women, 35 (t3.6)
Filipino immigrants, 11
Final Report: Japanese Evacuation from the West Coast 1942 (DeWitt), 12
Finley, Bruce, 16
Fix, Michael E., 42–43
Fletcher, Laurel E., 80–82
Flores v. Reno, 63
Florida, refugee settlement in, 61
Food stamps, 22
Ford, Gerald, 12, 13
Foreign governments, 61
Foreign Operations, Export Financing, and Related Programs Appropriations Act of 1990, 54
Foreign students
college students in U.S. by academic level, visa type, 110 (t7.10)
economic impact of, 109 (t7.9)
education in U.S., 107–110
fields of study for, 108 (t7.7)
foreign-student monitoring system, 24
foreign students by geographic area, 110f
funding source for, 109 (t7.8)
states with most, 108 (t7.6)
top 20 countries of origin for, 110 (t7.11)
U.S. businesses of, 106
visa restrictions, 25
Foreign visitors, nonimmigrant overstays, 70, 72
Foreign-born population
by age/region of birth, persons living in poverty, 38t
ages of, 34–35
by birth state/region, 33t
children by region of birth, living arrangements, 35 (t3.7)
employment, 33–34
family life of, 32
immigration methods, 35
location choices in U.S., 31–32
in New York City, 105

population by age/sex, 38f
population growth, top ten states, 34 (t3.3)
population projections, 32 (t3.1)
by region of birth, 31, 32 (f3.1)
by region of birth, family size, 34 (t3.5)
by region of birth, household income, 37 (t3.10)
by region of birth, industry of employment, 37 (t3.9)
by region of birth, marital status, 34 (t3.4)
by region of birth, occupation, 36t
women, fertility, 35 (t3.6)
See also Illegal aliens; Immigrants; Refugees
The Foreign-Born Population in the United States 2003 (Larsen), 41
Foreign-student monitoring system, 24
Form AR-3, 23
Form I-9 (Employment Eligibility Verification form)
example of, 17–19
requirement of, 16
Form I-30, 67
Form I-94
example of, 71f
tracking of nonimmigrant visitors, 70
Form I-151 (Alien Registration Receipt Card), 23–24
See also Green card
Form I-485, 67
Form I-600, 67
Form N-400, 67
Foster care, for child refugees, 64
French, Angela, 26
"From Colonial Times, Immigrants Have Changed, Invigorated the United States" (Bowman), 101
Funding, international students, 108, 109 (t7.8)

G

Gangs, 129–130
GAO. *See* U.S. Government Accountability Office
Geary Act of 1892, 8
Gender
asylum for persecution based on, 60–61
refugees arrivals by, 55, 56 (t4.2)
Gentleman's Agreement of 1907, 8, 10
Georgia
immigrant labor in, 84
immigration legislation, 28
German immigration, 2
Gibson, Campbell, 1
Gigliotti, Katherine, 94
Gilbert, Daniel, 59

Global Economic Prospects: Economic Implications of Remittances and Migration (World Bank), 95
Gold rush, California, 8
Gomez, Alan, 73
Gonzalez, Emilio T., 41
Goodman, Allen E., 107–108
Government. *See* Federal government; States
Great Depression, 11
Greater Antilles, map of, 140
Green card
  EADs and, 68
  history of, 23–24
  wait time for, 65
Greenwood, Michael J., 20
Griswold, Dan, 120
Group identity, persecution based on, 54
Group referrals category, 55–56
Guatemalan immigrants, use of welfare, 87
Guestworker programs
  Alan K. Simpson on, 115, 116
  Phyllis Schlafly on, 128, 129
  public opinion on, 113
Guidelines on International Protection: Gender-Related Persecution within the Context of Article 1A(2) of the 1951 Convention and/or Its 1967 Protocol Relating to the Status of Refugees (United Nations High Commissioner for Refugees), 60
Guzman, Lydia, 103

H

H1B program
  overview of, 46–47
  visas for scientists/engineers, 47
  visas issued by birth region, 47*f*
H1C program, 47–48
H2 program, 46
H2A program, 46, 46 (*t*3.17)
Haitians, asylum claims by, 59
Health and Health Care of Japanese-American Elders (Tanabe), 8
Health care
  Colorado state health care costs for illegal aliens, 94
  Texas state health care costs for illegal aliens, 92–93, 93 (*t*6.9)
Health insurance
  immigrant use of Medicaid, 86
  immigrants without, 85, 86*t*
Health issues
  AIDS, hepatitis A, tuberculosis cases by border county, 79 (*t*5.9)
  in border counties, 76–78
  diabetes rates by border county, 80*t*
  of documented/undocumented workers in New Orleans, 82, 83*t*

Henderson v. Mayor of the City of New York, 8
Hendricks, Tyche, 27
Hepatitis A, 77, 79 (*t*5.9)
Hernandez-Montiel v. INS, 61
High school dropouts
  competition with immigrants for jobs, 96–97
  dropout rates for 16- to 24-year-olds, 98 (*t*6.13)
"Hispanic Attitudes toward Learning English" (Pew Hispanic Center), 103
Hispanic immigrants
  Latin American impact on U.S., 102–105
  population shift and, 101
  public opinion on, 101–102
  See also Mexican immigrants
Historical Census Statistics on Population Totals by Race, 1790 to 1990, and by Hispanic Origin, 1790 to 1990, for the United States, Regions, Divisions, and States (Gibson and Jung), 1
Hollmann, Fred, 101
Homeland Security Act of 2002, 24
Homeland Security: Justice Department's Project to Interview Aliens after September 11, 2001 (U.S. Government Accountability Office), 28
Homestead Law, 2
Horn, Wade F., 61
House Judiciary Committee, 21
House Report 108-747—Security and Fairness Enhancement for America Act of 2003 (House Judiciary Committee), 21
Household income
  of foreign-born population, 34
  of native/foreign-born by region of birth, 37 (*t*3.10)
Housing, discrimination, 136
Hungarian refugees, 13, 53
Hungarian revolution, 53
Hurricane Katrina
  construction worker presence in hurricane-affected areas, 81 (*f*5.7)
  New Orleans, construction jobs held by documented/undocumented workers in, 82 (*f*5.8)
  New Orleans, educational status of documented/undocumented workers in, 81 (*f*5.6)
  New Orleans, health problems of documented/undocumented workers in, 83*t*
  New Orleans, overtime pay for documented/undocumented workers, 82 (*f*5.9)
  undocumented workers in New Orleans, 79–82
  work by illegal aliens, 84
Hutchinson, Asa, 69

I

IADB (Inter-American Development Bank), 95–96
ICE. *See* U.S. Immigration and Customs Enforcement
ID card
  national standards for, 25
  remittances and, 94–95
Identification
  for Medicaid coverage, 86
  national standards for, 25–26
  remittances and, 94–95
  for U.S-Canada border crossing, 74–75
Identity theft, 16
IIRIRA. *See* Illegal Immigration Reform and Immigrant Responsibility Act of 1996
Illegal aliens
  AIDS, hepatitis A, tuberculosis cases by border county, 79 (*t*5.9)
  barriers to legal immigration, 65–68
  birthplace of illegal immigrants in U.S., 69*f*
  borders on water, 73
  California's legislation against, 27
  construction worker presence in hurricane-affected areas, 81 (*f*5.7)
  cost of incarceration of, 90
  crime and, 83–84
  definition of, 68–69
  diabetes rates by border county, 80*t*
  disasters and, 78–82
  entry modes for unauthorized migrant population, 70*t*
  federal government programs, availability to, 92*t*
  Form I-94, 71*f*
  Illegal Immigration Reform and Immigrant Responsibility Act of 1996, 22–23
  immigrant labor, 84
  Immigration Reform and Control Act of 1986 and, 15–16
  impact of illegal immigration on southwestern border, 76–78
  income rankings, per capita, by state, 78*t*
  from Mexico, 75–76
  Mexico, twenty-four U.S. counties bordering, 77*f*, 79 (*t*5.8)
  Mexico's relationship with U.S., 75–76
  monitoring entry/exit, 69–70, 72–73
  New Orleans, construction jobs held by documented/undocumented workers in, 82 (*f*5.8)
  New Orleans, educational status of documented/undocumented workers in, 81 (*f*5.6)
  New Orleans, health problems of documented/undocumented workers in, 83*t*

New Orleans, overtime pay for documented/undocumented workers, 82 (f5.9)

number of, 69

post-9/11 policies, repercussions of, 28, 30

public opinion on, 111, 113, 114

public opinion on legal status of immigrants, 113 (t7.15)

public opinion on reduction of illegal Mexican immigration, 114 (t7.18)

quota laws and, 11

sanctuary laws, 129–131

state legislation against, 27–28

in Texas, financial impact of, 90, 92–93

U.S. Border Patrol, 73–75

US-VISIT appropriations, 72t

US-VISIT program, entering persons processed at land, air, sea ports by use of US-VISIT program, 72f

USCIS, fees collected by, 68f

visa classifications, U.S. nonimmigrant, 67 (t5.4)

wait time for employment-based immigrants, 66 (t5.1)

wait time for family-sponsored immigrants, 66 (t5.2)

wait time for visa interviews at key consular posts, 67 (t5.3)

See also Immigration policies, statements about

"Illegal Immigrants Are Bolstering Social Security with Billions" (Porter), 87

Illegal immigration

Illegal Immigration Reform and Immigrant Responsibility Act of 1996, 22–23

Immigration Reform and Control Act of 1986 and, 15–16

impact on counties along southwestern border, 76–78

Secure Fence Act of 2006, 26–27

See also Immigration policies, statements about

Illegal Immigration Reform and Immigrant Responsibility Act of 1996 (IIRIRA)

expedited removal under, 58

monitoring entry/exit of noncitizens, 70

options for inadmissible aliens, 50

provisions of, 22–23

Illiterate immigrants, 10

An Immigrant Nation: United States Regulation of Immigration, 1798–1991 (Immigration and Naturalization Service), 13

"Immigrant Policy" (National Conference of State Legislatures), 27

Immigrants

attitudes toward, 1–2

citizenship groups, characteristics, 43 (f3.6)

class of admission, 39 (t3.12)

defined, 31

discrimination against after 9/11, 122

early, 1

economy, immigrant contributions to, 105–107

food programs for legal immigrants, state-funded, 22t

health insurance, immigrants without, 86t

immigrant-founded, venture-backed firms, by state, 107f

immigrant-founded, venture-backed public companies, 106t

impact on U.S., 101

international students, education of, 107–110

jobs, native and immigrant competition for, 96–99

Latin American impact, 102–105

in New York City, 105

orphans adopted by U.S. citizens, 39 (t3.13)

public assistance and, 85–87

public opinion about immigrants' impact on government services, taxes, 113 (t7.17)

public opinion about Latin and Asian immigrants, 102 (t7.2)

public opinion of immigrants as burden/strength, 112f

public opinion on, 111 (t7.13)

public opinion on immigrants and jobs, 113 (t7.16)

public opinion on immigrants as local/national problem, 112t

public opinion on immigration, 101–102, 110–114

public opinion on immigration attitudes/experience with foreign-born people, 102 (t7.1)

public opinion on legal status of immigrants, 113 (t7.15)

public opinion on reduction of illegal immigration from Mexico, 114 (t7.18)

welfare cuts for legal immigrants, 21–22

See also Cost of immigration; Foreign-born population; Illegal aliens; Refugees

Immigrants at Mid-decade: A Snapshot of America's Foreign-Born Population in 2005 (Camarota), 69, 85

Immigration

barriers to legal immigration, 65–68

forms/fees, 67–68

organizations, contact information, 147–148

USCIS fees, 68f

See also Cost of immigration

Immigration Act of 1882, 8

Immigration Act of 1891, 9

Immigration Act of 1904, 8

Immigration Act of 1907, 9

Immigration Act of 1917, 8, 10

Immigration Act of 1965, 126

Immigration Act of 1990

asylum and, 59

provisions of, 20–21

Immigration and National Welfare (Cohen), 2

Immigration and Nationality Act Amendments of 1965

changes to, 20

provisions of, 12

Immigration and Nationality Act Amendments of 1976, 12

Immigration and Nationality Act Amendments of 1978, 12

Immigration and Nationality Act of 1952

parole authority with, 13, 53

provisions of, 12

Immigration and Naturalization Service (INS)

changes at, 11

child refugees and, 63

establishment of, 9

green card and, 23

monitoring entry/exit of noncitizens, 70

on parole authority, 13

as part of Department of Homeland Security, 69

reorganization of, 24

See also U.S. Citizenship and Immigration Service

"Immigration Appeals Pile Up" (Gilbert), 59

"Immigration: Diversity Visa Lottery" (Wasem and Ester), 20–21

Immigration Enforcement Actions: 2005 (Dougherty, Wilson, and Wu), 58

Immigration: From the Founding of Virginia to the Closing of Ellis Island (Wepman), 1

Immigration, history of

aliens excluded, by reason for exclusion, 10t

attitudes toward immigrants, 1–2

early immigrants, 1

first century of immigration, 2–5, 7–9

immigration as political issue, 13

immigration at turn of twentieth century, 9–10

immigration by region, selected country of last residence, 3t–7t

postwar immigration law, 12

refugees after World War II, 12–13

restrictions of immigration, 10–11

two-hemisphere system, 12

World War II, 11–12

Immigration, impact on United States

economy, immigrant contributions to, 105–107

foreign college students in U.S. by academic level, visa type, 110 (t7.10)

foreign students, economic impact of, 109 (t7.9)

foreign students, education of, 107–110

foreign students, fields of study for, 108 (t7.7)

foreign students, funding source for, 109 (t7.8)

foreign students, states with most, 108 (t7.6)

foreign students, top 20 countries of origin for, 110 (t7.11)

Latin American impact, 102–105

New York City, 105

population shift, 101

public opinion about immigrants' impact on local government services, taxes, 113 (t7.17)

public opinion about immigration concerns, 111 (t7.12)

public opinion about Latin and Asian immigrants, 102 (t7.2)

public opinion on biggest immigration issues, 114 (t7.19)

public opinion on immigrants, 111 (t7.13)

public opinion on immigrants and jobs, 113 (t7.16)

public opinion on immigration, 101–102, 110–114

public opinion on immigration attitudes/ experience with foreign-born people, 102 (t7.1)

public opinion on legal status of immigrants, 113 (t7.15)

public opinion on reduction of illegal immigration from Mexico, 114 (t7.18)

Immigration laws/policies

food programs for legal immigrants, state-funded, 22t

Form I-9, 17–19

green card, 23–24

Homeland Security Act of 2002, 24

Illegal Immigration Reform and Immigrant Responsibility Act of 1996, 22–23

Immigration Act of 1990, 20–21

Immigration Marriage Fraud Amendments of 1986, 16, 20

Immigration Reform and Control Act of 1986, 15–16, 115–116

Intelligence Reform and Terrorism Prevention Act of 2004, 25

post-9/11 backlash discrimination, 29t

post-9/11 changes, 24–25

post-9/11 policies, repercussions of, 28, 30

Real ID Act of 2005, 25–26

Secure Fence Act of 2006, 26–27

state legislation, 27–28, 27f

USA Patriot Act of 2001, 24

Welfare Reform Law of 1996, 21–22

See also Immigration, history of; Legislation and international treaties

Immigration Marriage Fraud Amendments of 1986, 16, 20

Immigration methods

adjustment of status, 35–36

description of, 35

employment-based admissions, 40

new arrivals, 35

new arrivals by adoption, 36, 38, 40

Immigration: Mexican (U.S. Library of Congress), 104–105

Immigration policies, statements about

Alan K. Simpson, 115–116

Ann E. Michalski, 116–117

Frank Sharry, 119–121

Heather MacDonald, 129–131

Laura R. Murphy and Timothy H. Edgar, 121–123

Margaret D. Stock, 118–119

Michael T. Dougherty, 131–133

Michael W. Cutler, 125–126

Phyllis Schlafly, 128–129

Ricardo Parra, 117–118

Steven A. Camarota, 118

Vernon M. Briggs Jr., 126–128

The Immigration Problem in the United States (National Industrial Conference Board), 9

Immigration Reform and Control Act of 1986 (IRCA)

amnesty program under, 125–126

lessons learned from, 115–116

provisions of, 15–16

"Immigration: Shaping and Reshaping America" (Martin and Midgley), 15

Immigration statistics

aliens refused entry, 49–52

aliens removed by nationality, 51t

aliens removed/reason for removal, 50t

baseball players in major leagues, foreign-born, 49f

baseball players/salaries, foreign-born, 48f

class of admission, immigrants admitted by, 39 (t3.12)

foreign-born by birth region, 32 (f3.1)

foreign-born by birth state/region, 33t

foreign-born population, 31–35

foreign-born population growth, top ten states, 34 (t3.3)

H1B visas issued by birth region, 47f

H2A workers, top ten states by, 46 (t3.17)

immigrant, definition of, 31

immigrant citizenship groups, characteristics of, 43 (f3.6)

immigrant orphans adopted by U.S. citizens by gender/age/region of birth, 39 (t3.13)

immigrants admitted by class of admission, 39 (t3.12)

major league foreign-born players, source countries for, 50f

methods for immigration, 35–40

native/foreign-born by age/region of birth, persons living in poverty, 38t

native/foreign-born by region of birth, family size of, 34 (t3.5)

native/foreign-born by region of birth, household income for, 37 (t3.10)

native/foreign-born by region of birth, industry of employment for, 37 (t3.9)

native/foreign-born by region of birth, marital status of, 34 (t3.4)

native/foreign-born by region of birth, occupation for, 36t

native/foreign-born children by region of birth, living arrangements of, 35 (t3.7)

native/foreign-born population by age/ sex, 38f

native/foreign-born women, fertility in, 35 (t3.6)

naturalization, 40–43

naturalized persons by decade/region of birth, 42f

naturalized persons by region of birth, 43 (f3.5)

nonimmigrant visas issued by classification, 44t–45t

orphans adopted by U.S. citizens, 39 (t3.13)

orphans adopted by U.S. citizens, top countries supplying, 40f

permanent resident status, persons obtaining by admission class/ occupation, 41t

population projections, native/foreign-born, 32 (t3.1)

science/engineering doctorate degrees awarded to citizens/noncitizens, 48t

tuberculosis cases by birth origin, 51f

tuberculosis cases by birth origin, drug resistant, 52f

visitors, 43–49

wage rates, adverse effect, 46 (t3.16)

The Impact of Immigration on the California Economy (Center for the Continuing Study of the California Economy), 99

The Impact of the Immigration Act of 1990 on U.S. Immigration (Greenwood and Ziel), 20

"In New York Immigration Court, Asylum Roulette" (Bernstein), 59

"In the News: Speaking English in the United States" (Kent and Lalasz), 103

Incarceration

civil rights of institutionalized persons, 137

of criminal aliens, cost to states, 90

Income

in border counties, 76

earnings growth for native/immigrant men by educational level, 99t

foreign-born household income, 34

immigrants' monthly income at first job in U.S., 96 (f6.4)

income rankings, per capita, by state, 78t

of native/foreign-born by region of birth, 37 (*t3.10*)

of naturalization candidates, 43

poll respondents' monthly income at first job in U.S., 96 (*f6.4*)

poll respondents' monthly income at last job in Latin America, 96 (*f6.3*)

Indentured servants, 1

India

  foreign students from, 107–108

  immigrant entrepreneurs from, 106

Individual referrals category, 55

Indochinese Refugee Act of 1977, 54

Industrial Revolution, 4–5

"Information on Certain Illegal Aliens Arrested in the United States" (U.S. Government Accountability Office), 83–84

Information resources, 149–150

Information-sharing, 122, 123

INS. *See* Immigration and Naturalization Service

INS, Hernandez-Montiel v., 61

Institute of International Education, 107–108, 109

Institutionalized persons, civil rights of, 137

Intelligence Reform and Terrorism Prevention Act of 2004, 25, 74–75

Inter-American Development Bank (IADB), 95–96

Internal Security Act of 1950

  green card and, 23

  provisions of, 12

International students. *See* Foreign students

Internet

  home technology access rates for 20 largest immigrant groups, 104*t*

  influence on education/language, 103–104

  youth access to computers/Internet, native and immigrant, 104*f*

Interpreters, Iraqi, 74

Interviews, voluntary, 28

Iowa, 116–117

Iraqis

  entry through U.S.-Mexican border, 74

  in U.S., 132

IRCA. *See* Immigration Reform and Control Act of 1986

IRCA Legalization Effects: Lawful Permanent Residence and Naturalization through 2001 (Rytina), 15

Irish immigration, 2

Irish Potato Famine, 2

"Is the New Immigration Really So Bad?" (Card), 99

Israel, immigrant entrepreneurs from, 106

J

Japan, 8, 10

Japanese immigrants, 8, 12

Japanese internment, 12

Jefferson, Thomas, 2

Jews, 9

Jobs

  illegal immigration's impact on, 129

  native and immigrant competition for jobs, 96–99

  public opinion on immigrants taking jobs from Americans, 111–112

  See also Employment; Work

John Ashcroft, Attorney General of the United States; Michael Creppy, Hon, North Jersey Media Group, Inc.; New Jersey Law Journal v., 28

Jolie, Angelina, 64

Jones, Rich, 92, 93–94

Jung, Kay, 1

Justich, Robert, 69

K

Kaiser Commission on Medicaid and the Uninsured, 86

Kasinga, Fauziya, 60–61

Katz, Lawrence F., 96

Kennedy, Edward, 20

Kennedy, John F., 12

Kent, Mary, 103

"Kin Struggle for Proof of Foreign 9/11 Victims" (Adams), 78

Kinzer, Stephen, 30

Know Nothing movement, 2

Koch, Wendy, 20

Kraut, Alan, 101

Ku Klux Klan, 5

L

Labor

  Bracero Program, 76

  illegal aliens and, 84

  immigrant labor, economic gain, 117

  Immigration Reform and Control Act of 1986 and, 15, 16

  See also Employment; Work

Labor Appropriation Act, 11

Lalasz, Robert, 103

Languages

  other than English spoken at home, 103*f*

  Spanish language, influence on U.S., 102–105

  voting and, 137–138

Larsen, Luke J., 41

Latin America

  immigration's impact on U.S., 102–105

  poll respondents' monthly income at last job in Latin America, 96 (*f6.3*)

  remittances, methods for sending to, 95*f*

  remittances sent to, 94–96, 98 (*t6.12*)

  remittances sent to, by state, 97*f*

  remittances sent to, frequency of, 96 (*f6.5*)

Latin American immigrants, 101–102, 102 (*t7.2*)

Lautenberg Amendment, 54

Law enforcement, 30

  See also Police

Lawful permanent resident (LPR)

  for asylees, 59

  with green card, 23

  Immigration Marriage Fraud Amendments of 1986, 16, 20

  refugees, asylees, other persons granted legal permanent resident status, 60 (*t4.7*)

Laws. *See* Immigration laws/policies; Legislation and international treaties

Legal Immigrants: Waiting Forever (Anderson and Miller), 65

Legal Immigration Family Equity (LIFE) Act of 2002, 35

Legalization, of undocumented population, 15–16

Legislation and international treaties

  Act to Repeal the Chinese Exclusion Acts, to Establish Quotas, and for Other Purposes, 8

  Agricultural Research, Extension, and Education Reform Act of 1998, 22

  Alien Act, 2

  Alien and Sedition Act of 1798, 2

  Alien Enemies Act, 2

  Articles of Confederation, 1

  Balanced Budget Act, 22

  Basic Naturalization Act of 1906, 9

  Child Status Protection Act of 2002, 64

  Chinese Exclusion Act, 8

  Civil Rights Act of 1964, 137

  Deficit Reduction Act of 2005, 86

  Displaced Persons Act of 1948, 13, 53

  Enhanced Border Security and Visa Entry Reform Act of 2002, 24, 73

  Fair Housing Act, 136

  Fair Share Refugee Act of 1960, 54

  Farm Security and Rural Investment Act of 2002, 22

  Geary Act of 1892, 8

  Gentleman's Agreement of 1907, 8, 10

  Homeland Security Act of 2002, 24

  Homestead Law, 2

  Illegal Immigration Reform and Immigrant Responsibility Act of 1996, 22–23, 58

  Immigration Act of 1882, 8

  Immigration Act of 1891, 9

  Immigration Act of 1904, 8

  Immigration Act of 1907, 9

  Immigration Act of 1917, 8, 10

  Immigration Act of 1965, 126

  Immigration Act of 1990, 20–21

  Immigration and Nationality Act Amendments of 1965, 12

Immigration and Nationality Act
 Amendments of 1976, 12
Immigration and Nationality Act
 Amendments of 1978, 12
Immigration and Nationality Act of
 1952, 12, 13
Immigration Marriage Fraud
 Amendments of 1986, 16, 20
Immigration Reform and Control Act of
 1986, 15–16, 115–116, 125–126
Indochinese Refugee Act of 1977, 54
Intelligence Reform and Terrorism
 Prevention Act of 2004, 25, 74
Internal Security Act of 1950, 12, 23
Labor Appropriation Act, 11
Lautenberg Amendment, 54
Legal Immigration Family Equity
 (LIFE) Act of 2002, 35
Medicare Prescription Drug,
 Improvement, and Modernization Act
 of 2003, 22
National Origins Act of 1924, 8, 11
Naturalization Act, 2
Nicaraguan Adjustment and Central
 American Relief Act, 21
Noncitizen Benefit Clarification and
 Other Technical Amendments Act of
 1998, 22
Omnibus Crime Control and Safe Streets
 Act of 1968, 137
Page Law, 7–8
Proposition 187, 27
Proposition 200, 27
Quota Law of 1921, 11
Real ID Act of 2005, 25–26, 59
Refugee Act of 1980, 13, 53, 54, 59–60
Refugee Relief Act of 1953, 13, 54
Secure Fence Act of 2006, 26–27, 74
Sedition Act, 2
state immigration legislation, 27–28
Torture Victims Relief Act of 1998, 61
Trafficking Victims Protection Act of
 2000, 61
Trafficking Victims Protection
 Reauthorization Act of 2003, 61
Trafficking Victims Protection
 Reauthorization Act of 2006, 61
Unaccompanied Alien Child Protection
 Act of 2005, 64
U.S. Constitution, 1–2
USA Patriot Act of 2001, 24
Victims of Trafficking and Violence
 Prevention Act of 2000, 20
Violence against Women Act of 1994,
 20
Violent Crime Control and Law
 Enforcement Act of 1994, 61
Voting Rights Act, 138
Welfare Reform Law of 1996, 21–22
Lending, 136–137
Lewis, Meriwether, 2

Lincoln, Abraham, 2
Literacy test, 10
Locale, choices of foreign-born population,
 31–32
Lockhart, James B., III, 87
Los Angeles Police Department, 129–130
"Lost in Translation: Iraq's Injured
 'Terps'" (Millman and Chon), 74
Lottery, Diversity Visa Program, 20–21
Louisiana. See New Orleans, Louisiana
Louisiana Health and Population Survey:
 Expanded Preliminary Results: Orleans
 Parish (Louisiana Department of Health
 and Hospitals), 80
Louisiana Purchase, 2
LPR. See Lawful permanent resident

M

MacDonald, Heather, 129–131
Maps
 Africa, 143
 East and South Asia, 144
 Europe, 142
 Middle East, 144
 North and Central America, Bahamas,
  and Greater Antilles, 140
 Oceania, 146
 South America, 141
 Southeast Asia, 145
Mara Salvatrucha, 129, 130–131
Marital status
 of foreign-born residents, 32
 of native/foreign-born by region of birth,
  34 (t3.4)
Marketing, in Spanish language, 102, 103
"Marketing en Español" (Aguilera), 102
Marriage, 16, 20
Martin, Jack, 92
Martin, Philip, 15
Martinez, Francisco, 130
Massey, Douglas, 120
Material Support Backgrounder (Refugee
 Council USA), 55
Mayor of the City of New York, Henderson
 v., 8
McGhee, Tom, 16
Measuring Protection by Numbers, 2005
 (United Nations High Commissioner for
 Refugees), 53
Measuring the Fallout: The Cost of IRCA
 Amnesty after 10 Years (Simcox), 16
Medicaid
 disability rights and, 135
 immigrant use of, 86, 87
 immigrants and, 85
 Texas state health care costs for illegal
  aliens, 92–93
 Welfare Reform Law of 1996 and, 21–22
Medicare Prescription Drug, Improvement,
 and Modernization Act of 2003, 22

Mehlman, Ira, 92
Mexican immigrants
 criminal violations of civil rights of, 135
 divorce among, 32
 illegal, 13
 influence on U.S., 104–105
 public opinion on reduction of illegal
  immigration from Mexico, 114 (t7.18)
 uninsured, 85
 U.S.-Mexico relationship, 75–76
 welfare use by, 87
Mexican Migration to the United States:
 1882–1992: A Long Twentieth Century
 of Coyotaje (Spener), 75
Mexico
 AIDS, hepatitis A, tuberculosis cases by
  border county, 79 (t5.9)
 relationship with U.S., 75–76
 southwest border, Border Patrol and,
  73–74
 totalization agreement, 88–89
 U.S. counties bordering, 77f, 79 (t5.8)
Miami, Florida, 130
Michalski, Ann E., 116–117
Middle East, map of, 144
Midgley, Elizabeth, 15
Military, active-duty, 41
Miller, David, 65
Millman, Joel, 74, 94–95
Minnesota, refugee settlement in, 61
"Modes of Entry for the Unauthorized
 Migrant Population" (Pew Hispanic
 Center), 69
Monitoring, U.S. entry/exit, 69–70, 72–73
Morse, Ann, 94
Moussaoui, Zacarias, 131
Murphy, Laura R., 121–123
Mutual Assistance Associations, 62–63

N

NAFTA (North American Free Trade
 Agreement), 76, 84
Names and addresses, 147–148
National Association of Counties, 77
National Association of Motor Vehicle
 Administrators, 26
National Center for Refugee and Immigrant
 Children, 64
National Center for Youth Law, 63
National Commission on Terrorist Attacks
 upon the United States (9/11
 Commission), 25
National Conference of State Legislatures,
 26, 27
National Governors Association, 26
National Industrial Conference Board
 (NICB), 9
National origin discrimination, federal
 protections against, 135–138
National origins, 41–42
National Origins Act of 1924, 8, 11

National origins quota system, 11, 12
National Research Council, 85
National Security Entry-Exit Registration System (NSEERS), 73, 132
Native-born population
    by age/region of birth, persons living in poverty, 38*t*
    by age/sex, 38*f*
    children by region of birth, living arrangements, 35 (*t3.7*)
    earnings growth for native/immigrant men by educational level, 99*t*
    immigrant impact on native wages, 98–99
    occupations of immigrants/native-born workers in California, 99*f*
    population projections, 32 (*t3.1*)
    by region of birth, family size, 34 (*t3.5*)
    by region of birth, household income, 37 (*t3.10*)
    by region of birth, industry of employment, 37 (*t3.9*)
    by region of birth, marital status, 34 (*t3.4*)
    by region of birth, occupation, 36*t*
    women, fertility, 35 (*t3.6*)
Nativism, 2, 9–10
Naturalization
    of active-duty military, 41
    Alien and Sedition Act of 1798 and, 2
    description of, 40
    general requirements, 40–41
    rates, 41
    special provisions, 41
    trends in, 42–43
Naturalization Act, 2
Naturalized persons
    by decade/region of birth, 42*f*
    national origins of, 41–42
    by region of birth, 43 (*f3.5*)
New arrivals
    by adoption, 36, 38, 40
    description of, 35
    orphans adopted by U.S. citizens, 39 (*t3.13*)
    top countries supplying orphans adopted by U.S. citizens, 40*f*
"New Enrollment of Foreign Students in the U.S. Climbs in 2005/06" (Goodman), 107–108
New Orleans, Louisiana
    construction jobs held by documented/undocumented workers in, 82 (*f5.8*)
    construction worker presence in hurricane-affected areas, 81 (*f5.7*)
    educational status of documented/undocumented workers in, 81 (*f5.6*)
    health problems of documented/undocumented workers in, 83*t*
    labor of illegal aliens, 84
    overtime pay for documented/undocumented workers, 82 (*f5.9*)

    risk exposure/information received by workers in, 83*f*
    undocumented workers in, 79–82
"New US Immigrants Creating Different Assimilation Patterns" (Schoetzau), 103
New York
    foreign students in, 107, 109
    immigrant welfare use in, 87
New York City Department of City Planning, 105
New York City, New York, 105
The Newest New Yorkers, 2000: Immigrant New York in the New Millennium (New York City Department of City Planning), 105
Ng, Betty, 69
Nicaraguan Adjustment and Central American Relief Act, 21
NICB (National Industrial Conference Board), 9
9/11 Commission (National Commission on Terrorist Attacks upon the United States), 25
Noncitizen Benefit Clarification and Other Technical Amendments Act of 1998, 22
Nongovernmental organizations (NGOs), 61, 62
Nonimmigrant overstays, 70, 72
Nonimmigrants
    baseball players, success of, 49
    overview of, 43–45
    temporary workers, 45–48
    visas and baseball, 48–49
    visas issued by classification, 44*t*–45*t*
North America, map of, 140
North American Free Trade Agreement (NAFTA), 76, 84
North Jersey Media Group, Inc.; New Jersey Law Journal v. John Ashcroft, Attorney General of the United States; Michael Creppy, Hon, 28
Northern border, 74–75
NSEERS (National Security Entry-Exit Registration System), 73, 132
"Nuevo Catholics" (Rieff), 105
Nuñez-Nito, Blas, 73–74
Nursing Relief for Disadvantaged Areas Act of 1999, 47
Nuschler, Dawn, 87–88

O

Occupations
    of foreign-born by region of birth, 36*t*
    of immigrants/native-born workers in California, 99*f*
    of native-born/foreign-born population, 33–34
    See also Employment; Work
Oceania, map of, 146
O'Connell, David, 105
Office of Immigration Statistics, 2

Office of Refugee Resettlement (ORR)
    benefits for refugees, 63
    function of, 61
    unaccompanied child refugees and, 63–64, 64*t*
Omnibus Crime Control and Safe Streets Act of 1968, 137
Open Doors 2006 (Institute of International Education), 107–108, 109
Operation Liberty Shield, 132
Operation Southern Focus, 133
Operation Tarmac, 132–133
Organizations, contact information, 147–148
Orphans
    adopted by U.S. citizens, top countries supplying, 40*f*
    new arrivals by adoption, 36, 38, 40
    orphans adopted by U.S. citizens, 39 (*t3.13*)
ORR. *See* Office of Refugee Resettlement
Orum, Anthony, 103
Outsourcing, 97
Overstays, nonimmigrant, 70, 72
Overtime pay, 82 (*f5.9*)
"Overview of INS History" (Smith), 9

P

P1 visas, 49
Page Law, 7–8
Parker, Allison, 28
Parole authority, 13, 53
Parra, Ricardo, 117–118
Passel, Jeffrey S.
    on illegal alien population, 69, 94, 111
    on naturalization, 42–43
Passports
    first requirement of, 10
    new requirements for, 73
    Western Hemisphere Travel Initiative, 74–75
Pearce, Susan C., 107
Pérez, Evan, 84
Permanent resident status, 41*t*
    See also Lawful permanent resident (LPR)
Pew Hispanic Center
    on foreign-born population, 31–38
    "Hispanic Attitudes toward Learning English," 103
    on illegal alien population, 69, 94
    public opinion on immigration, 101–102
Pew Research Center for the People and the Press, 101–102, 110–114
Pfaelzer, Mariana R., 27
Platzer, Michael, 105–106
Plyler v. Doe, 23, 27
Police
    cultural/religious awareness of, 30
    enforcement of immigration laws, 25

police misconduct, federal protections against, 137
sanctuary laws and, 129–131
Policies. *See* Immigration laws/policies; Immigration policies, statements about
Politics, 13
Population
of border counties, 76
foreign-born growth, top ten states, 34 (*t*3.3)
illegal alien population estimates, 69
immigrants, counting, 34
native/foreign-born by age/sex, 38*f*
projections, native/foreign-born, 32 (*t*3.1)
U.S. in 2006, 31
See also Foreign-born population; Native-born population
Population shift, 101
Porter, Eduardo, 87, 96–97
Portes, Alejandro, 103
A Portrait of "Generation Next" (Pew Research Center for People and the Press), 110, 114
Poverty, 38*t*
Privacy rights, 26
Processing priority system, 55–56
Proposition 103, 103
Proposition 187, 27
Proposition 200, 27
Public accommodations, discrimination in, 137
Public assistance, 85–87
Public opinion
on biggest immigration issues, 114 (*t*7.19)
on immigrants, 111 (*t*7.13)
on immigrants and jobs, 113 (*t*7.16)
of immigrants as burden or strength, 112*f*
on immigrants as local/national problem, 112*t*
on immigrants' impact on local government services, taxes, 113 (*t*7.17)
on immigration, 101–102, 110–114
on immigration attitudes/experience with foreign-born people, 102 (*t*7.1)
on immigration concerns, 111 (*t*7.12)
on Latin and Asian immigrants, 102 (*t*7.2)
on legal status of immigrants, 113 (*t*7.15)
on reduction of illegal immigration from Mexico, 114 (*t*7.18)
Public Opinion Research Study of Latin American Remittance Senders in the United States (Inter-American Development Bank), 95
"The Public's View of Immigration: A Comprehensive Survey and Analysis" (Center for Immigration Studies), 114

Q

"Q: Green Card Not Green?" (U.S. Citizenship and Immigration Service), 23
Quota Law of 1921, 11

Quotas
on Asian immigrants, 8
changes to quota, 12
first quota law, 10–11
impact of, 11

R

Racism
national origin discrimination, federal protections against, 135–138
nativism and, 9
9/11 backlash discrimination, 29*t*
Radio, Spanish-language, 102–103
"Raids at Swift Plants Target Identity Theft" (Finley and McGhee), 16
Reagan, Ronald
Immigration Reform and Control Act of 1986, 15
restitution for Japanese, 12
The REAL ID Act: National Impact Analysis (National Governors Association, National Conference of State Legislatures, and National Association of Motor Vehicle Administrators), 26
REAL ID Act of 2005
asylum and, 59
provisions of, 25–26
REAL ID: Big Brother Could Cost Big Money (French), 26
Rebuilding after Katrina: A Population-Based Study of Labor and Human Rights in New Orleans (Fletcher et al.), 80–82
Refugee Act of 1980
asylum criteria, 59–60
definition of refugee, 54
provisions of, 13
return of refugees to homeland, 53
Refugee Council USA, 55
Refugee Relief Act of 1953, 13, 54
Refugees
adjustment to life in U.S., 61–63
admission limits, annual, 54–55
age/gender of refugee arrivals, 56 (*t*4.2)
arrivals and persons granted asylum, 58*t*
arrivals by category of admission, 56 (*t*4.3)
arrivals by state of initial settlement, 62 (*t*4.9)
arrivals to U.S., 54*f*
asylees, annual flow of affirmative/defensive, 59*f*
asylum, persons granted affirmatively/defensively, 60 (*t*4.6)
asylum seekers, 57–61
children, unaccompanied, 63–64
children in Office of Refugee Resettlement custody, top countries of origin for, 64*t*
as conditional entrants, 13
cost of U.S. aid for, 89

Iraqis, 74
legally admitting, 53–54
number of U.S. admission, 53
parole authority and, 13
processing priority system, 55–56
Refugee Act of 1980, 54
refugees, asylees, other persons granted legal permanent resident status, 60 (*t*4.7)
refugees admitted, proposed admissions, 55*t*
regional ceilings by priority, 57*t*
special needs, response to, 56–57
State Department budget request for emergency refugee/migration expense, 92*f*
torture, victims of, 61
trafficking, tier placement of countries, 62 (*t*4.8)
trafficking/violence, victims of, 61
U.S. government costs for refugee resettlement, 63*t*
from World War II, 12–13
Refugees (UNHCR magazine), 53
Registration, alien, 11–12
Relatives, of immigrants, 35
Religion, 30, 105
Remittances
identification documents, 94–95
methods for sending to Latin America, 95*f*
percent of wages, 95–96
poll respondents' monthly income at first job in U.S., 96 (*f*6.4)
poll respondents' monthly income at last job in Latin America, 96 (*f*6.3)
sent to Latin America, frequency of, 96 (*f*6.5)
sent to Latin America by immigrant workers, by state, 97*f*
transmitting, 95
from U.S. to Latin America, 98 (*t*6.12)
value of remittances to families, 95
Remittances 2005: Promoting Financial Democracy (Inter-American Development Bank), 95
Removal
aliens excluded, by reason for exclusion, 10*t*
aliens removed by nationality, 51*t*
aliens removed/reason for, 50*t*
expedited, 58–59
proceedings, 49–50
Reno, Flores v., 63
Reno, Jamie, 26–27
Report of the Visa Office 2005, 49
"Report on U.S. Antiterrorism Law Alleges Violations of Civil Rights" (Shenon), 30
Reported Tuberculosis in the United States, 2005 (Centers for Disease Control), 51
Republican Party, 2

Residents, permanent, 41*t*

  See also Lawful permanent resident (LPR)

Resources, information, 149–150

Revenues

  economy, immigrant contributions to, 105–107

  illegal aliens' costs, revenues, and economic impact for Texas, 94 (*t*6.11)

  from illegal aliens in Texas, 93, 94 (*t*6.10)

  See also Economy; Taxes

"Reversal of Fortune: An Immigration Raid Aids Blacks—For a Time" (Pérez and Dade), 84

Rieff, David, 105

The Role of Immigrants in the U.S. Labor Market (Congressional Budget Office), 69, 98–99

Roosevelt, Franklin D.

  Chinese immigration and, 8

  World War II and, 11–12

Roosevelt, Theodore, 8

Rumbaut, Rubén G., 103

Russian immigrants, 87

Rytina, Nancy, 15

S

Salaries, of foreign-born baseball players, 48, 48*f*

San Diego, California

  border fence in, 73–74

  impact of illegal immigration on, 76

Sanctuary laws, 129–131

Sauerbrey, Ellen, 74

SAWs (special agricultural workers), 15, 116

SCAAP (State Criminal Alien Assistance Program), 90

Schlafly, Phyllis, 84, 128–129

Schmidt, Susan, 63–64

Schoetzau, Barbara, 103

School. *See* Education

Science, doctorate degrees awarded to citizens/noncitizens, 48*t*

SCIRP (Select Commission on Immigration and Refugee Policy), 13

Secret deportation hearings, 28

Secure America bill, 121

Secure Fence Act of 2006, 26–27, 74

Security

  immigration policies and, 118–119

  risks, tracking, 73

  terrorism and immigration policies, 121–123

Sedition Act, 2

Seeking Asylum Alone: Unaccompanied and Separated Children and Refugee Protection in the U.S. (Bhabha and Schmidt), 63–64

Select Commission on Immigration and Refugee Policy (SCIRP), 13

Sending Money Home: Leveraging the Development Impact of Remittances (Inter-American Development Bank), 95–96

September 11, 2001 (9/11) terrorist attacks

  antiterrorism laws after, 15

  backlash discrimination, 29*t*

  blame on immigration laws, 118–119

  Homeland Security Act of 2002, 24

  immigration system and, 131

  Intelligence Reform and Terrorism Prevention Act of 2004, 25

  post-9/11 changes, 24–25

  Real ID Act of 2005, 25–26

  terrorism and immigration policies, 121–123

  undocumented families of victims, 78–79

  USA Patriot Act of 2001, 24

SEVIS. *See* Student and Exchange Visitor Information System

Sexual orientation, 60–61

Sharry, Frank, 119–121

Shenon, Philip, 30

Simcox, David, 16

Simpson, Alan K., 20, 115–116

Sindelar, Daisy, 38

Siskin, Alison, 87–88

Size and Characteristics of the Unauthorized Migrant Population in the U.S. (Passel), 69, 94, 111

Slaves, 1

Smith, Marion L., 9

Smuggling, 133

Social group, 59–61

Social Security Administration (SSA)

  benefits for refugees, 63

  identity theft and, 16

  immigrants and, 87–89

Social Security Benefits for Noncitizens: Current Policy and Legislation (Nuschler and Siskin), 87–88

Social Security numbers (SSNs), 16

Social Security system

  benefits paid under U.S. totalization agreements, 90*t*

  immigrant earnings and, 87–89

  national standards for cards, 25

  taxes paid by immigrants, 117

Social services, public opinion on immigrants and, 112, 113 (*t*7.17)

South America, map of, 141

South Asia, map of, 144

Southeast Asia, map of, 145

Southwest border, 73–74

Spanish language

  influence on U.S., 102–105

  languages other than English spoken at home, 103*f*

  voting in, 137–138

Special agricultural workers (SAWs), 15, 116

Special provisions, naturalization, 41

Specialized Refugee Foster Care Program, 64

Spener, David, 75

Spouses, immigration/residency status of foreign-born, 16, 20

SSA. *See* Social Security Administration

SSI (Supplemental Security Income), 21–22, 85

SSNs (Social Security numbers), 16

St. Augustine, Florida, 1

State Children's Health Insurance Program, 86

State Criminal Alien Assistance Program (SCAAP), 90

State Legalization Impact Assistance Grant program, 16

The State of American Business (Donahue), 113–114

States

  food programs for legal immigrants, state-funded, 22*t*

  foreign student enrollment in, 107–108

  immigrant populations in, 31–32

  immigrant welfare use and, 87

  immigrant-founded, venture-backed firms, by state, 107*f*

  immigration legislation of, 27–28

  income rankings, per capita, by state, 78*t*

  international students, states with most, 108 (*t*7.6)

  loss of immigration role, 8

  REAL ID Act of 2005 and, 26

  refugee arrivals by state of initial settlement, 62 (*t*4.9)

  remittances sent to Latin America by state, 98 (*t*6.12)

  remittances sent to Latin America by immigrant workers, 97*f*

  spending on immigration, 90, 92–94

  state immigration-related legislation enacted, 27*f*

  Texas, illegal aliens' costs, revenues, economic impact for, 94 (*t*6.11)

  Texas state health care costs for illegal aliens, 93 (*t*6.9)

  Texas state revenue from illegal aliens, 94 (*t*6.10)

  welfare benefits for immigrants, 22

  welfare programs, top states ranked by immigrant households using, 89*t*

Statistical Abstract of the United States, 2007 (U.S. Bureau of the Census), 102

Statistical information

  aliens excluded, by reason for exclusion, 10*t*

  aliens removed by nationality, 51*t*

  aliens removed/reason for removal, 50*t*

  asylees, annual flow of affirmative/defensive, 59*f*

asylum, persons granted affirmatively/ defensively, 60 (*t*4.6)

baseball, major league foreign-born players, source countries for, 50*f*

baseball players in major leagues, foreign-born, 49*f*

baseball players/salaries, foreign-born, 48*f*

border county, AIDS, hepatitis A, tuberculosis cases by, 79 (*t*5.9)

border county, diabetes rates by, 80*t*

children in Office of Refugee Resettlement custody, top countries of origin for, 64*t*

class of admission, immigrants admitted by, 39 (*t*3.12)

construction worker presence in hurricane-affected areas, 81 (*f*5.7)

Department of Homeland Security budget by organization, 91*t*

dropout rates for 16- to 24-year-olds by race/ethnicity, 98 (*t*6.13)

earnings growth for native/immigrant men by educational level, 99*t*

entry modes for unauthorized migrant population, 70*t*

food programs for legal immigrants, state-funded, 22*t*

foreign college students in U.S. by academic level, visa type, 110 (*t*7.10)

foreign students, economic impact of, 109 (*t*7.9)

foreign students, fields of study for, 108 (*t*7.7)

foreign students, funding source for, 109 (*t*7.8)

foreign students, states with most, 108 (*t*7.6)

foreign students, top 20 countries of origin for, 110 (*t*7.11)

foreign students by geographic area, 110*f*

foreign-born by birth region, 32 (*f*3.1)

foreign-born by birth state/region, 33*t*

foreign-born population growth, top ten states, 34 (*t*3.3)

Form I-94, 71*f*

H1B visas issued by birth region, 47*f*

H2A workers, top ten states by, 46 (*t*3.17)

health insurance, immigrants without, 86*t*

home technology access rates for 20 largest immigrant groups, 104*t*

illegal immigrants in U.S., birthplace of, 69*f*

immigrant citizenship groups, characteristics of, 43 (*f*3.6)

immigrant orphans adopted by U.S. citizens by gender/age/region of birth, 39 (*t*3.13)

immigrant-founded, venture-backed firms, by state, 107*f*

immigrant-founded, venture-backed public companies, 106*t*

immigrants admitted by class of admission, 39 (*t*3.12)

immigration by region and selected country of last residence, 3*t*–7*t*

income rankings, per capita, by state, 78*t*

languages other than English spoken at home, 103*f*

native/foreign-born by age/region of birth, persons living in poverty, 38*t*

native/foreign-born by region of birth, family size of, 34 (*t*3.5)

native/foreign-born by region of birth, household income of, 37 (*t*3.10)

native/foreign-born by region of birth, industry of employment, 37 (*t*3.9)

native/foreign-born by region of birth, marital status of, 34 (*t*3.4)

native/foreign-born by region of birth, occupation for, 36*t*

native/foreign-born children by region of birth, living arrangements of, 35 (*t*3.7)

native/foreign-born population by age/ sex, 38*f*

native/foreign-born women, fertility in, 35 (*t*3.6)

naturalized persons by decade/region of birth, 42*f*

naturalized persons by region of birth, 43 (*f*3.5)

New Orleans, construction jobs held by documented/undocumented workers in, 82 (*f*5.8)

New Orleans, educational status of documented/undocumented workers in, 81 (*f*5.6)

New Orleans, health problems of documented/undocumented workers in, 83*t*

New Orleans, overtime pay for documented/undocumented workers, 82 (*f*5.9)

nonimmigrant visas issued by classification, 44*t*–45*t*

occupations of immigrants/native-born workers in California, 99*f*

orphans adopted by U.S. citizens, top countries supplying, 40*f*

permanent resident status, persons obtaining by admission class/ occupation, 41*t*

poll respondents' monthly income at first job in U.S., 96 (*f*6.4)

poll respondents' monthly income at last job in Latin America, 96 (*f*6.3)

population projections, native/foreign-born, 32 (*t*3.1)

public opinion about immigrants' impact on local government services, taxes, 113 (*t*7.17)

public opinion about immigration concerns, 111 (*t*7.12)

public opinion about Latin and Asian immigrants, 102 (*t*7.2)

public opinion of immigrants as burden/ strength, 112*f*

public opinion on biggest immigration issues, 114 (*t*7.19)

public opinion on immigrants, 111 (*t*7.13)

public opinion on immigrants and jobs, 113 (*t*7.16)

public opinion on immigrants as local/ national problem, 112*t*

public opinion on immigration attitudes/ experience with foreign-born people, 102 (*t*7.1)

public opinion on legal status of immigrants, 113 (*t*7.15)

public opinion on reduction of illegal immigration from Mexico, 114 (*t*7.18)

refugee arrivals, age/gender of, 56 (*t*4.2)

refugee arrivals by category of admission, 56 (*t*4.3)

refugee arrivals and persons granted asylum, 58*t*

refugee arrivals by state of initial settlement, 62 (*t*4.9)

refugee resettlement, U.S. government costs for, 63*t*

refugees, asylees, other persons granted legal permanent resident status, 60 (*t*4.7)

refugees, regional ceilings by priority, 57*t*

refugees admitted, proposed admissions, 55*t*

remittances, methods for sending to Latin America, 95*f*

remittances from U.S. to Latin America, 98 (*t*6.12)

remittances sent to Latin America by immigrant workers, by state, 97*f*

remittances sent to Latin America, frequency of, 96 (*f*6.5)

science/engineering doctorate degrees awarded to citizens/ noncitizens, 48*t*

Social Security benefits paid under U.S. totalization agreements, 90*t*

State Department budget request for emergency refugee/migration expense, 92*f*

state immigration-related legislation enacted, 27*f*

Texas, illegal aliens' costs, revenues, economic impact for, 94 (*t*6.11)

Texas, tuition cost of noncitizen college students, 93 (*t*6.8)

Texas state health care costs for illegal aliens, 93 (*t*6.9)

Texas state revenue from illegal aliens, 94 (*t*6.10)

trafficking, tier placement of countries, 62 (*t*4.8)

tuberculosis cases by birth origin, 51*f*

tuberculosis cases by birth origin, drug resistant, 52f

US-VISIT appropriations, 72t

US-VISIT program, entering persons processed at land, air, sea ports by use of US-VISIT program, 72f

USCIS, fees collected by, 68f

wage rates, adverse effect, 46 (t3.16)

wait time for employment-based immigrants, 66 (t5.1)

wait time for family-sponsored immigrants, 66 (t5.2)

wait time for visa interviews at key consular posts, 67 (t5.3)

welfare programs, top states ranked by immigrant households using, 89t

welfare programs/EITC, immigrant households using, 88t

welfare programs/EITC use for native, immigrant households, 87t

youth access to computers/Internet, 104f

A Statistical Portrait of the Foreign-Born Population at Mid-Decade (Pew Hispanic Center), 31–38

Stock, Margaret D., 118–119

Strayhorn, Carole Keeton, 90, 92–93

Student and Exchange Visitor Information System (SEVIS)

description of, 132

foreign student visas, tracking of, 109

function of, 25

Students. *See* Foreign students

Sucher, Kenneth, 42–43

Supplemental Security Income (SSI), 21–22, 85

"Survey of U.S. Border State Voters and Canadians about New Border Regulations" (Zogby International), 75

Swift and Company, 16

Swope, Linda, 84

T

T (nonimmigrant visa), 61

Taiwanese immigrants, 106

Tanabe, Marianne K. G., 8

Tancredo, Tom, 103

TANF (Temporary Assistance for Needy Families), 21–22, 85

Taxes

Earned Income Tax Credit, 86–87

financial impact of illegal aliens in Texas, 92

from illegal aliens in Colorado, 94

immigrant earnings and, 85

paid by immigrants, 117

revenues from illegal aliens, 93

Social Security system, 87–89

welfare programs/EITC, immigrant households using, 88t

welfare programs/EITC use for native, immigrant households, 87t

Technology

home technology access rates for 20 largest immigrant groups, 104t

immigrant workers and, 97

influence on education/language, 103–104

youth access to computers/Internet, native and immigrant, 104f

Temporary Assistance for Needy Families (TANF), 21–22, 85

Temporary foreign workers

H1B program, 46–47

H1B visas for scientists/engineers, 47

H1B visas issued by region of birth, 47f

H1C program, 47–48

H2/H2A program, 46

overview of, 45–46

Temporary nonimmigrant visa, 65–67

Temporary protected status (TPS), 21

Terrorism

amnesty and, 125, 126

counter-terrorism immigration enforcement, 132–133

immigration law and, 121–123

immigration policies and, 118–119

immigration system and, 131

Intelligence Reform and Terrorism Prevention Act of 2004, 25

post-9/11 policies, repercussions of, 28, 30

See also September 11, 2001 (9/11) terrorist attacks

Texas

financial impact of illegal aliens in, 90, 92–93

health care costs for illegal aliens, 93 (t6.9)

illegal aliens' costs, revenues, economic impact for, 94 (t6.11)

immigrant welfare use in, 87

revenue from illegal aliens, 94 (t6.10)

tuition for undocumented students in, 23, 93 (t6.8)

"This Month in Immigration History: June 1940" (U.S. Citizenship and Immigration Service), 11

"This Month in Immigration History: May 1987" (U.S. Citizenship and Immigration Service), 13

Time

wait time for employment-based immigrants, 66 (t5.1)

wait time for family-sponsored immigrants, 66 (t5.2)

wait time for visa interviews at key consular posts, 67 (t5.3)

waiting time for legal entry documents, 65

"Today's Immigrant Woman Entrepreneur" (Pearce), 107

Torture, victims of, 61

Torture Victims Relief Act of 1998, 61

Totalization agreements

description of, 87–89

Social Security benefits paid under, 90t

TPS (temporary protected status), 21

Trafficking

Anti-Smuggling Program, 133

tier placement of countries, 62 (t4.8)

victims of, 61

Trafficking Victims Protection Act of 2000 (TVPA), 61

Trafficking Victims Protection Reauthorization Act of 2003, 61

Trafficking Victims Protection Reauthorization Act of 2006, 61

Transportation, of refugees, 62

Transportation Security Administration, 89

Trends in Naturalization (Fix/Passel/Sucher), 42–43

Truman, Harry, 12

Tuberculosis

AIDS, hepatitis A, tuberculosis cases by border county, 79 (t5.9)

in border counties, 77

cases by birth origin, 51f

cases by birth origin, drug resistant, 52f

cases reported in U.S., 51–52

Tuition

cost of noncitizen college student tuition in Texas, 92, 93 (t6.8)

international students, funding source for, 108–109, 109 (t7.8)

for undocumented students, 23

TVPA (Trafficking Victims Protection Act of 2000), 61

Two-hemisphere system, for immigration, 12

2003 Yearbook of Immigration Statistics (U.S. Department of Homeland Security), 36

2005 Yearbook of Immigration Statistics (U.S. Department of Homeland Security)

on adoption statistics, 36, 38

on immigration after World War I, 10

on immigration in early twentieth century, 9

on naturalization statistics, 41–42

U

U-visa, 20

Unaccompanied Alien Child Protection Act of 2005, 64

Unaccompanied children, refugees, 63–64, 64t

The Underground Labor Force Is Rising to the Surface (Justich and Ng), 69

Undocumented aliens. *See* Illegal aliens

Undocumented Immigrants in Texas: A Financial Analysis of the Impact to the State Budget and Economy (Strayhorn), 90, 92–93

Unemployment, 76
United Nations High Commissioner for
 Refugees (UNHCR)
 asylum for gender/sexual orientation
  persecution, 60
 on Hungarian revolution refugees, 53
 processing priority system and, 55, 56
United States
 refugee adjustment to life in, 61–63
 relationship with Mexico, 75–76
United States, immigration's impact on
 economy, immigrant contributions to,
  105–107
 foreign students by geographic area,
  110f
 home technology access rates for 20
  largest immigrant groups, 104t
 immigrant-founded, venture-backed
  firms, by state, 107f
 immigrant-founded, venture-backed
  public companies, 106t
 international college students in U.S. by
  academic level, visa type, 110 (t7.10)
 international students, economic impact
  of, 109 (t7.9)
 international students, education of,
  107–110
 international students, fields of study for,
  108 (t7.7)
 international students, funding source
  for, 109 (t7.8)
 international students, states with most,
  108 (t7.6)
 international students, top 20 countries
  of origin for, 110 (t7.11)
 languages other than English spoken at
  home, 103f
 Latin American impact, 102–105
 New York City, 105
 population shift, 101
 public opinion about immigrants' impact
  on local government services, taxes,
  113 (t7.17)
 public opinion about immigration
  concerns, 111 (t7.12)
 public opinion about Latin and Asian
  immigrants, 102 (t7.2)
 public opinion of immigrants as burden
  or strengthening means, 112f
 public opinion on biggest immigration
  issues, 114 (t7.19)
 public opinion on immigrants, 111
  (t7.13)
 public opinion on immigrants and jobs,
  113 (t7.16)
 public opinion on immigrants as local/
  national problem, 112t
 public opinion on immigration, 101–102,
  110–114
 public opinion on immigration attitudes/
  experience with foreign-born people,
  102 (t7.1)

public opinion on legal status of
 immigrants, 113 (t7.15)
public opinion on reduction of illegal
 immigration from Mexico, 114 (t7.18)
youth access to computers/Internet,
 native and immigrant, 104f
University of Houston Law Center, 23
U.S. attorney general
 parole authority, 13
 temporary protected status granted by,
  21
U.S. border
 border security, need for reform, 120
 border security, importance of, 129
 borders on water, 73
 control challenges, 69–70
 DHS budget and, 89
 diabetes rates by border county, 80t
 Homeland Security Act of 2002 and, 24
 immigration policy reform, 118, 120
 impact of illegal immigration on
  southwestern border, 76–78
 Mexico, twenty-four U.S. counties
  bordering, 77f, 79 (t5.8)
 Mexico's relationship with U.S., 75–76
 Ricardo Parra on border security, 117
 Secure Fence Act of 2006, 26–27
 terrorism and immigration, 122
 U.S. Border Patrol, 73–75
 USA Patriot Act of 2001 and, 24
U.S. Border Patrol
 creation of, 11
 illegal aliens from Mexico and, 75
 northern border, 74–75
 responsibility of, 73
 southwest border, 73–74
 strengthening number of, 22
U.S. Bureau of the Census
 illegal alien population estimates, 69
 on immigrant population, 31
 information resources from, 149
 on languages spoken in U.S., 102
 on population in cities, 10
U.S.-Canadian border, 74–75
U.S. Citizenship and Immigration Service
 (USCIS)
 fees collected by, 68f
 on green card, 23
 immigration forms/fees, 67–68
 on immigration, qualifications for, 35
 information resources from, 149
 INS reorganization as, 24
 on politics of immigration, 13
 on temporary protected status, 21
 "This Month in Immigration History,"
  11
 visa service fees to, 65
U.S. Coast Guard
 budget of, 89
 migrant interdictions by, 73

U.S. Constitution
 Equal Protection Clause, 137
 on immigration, 1–2
U.S. Customs and Border Patrol (CBP)
 alien admissibility and, 49–50
 budget of, 89
 monitoring entry/exit, 69–70, 72–73
 Secure Fence Act of 2006, 26–27
 U.S. Border Patrol, 73–75
U.S. Department of Health and Human
 Services, 50
U.S. Department of Homeland Security
 (DHS)
 budget by organization, 89, 91t
 creation of, 24
 on immigration after World War I, 10
 on immigration during Civil War, 3
 on immigration in early twentieth
  century, 9
 information resources from, 149
 monitoring entry/exit, 69–70, 72–73
 Secure Fence Act of 2006 and, 26–27
 undocumented workers in New Orleans
  and, 80
U.S. Department of Housing and Urban
 Development, 136
U.S. Department of Justice
 on asylum claims, 57–58
 asylum for victims of trafficking/
  violence, 61
 battered brides and, 20
 civil rights violations and, 29t, 30
 Federal Protections against National
  Origin Discrimination, 135–138
 information resources from, 149
 INS transferred to, 11
 post-9/11 policies, repercussions of, 28
U.S. Department of Labor, 80
U.S. Department of State
 on aliens turned away from U.S., 49
 annual refugee admissions limits, 54–55
 budget request for emergency refugee/
  migration expense, 92f
 Diversity Visa Program, 21
 information resources from, 149
 refugee aid budget, 89
U.S. Department of State's Bureau of
 Consular Affairs, 65–67
U.S. General Accounting Office, 22
U.S. government. See Federal government
U.S. Government Accountability Office
 (GAO)
 ESF audit, 87
 on illegal aliens and crime, 83–84
 information resources from, 149
 on totalization agreement, 88
 on US-VISIT program, 70
 on voluntary interviews, 28

U.S. Immigration and Customs Enforcement (ICE)
  budget of, 89
  counter-terrorism immigration enforcement, 132–133
  foreign student visas, tracking of, 109
  function of, 69
  marriage fraud investigations, 20
  sanctuary laws and, 130–131
  on Swift raids, 16
U.S. Library of Congress, 104–105
U.S.-Mexican border
  Secure Fence Act of 2006, 26–27
  U.S. Border Patrol and, 73–74
  U.S.-Mexico relationship, 75–76
  See also U.S. border
US/Mexico Border Counties Coalition (USMBCC), 76–78
"The U.S.-Mexico Totalization Agreement" (Social Security Administration), 88
U.S. Office of Immigration, 9
U.S. Supreme Court
  Flores v. Reno, 63
  Henderson v. Mayor of the City of New York, 8
  Plyler v. Doe, 23
"US-VISIT: Current Ports of Entry" (U.S. Department of Homeland Security), 70
US-VISIT (U.S. Visitor Information and Immigrant Status Indicator Technology) program
  appropriations, 72t
  counter-terrorism immigration enforcement, 132
  description of, problems of, 70, 72
  entering persons processed at land, air, sea ports by use of, 72f
USA Patriot Act of 2001, 24
USCIS. *See* U.S. Citizenship and Immigration Service
USMBCC (US/Mexico Border Counties Coalition), 76–78

V

"Va. Case Highlights Fraudulent Marriages" (Koch), 20
Venture capital
  immigrant venture capitalists, 106
  immigrant-founded, venture-backed firms, by state, 107f
  immigrant-founded, venture-backed public companies, by industry, 106 (t7.5)
  immigrant-founded, venture-backed public companies, by year established, 106 (t7.4)
Victims of Trafficking and Violence Prevention Act of 2000, 20
Vietnam War, 13
Vietnamese refugees, 13
Viña, Stephen, 73–74
Violence against Women Act of 1994, 20
Violence, asylum for victims of, 61

Violent Crime Control and Law Enforcement Act of 1994, 61
Visa Waiver Program, 72–73
Visas
  annual limit on, 35
  baseball and, 48–49
  to Chinese orphans, 40
  cost of, 65–68
  denials of, 49
  for displaced persons, 13
  Diversity Visa Program, 20–21
  on first-come, first-served basis, 12
  of foreign students, 109
  H1B, issued by birth region, 47f
  for immigrant workers, 119, 120–121
  nonimmigrant, 43
  nonimmigrant visas issues by classification, 44t–45t
  post-9/11 changes, 24–25
  T visa, 61
  temporary foreign workers, 45–48
  visa classifications, U.S. nonimmigrant, 67 (t5.4)
  Visa Waiver Program, 72–73
  wait time for, 65
  wait time for visa interviews at key consular posts, 67 (t5.3)
Visitors. *See* Nonimmigrants
Voluntary interviews, 28
Voting, 137–138
Voting Rights Act, 138

W

Wages
  adverse effect rates by state, 46 (t3.16)
  earnings growth for native/immigrant men by educational level, 99t
  immigrant impact on native wages, 98–99
  rates, adverse effect, 46 (t3.16)
  See also Earnings; Income
Wait time
  for employment-based immigrants, 66 (t5.1)
  for family-sponsored immigrants, 66 (t5.2)
  for legal entry documents, 65
  for visa interviews at key consular posts, 67 (t5.3)
Wal-Mart, 102
Wasem, Ruth Ellen, 20–21
Washington State, 28
Waterman, Shaun, 26
Welfare
  cuts for legal immigrants, 21–22
  federal government programs, availability to, 92t
  public assistance programs, 85–87
  public opinion on immigrants, 101, 102
  top states ranked by immigrant households using, 89t

welfare programs/EITC, immigrant households using, 88t
welfare programs/EITC use for native, immigrant households, 87t
Welfare Reform Law of 1996, 21–22
Welfare Reform: Many States Continue Some Federal or State Benefits for Immigrants (U.S. General Accounting Office), 22
Wepman, Dennis, 1, 2
Western Hemisphere Travel Initiative, 75
White supremacists, 5
Why Am I Here? Children in Immigration Detention (Amnesty International), 63
WIC (Women, Infants, and Children) program, 85
Wilson, Denise, 58
Wilson, Woodrow, 10
"With Millions in 9/11 Payments, Bereaved Can't Buy Green Cards" (Buckley), 79
Wives, battered brides, 20
Women
  battered brides, 20
  immigrant women business owners, 107
  native/foreign-born, fertility of, 35 (t3.6)
Women, Infants, and Children (WIC) program, 85
Work
  construction worker presence in hurricane-affected areas, 81 (f5.7)
  demand for low-skilled labor, 119, 120
  Earned Income Tax Credit, 86–87
  earnings and Social Security, 87–89
  foreign-born in New York City workforce, 105
  guestworker program, 116
  of illegal aliens, amnesty program and, 125–126
  illegal immigration's impact on jobs, 84, 129
  immigrants for low-skilled labor, 127
  immigrants' monthly income at first job in U.S., 96 (f6.4)
  national origin discrimination, federal protections against, 136
  native and immigrant competition for jobs, 96–99
  New Orleans, construction jobs held by documented/undocumented workers in, 82 (f5.8)
  New Orleans, educational status of documented/undocumented workers in, 81 (f5.6)
  New Orleans, health problems of documented/undocumented workers in, 83t
  New Orleans, overtime pay for documented/undocumented workers, 82 (f5.9)
  occupations of immigrants/native-born workers in California, 99f
  public opinion on immigrants and jobs, 111–112, 113 (t7.16)
  remittances and, 95–96
  risk exposure/information received by workers in, 83f

undocumented workers in New Orleans, 79–82

U.S. competition with world, 113–114

See also Employment

Workers. *See* Employment; Labor; Temporary foreign workers; Work

World Bank, 95

World War I, 10

World War II

alien registration, 11–12

immigration and, 11–12

Japanese internment, 12

refugees from, 12–13

Wu, Amy, 58

Y

Yardley, Jim, 40

Yin, Sandra, 102

Youth

computers/Internet, influence on education/language, 103–104

dropout rates for 16- to 24-year-olds, 98 (*t*6.13)

dropouts, competition with immigrants for jobs, 96–97

youth access to computers/Internet, native and immigrant, 104*f*

See also Children; Foreign students

Z

Ziel, Fred A., 20

Zogby International, 75